Diversity Across the Disciplines

All the best,

Audrey

12/12/20

Diversity Across the Disciplines

Research on People, Policy, Process, and Paradigm

edited by

Audrey J. Murrell
University of Pittsburgh

Jennifer L. Petrie-Wyman
University of Pittsburgh

Abdesalam Soudi
University of Pittsburgh

INFORMATION AGE PUBLISHING, INC.
Charlotte, NC • www.infoagepub.com

Library of Congress Cataloging-in-Publication Data

A CIP record for this book is available from the Library of Congress
http://www.loc.gov

ISBN: 978-1-64113-919-9 (Paperback)
 978-1-64113-920-5 (Hardcover)
 978-1-64113-921-2 (eBook)

CONTENTS

PART II
PROCESS

PART III
POLICIES

PART IV

PARADIGMS

PREFACE

DIVERSITY ACROSS THE DISCIPLINES

Research on People, Policy, Process, and Paradigm

Diversity research and scholarship has evolved over the past several decades and is presently reaching a critical juncture. While the scholarship on diversity and inclusion has advanced within various disciplines and subdisciplines, there have been limited conversations and collaborations across distinct areas of research. Theories, paradigms, research models, and methodologies have evolved but continue to remain locked within specific areas, disciplines, or theoretical canons. Thus, we need to facilitate dialog and collaboration that extends across our traditional disciplinary boundaries in order to advance our understanding in theory, research, education, and practice.

During my tenure as Provost of the University of Pittsburgh, I sponsored a series of theme-based initiatives entitled the "Year of" to help facilitate focused collaboration across the university. This edited volume was developed as part of the "Year of Diversity." The primary goal then, as it is now, was to help the Pitt community recognize and appreciate one another's differences and to understand that unfamiliar ideas and perspectives are necessary prerequisites for the advancement of knowledge. Not only were these

Diversity Across the Disciplines, pages ix–x
Copyright © 2020 by Information Age Publishing
All rights of reproduction in any form reserved.

efforts aimed at laying a strong foundation for dialog across our various disciplines, they also renewed our commitment to diversity across stakeholders within the university community. Throughout the year, faculty, staff, students and community partners focused on achieving a better understanding of the importance of difference in terms of building learning communities and preparing us to value experiences unlike our own. We explored differences across race, gender expression, veteran status, disability status, politics, ethnicity, and religion. More broadly, we focused on diversity supports attached to social inequality and social status inequality.

Advancing knowledge, theory and practices focused on diversity advances the mission of higher education in many dimensions. It helps us recognize and appreciate the full range of differences among us. It allows us to reflect on the value of diversity and how it strengthens interactions across people, systems, and communities. Research on diversity can also challenge our understanding in ways that evoke how different ideas and perspectives are fundamental to the advancement of knowledge that creates meaningful and long-lasting social impact.

The authors who contributed to this volume embraced the opportunity before them and were challenged to think about diversity in new and different ways. It meant pushing their thinking about people, process, policy, and paradigms beyond the normal approaches or perspectives as defined by their traditional areas of expertise. This was a necessary yet disruptive endeavor because diversity can evoke challenging dialogs. It produces conflicting views and unknown frontiers to navigate. I am pleased that the authors of this book responded to this challenge by thinking about diversity in novel ways, thereby modeling for others how we can move outside of traditional disciplinary boundaries to confront necessary issues by engaging with others who may have different views from our own. Inevitably, their work displayed different approaches and modes of thinking. I see it as a source of strength that produced innovation in their research.

I am honored to have sponsored and been part of this collaborative edited volume examining diversity across the disciplines in higher education. It brings together contributions from the arts, sciences, and professional fields in order to advance diversity and inclusion across campuses, disciplines, paradigms, and traditions. An undertaking of this magnitude is even more important in our current higher education climate, which necessitates multicultural thinking and interdisciplinary collaboration. In both the present and the future, we must become more familiar with discussing diversity across disciplines. This volume represents one amazing step toward this ultimate destination.

—Patricia E. Beeson, PhD

PART I

PEOPLE

CHAPTER 1

BELIEFS ABOUT COMPETENCE

The Story of Self-Efficacy, Gender, and Physics

Z. Yasemin Kalender
University of Pittsburgh

Emily Marshman
University of Pittsburgh

Timothy Nokes-Malach
University of Pittsburgh

Christian Schunn
University of Pittsburgh

Chandralekha Singh
University of Pittsburgh

Diversity Across the Disciplines, pages 3–17

3

ABSTRACT

While there have been some efforts to increase the diversity in physics courses, female students are often underrepresented and underperform in these
courses. This chapter reports the findings of a longitudinal analysis of students' motivation in introductory physics course sequences. The findings
have implications for student academic and professional achievements as well
as faculty members and university administrators in regards to the development of interventions and pedagogies that take into account female students'
motivational characteristics in physics.

DIVERSITY IN STEM DISCIPLINES

The representation of women in many science, technology, engineering,
and mathematics (STEM) fields is unacceptably low. Although there have
been several efforts to increase women's involvement in STEM majors and
jobs, unequal gender participation among students majoring in a number
of STEM fields persists, with little change (National Science Board, 2014).
There is greater participation of women in biology, chemistry, industrial engineering, and chemical engineering, but physics, computer science, and
electrical engineering have made little progress in increasing the representation of women (Ivie, 2018; National Science Board, 2014).

In the United States, the discipline of physics has had a low level of participation from women at all educational levels (Ivie, 2018; National Science
Board, 2014). Even though the number of female students enrolling in regular high school physics classes has increased in the past several decades, female students are less likely to enroll in more advanced high school physics
courses (AP Physics B and C; Ivie, 2018). Similarly, the number of women
majoring in physics has increased since the 1980s, but the percentage of
all bachelor's degrees in physics earned by women is still only around 20%
(Ivie, 2018). The underrepresentation of women in physics exhibits similar
trends in PhD degrees. This pervasive issue surrounding the lack of gender
diversity in physics—beginning at high school and becoming increasingly
salient in college, in advanced degree programs, and in academic leadership positions—is of concern to the physics community. Despite existing
efforts to understand low diversity in physics (Hazari, Sonnet, Sadler, &
Shanahan, 2010), the reasons for women's low enrollment and participation in physics are not fully understood. In recent years, investigation of the
origins of the gender gap in physics and effective approaches to creating a
more inclusive and equitable learning environment has gained traction in
the physics education and broader science education research communities. In this chapter, we specifically focus on students' motivational characteristic differences by gender in a foundational college-level physics course

in which women are generally outnumbered by men. Investigating this specific physics course is a matter of great importance to identify the experiences of underrepresented groups, such as women, in STEM courses, and to enhance diversity in STEM disciplines.

BACKGROUND RESEARCH ON WOMEN'S REPRESENTATION IN PHYSICS

Prior research related to gender and physics indicates that male students outperform female students in physics at various learning levels (Taasoobshirazi & Carr, 2009). For instance, women underperform compared to men in calculus-based physics courses in college (Tai & Sadler, 2001). Similarly, Kost, Pollock, and Finkelstein (2009) found that female students perform lower than male students on a standardized conceptual test before instruction (lower pretest scores), and the gap persists, even after instruction, in posttest scores. Although many other studies have also documented the existing gender gap in physics performance (Karim, Maries, & Singh, 2018; Madsen, McKagan, & Sayre, 2013), the factors that underlie the gap have yet to be understood.

Researchers have hypothesized several factors to explain women's underrepresentation and underperformance in physics courses. Those hypotheses generally fall into two categories: those that address students' background and education and those that address motivational aspects of student learning. These factors impact students' engagement and achievements in physics courses. For instance, effective high school physics teaching methodologies have been found to be positively correlated with students' science career aspirations (Hazari et al., 2010). Likewise, advantages of better high school preparation in science courses can enhance students' learning and achievement in college science classes (Sadler & Tai, 2007). This result suggests that the gender gap in pretest scores might stem in part from the differences in high school physics education and preparation, which translate to an initial gender gap in college (Kost et al., 2009). Critically, social and environmental factors, such as social customs, gender biases, the lack of female role models, and traditionally attributed gender roles about who can succeed in physics (i.e., brilliant men), can also negatively influence women's attitudes, engagement, persistence, and performance in physics courses (Hackett & Betz, 1981). Interviews with female students majoring in physics have shown that male students usually take on the primary roles implementing lab work, while female students are assigned more menial supporting roles, a phenomenon referred to as "taking female roles" (Danielsson, 2012, p. 30). Those interviews also revealed that female students carry beliefs that there are differences between female and male brains, and that men are better at "getting physics" due to these biological differences in intelligence (Danielsson, 2012); in other words, women have internalized stereotypical messages against their abilities.

Students' motivational characteristics, such as self-efficacy, can also be related to students' academic choices related to whether to enroll in science courses, such as physics, or to major in physics-related fields (Wang & Degol, 2013). Self-efficacy, a concept established by Bandura (1977), is one aspect of students' motivation that refers to individuals' beliefs in their capability to perform well on a particular task. In other words, individuals' self-concepts about their competence and expectations for a specific task can influence their subsequent behavior (e.g., how they make academic choices; how much time and effort they are willing to spend on the task; Bandura, 1986). Gender biases in certain STEM disciplines can generate gender differences in self-efficacy and suppress women's participation in these disciplines.

Self-efficacy can also be one way to relate students' experiences and attitudes to their learning outcomes. There are several factors that contribute to the development of self-efficacy: social and cultural norms and persuasion experiences, achievement or failure on a previous task, observations of how others perform on similar tasks, and individuals' emotional state (Bandura, 1986). For instance, having support and encouragement from mentors can positively affect students' self-efficacy and motivate them to engage with difficult learning activities, whereas, experiencing stress and doubt due to classroom norms and cultural biases can negatively affect students' self-efficacy and performance. Low levels of self-efficacy might cause students to disengage or show less persistence. Cheryan, Ziegler, Montoya, and Jiang (2017) investigated causes of gender imbalance in some STEM fields and found that self-efficacy can be a strong predictor of unequal gender participation during class activities and enrollment in STEM fields such as physics.

GENERAL BELIEFS ABOUT PHYSICS: WHO CAN SUCCEED IN IT?

In the field of academic motivation, self-efficacy has been one focus of research in the past several decades, particularly in STEM disciplines (Pintrich & Schunk, 1995). Academic self-efficacy influences learners' goal-setting, the amount of effort they expend on tasks, the level of learning, and, ultimately, their career choices (Lent & Brown, 2006). Moreover, students' self-efficacy can be related to self-regulation strategies, task management, and engagement and interest in particular academic tasks (Schunk, 1994; Schunk & Pajares, 2002; Zimmerman, 2000). Having high self-efficacy might help students view difficult tasks as challenges rather than hurdles (Collins, 1982). In other words, the higher the student's self-efficacy in a particular learning activity, the more perseverance and resilience he or she is likely to show when faced with adversity. Research also indicates that there is a positive relationship between students' self-efficacy and their academic performance (Pintrich & Schunk, 1995). For instance, self-efficacy has been found to be a determining factor in measures of math performance (Pajares & Miller, 1994). In physics, self-efficacy has also been shown to be a strong predictor for students' post-conceptual test and final course grades, even after controlling for their prior knowledge (Cavallo, Potter, & Rozman, 2004).

The critical role of self-efficacy in academic engagement and achievement can explain some aspects of women's low participation and underperformance in physics courses. Prior research indicates that men and women have different levels of self-efficacy in physics, with men demonstrating higher confidence in high school and college physics courses (Cavallo et al., 2004; Kost et al., 2009; Shaw, 2004). Sawtelle, Brewe, and Kramer (2012) studied the retention differences in introductory physics courses across gender and found that self-efficacy was a strong latent variable predicting gender differentials in retention and persistence. Male and female students have also been shown to have different classroom interactions and experiences in first-year college courses, impacting their self-efficacy (Hutchison-Green, Follman, & Bodner, 2008). Stereotypical beliefs, gender biases, or brilliance attributions in physics courses can at least partly explain why female and male students have different classroom experiences. These biased beliefs can lower female students' self-confidence and their sense of belonging in physics courses. Recently, we have investigated the interactions among gender, physics self-efficacy, and students' performance in college-level calculus-based physics courses; we provide some of the key findings from this work in the next section.

Stereotype threat is one of the factors that can decrease the self-efficacy of women in physics courses (Steele, 1997; Steele & Aronson, 1995). Marchand and Taasoobshirazi (2013) found that women who are under stereotype threat in physics courses perform worse than men, whether the threat exists implicitly or explicitly. In general, the successful physicist is typically portrayed as male, and there is a perception that physics has a masculine culture and norms (Seymour & Hewitt, 1997). This type of gender socialization can create a stereotype threat, reduce women's self-efficacy, and make women feel that they do not belong in a physics classroom. Societal stereotypes about physics can be internalized by women, constraining their performance and negatively impacting their learning and achievement. Therefore, stereotype threat can reduce women's self-efficacy and performance and can contribute to their underrepresentation and underperformance in physics.

Similarly, a view that natural (innate) ability is a requirement for success in physics can activate an external stereotype threat for women (Leslie, Cimpian, Meyer, & Freeland, 2015). Because men are more commonly associated with higher intellectual ability than women (Upson & Friedman, 2012), the belief that succeeding in physics requires raw brilliance can disadvantage women. One study that examined the early formation of stereotypical beliefs showed that girls at the age of 6 start to think that their male peers are "really, really, smart" (Bian, Leslie, & Chimpian, 2017, p. 389). This study also demonstrated that girls lose their interest in and avoid the activities that are thought to require being "really, really, smart" (Bian et al., 2017, p. 389). In addition, those with a fixed mindset (who view brilliance and natural ability as gifts that one is born with) demonstrate less resilience in the face of difficulties than those with a growth mindset who view the brain as a muscle that can be developed through hard work and struggling (Dweck, 2006, 2007). Therefore, stereotypical beliefs that brilliance is fundamental to success in physics and that men naturally possess superior intellectual gifts might reduce women's self-efficacy and persistence in physics. In particular, research shows that field-specific ability attributions cause women to exhibit lower participation in disciplines that have expectations of brilliance, such as physics, which can lead to gender disparity (Leslie et al., 2015).

Stereotype threat or gender-biased brilliance attributions can also throw women into a negative feedback loop. Female students might initially have lower self-confidence than male students in physics courses because they are subject to external gender-biased societal beliefs. These beliefs can cause female students to internalize threats and adversely impact their learning and performance. Moreover, external and internal stereotype threats that women undergo in physics courses (Marchand & Taasoobshirazi, 2013) can generate feelings of anxiety and worries about failure, which can constrain women's performance and cause them to perform worse than they actually otherwise could, thus reinforcing the negative gender stereotypes (Beilock, Rydell, & McConnell, 2007). In a subsequent task, women might have higher anxiety and even lower confidence, creating a vicious negative cycle. One university course that can activate this feedback loop is the first-year calculus-based physics course.

In sum, beliefs about success in physics are often biased and can play a large role in harming performance, reducing engagement, and generally leading to increasingly negative outcomes. First-year calculus-based "physics" courses are potentially important pressure points. In studying this context, we aim to uncover root causes of low diversity by investigating the dynamics among self-efficacy, performance, and gender.

A RECENT STUDY: THE ROLE OF SELF-EFFICACY IN INTRODUCTORY PHYSICS

Recently, we studied male and female students' motivational characteristics in calculus-based physics courses. Specifically, we examined the role of self-efficacy beliefs as a part of students' motivational characteristics and the interaction of such beliefs with students' physics performance. In calculus-based physics courses, female students make up less than 30% of the population, thus making them likely to be subject to implicit stereotype threat. Because students in calculus-based courses are mostly freshmen, we were able to track their motivational beliefs starting early in the academic program. For these reasons, we chose to examine the relationship between self-efficacy and gender in introductory calculus-based physics courses. Students enrolled in these courses are typically majoring in physical science or engineering fields. In order to measure students' motivational characteristics, we developed a survey using previously constructed and validated instruments and revalidated our instrument with exploratory factor analysis (EFA) and individual student interviews (Marshman, Kalender, Schunn, Nokes-Malach, & Singh, 2017). The EFA showed that self-efficacy items factored as a coherent and separate latent variable with acceptable internal reliability. Furthermore, interviews with students were conducted to test whether students overall and those from different backgrounds interpreted the self-efficacy questions as intended. Our main study included data collected over a 2-year period investigating the motivational characteristics of approximately 1,000 students in calculus-based Physics 1 and Physics 2 courses. The brief self-efficacy survey was given to students in the recitation sections at the beginning of each course and at the end of the second course (i.e., three time points total). Students' responses to the survey were merged with demographic data obtained from university records, which also included students' physics grades. Analysis presented here includes data from Marshman et al. (2017), plus a second year of data collection. Although our dataset is limited to binary gender, we are aware that gender is a multidimensional, sociocultural construct with more than binary gender categories.

LONGITUDINAL ANALYSIS OF SELF-EFFICACY DIFFERENCES ACROSS GENDER

The results revealed a statistically significant gender gap in self-efficacy with a large effect size (Cohen's $d = 0.61$) at the beginning of Physics 1 (pretest) when female students scored lower than male students (see Figure 1.1). The gender gap in self-efficacy persisted at the beginning of Physics 2 and increased at the end of Physics 2 (Cohen's $d = 0.79$). In addition to the persistence of gender differences throughout the two physics courses (Physics 1 and Physics 2), the initial average self-efficacy score for female students was noticeably below 3 (the cutoff for a positive level of self-efficacy on the scale) and declined over time to a score approaching 2 (the cutoff for a negative level of self-efficacy on the scale). In contrast, average self-efficacy

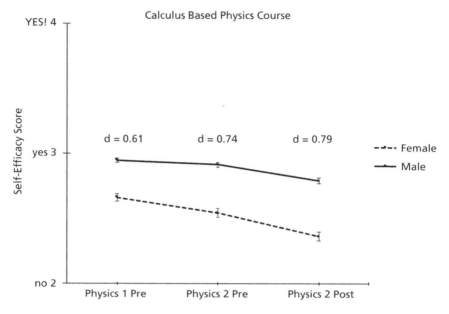

Figure 1.1 Mean longitudinal self-efficacy scores across gender in introductory physics courses for physical science and engineering majors. Error bars represent standard error (Marshman et al., 2018a). "YES!"; "yes"; and "no" correspond to "very positive," "positive," and "negative" mean self-efficacy survey responses, respectively.

of men initially was positive (score of about 3) and showed a much smaller average decline through the end of Physics 2.

The effect sizes suggest that the observed gender gap is large and even growing from Physics 1 to Physics 2. This increasing gender gap in self-efficacy between Physics 1 and Physics 2 was statistically significant. The fact that female students are a minority in physics courses and starting with an initial lower self-efficacy than male students can be one piece of evidence that female students are already under stereotype threat before they even begin to engage in classroom activities (Maries, Karim, & Singh, 2018). Female students who agree with gender stereotypes at the beginning of the course and are likely to have a greater stereotype threat performed worse than female students who disagree with gender stereotypes, despite having no initial difference in female students' performance in these two groups (Maries et al., 2018).

Self-Efficacy Gender Gap Between Similarly Performing Female and Male Students

We also investigated the interactions among self-efficacy, gender, and course performance by examining female and male students' self-efficacy for matched performance levels (Marshman, Kalender, Schunn, Nokes-Malach, & Singh, 2018). Using students' final course grades in Physics 1 and Physics 2, we grouped students into three grade categories: (a) C and C+; (b) B−, B, B+; and (c) A−, A, A+. Students with a grade of C− and below are required to repeat the course in order to move on to the next level, so we excluded them from this analysis.

In Physics 1, female students' average self-efficacy scores were statistically lower than those of male students, regardless of the performance group (see Figure 1.2). In other words, there was a gender gap in self-efficacy scores, even for male and female students who were performing similarly. The effect sizes for the gender gap in self-efficacy range from 0.60 to 0.87, which corresponds to medium to large effect sizes. This alarming gender gap was also apparent for female students in the high-achieving group (grades of A−, A, and A+). The average self-efficacy of female students who received As was equal to male students who received Bs. A positive grade outcome should have helped to close the gender gap in students' self-efficacy, but the self-efficacy gaps are actually similar.

In Physics 2, the large gender gap in students' self-efficacy for matched grade groups persisted. Female students had a statistically significantly lower level of self-efficacy in all matched performance groups. The effect sizes for the gender gap in Physics 1 show similar trends with Physics 2, and self-efficacy for high-achieving female students worsens: Female students receiving As had similar self-efficacy scores as male students receiving Cs.

Relatedly, we also analyzed the gender effect on self-efficacy, controlling for students' grades with different instructors and teaching methodologies (e.g., active engagement versus traditionally taught courses). Regardless of

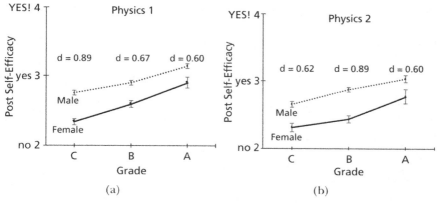

Figure 1.2 Mean posttest self-efficacy scores by gender and course grade in Physics 1 (a) and Physics 2 (b) courses. Error bars represent standard error of the mean. *Source:* Adapted from Marshman, Kalender, Schunn et al., 2018. Copyright 2018 by the American Physical Society.

the instructor or the teaching method, the gender effect on students' self-efficacy was always present and large (Marshman, Kalender, Nokes-Malach, Schunn, & Singh, 2018). Even with reform teaching methods or more effective instructors, women had lower self-confidence (Marshman, Kalender, Nokes-Malach et al., 2018). However, it is important to note that all instructors in this data set were male.

IMPLICATIONS FOR ACADEMIC AND PROFESSIONAL ACHIEVEMENTS

The experiences women have in physics classes play a significant role in developing their self-confidence (Zeldin & Pajares, 2000), and these self-efficacy beliefs can have both short-term and long-term consequences. That the gender gap increases across physics courses and that the gender differences in self-efficacy exist at matched performance levels, regardless of teaching style and instructors, has implications for physics instructors, physics education researchers, and educational policymakers and decision-makers. In addition, the lack of race/ethnic diversity in physics is also a potentially important underlying issue that may be entangled with and contributing to the lack of gender diversity in physics (Litzler, Samuelson, & Lorah, 2014).

In small-group activities, female students with lower self-confidence might allow male students to dominate conversation because these female students worry that their thoughts will be less valued or recognized by others, leading them to participate in group discussions at lower rates. In addition, female students are outnumbered in these classes, and the gender imbalance is reinforced by the fact that all the instructors are male. Because of these worries and anxieties, female students might not fully engage in the classroom, resulting in lower performance than men on high-stakes exams, which initiates the negative feedback cycle for women. In active engagement classes where students frequently interact with one another, instructors need to recognize that female students may not benefit from and participate in small-group activities as much as male students, due to initial disparities in self-efficacy. Unless every member of the group is encouraged to contribute equitably, active engagement courses might not stimulate and sustain women's engagement in physics as much as men's, and the gender gap may increase (Karim et al., 2018).

Additionally, some women with low confidence in physics can prematurely decide to withdraw from the course because they underestimate their competence. Women might also interpret their struggles in physics courses as proof that they are not good at physics or do not have the natural ability to succeed in physics, despite strong performance (Marshman, Kalender, Nokes-Malach et al., 2018). Since there are historically so few female role models in physics and so few female instructors currently teaching, female students might feel that they do not belong in the physics classroom. Another possible driver of the gender gap in self-efficacy is that men have been shown to overestimate their intelligence or competence (von Stumm, 2014). In particular, the self-efficacy gender gap among similarly performing students might be due to under-confidence of women, overconfidence of men, or a combination of both. Regardless of the source, it can hurt women's recruitment, retention, and advancement in STEM fields.

In addition, because the culture of physics is perceived as being masculine and more consistent with male students' needs, women can feel less welcome in the physics community, lowering their sense of belonging, self-confidence, and, ultimately, their motivation to remain in the field. Negatively biased judgements and low physics confidence might cause female students to lose interest in pursuing STEM as a career since physics is one of the fundamental and gateway courses for many STEM majors (Marshman, Kalender, Nokes-Malach et al., 2018).

The self-efficacy gender gap in physics may further influence students, even among those who choose to continue in physical science and engineering beyond the first year. Women who have similar academic achievement with men but lower self-confidence in their ability might have lower STEM success expectancies than do men (Robnett & Thoman, 2017). Because of low confidence and low expectations of success, female students may not take advantage of opportunities, such as internships or undergraduate research experiences, at the same rate as equally qualified male students, even though these experiences can greatly enhance their resume. Those highly qualified female students in the physical sciences or engineering may also have difficulties promoting their strengths in interviews for internships and jobs if they undervalue their skills, performance, and capabilities (Babcock & Laschever, 2007). Women with excellent credentials who undervalue their ability and performance may feel that they are lucky to land a job interview, especially in highly competitive fields; during the job interview, they may not perform as well because they feel anxious about not being qualified for the job. Furthermore, highly qualified women may shy away from competitive situations due to their low self-efficacy (Niederle & Vesterlund, 2007). Even high-achieving women in physics may also discredit their capabilities and undervalue their performance, possibly resulting in their exit from physical science or engineering tracks to non-STEM careers. In the future, we aim to explore students' STEM career pathways and track their college trajectories, as well as test whether early self-efficacy is related to later decisions to stay in STEM, through both quantitative and qualitative analyses. We also intend to investigate self-efficacy and gender dynamics in algebra-based physics courses in which women are often in the majority. Furthermore, we will examine students' self-efficacies in other

STEM domains to better understand the specificity/generality of the self-efficacy gaps and their combined effects on STEM course performance more generally.

Our research findings have implications for faculty members and university administrators in developing, implementing, and supporting interventions and pedagogies that take into account female students' motivations; we are particularly interested in interventions and reformed pedagogies that can help women feel more confident and more accurately assess their skills and performance in physics courses. Social psychological belonging and mindset interventions have been found to be effective in engaging diverse group of students, especially minorities such as women (Yeager & Walton, 2011). Belonging and mindset interventions can convey the message that most students in physics courses have competency concerns, regardless of whether or not they are from underrepresented groups (in physics, this may include women and ethnic/racial minorities); they can also advance the idea that struggling is a stepping stone to learning new material and should not be viewed as a sign of failure. Classroom feedback from instructors can also have a significant impact on women's motivational characteristics, and instructors can unintentionally signal stereotypical beliefs about brilliance by praising students' ability instead of their hard work and effort (Yeager & Walton, 2011). The positive and long-lasting effects of social psychological classroom interventions can help female students have more confidence, a sense of belonging, and persistence in physics.

Gender disparity in students' physics self-efficacy is a critical issue for the field of physics education as a whole. Positive, robust self-efficacy can help women become more resilient and persistent as they pursue more challenging academic and professional goals. The detrimental consequences of failing to address the underrepresentation and lack of supportive environments for women will be a persistent and perpetuating issue in physics and related fields and an unfortunate loss of well-qualified workforce members in STEM occupations. Hence, research into the motivational aspects of student learning has the potential to provide important insights regarding possible reasons for underrepresentation of certain groups of students in physics-related STEM fields. Investigating the origins of motivational characteristics gaps among students by gender or race/ethnicity informs not only physics education researchers but also educational policymakers, curriculum developers, and instructors from all levels of physics teaching in order to promote a more effective, diverse, and inclusive learning environment in the discipline of physics.

REFERENCES

Babcock, L., & Laschever, S. (2007). *Women don't ask: The high cost of avoiding negoitation—and positive strategies for change.* New York, NY: Bantam Books.

Bandura, A. (1977). Self-efficacy: Toward a unifying theory of behavioral change. *Psychological Review, 84*(2), 191–215.

Bandura, A. (1986). *Social foundations of thought and action: A social cognitive theory.* Englewood Cliffs, NJ: Prentice Hall.

Beilock, S. L., Rydell, R. J., & McConnell, A. R. (2007). Stereotype threat and working memory: Mechanisms, alleviation, and spillover. *Journal of Experimental Psychology: General, 136*(2), 256–276.

Bian, L., Leslie, S.-J., & Chimpian, A. (2017). Gender stereotypes about intellectual ability emerge early and influence children's interests. *Science, 355*(6323), 389–391.

Cavallo, A. M. L., Potter, W. H., & Rozman, M. (2004). Gender differences in learning constructs, shifts in learning constructs, and their relationship to course achievement in a structures inquiry, yearlong college physics courses for life science majors. *School Science and Mathematics, 104*(6), 288–300.

Cheryan, S., Ziegler, S. A., Montoya, A. K., & Jiang, L. (2017). Why are some STEM fields more gender balanced than others? *Psychological Bulletin, 143*(1), 1–35.

Collins, J. (1982, March). *Self-efficacy and ability in achievement behaviour.* Paper presented at the meeting of the American Educational Research Association, New York, NY.

Danielsson, A. T. (2012). Exploring woman university physics students "doing gender" and "doing physics." *Gender and Education, 24*(1), 25–39.

Dweck, C. (2007). Is math a gift? Beliefs that put females at risk. In S. J. Ceci & W. M. Williams (Eds.), *Why aren't more women in science? Top researchers debate the evidence* (pp. 47–55). Washington, DC: American Psychological Association.

Dweck, C. S. (2006). *Mindset: The new psychology of success.* New York, NY: Random House.

Hackett, G., & Betz, N. E. (1981). A self-efficacy approach to the career development of women. *Journal of Vocational Behavior, 18*(3), 326–339.

Hazari, Z., Sonnert, G., Sadler, P. M., & Shanahan, M.-C. (2010). Connecting high school physics experiences, outcome expectations, physics identity, and physics career choice: A gender study. *Journal of Research in Science Teaching, 47*(8), 978–1003.

Hutchison-Green, M., Follman, D. K., & Bodner, G. M. (2008). Providing a voice: Qualitative investigation of the impact of a first-year engineering experience on students' efficacy beliefs. *Journal of Engineering Education, 97*(2), 177–190.

Ivie, R. (2018). *Beyond representation: Data to improve the situation of women and minorities in physics and astronomy.* Retrieved from https://www.aip.org/sites/default/files/statistics/women/beyond-representation-18.2.pdf

Karim, N. I., Maries, A., & Singh, C. (2018). Do evidence-based active-engagement courses reduce the gender gap in introductory physics? *European Journal of Physics, 39*(2), 025701–025732.

Kost, L. E., Pollock, S. J., & Finkelstein, N. (2009). Characterizing the gender gap in introductory physics. *Physical Review Special Topics–Physics Education Research, 5*(1), 010101–010114.

Lent, R. W., & Brown, S. D. (2006). On conceptualizing and assessing social cognitive constructs in career research: A measurement guide. *Journal of Career Assessment, 14*(1), 12–35.

Leslie, S.-J., Cimpian, A., Meyer, M., & Freeland, E. (2015). Women are underrepresented in disciplines that emphasize brilliance as the key to success. *Science, 347*, 262–265.

Litzler, E., Samuelson, C. C., & Lorah, A. J. (2014). Breaking it down: Engineering student STEM confidence at the intersection of race/ethnicity and gender. *Research in Higher Education, 55*(8), 810–832.

Madsen, A., McKagan, S. B., & Sayre, E. (2013). Gender gap on concept inventories in physics: What is consistent, what is inconsistent, and what factors influence the gap? *Physical Review Special Topics–Physics Education Research, 9*(2), 020121. https://doi.org/10.1103/PhysRevSTPER.9.020121

Marchand, G. C., & Taasoobshirazi, G. (2013). Stereotype threat and women's performance in physics. *International Journal of Science Education, 35*(18), 3050–3061.

Maries, A., Karim, N. I., & Singh, C. (2018). Is agreeing with a gender stereotype correlated with the performance of female students in introductory physics? *Physical Review–Physics Education Research, 14*(2), 020119. https://doi.org/10.1103/PhysRevPhysEducRes.14.020119

Marshman, E., Kalender, Z. Y., Schunn, C. D., Nokes-Malach, T. J., & Singh, C. (2017). A longitudinal analysis of students' motivational characteristics in introductory physics courses: Gender differences. *Canadian Journal of Physics, 96*(4), 391–404.

Marshman, E., Kalender, Z. Y., Schunn, C. D., Nokes-Malach, T. J., & Singh, C. (2018, July/August). *Gender differences in students' motivational characteristics: Alarming trends*. Presentation presented at the summer meeting of the American Association of Physics Teachers, Washington, DC.

Marshman, E. M., Kalender, Z. Y., Nokes-Malach, T. J., Schunn, C. D., & Singh, C. (2018). Females students with A's have similar physics self-efficacy as male students with C's: In introductory courses: A cause for alarm? *Physical Review–Physics Education Research, 14*(2), 020123. https://doi.org/10.1103/PhysRevPhysEducRes.14.020123

National Science Board. (2014). *Science and engineering indicators 2014*. Retrieved from https://www.nsf.gov/statistics/seind14

Niederle, M., & Vesterlund, L. (2007). Do women shy away from competition? Do men compete too much? *Quarterly Journal of Economics, 122*(3), 1067–1101.

Pajares, F., & Miller, M. D. (1994). Role of self-efficacy and self-concept beliefs in mathematical problem solving: A path analysis. *Journal of Educational Psychology, 86*(2), 193–203.

Pintrich, P., & Schunk, D. (1995). *Motivation in education: Theory, research, and applications*. Englewood Cliffs, NJ: Merrill-Prentice Hall.

Robnett, R. D., & Thoman, S. E. (2017). STEM success expectancies and achievement among women in STEM majors. *Journal of Applied Developmental Psychology, 52*, 91–100.

Sadler, P. M., & Tai, R. H. (2007). The two high-school pillars supporting college science. *Science, 317*(5837), 457–458.

Sawtelle, V., Brewe, E., & Kramer, L. H. (2012). Exploring the relationship between self-efficacy and retention in introductory physics. *Journal of Research in Science Teaching, 49*(9), 1096–1121.

Schunk, D. H. (1994). Self-regulation of self-efficacy and attributions in academic settings. In D. H. Schunk & B. J. Zimmerman (Eds.), *Self-regulation of learning and performance: Issues and educational applications* (pp. 75–99). Hillsdale, NJ: Erlbaum.

Schunk, D. H., & Pajares, F. (2002). The development of academic self-efficacy. In A.Wigfield & J. S. Eccles (Eds.), *Development of achievement motivation* (pp. 15–31). San Diego, CA: Academic Press.

Seymour, E., & Hewitt, N. M. (1997). *Talking about leaving: Why undergraduates leave the sciences.* Boulder, CO: Westview Press.

Shaw, K. A. (2004). The development of a physics self-efficacy instrument for use in the introductory physics classes. *AIP Conference Proceedings, 720,* 137–140.

Steele, C. M. (1997). A threat in the air: How stereotypes shape intellectual identity and performance. *American Psychologist, 52*(6), 613–629.

Steele, C. M., & Aronson, J. (1995). Stereotype threat and the intellectual test performance of African Americans. *Journal of Personality and Social Psychology, 69*(5), 797–811.

Taasoobshirazi, G., & Carr, M. (2009). A structural equation model of expertise in college physics. *Journal of Educational Psychology, 101*(3), 630–643.

Tai, R. H., & Sadler, P. M. (2001). Gender differences in introductory undergraduate physics performance: University physics versus college physics in the USA. *International Journal of Science Education, 23*(10), 1017–1037.

Upson, S., & Friedman, L. F. (2012). Where are all the female geniuses? *Scientific American Mind.* Retrieved from https://www.scientificamerican.com/article/where-are-all-the-female-geniuses

von Stumm, S. (2014). Intelligence, gender, and assessment method affect the accuracy of self-estimated intelligence. *British Journal of Psychology, 105*(2), 243–253.

Wang, M.-T., & Degol, J. (2013). Motivational pathways to STEM career choices: Using expectancy–value perspective to understand individual and gender differences in STEM fields. *Developmental Review, 33*(4), 304–340.

Yeager, D. S., & Walton, G. M. (2011). Social-psychological interventions in education: They're not magic. *Review of Educational Research, 81*(2), 267–301.

Zeldin, A. L., & Pajares, F. (2000). Against the odds: Self-efficacy beliefs of women in mathematical, scientific, and technological careers. *American Educational Research Journal, 37*(1), 215–246.

Zimmerman, B. J. (2000). Self-efficacy: An essential motive to learn. *Contemporary Educational Psychology, 25*(1), 82–91.

CHAPTER 2

REALIST REVIEW

Promoting Diverse Stakeholder Engagement

Katherine W. Bogen
Rhode Island Hospital

Lisa D. Brush
University of Pittsburgh

Samantha Ciaravino
Child Trends, Washington, DC

Maria Catrina D. Jaime
University of California, Davis

Heather L. McCauley
Michigan State University

Elizabeth Miller
Children's Hospital of Pittsburgh

Diversity Across the Disciplines, pages 19–34
Copyright © 2020 by Information Age Publishing
All rights of reproduction in any form reserved.

ABSTRACT

Despite the recent expansion of diversity scholarship, related research often remains siloed within specific academic disciplines, limiting the capacity for cross-cultural and cross-disciplinary collaboration. Toward the goal of establishing interdisciplinary perspectives on diversity and inclusion, this chapter seeks to outline the realist review as a potentially useful method in promoting diverse stakeholder engagement. The chapter explores the theoretical context of interdisciplinary and diverse stakeholder engagement and describes different settings in which realist review methodologies have been successful. The chapter then outlines the realist review process and explains its relevancy to participatory research and diverse stakeholder engagement. By developing a theoretically-grounded model of stakeholder-engaged and cross-cultural research, this chapter aims to achieve a more dynamic interdisciplinary process and contribute to existing literature on best practices.

FUNCTIONAL SILO SYNDROME IN A RESEARCH CONTEXT

In 1988, Phil S. Ensor, a former director of Goodyear Tire and Rubber Company, coined the phrase "functional silo syndrome" to explain barriers to effective collaboration within organizational systems, writing that

> the overall organizational mentality is one of imposing control on people rather than eliciting commitment from them...The organization "behaves" out of a foundation of mistrust and lack of mutual concern. The genius of the people is wasted; individuals are uncommitted; groups are not cohesive. No shared vision exists for people to rally around. Gaping social chasms exist on both the vertical axis and the horizontal axis. (p. 16)

Ensor (1988) highlights the cost of favoring command and control over collaboration and creativity in hierarchical organizations. Actors with greater institutional power are isolated from mid- and low-level workers, preventing ideas from moving smoothly across differently (em)powered communities. This isolation contributes to the crisis of the "silo," making it challenging for lower-level employees or collaborators to have their voices heard and causing groups to self-segregate into communities that will allow them a voice. Actors' communication across tiers is limited. Ideas stop at a single level, and the organization faces significant challenges to bringing in multiple perspectives, disestablishing hierarchy, and empowering low-level collaborators to participate in organization-level progress. Notably, this stymied communication also decreases collaborative competency, especially across diverse stakeholder groups or between individuals with disparate cultural perspectives (Reich & Reich, 2006). In order to enhance attention to diverse voices, promote connection, improve cultural sensitivity, and enliven cross-power collaboration, even historically hierarchical organizations can intentionally counteract silo syndrome.

Though Ensor's (1988) thoughts were based on observations made in business organizations, his insights ring true across other fields, including academic scholarship. In recent years, researchers and practitioners in public health, education, linguistics, psychology, and policy have sought a remedy to hierarchy, internal homogeneity, and silo syndrome, developing mechanisms of collaboration and interdisciplinary work with a fundamental aim of bridging informational gaps, inspiring commitment to research processes, promoting both diversity and cohesion, subverting power differentials, and establishing trust between communities. Unfortunately, research often remains isolated within specific academic disciplines, limiting the capacity for cross-disciplinary collaboration. Substantive and disciplinary silos frustrate cross-cultural collaboration within academia, preventing individuals with social power—especially White upper-class academics—from understanding the needs and norms of "other" (read: othered) communities (Haggis & Schech, 2010; Kubota, 2002). Isolated, narrowly disciplined academics have trouble conducting effective community-based research, which depends on feedback loops among diverse participants in complex projects.

Silo syndrome devastates research reliant on collaboration *with* communities, rather than simply research *about* these communities. Even when scholars include community members and grassroots stakeholders in the research process, hierarchical structures emerge between researchers and community members that may limit the transformative value of this collaboration by—intentionally or otherwise—silencing community partners. Racism, classism, sexism, and other "isms" also impact the institutional life of academics, inhibiting the potential for underrepresented groups to be engaged in research design (Ahmed, 2012). Silos are generated not only by discipline but also by positionality within the collaboration (academic versus community member), race, class, gender, ability, sexual orientation, and social status. The same measures that could strengthen interdisciplinary research could also dismantle top–down evaluation methods, leading to research projects both being designed by diverse teams and benefiting diverse communities.

One field that has been plagued by silo syndrome is research on sexual and gender-based violence. Jordan (2009) maps the extent to which violence against women researchers are isolated in disciplinary siloes (e.g., nursing, psychology). Silo syndrome undermines efforts to address gender-based violence, which might usefully and synergistically engage medical professionals, law enforcement, mental health practitioners, university administrators, Title IX employees, policymakers, funders, and survivors of various social, racial, religious, and gender backgrounds. The infrastructure of violence prevention work is siloed because violence is complex and diverse, and unequal stakeholders often reproduce disciplinary isolation and hierarchies in the process of addressing and mitigating violence (Corrigan, 2013). When diverse stakeholders remain in disciplinary or institutional silos, production and dissemination of knowledge is challenging, stalling improvements in the health of violence survivors and commitment to intervention (Jordan, 2009). Breaking out of silos may help researchers establish best practices in stakeholder engagement across the social sciences and medicine (Cross, Singer, Colella, Thomas, & Silverstone, 2010); ensure cultural competency when working with diverse communities (Pecukonis, Doyle, & Bliss, 2008); and manage the needs and goals of multiple stakeholder groups (Nissen, Merrigan, & Kraft, 2005).

Toward the aim of establishing interdisciplinary perspectives on research, promoting diversity in community-based projects, and working to combat silo syndrome, this chapter presents the realist review (RR; Pawson, Greenhalgh, Harvey, & Walshe, 2005) as a method of stakeholder engagement. Realist Reviews involve collaborative dialogue among stakeholders, allowing multiple perspectives to impact research goals, design, implementation, and feedback. Current practice presents the essential RR research question as "What works for whom in what circumstances, how, and why?"—establishing causality and impact of research in a given context, with specific actors (Greenhalgh, Macfarlane, Steed, & Walton, 2016). Within this context, the "realism" in RR is the focus on description and explanation, rather than normative judgment. Realist Reviews allow participants to set aside normative concerns when approaching a question; the concern is not whether research "should" work a certain way, but simply whether it does and, if so, what circumstances allow it to do so. Throughout this chapter, we introduce settings in which RR could be beneficial, describe the theory behind RR methods, explore stakeholder groups that could participate in RRs, and list potential methodological pros and cons, thereby providing a usable guide for academics collaborating across areas of specialized knowledge and expertise. We seek to establish RR as a theoretically grounded model of stakeholder-engaged and cross-cultural research that encourages a dynamic interdisciplinary process and promotes diversity both in research teams and as an object of study.

SUCCESSFUL CONTEXT(S)

Research teams have documented using RR to approach complex questions regarding research design, impact, evaluation, and feedback. Contexts in which RR has been effectively utilized include planning and implementing a large-system healthcare transformation (Best et al., 2012), developing feasible clinical practice guidelines for medical practitioners (Kastner et al., 2015), making high-impact policy in response to time-sensitive and emerging issues for marginalized communities (Saul, Willis, Bitz, & Best, 2013), designing and implementing malaria control interventions (Donnelly, Berrang-Ford, Ross, & Michel, 2015), and studying and communicating about climate change (Berrang-Ford, Pearce, & Ford, 2015). Realist Reviews are applicable to multiple academic, social, and political contexts in which researchers draw on diverse groups' expertise. However, researchers focused on marginalized or diverse communities that have yet to adopt RR to enhance work with indigenous partners (Jones, Cunsolo, & Harper, 2018) or medical patients with chronic health problems (Jilka, Callahan, Sevdalis, Mayer, & Darzi, 2015).

Moreover, there is limited evidence to suggest that academics in competing or isolated disciplines have adopted RR to facilitate rich cross-disciplinary collaboration, possibly as a result of competing or unequal power dynamics across fields. Research focused on marginalized communities, as well as those isolated in hierarchical research organizations, seem likely to benefit from the synergies of RR, which can foster robust partnerships across numerous disciplines.

SUPPORTIVE THEORIES

The RR method combines complementary informed/analytic and intuitive problem-solving models to enhance the context, mechanisms, and outcomes of research (Jagosh et al., 2012). "Informed" responses—also referred to as analytic responses—are considered deliberate and effortful, and they are reached by a process that can be made explicit (analysis). That is, the processes used to arrive at a conclusion can be clearly explained from start to finish (Hammond, 1996; Hogarth, 2014). "Intuitive" responses are informed by experiential learning, or implicit knowledge of one's own values, the social context of one's communities, and one's own biases. Informed responses are frequently perceived as conscious, whereas intuitive reactions may be subconscious, occurring without a "logically defensible step-by-step process" (Hammond, 1996, p. 60). Both types of responses may be critical in developing an effective RR process and promoting research when researchers and communities are diverse, hierarchical, or potentially plagued by silo syndrome (Hogarth, 2014). Dual problem-solving models can allow participants in an RR to discuss not only how they would logically approach a problem—incorporating multiple perspectives and diverse expertise—but also how they feel about the problem itself, as well as their subconscious (intuitive or instinctual) response to the proposed problem-solving strategy. Dual process theory, the theoretical basis for development of dual problem-solving models, asserts that increased awareness of both of these thought processes, and inclusion of both in research and practice, can allow people greater use of their full cognitive resources (Hogarth, 2014). Valuing both problem-solving approaches allows individuals engaged in RR to react to a proposed scenario through indicating (a) how most people in their community would react to a given research study or project (context); (b) how they themselves would react (perception); and (c) how a person given relevant information regarding the project at hand could be expected to react (Epstein, Lipson, Holstein, & Huh, 1992; adapted from Hogarth, 2014). This effect may be similarly compounded when there are multiple stakeholders engaged in the RR process—when the cognitive resources of an entire group are enhanced for the greater benefit of a community. These multiple voices and perspectives are often left out of traditional research.

Dynamic and inclusive processes, such as dual process theory, are particularly relevant to diversity research. Researchers may observe, measure, and try to remedy some disparities and inequalities, such as racist hiring practices, ensuing wage gaps, and interventions focused on increasing access to high-wage positions (Reardon & Robinson, 2008). However, other processes and outcomes of inequality may be more intuitive or unconscious (e.g., experiences of minority stress and somatization [physical symptoms] from everyday life that may or may not be consciously linked to experiences of racial oppression; Vega & Rumbaut, 1991). As a result, individuals with diverse racial or ethnic perspectives may react differently to proposed research, interventions, methods, or outcomes, given both the conscious and unconscious processing of their lived experiences. Combined informed/ intuitive research processes are therefore especially useful when addressing the needs of diverse communities, as these dual processes create space for dialogue regarding both approaches to knowledge. Not only are diverse actors given the space to analyze their lived experiences and consider how these experiences should impact a research design, but they also are empowered to problem-solve as collaborative peers. The way the problem-solving process *feels* to engaged parties—the extent to which their voices are valued, their individual experiences are taken seriously, and they have opportunities to contribute historically underrepresented perspectives—is therefore given comparable weight to the importance of addressing the problem itself, a balance of priority that is often excluded from traditional research.

In addition to dual process theory, theories of collaborative learning and shared decision-making also undergird the RR method and may increase stakeholder investment in potential positive outcomes. Collaborative learning theory relies on an individual's belief that other people have information to share that is valuable to that individual. Gillam (1994) explores collaborative learning as a means of tutoring peers, decentralizing authority, eliminating hierarchy, reinforcing professional respect, and allowing each participant to feel a sense of agency (e.g., "together, we are part of each other's learning process and can validate each other's experiences"). Such processes may help to establish mutual respect across hierarchal differences, including gender, race, ethnicity, education, and socioeconomic statuses, as well as disciplinary prestige. Collaborative learning is therefore a way to counter silo effects of social hierarchies that privilege certain actors, particularly White men, over others.

Collaborative learning is especially important to counter methodological and disciplinary bigotry. Hammarberg, Kirkman, and De Lacey (2016) discuss disparities between perceptions of qualitative versus quantitative research:

> In quantitative circles, qualitative research is commonly viewed with suspicion and considered lightweight because it involves small samples which may not be representative of the broader population, it is seen as not objective, and the results are assessed as biased by the researchers' own experiences or opinions. In qualitative circles, quantitative research can be dismissed as oversimplifying individual experience in the cause of generalisation, failing to acknowledge researcher biases and expectations in research design, and requiring guesswork to understand the human meaning of aggregate data. (p. 498)

Similar observations have been made regarding prioritizing science, technology, engineering, and mathematics, or STEM, over humanities learning in higher education (Axelrod, 2017). Hierarchy, bigotry, and competition are mutually reinforcing. Collaborative learning undermines these all simultaneously. Collaborative learning enhances the possibilities both for interdisciplinary, multimethod research teams (one sense of diversity) and for community, based on collaborations with historically invisible or silenced constituencies (a second sense of diversity).

The process of shared decision-making reinforces collaborative learning (Gillam, 1994); helps to mitigate potential group conflict (Daniels & Walker, 2001); and reinforces feelings of agency (Elwyn et al., 2012). Traditionally excluded stakeholders take space and power to engage in and take responsibility for a successful outcome, participate in each step of the program or study design, and contribute to the problem-solving activities of the group. Maintaining the dignity of each participant involved in research—that is, ensuring that participants feel that they have the respect of the group and that they themselves respect other opinions being brought to the table—improves feelings of investment in the study goals and creates a stakeholder group more likely to commit passionately to the study than if decisions were all top-down (Satcher, 2005). Such processes may be especially important when the topic arouses controversy, such as sex education in schools, healthcare policies for state and federal aid recipients, or legalization of marijuana. Realist Reviews may be particularly useful in engaging with problems better conceived not in terms of technical solution but rather as various potentially politically motivated possibilities, among which researchers and communities need to choose. Clarifying possibilities and the basis for choices is key in research.

OUTLINING THE REALIST REVIEW PROCESS

Critical steps in the RR process include clarifying the scope of the research question (Step 1); searching for evidence regarding existing approaches to the question (Step 2); appraising studies and extracting data (Step 3); synthesizing evidence and drawing conclusions (Step 4); and disseminating, implementing, and evaluating the research (Step 5; for explicit details of the RR methodology, see Pawson et al., 2005). We discuss Steps 4 and 5 because these final two steps in the review process most intentionally involve the perspectives of multiple stakeholder groups and create the opportunity for cross-cultural and cross-disciplinary collaboration. Importantly, before stakeholders are integrated into the review process, a research question must be identified, the purpose of the review refined for clarity of goals, and key relevant theories explored (Step 1). Once this has been accomplished, researchers examine relevant literature and compile a sampling of articles that will eventually be shared with the stakeholder group (Step 2). Researchers appraise methods and findings and consider fitness, relevance, and rigor of previous studies in order to provide stakeholders with tools for informed decisions about community buy-in (Step 3).

Ideally, researchers invite or encourage academics from outside disciplines to engage in Steps 1–3, exploring theories and literature relevant to their own disciplines and bringing forward promising literature to support an initial project design. That is, rather than simply providing recommendations, academics from other disciplines are integrated into the study design and subsequent evaluation procedures. Moreover, toward the goal of robust and authentic collaboration with community members, all non-research stakeholders should be invited to participate in Steps 1–3 as well, bringing relevant literature and community information to the table to share with the research group. This information could take the form of anecdotes relevant to community needs, data that the community have already collected regarding the problem to be addressed, literature that community members are familiar with or interested in discussing, interventions that have been attempted in the past, and information regarding particular community leaders or institutions that should be involved in sharing expertise. Although this is not made explicit in extant literature regarding the RR process, incorporating community stakeholders into Steps 1–3 of procedures strengthens the capacity of researchers to engage historically invisible, silenced, and marginalized community members throughout the entirety of the research process, including the early steps of establishing critical data to be shared with the larger stakeholder team.

Once the collaborative team has set goals, explored theories, reviewed empirical literature, and collected relevant data from community members, the collaboration becomes more fully rooted, as group members are invited to engage in a facilitated dialogue. Here, researchers seek to contextualize the work, gain perspective from populations involved or impacted, enhance support for the project, and address community concerns. Step 4 of the RR procedure requires participants in the review process to synthesize data and refine theories relevant to the proposed program; this addresses the primary question of determining what works for whom, how, and under what circumstances (Pawson et al., 2005). During this process, researchers, program facilitators, and interventionists frequently pose questions to community stakeholders to assess why a given program would or would not be effective for their community. It is ideal that this step take place in the form of an in-person meeting, allowing all involved parties to literally have a seat at the table. Individuals with decision-making power (frequently those designing or facilitating the project) may summarize disseminated literature and introduce contradictory literature or evidence to generate a dialogue with stakeholders about the specific context in which the project will take place. This discussion enables actors to map out potential outcomes of the social context and programmatic "ingredients," as described by Pawson et al. (2005): "'If A, then B' or 'In the case of C, D is unlikely to work'" (p. 24).

For instance, in the case of a school-based intervention in a low-resource community facing budgetary restrictions—presume this district has been unable to provide teachers with regular contracts—a program may be successful if and only if outside staff implement the intervention. Adding additional responsibilities to overwhelmed teachers would undermine the intervention, no matter how well-designed, theoretically driven, and evidence-based. In such an instance, it is critical that the needs of school staff are addressed during the process of program design and that teachers are allowed the opportunity to voice their insistence that outside facilitators be provided to protect their time, dignity, and buy-in to the project.

In Step 4 of the RR process, community members and other engaged stakeholders become the educators. The goal is to shift attention and power from researchers to local leaders and individuals with deep knowledge of the community. Though interventionists and academics in specific disciplines may have a demographic understanding of community characteristics, the experiential expertise of local stakeholders is critical to successful implementation (and sustainable community change). Stakeholders provide keen, practical insights into their community's needs, organizational structures, internal politics, composition, recent crises, and other factors that may impact the success of the proposed program. Step 4 offers the opportunity to bring in diverse knowledge and perspectives to provide feedback on existing interventions, evaluate whether models developed elsewhere would be effective for their community, and assist in the design of a new intervention. Moreover, it is not enough for researchers to "invite" stakeholders to participate. Rather, the RR process necessitates a commitment to maximizing participation. Maximizing participation means scheduling group meeting times that all parties will be able to attend; subsidizing or providing participant travel; choosing "unconventional" meeting locations (i.e., not ruling out living rooms, community centers, local libraries, and so forth); determining the availability of translators; working around competing schedules; and scheduling multiple meetings with stakeholders so that all relevant groups are able to participate.

Further, Step 5 of the RR method invites community stakeholders to join researchers to draft and test recommendations and conclusions, paying particular attention to changeable factors (e.g., program design, program location, involved participants) and present contexts. Importantly, Step 5 incorporates a revisitation of the review and recommendation processes—especially Step 4—after the program has been rolled out. Such meetings allow stakeholders to examine evidence-based findings from the program or intervention, identify appropriate recommendations, highlight what presently works, and revisit what has been ineffective (Adams, Sedalia, McNab, & Sarker, 2015). Reengagement during Step 5 also helps to build cohesion and strengthen collaboration between researchers and community members, as it reasserts the value of the stakeholders' perspectives. Specifically, reengagement allows researchers to communicate the message that stakeholder feedback was indeed incorporated into the project, to praise stakeholders for the successes of the program, and to seek guidance from stakeholder groups in addressing challenges.

The iterative organization of collaboration in RR puts researchers, academics, and interventionists in a "learning" position, subverting the oft-accepted hierarchy within academia of researchers, academics, and interventionists having power over community members. For a number of reasons, this subversion of hierarchy is an especially critical mandate when doing diversity research and when working across academic disciplines. Consider that as recently as 2016, 76% of full-time faculty in postsecondary institutions in the United States were White (41% White men, 35% White women; U.S. Department of Education, 2018). To counteract White privilege in research, academics must act as learners when working on community-oriented projects, especially when in collaboration with communities of color or communities experiencing multiple marginalizations. Only when community members permit, guide, approve of, and review proposed interventions will projects address the needs of diverse actors, disestablish hierarchy, and potentially counter the prevailing Whiteness of academia and historical racialization, exploitation, and malign neglect of communities of color and other marginalized populations.

THE REALIST APPROACH TO PARTICIPATORY RESEARCH AND STAKEHOLDER ENGAGEMENT

Scenario: A team of tobacco use treatment and prevention advocates develops a school-based intervention to prevent "vaping" (smoking of e-cigarettes) among high school students. The intervention is two hours long, is conducted as an aspect of the in-school health curriculum, and focuses primarily on the health risks of vaping in an attempt to dissuade students from engaging in this behavior. The school is in a large city in the northeast United States and has a racially and ethnically diverse student population: 28% Non-Hispanic White, 33% Black, 22% Latinx, 11% Asian or Pacific Islander, 3% Native, and 3% other/multiracial. Of the student population, 62% receive subsidized lunch. Budgets for the school have been limited, and the district was not able to renew teacher contracts for the year. Facilitators of the intervention receive the following critical feedback from various groups:

- *School health staff:* "Two hours is a long time to take away from the general health curriculum. How do we know this was the best time frame for delivery? Why not incorporate it into after-school programs instead?"
- *Students:* "Adults tell us that vaping is bad all of the time, but a lot of my friends vape socially. Why didn't the class cover ways to turn down vaping but still look cool?"
- *Administrators:* "Our teachers are frustrated at having to give up regular curriculum time for this intervention, and it is very important that we keep in mind teacher needs given contract difficulties this year. How do I communicate to them that it's worth the time?"
- *Parents:* "We didn't know that this program was being run in the school; it would have been nice if researchers kept us more in the loop. What are the warning signs to watch out for? How can I tell if my child has started vaping? How do I talk to my child about the potential health risks?"
- *Local community health center staff:* "We have specialized knowledge of the community and socioeconomic factors that might drive young people in the area to vape. The intervention may be more successful if we are able to give input and point out factors that increase risk."
- *School counseling staff:* "We've noticed that more boys have been getting in trouble for vaping than girls, and that a lot of these boys

come from higher-income families. They might be using their allowance or money from their parents to buy vapes. Did the intervention address how ideas and material privileges of gender and affluence organize vaping habits? How do we make sure that this intervention is relevant for all of our students?"

- *School board:* "It's nice to have outside educators come in and run an intervention, but budgets are tight and we can't pay for this every year. How could we train other people to implement this program? What would it take to make a program like this financially feasible and sustainable?"
- *Intervention design experts:* "Interventions that are positively framed tend to have a better impact than scare-tactic interventions. Why did the intervention team choose to focus on the health risks of vaping, rather than the potential health benefits of not vaping?"

Realist Reviews allow multiple community stakeholders to be engaged in the collection of key information, thereby bolstering the strength of grassroots, participatory research. When diverse members of a community and experts across disciplines are left out of the development and decision-making processes, important questions go unasked, and individual stakeholder groups may struggle to buy into a research project. Fostering feelings of engagement and receiving feedback from multiple stakeholder groups through an inclusive RR process could significantly strengthen this intervention. Incorporating stakeholder concerns and initial observations into the intervention's initial planning phases, rather than adopting the traditional method of amending the intervention after receipt of feedback, could also save valuable resources, including time and financial expenditures.

IMPORTANCE OF STAKEHOLDER ENGAGEMENT AND PARTICIPATORY RESEARCH

Fundamentally, the RR method develops participatory research partnerships among researchers/academics, the populations they aim to serve, and the study participants themselves. Jagosh et al.'s (2012) review of participatory research literature examines the importance of partnership synergy and the larger impact of collaboration on process outcomes. According to Jagosh et al. (2012), participatory research partnerships

(1) ensure culturally and logistically appropriate research, (2) enhance recruitment capacity, (3) generate professional capacity and competence in stakeholder groups, (4) result in productive conflicts followed by useful ne-

gotiation, (5) increase the quality of outputs and outcomes over time, (6) increase the sustainability of project goals beyond funded time frames and during gaps in external funding, and (7) create system changes and new unanticipated projects and activities. (p. 312)

Realist Review serves as a particularly promising method to achieve these goals, especially when the context (sociocultural backdrop of a given program or research project) is supportive. Realist Review assesses the level of contextual support and challenges by asking community partners the following questions: How will my environment/community impact the success of the proposed project, and what do all engaged groups foresee as being the most difficult part of working together? Specifically, understanding the degree to which the community might support the proposed project and the potential obstacles to a successful intervention can strengthen design, content, implementation, evaluation, and eventual dissemination of innovative interventions with diverse populations.

Steps 4 and 5 of the RR process allow all collaborating groups to work toward the flattening of hierarchy by recognizing diverse expertise and sharing critical tools, including knowledge of previous findings and efforts as well as intimate understandings of community values, dynamics, and needs. Without incorporating the voices of diverse actors from different racial, socioeconomic, educational, professional, and academic backgrounds, it is unlikely that proposed research projects will be relevant to populations that span these intersecting dimensions of inequality. Moreover, when research aims to address a very specific community or need, receiving input, buy-in, and guidance from the target community—indeed, empowering these communities to lead discourse and design—is critical. Only members of the target community will have the insider knowledge to plan a relevant project, address pushback from other community members, and ethically execute stakeholder-engaged participatory research.

POTENTIAL CHALLENGES TO BE ADDRESSED

Although RR provides promising opportunities to challenge hierarchical research models, address silo syndrome, contribute to cross-disciplinary collaboration, and enhance the inclusion of diverse perspectives within the academy, challenges remain. First, given existing hierarchies and social powers, a single dominant voice (or several dominant voices) may monopolize the review process (Luntz, 1994). Research on political focus groups in the United States highlights the need for a group moderator or session facilitator to ensure that no one member of the review process dominates the collaborative space. Of course, this facilitator must guard against the likelihood that they—intentionally or unintentionally—steer or direct a conversation that is supposed to be driven by the interests and concerns of stakeholders.

Additionally, RR, if improperly conceived or executed, may reinforce hierarchy and position groups already in power by appearing to be patronizing and doing a favor by listening to marginalized perspectives. This phenomenon has been examined in terms of "White savior" and "male savior" complex (Frey, 2016; Madsen & Mabokela, 2016), wherein White individuals and masculine individuals, as a function of their relative social status and power, seek to "rescue" a population perceived as "needy." Such efforts may unintentionally disempower already marginalized actors by treating them as charity cases, acting condescending toward them, or eliding the privileging of certain people engaged in the project (particularly men, White people, wealthy people, and people with higher degrees). It is therefore the responsibility of the facilitator, preferably with active collaboration of the group as a whole, to create a plan to disestablish hierarchy throughout the RR process, planning regular check-ins and establishing ground rules to ensure that the voices of all participants are both heard and valued.

Potential challenges notwithstanding, RR models a community-based research approach that may confront silo syndrome; magnifying diverse voices in academia, establishing appropriate research designs and interventions tailored to specific populations, and encouraging interdisciplinary collaboration. Intentional integration of multiple perspectives through review Steps 1–5 (especially Steps 4 and 5) provides ample opportunity to bridge what Ensor (1988) called the "gaping social chasms" (p. 16) plaguing hierarchical organizations, including the ivory tower. Realist Review is a valuable addition to the best practices toolbox of researchers, practitioners, grassroots organizers, program directors, and teams attempting to engage in a theoretically grounded model of inclusive program planning, design, implementation, and evaluation.

REFERENCES

Adams, A., Sedalia, S., McNab, S., & Sarker, M. (2015). Lessons learned in using realist evaluation to assess maternal and newborn health programming in rural Bangladesh. *Health Policy and Planning, 31*(2), 267–275.

Ahmed, S. (2012). *On being included: Racism and diversity in institutional life.* Durham, NC: Duke University Press.

Axelrod, P. (2017, October 26). *Are STEM fields over-prioritized in higher education?* Retrieved from https://yaleglobal.yale.edu/content/are-stem-fields-over-prioritized-higher-education

Berrang-Ford, L., Pearce, T., & Ford, J. D. (2015). Systematic review approaches for climate change adaptation research. *Regional Environmental Change, 15*(5), 755–769.

Best, A., Greenhalgh, T., Lewis, S., Saul, J. E., Carroll, S., & Bitz, J. (2012). Large-system transformation in health care: A realist review. *Milbank Quarterly, 90*(3), 421–456.

Corrigan, R. (2013). *Up against a wall: Rape reform and the failure of success.* New York, NY: New York University Press.

Cross, R., Singer, J., Colella, S., Thomas, R. J., & Silverstone, Y. (2010). *The organizational network fieldbook: Best practices, techniques, and exercises to drive organizational innovation and performance.* San Francisco, CA: Jossey-Bass.

Daniels, S. E., & Walker, G. B. (2001). *Working through environmental policy conflict: The collaborative learning approach.* Westport, CT: Praeger.

Donnelly, B., Berrang-Ford, L., Ross, N. A., & Michel, P. (2015). A systematic, realist review of zooprophylaxis for malaria control. *Malaria Journal, 14*, 313. https://www.doi.org/10.1186/s12936-015-0822-0

Elwyn, G., Frosch, D., Thomson, R., Joseph-Williams, N., Lloyd, A., Kinnersley, P., . . . Barry, M. (2012). Shared decision making: A model for clinical practice. *Journal of General Internal Medicine, 27*(10), 1361–1367.

Ensor, P. S. (1988). The functional silo syndrome. *AME Target, 16*, 16.

Epstein, S., Lipson, A., Holstein, C., & Huh, E. (1992). Irrational reactions to negative outcomes: Evidence for two conceptual systems. *Journal of Personality and Social Psychology, 62*(2), 328–339.

Frey, C. (2016). The White savior in the mirror. In A. W. Wiseman (Ed.), *Annual review of comparative and international education 2016* (Vol. 30; pp. 185–198). Bingley, England: Emerald Group.

Gillam, A. M. (1994). Collaborative learning theory and peer tutoring practice. In J. A. Mullin & R. Wallace (Eds.), *Intersections: Theory-practice in the writing center* (pp. 39–53). Urbana, IL: National Council of Teachers of English.

Greenhalgh, T., Macfarlane, F., Steed, L., & Walton, R. (2016). What works for whom in pharmacist-led smoking cessation support: Realist review. *BMC Medicine, 14*, 209. https://doi.org/10.1186/s12916-016-0749-5

Haggis, J., & Schech, S. (2010). Refugees, settlement processes and citizenship making: An Australian case study. *National Identities, 12*(4), 365–379.

Hammarberg, K., Kirkman, M., & De Lacey, S. (2016). Qualitative research methods: When to use them and how to judge them. *Human Reproduction, 31*(3), 498–501.

Hammond, K. (1996). *Human judgement and social policy.* Oxford, England: Oxford University Press.

Hogarth, R. M. (2014). Deciding analytically or trusting your intuition? The advantages and disadvantages of analytic and intuitive thought. In T. Betsch & S. Haberstroh (Eds.), *The routines of decision making* (pp. 97–112). New York, NY: Psychology Press.

Jagosh, J., Macaulay, A. C., Pluye, P., Salsberg, J., Bush, P. L., Henderson, J., . . . Seifer, S. D. (2012). Uncovering the benefits of participatory research: Implications of a realist review for health research and practice. *The Milbank Quarterly, 90*(2), 311–346.

Jilka, S. R., Callahan, R., Sevdalis, N., Mayer, E. K., & Darzi, A. (2015). "Nothing about me without me": An interpretative review of patient accessible electronic health records. *Journal of Medical Internet Research, 17*(6), e161.

Jones, J., Cunsolo, A., & Harper, S. L. (2018). Who is research serving? A systematic realist review of circumpolar environment-related Indigenous health literature. *PloS One, 13*(5). https://doi.org/10.1371/journal.pone.0196090

Jordan, C. E. (2009). Advancing the study of violence against women: Evolving research agendas into science. *Violence Against Women, 15*(4), 393–419.

Kastner, M., Bhattacharyya, O., Hayden, L., Makarski, J., Estey, E., Durocher, L.,... Brouwers, M. (2015). Guideline uptake is influenced by six implementability domains for creating and communicating guidelines: A realist review. *Journal of Clinical Epidemiology, 68*(5), 498–509.

Kubota, R. (2002). The author responds: (Un)raveling racism in a nice field like TESOL. *TESOL Quarterly, 36*(1), 84–92.

Luntz, F. (1994). Focus group research in American politics. *The Polling Report, 10*(10), 1. Retrieved from http://www.pollingreport.com/focus.htm

Madsen, J. A., & Mabokela, R. O. (2016). Critical consciousness in the cross-cultural research space: Reflections from two researchers engaged in collaborative cross-cultural research. In A. W. Wiseman (Ed.), *Annual Review of Comparative and International Education 2016* (pp. 147–163). Bingley, England: Emerald Group.

Nissen, L. B., Merrigan, D. M., & Kraft, M. K. (2005). Moving mountains together: Strategic community leadership and systems change. *Child Welfare, 84*(2), 123–140.

Pawson, R., Greenhalgh, T., Harvey, G., & Walshe, K. (2005). Realist review—A new method of systematic review designed for complex policy interventions. *Journal of Health Services Research & Policy, 10*(Suppl. 1), 21–34.

Pecukonis, E., Doyle, O., & Bliss, D. L. (2008). Reducing barriers to interprofessional training: Promoting interprofessional cultural competence. *Journal of Interprofessional Care, 22*(4), 417–428.

Reardon, S. F., & Robinson, J. P. (2008). Patterns and trends in racial/ethnic and socioeconomic academic achievement gaps. In H. F. Ladd & E. B. Fiske (Eds.), *Handbook of research in education, finance, and policy* (pp. 497–516). New York, NY: Routledge.

Reich, S. M., & Reich, J. A. (2006). Cultural competence in interdisciplinary collaborations: A method for respecting diversity in research partnerships. *American Journal of Community Psychology, 38*(1–2), 51–62.

Satcher, D. (2005). *Methods in community-based participatory research for health.* San Francisco, CA: Wiley.

Saul, J. E., Willis, C. D., Bitz, J., & Best, A. (2013). A time-responsive tool for informing policy making: Rapid realist review. *Implementation Science, 8*, 103. https://doi.org/10.1186/1748-5908-8-103

U.S. Department of Education. (2018). *The condition of education 2018.* Retrieved from https://nces.ed.gov/pubs2018/2018144.pdf

Vega, W. A., & Rumbaut, R. G. (1991). Ethnic minorities and mental health. *Annual Review of Sociology, 17*(1), 351–383.

CHAPTER 3

TAKING REFUGE/SYRIA

A Case Study for Interdisciplinary Collaboration

Cynthia Croot
University of Pittsburgh

ABSTRACT

The chapter examines the interdisciplinary project, Taking Refuge, which aimed to humanize the situation of Syrian refugees, by giving voice to the crisis through works of classical and contemporary theatre, film, journalism, and academic research. The first part of this chapter explores the need for interdisciplinary dialogues regarding Syrian refugees with special attention to the refugee experience in Pittsburgh. The second part of the chapter describes the innovative programming of Taking Refuge at the University of Pittsburgh and at other college campuses emphasizing the power of collaboration and interdisciplinary partnerships to educate students about the Syrian refugee experience.

In this chapter, I will explore how Diversity Across the Disciplines, an initiative funded by the Year of Diversity and the David Berg Center for Ethics and Leadership at the University of Pittsburgh, helped catalyze Taking

Diversity Across the Disciplines, pages 35–52
35

Refuge (http://www.takingrefuge.net), a series of performances and events exploring the lives of Syrian refugees. I'll discuss how the support from Pitt's Year of Diversity helped spur an international conversation about displacement, the Syrian refugee crisis, and our notions about what it means to belong in a community and the world. In addition to describing that initial institutional support, I will discuss the other collaborators, funders, and organizations who helped bring this project to life at Pitt and other schools in the United States and the United Kingdom, expanding the project with subject area expertise, unique perspectives, and professional and artistic connections. These pivotal collaborators included students and colleagues, artists and journalists, community leaders, and Syrian refugees who came together during our weeklong examination of the Syrian refugee crisis in a project called Taking Refuge.

The success of this project, reaching across the divides of discipline and geography that often impede scholars attempting multidisciplinary ventures, may provide a model for new and sustained interdisciplinary efforts. It is my hope in this chapter to create a space for reflection on interdisciplinary global collaborations like Taking Refuge and offer recommendations for future work. I also describe the relevance of my time as a U.S. delegate in a 2004 cultural exchange with the Center for International Conflict Resolution (CICR) at Columbia University, which provided the subterranean scaffold that made this project possible. The impact of that experience illustrates the power of international exchange programs to influence young scholars and leave an indelible mark on their work to come.

BACKGROUND: INTERDISCIPLINARY DIALOGUES ABOUT SYRIA

In 2004, I was a freelance director living in New York City, having completed my Master of Fine Arts in Theatre Directing at Columbia University. Knowing of my commitment to theatre and social justice, a colleague forwarded an opportunity she thought might interest me. Columbia University's CICR, under the stewardship of Andrea Bartoli (in partnership with Damascus University and the U.S. Department of State), was hosting an interdisciplinary cultural exchange. Hoping to forge cultural connections where state connections were failing, they were building a U.S.–Syria citizens exchange to allow participants to experience the other's country firsthand. CICR was especially interested in U.S. delegates who had never traveled to the region. They issued a call for academics, educators, environmentalists, and artists interested in participating for several weeks in the United States and Syria. Events ranged from enervating to euphoric, from a candid political conversation with Noam Chomsky at the Massachusetts Institute of Technology, to a sunrise tour of the ancient city of Palmyra. I was struck by my vast ignorance of Syria and the staggering number of assumptions, stereotypes, and narratives I inherited from the U.S. media before I saw the country for myself. Those weeks of cognitive dissonance changed me. I returned to the United States determined to educate the public about misinformation about the region. Conducting research over ensuing years in Syria, Palestine, Israel, Jordan, and Iran (an area I will refer to as the Middle East), my passion for the region has deepened. But from the outset, CICR was the catalyst. As a direct result of that initial cultural exchange in 2004, I created Taking Refuge in 2017, and universities across the United States and in the United Kingdom took part in projects exploring the plight of Syrian refugees from cross-cultural and cross-disciplinary perspectives.

BACKGROUND: CONFLICT IN SYRIA

Located along the Mediterranean Sea between Turkey, Iraq, Jordan, Lebanon, and Israel, Syria was little known to much of the U.S. public before the civil war began in 2011. The country was often considered only as it related to U.S. conflicts with Afghanistan, Iraq, or ISIS. Terms like "Arab" or "Islamic" or "Middle Eastern" were incorrectly regarded as interchangeable in reporting on the region, and whole countries were reviled as dangerous (Barakat, 2018). When we undertook Taking Refuge in the Spring of 2017, the civil war in Syria had been going on for 6 years, and the number of refugees from Syria had just reached 5 million. Today that figure tops 6.5 million (UNHCR, 2018).

To call the Syrian refugee situation a crisis is to understate it dramatically. Not only are individual citizens displaced, but Syria and the surrounding region have also been transformed through violence and war. The sheer number of people seeking resettlement are reshaping the geopolitical world. In 2018, nearly 7 years into the conflict, there was little evidence that former residents of Syria would return home. Many had no home to return to (Chulov, 2018). As a result, most refugees are attempting to pursue permanent citizenship in their new geographies. For countries where the refugee population is plentiful, this creates a strain on resources. Countries like Lebanon are experiencing a cultural shift of seismic proportions. According to the World Bank (n.d.), Lebanon is home to the largest number of refugees per capita in the world—one Syrian refugee for every four Lebanese in the country.

PITTSBURGH AND THE SYRIAN REFUGEE CRISIS

While the University of Pittsburgh has nine registered student clubs associated with Middle Eastern cultures and the Cathedral of Learning boasts an international room dedicated to Syria, no official Syrian student club exists on campus (L. Miller, personal communication, September 26, 2018).

And although nearby Allentown, Pennsylvania, is home to the largest Syrian community in the United States, Pittsburgh residents have had a mixed reaction to assisting in the continuing refugee crisis. Pittsburgh Mayor Bill Peduto pledged to take in 500 refugees when he took office (WXPI, 2015), but by 2017, that number had still not been met. Instead, Peduto found opposition from people around the city. Many expressed misgivings about resources already stretched thin for current city residents. Some people made xenophobic and anti-Muslim remarks, and others expressed outsized security concerns (St-Esprit, 2017).

To my students at the University of Pittsburgh, the impact of the Syrian refugee crisis was very remote. While news outlets reported on Syrians crammed into boats and dead children on beaches, most of the undergraduates I spoke with about the crisis seemed uninformed, misinformed, or disinterested in events occurring half a world away. In this climate, I found it imperative to address the crisis in a manner that humanized the conflict and the personal toll of the war. I wanted to find a way to concretize this conflict for my students. It was also vital to me to foreground the artistic expression and experiences of Syrians by providing a space for marginalized voices to take center stage. Within my department at the University of Pittsburgh, part of our ongoing mission is to increase visibility for underserved populations, celebrate diversity, and empower voices from outside the mainstream to be heard. The project I was envisioning fell solidly in line with these goals, and quickly found a home in the Department of Theatre Arts.

CREATING TAKING REFUGE

I planned Taking Refuge in concert with the annual celebration of World Theatre Day. Founded in 1961 by the International Theatre Institute (ITI), World Theatre Day is celebrated each year on March 27. Since its creation by UNESCO in 1948, along with leading theatre and dance experts, ITI has worked to foster peacemaking through the arts at its centers around the world. The celebration is marked by messages from theatre luminaries and an open call for events around the world to celebrate the potential of the creative arts. Aligned with the core values expressed by ITI and their founding partner, UNESCO, World Theatre Day emphasizes inspiration, inclusiveness, collaboration, and transparency. The occasion provided a perfect opportunity to address the situation of human displacement through the performance of a play. I resolved to present the critically acclaimed text *Oh My Sweet Land* by Amir Zuabi as part of the larger Taking Refuge project.

Zuabi is a playwright and director who grew up in a conflict zone and is familiar with displacement, historical injustice, and political struggle. Written in 2013 and produced in London in 2014, *Oh My Sweet Land* was praised in the press. The *New York Times* described it as "a forceful and absorbing play about a Syrian-American woman who goes searching for her married lover, Ashraf" (Soloski, 2017, para. 3). The solo piece is structured as a series of vignettes told by a woman busy cooking kibbeh: croquettes made of lamb (or sometimes goat or beef), bulgur wheat, onions, pine nuts, and spices. The food is a staple of Syrian cuisine. The play has been presented around the world in wildly different venues, from London's Young Vic to kitchens in private homes around New York City. Zuabi's play helped ground audiences in a cross-cultural experience of the Syrian refugee crisis, making a distant conflict relevant for the American audience. As *New York Times* reviewer Alexis Soloski put it:

> Probably most of us read news articles and absorb reports about fighting in Syria or similarly fraught regions. Maybe we have signed petitions or made donations. But I doubt we have let ourselves feel the full extent of these horrors, like the revelation that many children have been killed in chemical weapons attacks. Mr. Zuabi's play implicates its audience for wondering whether this woman, with her American passport and more or less comfortable life, will ever find her lover when women who look just like her are being suffocated. Yet this isn't a scolding play or a holier-than-thou one. The woman is realizing the limits of her own awareness right alongside us. "Decent people can't look away from what is happening," she tells herself. But people can and people do, like the woman who will soon look away from us as she removes the kibbe from boiling oil. So we go on—cooking, cleaning, watching plays—and we put slaughter out of our minds. What else can we do? (Soloski, 2017, paras. 8–9)

Zuabi enthusiastically agreed to participate in Taking Refuge and granted permission for a staged reading at the University of Pittsburgh. Given the international connections the artists involved already had in place, I decided to attempt to coordinate additional programming across the United States. The national platform would help draw attention to the artistry of Zuabi and others while enlightening audiences about the reality of a life displaced. Zuabi's reading at the University of Pittsburgh acted as an anchor for presentations and discussions contextualizing Syria from the vantage point of other disciplines as well.

TAKING REFUGE: CROSS-DISCIPLINARY DIALOGUES AT THE UNIVERSITY OF PITTSBURGH

Overview

The University of Pittsburgh hosted eight separate events for Taking Refuge. The project expanded and gained momentum through the critical cooperation of partners Jacques Bromberg (Classics), Lisa R. Bromberg (Global Studies), and Michael Goodheart (Global Studies), along with collaborators and allies Annmarie Duggan (Theatre Arts), Randall Halle (Film Studies), Daniel Kubis (Humanities Center), Jonathan Arac (Humanities Center), and Elaine Linn (Consortium for Educational Resources on Islamic Studies), among others. Our weeklong slate of events would not have been possible without everyone's hard work and stewardship. Taking Refuge: An examination of the Syrian Refugee Crisis by Artists, Activists, Academics, and Individuals Directly Affected by War and Political Violence took place March 22–29, 2017, and included the following:

- Syria in Context: a conversation with Joseph Bahout, visiting lecturer with the Carnegie Endowment for International Peace, and Luke Peterson (Global Studies), with an introduction by Michael Goodhart (Global Studies)
- Pittsburgh Perspectives: a roundtable discussion featuring Leslie Aizenman, director of Refugee and Immigrant Services, Jewish Family and Children's Services; Wiam Younes (Computer Sciences), cofounder of Pittsburgh Refugee Center; Kristen Tsapis, community volunteer, Somali Bantu Community Association; Jenna Baron, executive director, Alliance for Refugee Youth Support and Education; Jaime Turek, senior reception and placement cast manager at Northern Area Multi-Service Center; and members of the local Syrian community, moderated by Lisa R. Bromberg (Global Studies)
- Presentation and talk with photojournalist Maranie Rae and Human Refuge(e)
- Reading of *Oh My Sweet Land* by Zuabi, performed by Lameece Issaq, founding director of Noor Theatre and dedicated to the work of theatre artists of Middle Eastern descent, followed by a discussion facilitated by Cynthia Croot
- Screening of *Mare Nostrum* and *Searching for the Translator*: two short films by Rana Kazkaz and Anas Khalaf
- Reading of selections from *Trojan Women* by Euripides, followed by a community discussion facilitated by Cynthia Croot with Jacques Bromberg
- Screening of *Queens of Syria* documentary
- Screening of Queens of Syria performing their adaptation of *The Trojan Women* by Euripedes, followed by a conversation with Mohammed Bamyeh (Sociology), editor of *International Sociology Reviews*

Taking Refuge: Providing Context to the Conflict

Taking Refuge incorporated cross-disciplinary and multimedia events, including performance, film, discussion, and keynote lectures. This provided students with a variety of entry points for understanding the sociopolitical situation in Syria, and background and context for the artistic work they were viewing. At the outset, the conversation between Joseph Bahout and Luke Peterson gave the conflict greater immediacy, grounding us in the geopolitical situation on the ground. It also seemed to offer some hope, describing nascent systems emerging in the absence of traditional government in Syria and how people were attempting democratic organization amidst the conflict.

Voices From Syria

Our project also welcomed the views of Syrians, both as artists and citizens. To involve our extended campus community directly, we invited several local leaders who work with refugees and immigrants, along with recently relocated refugees living in Pittsburgh, to join us. Their comments proved some of the most poignant of the sessions I attended. One woman, asking about ways she could help Syrian refugees, was chastised by an audience member who reminded her that many residents in Pittsburgh had lived in the city all their lives and also needed help. One of the Syrian refugees on the panel spoke up then, affirming that, yes, help was needed by her community, and help was welcome. This exchange spurred a conversation about the needs of refugees as they related to ongoing inequities in the Pittsburgh community, a topic that threaded through other events in the series. It was a fruitful discussion where people were able to ask questions, offer services, make connections, and see the topic in the broader context of our city and the challenges it faces.

Taking Refuge: Depictions of Syria Through Performance, Photography, and Film

Taking Refuge featured artwork examining the Syrian conflict and human displacement through genres including performance, photography, and film. The centerpiece of our series was a staged reading of *Oh My Sweet Land*. Performed by Lameece Issaq, it was a complex and humanizing portrait of life in exile. Providing another site of artist-witness, Maranie Rae shared her images from the Zaatari refugee camp in Jordan, as well as the stories residents told her. These first-person accounts accompanied by Rae's photos proved a moving testimony of the human cost of war. Screenings were also presented by Syrian refugee filmmakers Rana Kazkaz and Anas Khalaf. Their extraordinary short film *Mare Nostrum* was especially effective at complicating assumptions an audience might make about the crisis. Thirteen minutes long, it depicts a Syrian father putting his daughter's life at risk on a Mediterranean shore, with the ultimate goal of helping her make her way to safety across the sea. It is a film that humanizes the plight of refugees, making plain the impossible decisions they face. Since its release, it has been selected at over 100 international film festivals, including Sundance, and has won more than 40 international prizes.

Spearheaded by Jacques Bromberg, two full-length films were also screened: the *Queens of Syria* documentary chronicling their play development and adaptation process, and the Queens of Syria's performance of *Trojan Women*. Documentary director Yasmin Fedda's Tell Brak Films website ("Queens of Syria," 2017) describes how

> fifty women from Syria, all forced into exile in Jordan, came together in Autumn 2013 to create and perform their own version of the *Trojan Women*, the timeless Ancient Greek tragedy all about the plight of women in war. What followed was an extraordinary moment of cross-cultural contact across millennia, in which women born in 20th century Syria found a blazingly vivid mirror of their own experiences in the stories of a queen, princesses and ordinary women like them, uprooted, enslaved, and bereaved by the Trojan War.

In their review in 2016, the *Guardian* called the live performance of this adaptation of *Trojan Women* "the most urgent work on the London stage" (Clapp, 2016, para. 1).

The films provided different points of view on the performance: one from the perspective of the audience and the other from behind the scenes, documenting the creation of the piece itself. The documentary won various awards, including for Best Documentary Director from the Arab World at the Abu Dhabi Film Festival, and collecting accolades at festivals in Morocco, Argentina, and Minneapolis–St. Paul.

Finally, Taking Refuge at Pitt included a live staging of Euripides' version of *Trojan Women*. It was essential to help students understand historical precedents of displacement in the region and the source material upon which the work of the Queens of Syria was based. Excerpts from the play were performed by professional members of the arts community and the Department of Theatre Arts (Kimberly Parker Griffin, Brendan Griffin, Elizabeth Ruelas, Julia de Avilez Rocha, and Bri Scholar) under my direction. The performance was moving in itself, as well as in relation to the other events, screenings, and talks that week. But it was an especially useful foil to the film adaptation and documentary about the work of the group Queens of Syria.

Project Outcomes

Reflecting on the project and the feedback we received, Taking Refuge at the University of Pittsburgh was an artistic, programmatic, and pedagogical success. We documented attendance from students across the campus pursuing different majors and felt that the variety of events gave multiple opportunities for undergraduate and graduate students to engage with the subject critically, personally, and artistically. Several sessions even incorporated authentic food, sometimes serving as an additional draw for audiences. We were fortunate to find a local chef who prepared Syrian cuisine, allowing students to experience Syrian culture firsthand. It was an ambitious slate, but each gathering served a specific purpose in our design. From describing the immediate needs of refugees and the precedents that contributed to the current situation to exploring the historical struggles of the region as dramatized in ancient texts, Taking Refuge painted a sweeping portrait of the crisis.

In addition to our Pitt team of artist-practitioners, administrators, and scholars, we were aided in our efforts through several pivotal funding sources. Financial support for the project came from the Kabak Endowment (Babette Kabak was a 1939 Pitt graduate whose legacy lives on through this endowment, as does her passion for justice and peaceful conflict resolution); the departments of Film Studies, Classics, Global Studies, and Theatre Arts; the Humanities Center, the David Berg Center for Ethics and Leadership, and the University of Pittsburgh's Year of Diversity.

TAKING REFUGE PARTNER PROGRAMMING

This section describes some of the other campuses where Taking Refuge events took place and partners who were instrumental in the depth and breadth of this project in the United States and the United Kingdom. As I began to share promotional news of our upcoming series at Pitt, several colleagues inquired about how they might be involved on their own campuses. Theatre departments were ideal spaces to host a reading of *Oh My Sweet Land*, and World Theatre Day was a strong anchor that helped unify involvement on other campuses, including participants at the University of Roehampton in the United Kingdom, College of the Holy Cross, Colgate University, Indiana University of Pennsylvania, Louisiana State University, and the College of Charleston.

University of Roehampton

Glenn Odom's approach was unique, integrating an exploration of the refugee situation into his curriculum in advance of our World Theatre Day events. To start with, I visited the campus and worked with several of his students who had been conducting research on Islamic culture and theatre. We explored a variety of movement exercises based on Viewpoints (Anne Bogart's system adapted from the work of Mary Overlie) and engaged in discussions about notions of migration and home. Odom described how

> students then read several plays from the Arab world more broadly and visited London's Islamic Cultural Centre and Mosque. We followed this up by an informal public reading of *Oh My Sweet Land,* aimed at students. This was the first event of this sort the department had participated in three years. (G. Odom, personal communication, October 10, 2018)

The reading his students undertook was "very informal...in which students volunteered for the parts and underwent minimal preparation" (G. Odom, personal communication, October 10, 2018). While the group was small (12 participated), they were "excited by the work and commented that they appreciated seeing more representation of the Middle East in our curriculum" (G. Odom, personal communication, October 10, 2018). On some campuses, the identity of the central character in the play presented a casting challenge. This did not seem to be a problem at Roehampton, which had a higher percentage of students of color than some other participating schools. As Odom explained, "we are 70% BAME [Black, Asian, and minority ethnic] with roughly 20% identifying with Islam culturally or religiously" (G. Odom, personal communication, October 10, 2018).

I asked Odom in a follow-up interview if the event had any immediate or long-term impact. He responded that "one student who was part of the rehearsal process began attending his modules more regularly and also wrote his dissertation on issues of representation in theatre" (G. Odom, personal communication, October 10, 2018). While it is difficult to credit Taking Refuge for such a significant shift in attention and direction, the value of students recognizing themselves in the art they encounter is well documented (Keto, 2016). Odom's experience suggests that *Oh My Sweet Land* opened a door for this particular student—and helped make visible an opportunity that was not obvious before.

College of the Holy Cross

Associate professor Nadine Knight at College of the Holy Cross in Worcester, Massachusetts, hosted a live reading of *Oh My Sweet Land* to mark the occasion of World Theatre Day in coordination with the Peace and Conflict Studies program and the Department of Art History on campus. Her collaboration with the Peace and Conflict Studies program was a natural fit, given that they had created a series in support of the JUHAN (Jesuit Universities Humanitarian Action Network) Conference that summer. The 2017 conference theme, as described to her by one of the student co-organizers, was Principles in Crisis: Refugees and Responsibility. Knight described that

> Holy Cross, as a Jesuit liberal arts college, is deeply committed to social justice as part of our mission, though I would say that issues in the Middle East are possibly less familiar to our students than other regions of the world. (N. Knight, personal communication, March 26, 2019)

She was concerned about issues of casting and representation, so it was important to her to clarify that she was presenting a reading instead of a performance. She gathered a racially and ethnically diverse group of eight women comprised of students; faculty from the departments of English, history, political science, and biology; and a staff member with the Office of Community-Based Learning. She also sought out coaching on Arabic pronunciations to be as respectful of the script and its language as possible.

Accompanying the reading was the film *The Destruction of Memory*, written, directed, and produced by Tim Slade. The film examines how culture has been destroyed by ISIS in Syria and Iraq, along with the attempts to preserve and restore those treasures of civilization. The discussion that followed the reading and screening was led by Pamela Karimi, a professor of art and architecture at the University of Massachusetts Dartmouth who specializes in the modern Middle East. Knight characterized Taking Refuge as a success on campus, recalling 70–80 people in attendance at her event, which was free and open to the public.

Colgate University

Associate professor April Sweeney coordinated events on her campus at Colgate University in Hamilton, New York in collaboration with colleagues in the departments of Theater; Film and Media Studies; History; and Middle Eastern and Islamic Studies. The multiday schedule at Colgate was co-sponsored by the Humanities Division, the Lampert Institute for Civic and Global Affairs, and the Department of Theater, and included the following:

- Performance Activism and the Syrian Uprising by Edward Ziter, associate professor of drama at New York University;

- Friday Night Film Series: *Another Kind of Girl* (directed by Khaldiya Jibawi) and *At Home in the World* (directed by Andreas Koefoed), followed by a Skype question and answer session with Koefoed; and
- International Theater Day: Staged reading *Oh My Sweet Land*, read by Noor Khan, associate professor of History and Middle Eastern and Islamic Studies, and directed by April Sweeney.

In my follow-up interview with Sweeney, she noted that "collaboration between different departments to present a series on a topic, while not a frequent occurrence, seems to happen every four to five years" (A. Sweeney, personal communication, September 20, 2018). She remarked that the work was well received and that the "students and faculty were particularly quite moved, and this stimulated many questions both from the reading of the play and Professor Ziter's talk on the Syrian uprising" (A. Sweeney, personal communication, September 20, 2018). Sweeney felt that the events "strengthened ties between the History and Theater departments, and gave students a deeper understanding of the power of art in relation to the political sphere in the context of the Syrian uprising" (A. Sweeney, personal communication, September 20, 2018). In terms of takeaways from Taking Refuge, she expressed her desire to work further in advance and to connect such projects more directly to the curriculum. Sweeney said she "would love to collaborate like this again and find ways to share resources and ideas. It was a great thing to model for students and include them in" (A. Sweeney, personal communication, September 20, 2018).

College of Charleston

Assistant professor Vivian Appler at the College of Charleston in Charleston, South Carolina, was another collaborator who rooted her exploration of the Syrian refugee crisis in the context of an ongoing class: Her feminist theatre class performed a staged reading of *Oh My Sweet Land* on World Theatre Day. This was the second major project for the course that was practical in nature. Instead of having one woman speak all of the text, it was broken up, allowing more students to participate. After the reading, a talk-back where audiences members could share their responses was offered. Appler noted that although there were not too many people in attendance (it was a busy time of the year). those who did come had "great conversations about the play and about the characters" (V. Appler, personal communication, September 10, 2018). Appler has since written a review of the play that she saw performed in New York City and reached out to producers to see if she might be able to bring the production to Charleston. She feels it could be really productive for the students and for me, and for more people in Charleston. People in Brooklyn are already sympathetic, but not necessarily in Charleston. I think it would be good to reach a lot of people who might not already be on the same page. (V. Appler, personal communication, September 10, 2018)

The decision to have her students speak the words of the female character (and other voices) from Syria prompted a great deal of discussion regarding race and representation. As Appler recounted,

a lot of students . . . had questions or queasiness about performing the words of a person of a different race . . . They asked, "Is it OK for us to be performing this?" Well, I told them, "It's an educational experience. Should we not do this play? Even as a reading, should we exclude this voice as part of our community's conversations?" . . . We had great conversations, and they were all really moved by the play. I thought it was powerful. (V. Appler, personal communication, September 10, 2018)

Place matters in Charleston, and Appler is aware of the context in which she is working. The history of the region is still very much alive in the building, the land, and the people. Appler remarked that

the community is still healing from very specific tensions and violence ([Emanuel African Methodist Episcopal Church] is two blocks from where I teach here). We get so caught up in Black and White, and all these other questions about integration and diversity get lost. There's a mosque here. One could assume there are Syrian immigrants here too . . . they are just not seen. (V. Appler, personal communication, September 10, 2018)

After the project, her students reflected on the experience. Some appreciated the humanizing impact of the protagonist's story, and others noted that the event created conversation even among students who were not able to attend. In addition, some students were in support of the project as emblematic of positive feminist representation.

Appler collaborated on organizing related events this spring, which were well-attended.

"Refugee Life/Refuge of Food: Syrian Culture in the Wake of Wartime Diaspora," was funded by SC Humanities and produced as a part of the Global Foodways year-long series organized by Dr. Lauren Ravalico. Our signature event involved Osama Alomar's poetry, a talk with Shadi Martini, a dance lesson with Dr. Shayna Silverstein, and a cooking demonstration with Mayada Anjari, and was sold out. (V. Appler, personal communication, April 23, 2019)

Louisiana State University

Assistant professor Stacey Cabaj at Louisiana State University in Baton Rouge, Lousiana, organized events on her campus as well. Interestingly, Lousiana State University also incorporated food into their programming. This presentation of *Oh My Sweet Land* was in cooperation with Swine Palace (a nonprofit theatre company associated with Lousiana State University). It took place on campus on World Theatre Day. The reading was performed by guest artist Leila Buck, a Lebanese-American actress, writer, teacher, and facilitator based in New York City. The performance was paired with a dinner. A panel discussion about the script followed the reading and focused on the Syrian refugee crisis in particular. Cabaj characterized the event as a success, one that spurred dialogue that evening and throughout the semester. The powerful impact of Buck's performance was an inspiration. In addition to the stimulating talk-back after the play, the work continued to resonate with students, including one woman who shifted the focus of her Master of Fine Arts thesis as a result.

Indiana University of Pennsylvania

At Indiana University of Pennsylvania in Freeport, Pennsylvania, assistant professor Rachel DeSoto-Jackson coordinated a reading of *Oh My Sweet Land* with the Simulated Patient and Applied Theatre Ensemble, which is part of the Department of Theater and Dance and led by DeSoto-Jackson. This reading was open to the public and performed on World Theatre Day.

TAKING REFUGEE: LOOKING BACK AND LOOKING FORWARD

This section reviews the critical outcomes of the project Taking Refuge and offers suggestions and a way forward for future global collaborations. From my first visit to Syria, my research has been interdisciplinary in nature. I consider that one of the strengths of the opportunity I had through the Center for International Conflict Resolution back in 2004. Without that initial exchange, I doubt Taking Refuge would have happened. In the years that followed, other institutions helped encourage and support my interest. Whitman College in Walla Walla, Washington (where I had my first tenure-track position), granted me a second opportunity to explore Syria, in the hopes of building an educational exchange with colleagues at the University of Damascus. While the civil war crushed those aspirations, I remain hopeful that other institutional partners will support cross-cultural exchange, including institutions in Lebanon and Jordan. Thanks to additional travel funding from Whitman College, I was able to answer the invitation to speak at the Fadjr International Theatre Festival in Iran. Support at critical moments in my career kept my connection to the region alive. I was able to conduct research and forge collaborations in Israel and Palestine through the generosity and hard work of Tavia La Follette and Artup. Today, I consider it an ongoing part of my work to share stories from this region across disciplinary boundaries. Since Taking Refuge launched, I've collaborated with two undergraduate students as part of the First Experience of Research program at Pitt: Thomas Swigon and Theresa Lim (neither Swigon nor Lim is a theatre student). We worked to create a database of dramatic works depicting refugees and displaced peoples. It will be added to the Taking Refuge website to help others interested in organizing events or staging productions. Swigon and Lim have also expressed an abiding interest in the future of the project, despite their academic paths outside of my department—another interdisciplinary foothold in the imaginations of our students.

Similarly, colleagues at other campuses involved in Taking Refuge noted growth in interdepartmental and interdisciplinary collaboration as a result (and a necessity) of their events. Many hoped that relationships would grow and evolve, but expressed guarded optimism, given limited bandwidth. While most of us are working at schools that encourage cross-disciplinary projects, few provide the space for planning or the opportunity to meet people beyond our well-worn paths. One of the pivotal events that made Taking Refuge possible for me was the David Berg Center for Ethics and Leadership at the University of Pittsburgh's Diversity Retreat, supported by the provost, which I took part in the spring before Taking Refuge. I saw a variety of models and possibilities for collaboration that bolstered my enthusiasm.

Most partners in Taking Refuge characterized their participation as a success. Though audience size and impact varied, all noted an increase in student awareness, and at least two colleagues observed a direct and meaningful effect on the continued study of graduate-level students. This gives credence to my suspicion that especially in contexts where such opportunities are scarce, the presentation of works by minority or underrepresented voices can have an outsized impact on audiences. In addition, meaningful conversations about representation and casting happened at our school, the College of Charleston, and the College of the Holy Cross. Colleagues found a variety of ways to embody the subject matter (through inviting guest artists, splitting up the text through multiple speakers, and performing it in the context of a class) that felt respectful to the intent of the playwright. As for the persisting question of "Who is allowed to tell what story?" in contemporary theatre it seems we are each formulating answers for ourselves, dependent on the context, politics, and people involved in each theatrical collaboration.

Taking Refuge events also benefited the artists represented with name recognition and/or financial support. Some received additional performance and screening requests once Taking Refuge had concluded. Based on the discussions I observed at Pitt, Taking Refuge helped raise visibility for local organizations working to bring aid to refugees in Pittsburgh, and may have helped connect volunteers with those groups. These are all anecdotal benefits, based on the evidence of my own observations and the interviews I conducted with sites outside of Pittsburgh. But there is much to be proud of.

There is also room for improvement. In many of the events staged, it would be fair to say that conversations were limited to people inside academia. Could the project have had more impact if first-person stories of refugees and/or the people who work with them had been part of the initial phase of programming at each site? Especially in geographies where refugee populations seem invisible, providing an opportunity for displaced peoples to be heard could be a tremendous educational opportunity for students and the local community, as well as a site of simple human connection where we can share stories, resources, and support.

Some faculty members were enervated by the difficulty of staging such events, given their heavy workload of teaching and administrative duties. Community engagement (a cornerstone of this project) can be valued inconsistently at schools during the tenure and promotion process, resulting in faculty feeling de-incentivized toward such work. Institutional support is not ensured, and the time to plan (let alone develop relationships with new collaborators) can be hard to come by. Follow-through can be especially tough. Once a project is complete, it can feel like a one-off unless a foundation is laid for future conversations.

How might we encourage deeper integration of events into the curriculum and lasting local engagement? We could explore grassroots partnerships in which local community members have an equal voice in programming choices and intended outcomes. Looking back on our work at Pitt, many of the contacts we forged are now cold. It would not be impossible to reestablish dialogue, but within what framework would those conversations exist? Two- or three-year project funds could provide a multiphase approach to relationship building and event curation rather than planning for outcomes in a single term. Second-phase projects could be drafted at the same time as inaugural efforts and adjusted based on results during the first year. Partnerships across geographical boundaries could be supported through a travel and research phase. While projects need to be agile and responsive to world events, much of what we accomplished with Taking Refuge happened through the trust and coordination of people with whom I already had established, collegial relationships. Though interdisciplinary cooperation was the aim, I am equally proud that we forged interdisciplinary collaborations and leveraged resources from many campuses to raise the profile of the project, rather than position ourselves as isolated competitors within our field.

Institutions might also consider department-specific funding for long-range projects and ongoing interdisciplinary work. Maybe a grant to a department of theatre arts would come with the caveat that two other departments must also benefit from the resulting guest lecture or event series and join in the planning. A university interested in programming that fed directly into the curriculum could support proposals a year or two in advance, while there is still time to conduct adjacent research and build syllabi. And we might forge professional partnerships with organizations that already provide a bridge. The Pulitzer Center on Crisis Reporting is an excellent example of an organization supporting diverse approaches to international journalism. Using their organizational structure and body of work as the starting point, one could build a series of campus events of interest to many different departments, jumpstarting interdisciplinary conversations with the Pulitzer Center as a catalyst.

Even with the lessons learned and goodwill created by Taking Refuge, the work is far from over. Refugees from Syria experienced a brutal winter in camps in Lebanon this year, and the statistics on displaced peoples living in poverty, as well as the rise in hate crimes, are hard to bear. It is vital that we continue to fight for visibility for these concerns in our theatres, on our campuses, and within our communities. While I offer my sincerest thanks to everyone who helped make our first incarnation of Taking Refuge such a great success, I also offer a challenge: Let's keep the conversation going.

REFERENCES

Barakat, N. (2018, April 18). Let's banish the term "Arab world." What does it mean anyway? *The Guardian.* Retrieved from https://www.theguardian.com/commentisfree/2018/apr/18/lets-banish-the-term-arab-world-what-does-it-mean-anyway

Chulov, M. (2018, August 30). 'We can't go back': Syria's refugees fear for their future after war. *The Guardian.* Retrieved from https://www.theguardian.com/world/2018/aug/30/we-cant-go-back-syrias-refugees-fear-for-their-future-after-war

Clapp, S. (2016, July 16). Queens of Syria review—The most urgent work on the London stage. *The Guardian.* Retrieved from https://www.theguardian.com/stage/2016/jul/10/queens-of-syria-review-young-vic-euripides-trojan-women

Keto, E. C. (2016, December 9). Making space: Diversity, inclusion, and the arts at Harvard. *The Harvard Crimson.* Retrieved from https://www.thecrimson.com/article/2016/12/9/arts-diversity-cover

Queens of Syria. (2017, December 16). Retrieved April 26, 2019, from https://tellbrakfilms.com/films/queens-of-syria/

Soloski, A. (2017, September 17). Review: In 'Oh My Sweet Land,' dinner is served. Don't come hungry. *The New York Times*. Retrieved from https://www.nytimes.com/2017/09/17/theater/oh-my-sweet-land-review.html

St-Esprit, M. (2017, September 7). Pittsburgh promised to welcome Syrian refugees. These youth give the efforts a mixed review. *PublicSource*. Retrieved from https://www.publicsource.org/pittsburgh-promised-to-welcome-syrian-refugees-these-youth-give-those-efforts-a-mixed-review

UNHCR. (2018). *Seven years on: Timeline of the Syria crisis*. Retrieved from https://www.unhcr.org/ph/13427-seven-years-timeline-syria-crisis.html

WPXI. (2015, November 23). *Syrians living in Pennsylvania's 'Little Syria' react to refugee crisis*. Retrieved from https://www.wpxi.com/news/local/syrians-living-pennsylvanias-little-syria-react-re/26888612

CHAPTER 4

RESEARCHING OURSELVES

Naikan Meditation and Making Diversity Work

Clark Chilson
University of Pittsburgh

ABSTRACT

This chapter introduces how contemplative pedagogy and an innovative meditative practice called Naikan can contribute to a learning process that creates environments in which diversity can thrive in higher education. The Naikan practice develops a self-reflective social process that enhances the capacity for humility, gratitude, and seeing situations from the perspective of others, which in turn helps diverse individuals work better together on campuses. This chapter examines the Naikan practice within the context of diversity in higher education and then describes a faculty development model to implement the Naikan practice in higher education.

Daryl Smith (2015) points out that "opportunities and challenges [of diversity] can no longer be framed in terms of pursuing diversity or not pursuing diversity. *Diversity is.* Rather, we must establish conditions under which diversity works" (p. ix). This statement by Smith (2015) raises two questions:

Diversity Across the Disciplines, pages 53–65
Copyright © 2020 by Information Age Publishing
All rights of reproduction in any form reserved.

First, what does it mean to say diversity works? Second, what conditions could we establish to help it work?

To say "diversity works," we need to clarify what we mean by the terms "diversity" and "works." No one particular definition of diversity dominates studies of diversity. But however we define it, the term "diversity," at its core, involves difference, including inter alia differences in race, gender, physical abilities, sexual orientation, religion, politics, and socioeconomic class. The term "work" implies that it effectively achieves some goal. In other words, something works if it fosters the realization of what we seek to achieve.

If the goals of institutions of higher education are to produce and distribute knowledge, we can say "diversity works" if it contributes to achieving those goals. If diversity, for example, promotes discoveries on how social and natural worlds operate, then it is working. If it is helping students and the public learn what research has revealed, then it is working. If it is not doing these things, then it is not working.

The mere existence of a diverse population, however, does not make diversity work. Oppression in a diverse university population by a dominant group can undermine the university's goal of producing knowledge by restricting what is regarded as important knowledge and areas and methods of inquiry to those that the dominant group endorses. Marginalization of others can also undermine a basic aim of institutions of higher education: the distribution of knowledge. When knowledge is presented in a way suited primarily to a dominant group, it undermines the potential for others to engage with that knowledge and thus limits the extent of its distribution.

The key question then becomes this: "How can we get it to work?" No simple answer will suffice for this question. But we must address it to build on the diversity we currently have at universities and allow for greater inclusion going forward. As a means for making diversity work, we can learn methods for becoming more self-aware. One such method is a self-reflective type of meditation called Naikan, which is a Japanese term that literally means "introspection." Unlike meditation methods that focus on the breath or body sensations, Naikan gives attention to how we interact with others. Through practicing Naikan, faculty become more aware of their actions and how they relate to students. As a result, they create interior states that enhance their ability to make diversity work in the courses they teach.

WHAT MAKES DIVERSITY DIFFICULT: LIVING WITH FUNDAMENTAL DIFFERENCES

Most of us assume our ways of thinking are correct. In her TED Talk *On Being Wrong*, Kathryn Schulz (2011) points out that although we all know that every human makes mistakes, in the present moment, right now, it is hard for us to think of any belief or idea that we have that is wrong. Schulz notes that because of our tendency to see our beliefs as an accurate reflection of reality, we make assumptions about those who disagree with us: We assume they are ignorant or idiots, or if they are not ignorant or stupid, we too often conclude that they are evil. This tendency to think our beliefs are right and those who disagree with us are ipso facto wrong makes diversity difficult.

In the abstract, it is easy to celebrate diversity—it makes us more aware of social inequalities, it gives us new perspectives, it allows us to learn from the experiences of others, it can help us gain a deeper understanding of the human condition, and it can give access to power to those it has been unfairly denied. Diversity is easy when differences are at a distance and do not impinge on the living situations we create for ourselves. But on the ground, in the places where we spend our time and interact with others, diversity brings challenges.

When confronted with people different from us, and particularly with people who have different values and who demand things in the spaces in which we live that we do not like, the celebration of diversity can turn into a protest. In other words, diversity is fine as long as people do not fundamentally challenge us. Once that happens, there are two common but flawed strategies for dealing with it. The first is to try to avoid diversity, and the second is to try to eradicate it.

Attempts to avoid diversity have commonly been made to maintain power and privileges. Those with dominant power have long tried to exclude those different from themselves. Throughout the history of North America, this meant that White, Protestant, heterosexual men, who held most of the power, excluded women, non-Protestants, gay men, and people of color. Attempts by those in power to maintain their privileges by excluding others are widely recognized today as social injustice; this problem has undermined the ability of our society to thrive. Much of the discourse on diversity focuses on this problem, and policies of inclusion aim to solve it.

Another flawed strategy is that of trying to eradicate diversity by attempting to make people seem less different. Most people acknowledge that race, physical abilities, sexual orientation, gender, and gender expression all have an impact on how we experience the societies in which we live. Although diversity may appear to work better when differences are seen as not so important, to make diversity work effectively, we benefit by learning how to live with fundamental differences. We all do better when we learn how to live with diversity, including with those who have beliefs and ways of living that differ from our own. It would be worse than ironic if those who preach the merits of diversity demanded that others adopt their views of the world as superior. Cognitive coercion is not an effective strategy for promoting healthy diversity.

This does not mean that we should not fight for what we believe in—of course we should. Rather, as we strive to make diversity work to achieve wider social and educational goals, we should not exclude or disparage those not like us, including those with whom we disagree. Religious diversity can be an area of conflict because different religious (and nonreligious) worldviews often oppose one another.

RELIGIOUS DIVERSITY AND DIFFERENCE

We teach students who have a wide variety of religious identities and perspectives. In any particular classroom at a major university, we are likely to encounter students who identify as Christian, Muslim, Jewish, Hindu, atheist, or something else. Some students are actively engaged in a religion and devoutly follow it. Others were brought up in religious households, so identify with a religion but hardly practice it. The differences among the religious worldviews of these students are significant, but so are the differences among those students within a particular religion. In fact, those who identify as belonging to the same religion can often be more vehement in their disagreements with one another than they are with those of another religion.

Although there is a wide range of religious beliefs and practices among university students, it would be wrong to think of religious diversity as being solely about different religions; atheists and agnostics must be included. There are many students who do not affiliate with any religion. Some of them find religion interesting and are sympathetic toward it, while many others are hostile to religion and think religious people are ignorant. Conversations between religious and anti-religious people may be even harder than those between people of different religions. As the philosopher Richard Rorty (1994) famously pointed out, religion is a conversation-stopper.

Because religious differences are hard to reconcile, discussions about them are avoided. Even in the discourse on diversity, religion is often ignored. Eboo Patel (2015), in his *Chronicle of Higher Education* article titled "In Promoting Campus Diversity, Don't Dismiss Religion," states that "while higher education has stepped forward to do the hard—even heroic—work of engaging diversity issues related to race, gender, ethnicity, and sexuality, religious identity has too frequently been dismissed or treated with derision" (para. 5). An examination of the literature on diversity bears out this claim. Major works in the field often give little attention to religion. One large-scale study titled "The Interfaith Diversity Experiences and Attitudes Longitudinal Survey" conducted by the Interfaith Youth Core suggests that students are actually getting less exposure to different religions as college freshmen than they got as high school students (Bauer-Wolf, 2018; Quilantan 2018). However, ignoring religion does not solve problems that can arise from it, including issues stemming from different dress, understandings about gender, the role of the state in religion, and the relationship between scientific inquiry and religious belief.

Some professors believe that religion undermines scientific and scholarly inquiry and, therefore, oppose evidence-based learning. But when professors are dismissive of certain religious beliefs, they undermine student engagement with what they are teaching. This does not, of course, mean that an evolutionary biologist has to assess a religious student who denies evolution differently than a student who does not doubt it. Students need to learn about major fields of study, even if they disagree with them. However, this does not necessitate disrespecting the student's religion. In fact, more sensitivity toward students' who have difficulties related to course content might help the instructor improve his or her teaching of the material. Christian history professors also should not view atheist students as stubborn or dogmatic individuals who have a hard time seeing how Christianity did anything good in history. Doing so does not support student learning.

Rather than dismiss students or spend all our pedagogical energy on convincing them that our perspective is the correct one, we can become better instructors by becoming more aware of how we interact with students. To do this, however, we need practice in training our attention in particular ways. This is where meditation can contribute to making diversity work.

NAIKAN MEDITATION FOR EFFECTIVE DIVERSITY

Since the late 1990s, an increasing number of university faculty have taken an interest in contemplative pedagogy and started to introduce students to meditation to achieve learning goals (Shapiro, Brown, & Astin, 2011). Contemplative pedagogy involves meditation, attention training, awareness cultivation, concentration, and the ability to sustain contradictions (Coburn et al., 2011; Zajonc, 2013). Fisher (2017) explains that "contemplative inquiry focuses on direct first-person experience as an essential means of knowing that has been historically overshadowed and dismissed by an emphasis on analytical reasoning" (p. 4).

The meditative practice most closely aligned with contemplative pedagogy is mindfulness, which Jon Kabat-Zinn (1994), a leading proponent of mindfulness, defined as "paying attention in a particular way: on purpose, in the present moment, and nonjudgmentally" (p. 4). In contrast to this, there is Naikan meditation.

Naikan has a number of similarities to mindfulness meditation: It is a way of training our attention; it originated in Buddhism but requires no belief in Buddhist doctrine or any knowledge of Buddhism; it has been used with a wide range of people, from students to prisoners, to help them better cope with their lives; it has been a psychotherapeutic intervention for addiction and depression; and it is done in retreat-like settings or as part of a daily practice. Unlike mindfulness, however, Naikan focuses on social relationships and gives attention to our actions in the past. In particular, it gives attention to three questions: What have I received from others? What have I given back to them? What troubles and difficulties have I caused them? (Chilson, 2018).

There are two types of Naikan practice: intensive Naikan and daily Naikan. Intensive Naikan is mostly done at training centers, which offer a retreat-like setting where people stay for a week and during which all meals are provided. During intensive Naikan, people spend from Sunday afternoon to Saturday morning sitting alone behind a screen contemplating the three Naikan questions in relation to different intimate others (e.g., mother, father, spouse) at different times in their own lives, often in 3-year increments. Those who do Naikan, called *naikansha*, commonly start by reflecting on their mother and search for answers to the three questions in relation to her when they were between the ages of 5 and 7. For about two hours, they try to remember what they received from their mother between the ages of 5 and 7, what they gave back to her then, and what troubles and difficulties they caused her during that time.

After about two hours, an interviewer comes in; the *naikansha* then report, in less than five minutes, brief but concrete answers to the questions. For example, an individual may say that between the ages of 5 and 7, his mother baked his favorite type of chocolate cake for his sixth birthday. What he gave to her in the first grade was a painted picture of the family dog. He caused her trouble when, while playing fetch with the family dog, he broke a vase his mother received as a wedding gift.

The *naikansha* then use the three Naikan questions in relation to their mother for the next 3 years, from ages 8 to 10. They continue doing Naikan on their mother up to the present or to their mother's death. They then use the questions to contemplate their relationship with their father, their spouse (if married), and others in their lives that they have been close with, such as siblings and friends.

The other type of Naikan, called daily Naikan, is done as part of an individual's daily or weekly routine. In daily Naikan, an individual might reflect on his or her life using the three questions for short periods of time, such as what she received from a friend during the previous day or week, what she gave back to that friend during that time, and what troubles she caused her friend.

Daily Naikan meditation can also be focused on what happened during a particular period of time. For example, an individual might reflect on the previous day or week and ask the following questions: What did I receive this week from others? What did I give back to them? What troubles and difficulties did I cause? This is more expansive because rather than focusing on a particular person, attention is given to how the person doing Naikan interacted with various people during a certain period of time. So, if a woman is doing Naikan concerning the previous week, she might contemplate the questions for 15 minutes and realize that she received coffee from a colleague who made it before a meeting and how her son fixed a broken piece of furniture. What she gave back to others was holding the door for someone who was entering a building while carrying boxes and giving a large tip to a waitress. She might find that she caused trouble to her brother when she forgot to ask about his surgery and to her elderly neighbor when her empty plastic trash cans blew into his yard and she did not retrieve them until the evening when she got home from work.

Whether doing Naikan in an intensive setting or as a daily practice, it is important that answers be concrete in a way that can be visualized rather than be abstract concepts (e.g., kind, love, mean, generous) because concrete language is more precise and has stronger psychological impact. With daily Naikan, a person may write down answers to the three questions in a journal kept daily, weekly, or some other interval of time. Keeping a journal often increases concentration on Naikan. It provides a record of what happened and allows people to become more aware of how they relate to others. In writing down Naikan, an individual might find that he often receives more than he gives. It also clarifies the types of things we repeatedly receive, give, and do to cause others trouble.

NAIKAN AS METHOD FOR MAKING DIVERSITY WORK

How does Naikan relate to making diverse groups function when it does not deal directly with a diversity problem? As with other training methods, Naikan enhances relevant abilities without directly mimicking a particular realm it enhances. Sports analogies are apt here. Running as a training method for volleyball players may seem irrelevant because games of volleyball do not involve running long distances without stopping. Similarly, a boxer hitting a speed bag can seem irrelevant to becoming a better fighter because boxers in matches do not punch in the manner that they hit a speed bag. However, these training methods improve endurance and strength, which are necessary in both sports. Training methods can enhance capacities relevant to performance without mirroring what they are aimed at improving.

So it is with Naikan and diversity. Naikan is a training method for enhancing our ability to regulate our attention. It develops our capacities for humility, gratitude, and seeing situations from the perspective of others, which are all qualities that improve social functioning. Naikan enhances humility by showing us how we are not simply victims of others' actions we do not like but that we ourselves are also responsible for the difficulties others have. When we become more aware of how others have benefited us, and how we have caused others problems, self-righteousness slips away. We become less self-centered.

Naikan often leads to gratitude by making us more aware of what others have done for us, even when we have not been as generous with them. Naikan leads us to practice what Ozawa-de Silva (2015) called "mindfulness of the kindness of others." When we see how others have given to us in ways that we have not given to them, a sense of gratitude ensues. It is not uncommon for those doing Naikan to find that even people they are having difficulty with have benefited them in some way. Gratitude improves relationships in diverse populations because it allows us to appreciate more fully how others enrich our lives.

Naikan also requires that we practice seeing things from the perspective of others. In the process of trying to answer Naikan's questions, we become aware of the points of view beyond our own. We might remember, for example, not only that our father taught us to drive, but that he taught us to drive even when he was suffering from migraines or even when we were impatient with him. From his perspective, taking us out to drive probably seemed less attractive than staying home, yet he did it. When we are able to give more attention to how things look from the perspective of others, we are more likely to be understanding and empathetic and less likely to judge them negatively.

RESEARCHING OURSELVES: NAIKAN FOR FACULTY DEVELOPMENT

Publications about meditation at universities often focus on how getting students to do it can improve learning (Galante et al., 2018; Lin & Mai, 2018). With Naikan, rather than asking students to do it, it is best if instructors start with themselves. We can begin to use Naikan to research our lives to understand how we have interacted with others. In addition to family, Naikan may be done on friends, neighbors, or colleagues. It can also be done by professors in relation to their students as a way of getting faculty to see how they relate to their students.

To illustrate how instructors can do Naikan on their students, three concrete examples are provided: Naikan on an entire class, Naikan with a good student, and Naikan on a difficult student. As with other skills, such as swimming or skiing, it is often best to start with what is easiest and then move on to what is harder. Because it is important to be concrete in Naikan, the stand-in for the professor doing Naikan is given the name Dr. Brown.

Naikan on a Class

Doing Naikan on a class involves focusing on a specific length of time in relation to everyone in the class, rather than just on a specific person. It is similar to doing daily Naikan on a particular day rather than on a particular person. The length of time period to examine can be as short as a 1-minute interaction or as long as the entire term a class is taught. Below is an example of Naikan on a 75-minute class. Dr. Brown proceeds through the three questions in relation to his class as follows:

- What did I receive from students during the class session?
  - Amanda asked a question that helped clarify what I was trying to say.
  - Marcus made a statement that others found useful for analyzing the data.
  - Overall, students gave me their attention while I did most of the talking.
  - Many in the class borrowed money to pay for tuition to be there.
  - They showed that they took the course seriously by handing in their reading responses at the beginning of class.
- What did I give the class?
  - I taught them ways to read titles of texts that can help them better comprehend academic articles.
  - I told them a personal anecdote that made them laugh.
  - I gave everyone in the class a rubric to follow after many of them did poorly on their first essays.
- What trouble did I cause the class?
  - One of the points on my PowerPoint slide was vague and included an error I needed to fix.
  - John raised his hand to make a comment, but I failed to call on him.
  - I called on Marcie when she seemed to be distracted by something on her computer; thus, I called on her when I knew she would have preferred to be left alone.
  - I failed to give my full attention to what a student was saying because I was trying to figure out how I would respond when the student was still talking.
  - I used a metaphor to try to illustrate a point that confused some students.

In this example, we can see that the professor is reflecting on a range of interactions with students in the class. By doing this, Dr. Brown is getting a better understanding of who he is as an instructor for the students and how students may see him.

Naikan on a Good Student

Jane is the kind of student who is a joy to teach and who makes you feel that you are doing worthy, life-changing work. Below is an example of Dr. Brown doing Naikan on Jane over a 15-week semester.

- What did I receive from Jane?
  - When I asked the class a question one day and no one raised a hand, Jane volunteered an insightful answer that built on the reading for the day.
  - Jane showed me she cared about what I was teaching by paying attention in class, asking questions, and showing in her essay and exam answers intellectual engagement with the ideas discussed in the course.
  - She told me how what we were learning about ritual in the course gave her insight into some of her own actions.
- What did I give back to Jane?
  - I wrote a recommendation for her to get into graduate school.
  - I gave her advice on how to get into a good graduate school program.
  - I read a rough draft of an essay she wrote and gave her suggestions on how to improve it.
- What troubles and difficulties did I cause Jane?
  - I put off writing my letter for recommendation for her until the day it was due, which caused her anxiety.
  - I made her wait when I showed up late to my office hours one day.
  - I made a forceful criticism of something she wrote that was not necessary and probably made her feel bad.

Naikan on a Bad Student

Jason often arrives late to Dr. Brown's class; he goes on Facebook while Dr. Brown is lecturing; he sometimes loudly yawns; he sometimes whispers to students next to him, then laughs; and he complains that Dr. Brown assigns too much reading. Doing Naikan on him is difficult because when Dr. Brown thinks about him, what comes to mind is what bothers him about Jason. Dr. Brown finds it much easier to answer the following question:

"How does this person cause me trouble?" But there is no such question in Naikan because answering that question comes naturally to us, and so we do not need to practice it. Below is an example of Dr. Brown doing Naikan on Jason toward the end of a semester.

- What did I receive from Jason?
  - He made an appropriate joke in class once that was funny and made something I was trying to say more memorable.
  - He helped me develop patience and showed me how my tendency to get irritated can undermine the atmosphere in the class and my ability to articulate my thoughts.
  - In an in-class writing activity, I could see he was trying to understand what I was saying.
  - He agreed to be the group leader for a class activity and took his role as leader seriously.
- What did I give back to Jason?
  - I gave him feedback on his midterm exam so he could do better on his final exam.
  - When he came to my office, I offered him some chocolate that I had.
- What trouble and difficulties did I cause Jason?
  - I made a joke at his expense when I used him as an example of a person who loves to talk.
  - I required him to read difficult material.
  - I asked him to carefully consider an idea that he disagreed with, then I failed to carefully listen to or consider his interpretation of a text that differed from mine.
  - I expressed doubt and frustration when he told me why he was not in class on the day an assignment was due and why he did not hand it in on time.

Doing Naikan on Jason is hard, but as Dr. Brown does it, he begins to see that he has done things for him. While Jason might not be the perfect student, Dr. Brown realizes that he is also not the perfect teacher, seeing that he may have been annoying to him as well. This allows him to get out of his own self-centered perspective and start to think about how he might be more patient and try to respond to Jason empathetically.

CONCLUSION

Although increasing diversity is now welcomed at many institutions of higher education, more still needs to be done to promote inclusion. We can move further along the path of achieving the missions of our universities by effectively responding to the different types of diversity that already exist, including religious diversity.

Developing multiple strategies for inclusion and making it work has social value and contributes to educational goals. One strategy for supporting diversity involves enhancing our awareness of who we are as teachers and how we interact with students. A means for doing this is the self-reflective meditation method of Naikan. By practicing Naikan, professors can gain new understandings of themselves and their students that give them the capacity to foster learning in diverse classes and appreciate differences.

Making diversity work is a "we" problem, not a "them" problem. By learning how to use our attention to better understand ourselves, we can more powerfully model the ideals we espouse. In short, by becoming aware of how we engage with people, we can improve our ability to teach with our lives, not just our words.

REFERENCES

Bauer-Wolf, J. (2018, January 24). Declining exposure to religious diversity. *Inside Higher Ed.* Retrieved from https://www.insidehighered.com/news/2018/01/24/study-shows-drop-new-college-students-exposure-other-religions

Chilson, C. (2018). Naikan: A meditation method and psychotherapy. *Oxford Research Encyclopedia of Religion.* Retrieved from http://oxfordre.com/religion/view/10.1093/acrefore/9780199340378.001.0001/acrefore-9780199340378-e-570

Coburn, T., Grace, F., Klein, A. C., Komjathy, L., Roth, H., & Simmer-Brown, J. (2011). Contemplative pedagogy: Frequently asked questions. *Teaching Theology and Religion, 14*(2), 167–174.

Fisher, K. M. (2017). Look before you leap: Reconsidering contemplative pedagogy. *Teaching Theology and Religion, 20*(1), 4–21.

Galante, J., Dufour, G., Vainre, M., Wagner, A. P., Stochl, J., Benton, A., . . . Jones, P. B. (2018). A mindfulness-based intervention to increase resilience to stress in university students (the Mindful Student Study): A pragmatic randomised controlled trial. *Lancet Public Health, 3*(2), e72–e81.

Kabat-Zinn, J. (1994). *Wherever you go, there you are: Mindfulness meditation in everyday life.* New York, NY: Hyperion Books.

Lin, J. W., & Mai, L. J. (2018). Impact of mindfulness meditation intervention on academic performance. *Innovations in Education and Teaching International, 55*(3), 366–375.

Ozawa de-Silva, C. (2015). Mindfulness of the kindness of others: The contemplative practice of Naikan in cultural context. *Transcultural Psychiatry, 52*(4), 524–542.

Patel, E. (2015, March 11). In promoting campus diversity, don't dismiss religion. *Chronicle of Higher Education.* Retrieved from https://www.chronicle.com/article/In-Promoting-Campus-Diversity/228427

Quilantan, B. (2018, January 24). How college may actually limit students' exposure to different religions. *Chronicle of Higher Education.* Retrieved from https://www.chronicle.com/article/How-College-May-Actually-Limit/242330

Rorty, R. (1994). Religion as conversation-stopper. *Common Knowledge, 3*(1), 1–6.

Schulz, K. (2011, March). *On being wrong* [Video file]. Retrieved from https://www.ted.com/talks/kathryn_schulz_on_being_wrong

Shapiro, S. L., Brown, K. W., & Astin, J. A. (2011). Toward the integration of meditation into higher education: A review of research evidence. *Teachers College Record, 113*(3), 493–528.

Simmer-Brown, J., & Grace, F. (Eds.). (2011). *Meditation and the classroom: Contemplative pedagogy for religious studies.* Albany: State University of New York Press.

Smith, D. G. (2015). *Diversity's promise for higher education: Making it work* (2nd ed.). Baltimore, MD: John Hopkins University Press.

Zajonc, A. (2013). Contemplative pedagogy: A quiet revolution in higher education. *New Directions for Teaching and Learning, 134,* 83–94.

CHAPTER 5

USING PICTURE BOOKS TO PROMOTE YOUNG CHILDREN'S UNDERSTANDING OF GENDER DIVERSITY AND GENDER EQUITY

Katrina Bartow Jacobs
University of Pittsburgh

Thomas Hill
University of Pittsburgh

ABSTRACT

This chapter explores young children's awareness and perception of gender diversity in picture books. This chapter uses critical literacy and qualitative methods appropriate for early childhood education to explore the use of picture books as a way to both research young children's perceptions of gender norms and to foster a more equitable and diverse understanding of gender

Diversity Across the Disciplines, pages 67–81
Copyright © 2020 by Information Age Publishing
67

identity and representation. This chapter reports and discusses the outcomes of picture book readings in two kindergarten classes focusing on children's understanding of gender identity and gender equity in the books.

In the past few years, the development of the Twitter hashtag and interconnected social media campaign #WeNeedDiverseBooks has taken on issues of representation, authenticity, and identity in the field of picture books and books for young children, bringing to light the overwhelming lack of diversity in these texts (Bishop Killeen, 2015; Dávila, 2015; Thomas, 2016). This campaign has focused not only on the lack of diversity within publications, but also on the critical importance for both authorship and representation in K–12 classrooms to include a much broader range of social identities and perspectives. While much of the focus has been specifically on racial and ethnic identity (Dávila, 2015), there is a growing appreciation for the need to include issues of gender identity and sexuality in these conversations. There is an increasing focus within the field of education for the need to create safe spaces that promote gender equality and equity for all students, including those whose gender identities do not follow traditional "boy" or "girl" norms. In addition to being more supportive of students who identify as transgender or gender fluid, it is also critical that we continue to promote texts that offer wider perspectives for what it means to live as a boy or as a girl by continuing to disrupt stereotypes around gendered identities.

As important as the issues of the texts themselves are, it is also critical to understand how texts—both those that represent marginalized individuals and communities, and those that do not—are taken up by their audiences: children, parents, and teachers. In addition to an emerging awareness of students who identify as transgender (biologically male or female but identifying as the opposite), there is a growing appreciation for children who are developing along a continuum of more fluid gender representations (Reay, 2015). Questions of how to create communities where all children feel safe and capable of learning require attention on many levels, from procedures to school design to curriculum. However, far too often the focus ends at legal discussions of policies, such as bathroom usage or the right of a family to change their child's gender on official forms. What has been missing from the conversation is how teachers can use classroom instruction and books to build a community centered on equity and appreciation for gender fluidity. To guide productive instruction in these areas, it is critical that research within the field of education and literacy studies develops a greater sense of children's developmental understandings of gender diversity and identity, and of how literature might be used to disrupt social norms around gender expression and identity.

The project[1] described in this chapter focused on inviting young children to share their awareness and perception of gender identity and beginning to find ways to disrupt harmfully narrow social constructs of gender in ways that were age-appropriate for early childhood educational settings. This approach focused on an understanding of self, rather than of sexuality; started from the children's own comments and questions; and worked to build knowledge constructively. Working with two kindergarten classes and their teachers, we facilitated conversations around texts that were designed to explicitly address perceptions and questions of gender identity during shared read-alouds with the children. For this research project, Katrina entered the site and worked with the teachers to conduct the research. Tom was later brought on to help with analysis of the data. There were two main research questions that guided this work:

1. What cues, both visual and textual, do young children draw on when constructing understanding of gender during picture book read-alouds?
2. How can picture book read-alouds be used to disrupt narrow assumptions of gender identity and broaden children's understanding of gender fluidity and equity?

WHY STUDY GENDER DIVERSITY IN EARLY CHILDHOOD EDUCATION?

Because it is frequently linked with sexuality and sexual orientation, there is at times an uneasiness with addressing issues of gender and gender diversity with young children. However, research has demonstrated that children at a very young age become highly aware of gender, including how gender is performed through dress, physical appearance, and activity choices (Andrews, Martin, Field, Cook, & Lee, 2016; Baron, Schmader, Cvencek, & Meltzoff, 2014; Dunham, Baron, & Banaji, 2016; Yee & Brown, 1994). These understandings directly impact students' understandings and interpretations of texts and experiences in early childhood educational contexts. Just as students bring their racial, ethnic, and religious identities to bear on their sensemaking of narratives, it is imperative that we leave room in the literacy curriculum for students to both express and interrogate their own understandings of what gender means and how it is performed (Brooks & Browne, 2012). Drawing on the history of reader response theory (Rosenblatt, 1982; Sipe, 1998), Brooks and Browne (2012) argue that we need to intentionally include an understanding of how children's various cultural and social identities map onto the ways in which they engage texts and develop understandings of narratives during read-aloud sessions. In this work,

I utilized this framework to engage students in both presenting and thinking through their own gendered identities and understandings of picture book texts.

Taking this focus also allows us to separate sexuality from gender identity; while the two have obvious links, it is important to recognize the critical differences between gender—one's own perceptions and performance of identity—and sexuality, where the focus is on attraction between humans. This focus not only supports a healthy and developmentally appropriate concentration on the self and how one functions within community, but it also begins conversations that can lead in later grades to more complex discussions around attraction, identity, consent, and sexuality. Furthermore, we are becoming increasingly aware—both in formal research and through media outlets—that gender diversity is a leading cause of bullying in elementary school settings (Dake, Price, Telljohann, & Funk, 2003). Theorists find that not only are these conversations considered taboo in many settings, often being addressed only once an incident has occurred, but also that teachers and administrators are unsure of how to begin to discuss these topics. However, studies have also shown that providing a direct focus and specific programming in schools for addressing both sexuality and gender can help all students feel welcome and safe. The Gay, Lesbian, and Straight Education Network (GLSEN), a leading nonprofit in promoting equity and inclusion of all gender expressions and identities, found that all students, including those who identified as gender conforming and gender fluid, felt safer and more welcome in schools where conversations around gender diversity and equity were explicit and officially sanctioned (Kosciw, Greytak, Giga, Villenas, & Danischewski, 2016). However, these conversations frequently do not begin until the upper elementary, middle, or high school years. The current study aimed to address this gap by engaging these issues in the early elementary years through literacy practices that are common to almost all early childhood educational contexts. The goal here is to disrupt rigid social norms and stereotyping at an age before bullying is frequent, ideally reducing these issues before they even begin.

Finally, there is also the question of the texts themselves. Research has also shown that there remain significant issues regarding gender representation in young children's literature, even among books that are widely acclaimed (Crisp & Hiller, 2011; Mattix & Sobolak, 2014). Toward that end, this project deliberately used texts with characters who present a wide array of gender identities and representations, including texts where questions of gender diversity are central to the plot. There is a need to study children's responses to questions regarding gender in picture books to better understand the relationships between their developing understanding of gender and their interpretations of fictional and nonfictional narratives. In addition to working toward creating more picture books with inclusive gender identities and a broader range of gender diversity, there is also a need to determine some of the best ways to engage young children in discussing these topics, as well as to provide teachers with supports and structures that facilitate supportive conversations that promote both literacy development and social equity.

ENGAGING YOUNG CHILDREN
IN CRITICAL LITERACY PRACTICES

Beyond the question of which texts to use for this project, it was also important to consider the nature of how children were invited to discuss and engage with the picture books during the classroom read-aloud sessions. In designing the classroom engagements, I drew heavily on the work of critical literacy practices in early childhood settings. This approach centers children's understanding of the narratives in terms of plot or fundamental comprehension of story, as well as utilizes these textual interactions to engage young children in critical thinking about the context of both the story and the classroom or community itself. While this may seem like a stretch for young children, research has shown that this approach is highly effective with children as young as preschool age (Vasquez, 2014). This approach involves creating opportunities through reading, discussion, and activity for young children to actively question their understandings of the world, along with questions of equity, diversity, and fairness.

The project explored how young children negotiate conflict or differences of opinion in the classroom (Souto-Manning, 2014), and also how larger questions of diversity and equity can be addressed in early childhood educational settings in ways that foster young children's sense of agency in addressing these topics within their school contexts. Through both text selection and the use of a guided inquiry approach to the conversations around the books, this project aimed to support the kindergarteners in sharing their understandings and respectfully dialoguing around these perspectives. Taking this approach not only promoted a broader understanding of gender equity and diversity, but also more widely encouraged the children to develop an ability to reflect on their own perspectives and those of others in respectful and dialogic ways.

CURRICULUM AND RESEARCH DESIGN

This project was designed as a naturalistic curricular unit that took place in two kindergarten classrooms during a one-month period. While I, as the researcher and guest teacher, primarily took responsibility for designing and enacting the project, the classroom teachers were involved at all steps of the process. The project was designed around two phases of read-alouds with the children, some with the whole class and others with small groups of children. The goal for the text selection and the text-based questions was to give the children opportunities to offer their perspectives and understandings of the gender identities of the characters in the books. All of the books were readily available, high-quality picture books, many of which have been recognized with various awards from the American Library Association or similar organizations.

The first phase of read-alouds focused on books where the main characters are not specifically identified regarding their gender. In other words, these picture books had a main character who was not specifically identified in the text as either a boy or a girl. Books used included *My Friend Rabbit* (Rohmann, 2002); *The House in the Night* (Swanson, 2008); *Owl Moon* (Yolen, 1987); and *Don't Let the Pigeon Drive the Bus!* (Willems, 2003). During this first phase of read-alouds, I asked the students to share their understandings of the characters' gender.[2] At certain times during the reading, I would ask students whether they thought the character was a boy or a girl, and why. I also would ask if their opinions changed at any point in the story. I encouraged the children to think about both the words in the text and the images, as well as larger questions around the topics in the stories themselves. I recorded their observations on chart paper and with audio recordings to establish a baseline understanding of the students' perceptions of gender norms and what evidence they relied on regarding the texts' pictures, words, and topics. I also used this period to establish norms around answering questions that were inherently open-ended, including how to respectfully disagree with another child's perspective.

In the second phase of read-alouds, the focus shifted from understanding the children's perceptions around gender to directly working to create a broader, more fluid appreciation for gender diversity and representation. Books for this phase included *You Forgot Your Skirt, Amelia Bloomer!* (Corey, 2002); *Oliver Button Is a Sissy* (DePaola, 1979); *Pirate Girl* (Funke, 2005); *Dogs Don't Do Ballet* (Kemp, 2011); *The Worst Princess* (Kemp, 2012); *My Princess Boy* (Kilodavis, 2010); and *William's Doll* (Zolotow, 1972). During this phase, I continued to focus on holding inquiry-based, open-ended discussions with the children about the texts. However, the conversation shifted to actively discussing and challenging some of the ideas and themes that had emerged during the first phase of read-alouds. Using the chart that we had co-constructed, the children were asked to think about their collective assumptions about gender, along with the impact that similar assumptions had on the characters' well-being and happiness in the second series of books. The objective of this phase was not to make students feel shame or embarrassment, or to prove them wrong, but instead to explore which types of conversations and texts help students understand the pervasive discourse around gender norms and the painful impact this can have on characters and people who do not fit into these boxes. Following these conversations, the children were encouraged to think about their own classroom and school and how these spaces could be made welcoming to students of all gender identities and representations.

After completing the project in the classroom, the audio recordings (12 in total, ranging from 10 to 40 minutes in length) were transcribed by a doctoral student, focusing on verbatim transcription whenever possible. These documents were then analyzed for themes that emerged from the data around children's perceptions of gender, what aspects of the picture books they drew most heavily on for their understandings of characters' gender, and on which conversations seemed to most promote gender equity and acceptance in the classroom. We began with a priori codes based on our research questions and objectives and then did a cross-comparison analysis of the data to look for emic themes that emerged from the students themselves. These findings were shared with the classroom teachers and the parents to foster an ongoing discussion regarding these topics in the classroom and the children's homes.

"IN BOOKS, BOYS DON'T HAVE EYELASHES"

While gender is for many adults an uncomfortable topic in early childhood classrooms, it was clear through the discussions that the children already had strong perceptions around how to determine if a character was a boy or a girl. They jumped into these conversations willingly and extensively, and there was a generalized shared perception that one could tell if a character was a boy or a girl by how they appeared and by what they liked to do. In response to the first research question, which focused on how young children make sense of gender in picture books, the kindergarteners relied heavily on the visual representations in making their determinations around gender. This approach was likely in part because most of these children could not yet read independently. Children used visual cues more than 60% of the time they responded to the question of how they could tell if a character was a boy or girl. The majority of their visual cues relied on types of clothing (58% of the visual responses), with physical appearance (28%) and color (12%) being the other two most common points of connection. The children were able to draw on specific details of the drawings in making these determinations, which demonstrated not only their assuredness around gender representation but also their ability to construct meaning of the picture books themselves.

Perhaps unsurprisingly, given the strong association in the marketing of clothing and toys for girls to pink and purple and for boys to black, dark blue, and red, the children frequently utilized color as a way to determine a character's gender. During a read-aloud of *Owl Moon* (Yolen, 1987), a story of a young child and father going owl sighting during a winter night, one child firmly stated that the young child must be a girl because "the coat is a light purplish color. So it's a girl." Another child chimed in with, "Well, it could be a boy who has to wear his sister's hand-me-down coat. But then he would look mad." During a reading of *My Friend Rabbit* (Rohmann, 2002), where Rabbit (named as a he) gets his friend Mouse into some trouble with a toy airplane, the children overwhelmingly agreed that Mouse was a boy because, as one child stated, "the airplane is yellow and red. If it was a girl's plane, it would probably be pink or something." It is interesting to note that often it seemed as though the children presumed a male character unless there was a specific marker that signaled girl to them; at times, students even referenced what was not there to signify a girl character, with one child stating, "Well, Mouse would have a bow, if it were a girl."

Less expected was the children's deep focus on other physical features or attributes that widely signified gender to them. In particular, eyelashes became a central theme or reference point for the children. Overwhelmingly, they felt that if the eyelashes of a character were present, then the character was in fact a girl. As the adult reader, I was surprised by this statement the first time it came up and was equally surprised at how readily the other children agreed with the initial speaker. When I pointed out that all of the children in the class had eyelashes, the original student patiently explained to me, "Well, yeah, but that's in real life. In books, boys don't have eyelashes."

Interestingly, throughout the project, the children demonstrated a deep sense of understanding that books used shortcuts or common tropes to signify aspects of the characters and their identities. Excerpts from many of the transcripts demonstrated how deeply the children understood the idea that there was something special or particular around the ways that books present information, as opposed to real life:

Reading *Owl Moon* (Yolen, 1987)

> **Otto:**[3]She's wearing purple. So she's gotta be a girl.
> **Alice:** But, Otto, you're my friend and we both love purple.
> **Otto:** I know. But I'm talking about the book. Purple is how books say "girl."

Reading *The House in the Night* (Swanson, 2008)

> **Tom:** Oh, definitely a boy. Look at that short hair.
> **Me:** But I'm a girl. Well, a woman. And I have short hair, see?

Tom: But you're not in a book. You're in our classroom.
Ruth: Well, Louis [another child in the class] has long hair.
Tom: Yeah. But in a book, he might have short hair. Because, to show boy.

Related to the clear and consistent evidence that children understood that books draw on particular stereotypes or norms in order to demonstrate gender, the students also frequently referenced the idea of norms or expectations when making determinations around gender. Indeed, they often used this logic to refute times when other classmates (or myself) brought up counterexamples:

Reading *My Friend Rabbit* (Rohmann, 2002)

Michael: So Rabbit is a boy, right? Because it said "he." So then Mouse is a boy. A Rabbit Boy just would not play with a Mouse Girl.
Allie: Well, sometimes boys and girls are best friends.
Michael: Yeah. But not usually. I mean, not often. Boys usually play with boys.

Together, these trends in the data demonstrated the deep and highly traditional (even stereotypical) understandings of gender that the students held, as well as their already sophisticated understanding that books intentionally draw on these norms to help signify meaning or character attributes. This finding points to the fact that, at a young age, these children had not only absorbed many of the aspects of normativity around gender identity and representation, but also that they understood how these tropes or norms were used in creating meaning through texts. These trends point to the relevance of these topics within early childhood educational contexts, along with the importance of beginning to question these norms and assumptions in these early literacy experiences.

"BEING A GIRL DOESN'T MEAN YOU HAVE TO LIKE PINK"

After completing the first phase of read-alouds, we started reading the texts that deliberately introduced characters who either represented a broader range of gender identities or whose preferred activities or style of dress did not fit preconceived notions for their gender. Again, the guiding question was whether or not addressing gender in picture books helped children consider gender diversity in their own lives. For these read-alouds, I chose books and discussion questions that intentionally related to the topics that emerged during the first set of read-aloud sessions. During our conversations, I continued to ask about gender identity and representation, as well as deliberately turned the conversation toward thinking about the characters' states of mind or emotions within the texts. Because one of the goals of this research was to utilize picture book read-alouds to support more just and equitable spaces for children of diverse gender identity, I wanted to see if children could, when guided, link these book conversations to larger issues within their classrooms and communities.

Considerable research has demonstrated that young children show a strong ability to develop an empathetic stance when given opportunities to foster these skills in early elementary settings (Berliner & Masterson, 2015; Eisenberg & Strayer, 1990). The results of the discussions from this project aligned with these findings, as the children not only readily discussed the emotional responses of the characters—particularly those who felt uncomfortable with how their genders were defined, or those who faced bullying or derision for their choices regarding personal appearance and activity—but also made their own links to personal experiences. Sipe (2000) noted that one of the core types of responses that children offer to picture books is what he termed "personal connections." In these responses, children directly link what they see or hear in the story to experiences or contexts within their own lives. Often the children focused on small specifics, such as color:

> **Ruth:** I really don't like pink. And that's OK. But people give me stuff that is pink. Being a girl doesn't mean you have to like pink.
> **Robbie:** I love purple. But I don't, like, want to wear girl shirts. And it's hard to find boy shirts that are purple.
> **Otto:** I wanted to do ballet, but I was the only boy in the class. So that wasn't fun for me.

While these types of responses did occur in the initial phase of read-alouds, there was a significant increase during this phase of reading books that explicitly addressed gender norms, stereotypes, and diversity. Furthermore, as the included examples show, children were more willing to express times when they themselves faced similar issues to those in the texts.

Although children had shared stories of themselves or their friends who broke the rules of gender performance during the initial phase of reading, during these read-alouds they not only brought up these stories but also went more deeply into the impact that these experiences might have on real people. During a read-aloud of *My Princess Boy* (Kilodavis, 2011), the children spontaneously returned to the conversation about Louis's hair that was previously described:

Child: Remember we talked about Louis and how he has long hair?
Louis: Yep, I do.
Child: Well, people made fun of Princess Boy because he wore dresses. But people don't make fun of Louis.
Louis: Not at school. But lots of time, people think I'm a girl. And I have to tell them, "I'm a boy!" I don't like that I have to do it all the time.
Ruth: Right. Like, Princess Boy—he just wants to wear dresses. He doesn't like when they laugh at him for sparkly things.

In these moments, the children were able to work through concepts around teasing, assumptions, self-expression, and the impacts that these experiences can have on others' well-being and happiness. While in the earlier conversations there was a readiness to waive off an individual's gender diversity as simply an exception to the rule, during these conversations, there were many more conversations where children were able to really consider how these small moments could have larger impacts on those involved. In the previously described conversation, Louis was even able to discuss the subtle nuance between being actively teased versus just being misidentified, sharing that both can be painful.

In addition to talking about their classmates, children also were able to bring in stories from the news or from their own families to share:

Mary: So, um, there was a girl in the news. Well, I think she's a girl. She, um, she was a boy and now she's a girl, but her school wants her to use the boy bathroom and her parents think she should use the girl bathroom.
Charlie: My cousin. Um, her name is Michelle. Well, it was Michelle. But, um, she always liked sports and, like, wore clothes that boys wear. And, um, when she was in high school or college, I think it was high school, her mom wrote and said we should call her Michael. I mean, call him Michael. It's kind of confusing.

As these excerpts from the data show, there were times when the children expressed confusion around issues related to gender diversity but also shared their willingness to think through these issues together. Furthermore, by expanding discussions of gender diversity to include both transgender/gender fluidity and gender norms or assumptions, children were able to make personal connections and begin to understand how all of these issues relate to one another, broadening their knowledge and perspectives on gender diversity and gender identity.

IMPLICATIONS FOR RESEARCH
AND CLASSROOM PRACTICE

The findings from this project offered insights into possibilities for using picture books in research and practice to foster increased understanding of gender diversity in early elementary schooling contexts. In both classrooms, it was clear that using picture books and read-alouds provided a powerful way to link the children's experiences and questions with larger questions of gender representation, identity, and diversity. Furthermore, utilizing these texts helped to integrate these issues into the regular practices of language arts instruction in the classroom; these links allowed for a deeper investigation of these issues, rather than a single experience or discussion on a particular day. In addition, these interventions also ensured that there were texts available to the students that demonstrated a diverse range of gender expression and identity in their classroom contexts. Taken together, the research demonstrated that teacher-directed read-alouds can be a powerful way to engage students in thinking about gender diversity and in broadening the diversity of the classroom library.

Although this research was done exclusively in a kindergarten setting, the findings from this study also suggest that work around gender diversity using picture books would also be a valuable experience for students in older elementary grades; research has demonstrated that picture books continue to be powerful texts for older readers (Smith, 2008). In particular, using texts that are simpler in format but complex in terms of concepts or concerns could be a strong way to begin these critical conversations in upper elementary grades, where the beginnings of puberty can add more pressures and questions around gender that should be addressed in positive and accepting ways.

In terms of future research, using similar approaches in multiple grade levels could also offer a more nuanced understanding of how and when issues of gender identity and diversity impact children across the elementary age span. Furthermore, longitudinal work could explore how addressing these concerns in kindergarten and then following up over the elementary years could also provide insights into how schools and districts can develop curricula that support ongoing learning about gender equity and diversity in intentional and systemic ways. It would also be interesting to engage in research that explores issues of intersectionality in regard to gender identity, investigating the roles that race, ethnicity, and even religion play in how students understand and address these topics in their school contexts.

There is a clear need for teachers and educational researchers to work together to address topics of gender diversity and gender equity in positive and proactive ways, both in the classroom and in future academic research.

Given the strong links between student well-being and gender identity, we, as a field, need to continue to promote the discussion of gender and gender diversity throughout the curriculum. We also need research-based evidence that demonstrates the critical importance of engaging in these topics in early elementary contexts, before bullying and social pressures are as deeply entrenched. Based on the work of this project, it is clear that one strong point of entry is through the use of picture books and the common practice of teacher-led read-alouds to promote a broader understanding of gender identity, diversity, and equity in early elementary classroom contexts.

NOTES

1. This project was approved by the University of Pittsburgh's institutional review board for human subject research.
2. One of the questions that I struggled with in designing this work was how to define gender for young children, since part of the goal was to understand their own perspectives. In discussions with the teachers, it became clear that the children routinely used the binary of "boy/girl" in talk around books, toys, and themselves. For that reason, I initially asked children if they thought characters were boys or girls. Later, we did discuss a broader understanding of what gender identity might be.
3. All names are pseudonyms.

REFERENCES

Andrews, N. C., Martin, C. L., Field, R. D., Cook, R. E., & Lee, J. (2016). Development of expectancies about own- and other-gender group interactions and their school-related consequences. *Child Development, 87*(5), 1423–1435.

Baron, A. S., Schmader, T., Cvencek, D., & Meltzoff, A. N. (2014). The gendered self-concept: How implicit gender stereotypes and attitudes shape self-definition. In P. J. Leman & H. R. Tenenbaum (Eds.), *Gender and development* (pp. 109–132). New York, NY: Psychology Press.

Berliner, R., & Masterson, T. L. (2015). Review of research: Promoting empathy development in the early childhood and elementary classroom. *Childhood Education, 91*(1), 57–64.

Bishop Killeen, E. (2015). #WeNeedDiverseBooks! *Teacher Librarian, 42*(5), 52.

Brooks, W., & Browne, S. (2012). Towards a culturally situated reader response theory. *Children's Literature in Education, 43*(1), 74–85.

Corey, S. (2000). *You forgot your skirt, Amelia Bloomer!: A very improper story.* New York, NY: Scholastic Press.

Crisp, T., & Hiller, B. (2011). "Is this a boy or a girl?": Rethinking sex-role representation in Caldecott Medal-winning picturebooks, 1938–2011. *Children's Literature in Education, 42,* 196. https://doi.org/10.1007/s10583-011-9128-1

Dake, J. A., Price, J. H., Telljohann, S. K., & Funk, J. B. (2003). Teacher perceptions and practices regarding school bullying prevention. *Journal of School Health, 73*(9), 347–355.

Dávila, D. (2015). #WhoNeedsDiverseBooks?: Preservice teachers and religious neutrality with children's literature. *Research in the Teaching of English, 50*(1), 60–83.

DePaola, T. (1979). *Oliver Button is a sissy.* Boston, MA: Houghton Mifflin.

Dunham, Y., Baron, A. S., & Banaji, M. R. (2016). The development of implicit gender attitudes. *Developmental Science, 19*(5), 781–789.

Eisenberg, N., & Strayer, J. (Eds.). (1990). *Empathy and its development.* Cambridge, England: Cambridge University Press.

Funke, C. (2005). *Pirate girl.* Somerset, England: Chicken House.

Kemp, A. (2011). *Dogs don't do ballet.* New York, NY: Simon & Schuster.

Kemp, A. (2012). *The worst princess.* New York, NY: Simon & Schuster.

Kilodavis, C. (2010). *My princess boy.* New York, NY: Aladdin Press.

Kosciw, J. G., Greytak, E. A., Giga, N. M., Villenas, C., & Danischewski, D. J. (2016). *The 2015 National School Climate Survey: The experiences of lesbian, gay, bisexual, transgender, and queer youth in our nation's schools. New York, NY: GLSEN.* Retrieved from https://www.glsen.org/research/2015-national-school-climate-survey

Mattix, A., & Sobolak, M. J. (2014). Focus on elementary: The gender journey in picturebooks: A look back to move forward. *Childhood Education, 90*(3), 229–233.

Reay, D. (2015). The impact of gender, race and class on learning dispositions in schools. In D. Scott & E. Hargreaves (Eds.), *The SAGE handbook of learning* (pp. 363–372). Thousand Oaks, CA: SAGE.

Rohmann, E. (2002). *My friend Rabbit.* New York, NY: Macmillan.

Rosenblatt, L. M. (1982). The literary transaction: Evocation and response. *Theory Into Practice, 21*(4), 268–277.

Sipe, L. R. (1998). How picture books work: A semiotically framed theory of text-picture relationships. *Children's Literature in Education, 29*(2), 97–108.

Sipe, L. R. (2000). The construction of literary understanding by first and second graders in oral response to picture storybook read-alouds. *Reading Research Quarterly, 35*(2), 252–275.

Smith, M. (2008). Is "E" really for everybody? Picture books for older readers in public libraries. *Education Libraries, 31*(1), 5–12.

Souto-Manning, M. (2014). Making a stink about the "ideal" classroom: Theorizing and storying conflict in early childhood education. *Urban Education, 49*(6), 607–634.

Swanson, S. M. (2008). *The house in the night.* Boston, MA: Houghton Mifflin.

Thomas, E. E. (2016). Stories *still* matter: Rethinking the role of diverse children's literature today. *Language Arts, 94*(2), 112–119.

Vasquez, V. M. (2014). *Negotiating critical literacies with young children.* New York, NY: Routledge.

Willems, M. (2003). *Don't let the pigeon drive the bus!* New York, NY: Hyperion Books.

Yee, M., & Brown, R. (1994). The development of gender differentiation in young children. *British Journal of Social Psychology, 33*(2), 183–196.

Yolen, J. (1987). *Owl moon*. New York, NY: Philomel Books.

Zolotow, C. (1972). *William's doll*. New York, NY: HarperCollins.

PART II

PROCESS

CHAPTER 6

RELATIONSHIPS, RESOURCES, AND RECIPROCITY

Lessons on Engaging With Marginalized and Diverse Communities Through Asset-Based Participant Evaluation Research

Lori Delale-O'Connor
University of Pittsburgh

Ira E. Murray
United Way of Jackson Mississippi

ABSTRACT

This chapter examines the ways faculty members can engage in community-centered participant evaluation projects to connect with and support diverse communities while also potentially addressing the internal requirements of working in a university. Using qualitative data gathered from interviews and focus groups, as well as observations, and reflections, this chapter provides insights into the struggle in balancing myriad needs—broader community needs, the needs of particular community organization, university needs, and the needs of individuals, to complete a project that supports marginalized

Diversity Across the Disciplines, pages 85–100

and diverse communities. The chapter pays attention to the relationships, resources, and reciprocity needed when creating and implementing community-centered participation evaluation projects as a way to support marginalized communities.

Universities in the United States are typically relatively resource-rich institutions located in, if not always fully engaged with, communities. Literature has documented both the challenges (El Ansari & Weiss, 2005; O'Mara, 2012) and the innovative partnerships that result from relationships between communities and institutions of higher education (IHEs; Cotter, Welleford, Vesley-Massey, & Thurston, 2003; Dostilio, 2014; Martin, Smith, & Phillips, 2005; Mayfield, 2001). This work takes on a variety of formats, including service learning, university-led programming, and research (Bringle & Hatcher, 2002). Faculty members and other researchers occupy a central but sometimes conflicting role in the relationships between universities and communities (Weerts & Sandmann, 2010). They face professional expectations to advance the scholarly work of the university (e.g., publishing, presenting at conferences, obtaining grants) and the university community (e.g., teaching, mentoring students; Adams, 2002). This work does not always connect directly to—and sometimes comes into conflict with—the needs of the community in which the university resides and the interests and commitments of faculty with a desire to engage with the community (Dempsey, 2010; Dostilio, 2015). Further, they may have limited connection with the community (Dempsey, 2010). This conflict merits particular attention when the IHE population is racially and economically different from the community in which it is located (Mitchell, Donahue, & Young-Law, 2012).

Historically, divisions between communities and universities have stemmed from the deliberate spatial separation that the development of campuses initially espoused (McGirr, Kull, & Enns, 2003). Research that focuses explicitly on diversity in IHEs and community diversity has pointed to both the spatial and nonspatial divisions experienced in and across these relationships. In particular, case studies have pointed to tense or negative relationships between minoritized communities and IHEs connected to IHE expansion and competition for resources, such as space, housing, and funding (Bruning, McGrew, & Cooper, 2006; Evans, Taylor, Dunlap, & Miller, 2009; Mitchell et al., 2012; Uehling, 2009).

In this chapter, we draw from data and personal reflection on a yearlong community-centered participant evaluation project. This project, headed by university faculty and graduate students as part of a school district–led project, offers a study of one way that university researchers can use participatory evaluation to connect with and support diverse and marginalized communities while also meeting the requirements of working in a university. In particular, we address the following overarching question: How can participant evaluation serve as a way to connect faculty members and racially and ethnically marginalized communities?

Drawing from data gathered in interviews and focus groups with community members, as well as through community mapping, meeting participation, and reflections, this chapter provides insight into the struggles in balancing myriad needs in projects connecting IHEs and diverse communities. This focus includes needs of the broader community, of particular community organizations, of the university, and of individuals (faculty and students) to complete a project that offers benefits across parties. We focus our work around the concepts of relationships, resources, and reciprocity to provide insight into the aspects of this process, as well as ways to enhance this work, especially in the context of research on diverse communities. Our contribution includes the importance of taking an assets-based approach to the work and bringing resources and making connections beyond those required of the project versus traditional models. We contend that despite challenges, participant evaluation that takes an asset-based approach and considers particular relationships, resources, and reciprocity can facilitate connections to support the positive development of communities and to forward the work of IHE researchers. It is our intent that this chapter pushes the evaluation relationship into one that focuses on asset-based models of IHE–community relationships, as engendered in the work of individual faculty members (Donaldson & Daughtery, 2011). It is also our intent that this work informs conversations and considerations around diversity and inclusion as they pertain to the work of IHEs. To that end we focus on understanding the ways that evaluation can support IHEs in thoughtfully connecting with communities that are racially, ethnically, and economically different from the IHEs, and in particular engaging these communities in ways that serve to recognize the community's assets and support their development.

BACKGROUND

Community-based participatory research and evaluation is drawn from a Freirean understanding of knowledge creation (Freire, 1982)—that is, that knowledge belongs to and can (and should) be created by communities. Across fields such as education, health, economic development, and environmental change, community-based participatory evaluation offers an approach that has the potential to be relevant and build community capacity. In other words, by engaging the community in the ongoing research and evaluation in which they are equal thought partners and have a clear stake, the processes will not only be more meaningful but the outcomes also will be more relevant and more likely to be applied (Ahmed & Palermo, 2010;

Cousins & Whitmore, 1998). Despite this recognized value, community-based participatory research and evaluation face a variety of ethical challenges and practical considerations for IHE researchers (Minkler, 2004).

While models, approaches, and contexts vary, there are some key themes for researchers to consider across the literature on IHE–community collaboration as they seek to build and engage in evaluation embedded in or connected to a community, as well as reflect on such partnerships. For the purposes of this chapter, we highlight three key issues that operate in tandem as integral to the success of this work: relationships, resources, and reciprocity. Below we provide brief insight into each of these areas that we use to frame our work and experiences, focusing in particular on the assets of the community and the IHE. Taking such an asset-based approach is critical to community support and longevity of IHE–community partnerships (Holland & Gelmon, 1998). In addition, the relationships, resources, and reciprocity that can serve to better connect IHEs and diverse communities act as interdependent aspects to support joint work and processes. While we will separate these three Rs in defining and applying them to our case, these three dimensions are intertwined and ongoing in nature as connected to IHE–community collaboration.

Relationships

At the core of IHE faculty, staff, and student engagement with community-based research and evaluation are the relationships between IHEs and communities, which numerous studies have examined both theoretically and empirically (Bruning et al., 2006; Fisher, Fabricant, & Simmons, 2004; Ostrander & Chapin-Hogue, 2011; Strier, 2011). Case studies demonstrate the ways that successful IHE–community partnerships are rooted in relationships that are ongoing and multifaceted, and extend beyond research and academic connections (Cox, 2000; Walsh, 2006). While such relationships broadly involve the IHE, they are often made manifest in the work of individual faculty and students. Studies that focus on the themes of relationships and relationship building highlight the need for clarity as a core element of this work (U.S. Department of Housing and Urban Development, 2011). Specifically, research on the development and maintenance of relationships between IHEs and communities points to the need for all parties to develop a clear vision and goals for the relationship so that the work is clearly delineated and roles clearly defined (U.S. Department of Housing and Urban Development, 2011). In addition, for IHEs to establish strong relationships with communities, their representatives must have clear historical awareness and understand and acknowledge the assets of the community and community partners (U.S. Department of Housing and

Urban Development, 2011). Continual cultivation of these relationships—which Collins, Weinbaum, Ramón, & Vaughan (2009) refers to as "constant gardening" (p. 409)—also means that relationships may be more effective when they are part of a larger, sustained effort.

Resources

Literature has pointed to resources as another critical aspect of IHE–community collaborations—that is, the recognition and acknowledgement of the resources that both parties bring to bear (Williamson et al., 2016). For instance, IHEs are often seen through the lens of their resources—financial capital, time, research knowledge, processes (Weinberg, 1999)—and the provision of these resources. However, in partnerships, communities are frequently viewed either as in need of the resources IHEs have or as a place to study (Henry & Breyfogle, 2006). Recognition that communities possess many assets of their own is critical to IHE–community relationships (Cruz & Giles, 2000). This is particularly critical within minoritized, diverse communities, as well as within high-poverty communities (Howarth, Currie, Morrell, Sorensen, & Bengle, 2017). Positioning resources through the lens of mutual benefit and improvement offers a valuable perspective on resources, as they can support or undermine IHE–community connections (Collins et al., 2009).

Resources further include understanding and acknowledging the history of both the place and the relationship as relevant, as well as acknowledging potential power differentials (Bringle & Hatcher, 2002; Buys & Bursnall, 2007). In general, IHE–community collaborations benefit from a clear understanding of and a sharing of resources, as well as an acknowledgement of potential differentials in the types of resources they bring to the work.

Reciprocity

As Dostilio et al. (2012) discuss, reciprocity is frequently underspecified and misunderstood; however, they clarify that reciprocity can be understood as taking on three primary orientations based on exchange of benefits, resources or actions, influence of relationships and contexts, and/or generativity. We highlight in particular the third conceptualization of generative reciprocity that Dostilio et al. defines as participants jointly producing or co-creating something that would not have otherwise existed. Generative reciprocity also has potential for social justice by overcoming the boundaries of who is the server and who is served (Davis, Kliewer, & Nicolaides, 2017; Henry & Breyfogle, 2006). Generative reciprocity involves transformations in ways of knowing and in broader systems (Dostilio et al., 2012). Dostilio et al. describe, for instance, the development of a new organization focused on addressing a joint issue that would not have existed without the collaboration between a university and community. Generative reciprocity in IHE–community collaboration can lend support to deepening relationships and cultivating trust, as well as to opportunities to engage and bring in disparate groups, share power, and more fully engage (Cherry & Shefner, 2004). At its core, generative reciprocity involves the recognition of the interrelatedness and connectedness of systems—in this case, the connectedness of the IHE and community (Dostilio et al., 2012). Generative reciprocity offers additional value for diverse communities that may practice and value different ways of making meaning than IHEs, particularly as we consider IHEs' engagement in supporting more socially just outcomes for these communities (Asghar & Rowe, 2017; Davis et al., 2017).

PROJECT BACKGROUND

During the academic school year, a team of faculty and graduate students from City University,[1] a research institution located in one of the 100 largest cities in the United States, embarked on a yearlong evaluation of a planning and improvement initiative located in the same city. The initiative was focused on understanding and engaging the resources, organizations, and people within a neighborhood proximate to City University and the broader city community to better meet the needs and improve the lives and academic and social outcomes of the students and staff at one of the neighborhood's schools (Grades 6–12). The school district's underlying belief behind forwarding this initiative was that coordinating efforts and resources across the community would yield the greatest positive impact (or set of outcomes) for this school. The initiative included both planning and implementation. The evaluation team engaged in a variety of tasks, including developing a community asset map and conducting observations, interviews, and document reviews.

Community and School Context

The majority of the participatory evaluation work was set in Westmont, a historically Black neighborhood in the city where the university is located. Current census data indicate that the area is made up of primarily Black residents, with population estimates ranging from 72% to 95% by census tract. Westmont has experienced redevelopment and associated displacement, including the loss of thousands of residences, at the hands of the city and developers since the 1970s. The neighborhood is immediately adjacent to City University.

The school selected by the school district for evaluation is physically located in Westmont and was initially established as a partnership school run collaboratively by the school district and City University. The school is a combined middle and high school enrolling approximately 550 students, over 90% of whom identified as Black/African American, while the remaining 9% identified as White/Caucasian, multiracial, Asian, Hispanic/Latino, or Pacific Islander. The school was classified as a Title I school. At the time of the evaluation, nearly 90% of the attending students were classified as economically disadvantaged.

The partnership was initially developed to administer a collaboratively run college preparatory school within the Westmont community. In the earliest years of the partnership, the University had instructional coaches and other faculty and staff embedded in the building, and it played a variety of roles in supporting both teachers and school programming. This strongly linked relationship lasted for a few years, but for a variety of reasons connected to both City University and school district administration, the partnership was not fully realized and ultimately diminished in scope. At the time of the evaluation, the partnership was limited to a few programs led by City University, such as tutoring and after-school activities, occurring at the school.

City University

The evaluation team came from an urban university boasting over 20,000 undergraduate and graduate students. A member of the Association of American Universities, the IHE is a predominantly White university, with over 70% of undergraduate students and 75% of faculty identifying as White. The research team, however, consisted primarily of people of color, specifically a Latina faculty member, a Black male graduate student, a Latino graduate student, a White female undergraduate student, and a White female research assistant.

DATA AND METHODS

As part of the project, the IHE research team conducted interviews and focus groups at the start and conclusion of the project with approximately 70 members of adjacent communities. The focus group questions focused on the perceived strengths and weaknesses of the school, their understanding of the vision and purpose of the process, and their hopes for the students and the school. For instance, we asked participants the following questions: What opportunities do young people in Westmont have that you think would help them to forward their development (this could be academic, social, emotional, physical, or spiritual)? What barriers or obstacles do you think young people in Westmont encounter that may make it difficult to make the most of learning opportunities?

Interview and focus group participants included parents, students, educators, nonprofit leaders, leadership at local IHEs, and school district project staff. We also attended all planning meetings and observed, took notes, and participated in meeting activities. Our observation protocol noted the physical setting, meeting purpose, background, handouts, and running meeting notes. After each meeting and interview, the research team conducted debrief meetings.

As part of the project, the research team also developed an asset map and community directory. This work documented (on an interactive map, including phone numbers, addresses, and websites) the educational, health, religious, and social service organizations and programming available within the physical boundaries of Westmont, as well as those that served the school community from other parts of the city. These products were distributed for use by the school district, school, and community organizations. Completing them offered the research team a concrete understanding of the geography of the community and its resources.

For this study, we focused our analysis on understanding the connections between our involvement in the evaluation and both respondents' and the research team's impressions of the university and our work. To that end, we drew primarily from focus group, interview, and observational data, as well as our reflections on the evaluation process and the products that developed as a result of the process. Using these data, we focused on finding themes and patterns across the data sources—in particular, what the university can, could, and should do; connections and relationships across entities; and successes and shortcomings. Drawing from those themes, we linked back to prior literature on IHE–community connections to both better understand and refine where our case might fit, as well as note differences between our data and prior literature. Using this approach, we narrowed our focus to understand the data through the terms and lenses already discussed in the literature, as well as in particular relationships, resources, and reciprocity.

FINDINGS

While there are certainly challenges for researchers wanting to engage with communities, we learned from our work that participatory evaluation may provide one way to support these connections in ways that are beneficial to both parties and that further align with broader, positive IHE–community connections. In particular, participatory evaluation may be particularly beneficial as these relationships are formed between IHEs and ethnically and racially diverse communities. While engaged in this work, our data collection and analysis, as well as our written reflections, yielded a variety of findings that point to the valuable nature of evaluation and to the lessons learned around community–university evaluation partnerships. In what follows, we describe some ways we found that participant evaluation can serve as an asset-based approach to connect IHE researchers and communities. We frame our results in the literature discussed previously—in particular, related to the importance of (a) relationships, or building and cultivating relationships; (b) resources, or understanding and establishing clarity around the resources that we as evaluators and the community members and organizations with whom we engaged bring to bear; and (c) reciprocity, or the importance of reciprocity in understanding and engaging with one another.

Relationships

One of the positive outcomes of this work were the connections that we made with the school district and other partners in the work. The project itself provided relatively clear tasks and associated outcomes to consider when engaging the community. The community assets, mapping, and other parts of the evaluation required a substantial amount of time in the community and in the school, attending meetings and conducting focus groups and interviews, as well as offering feedback. Because of the evaluation work, we met and spoke with many school and community members repeatedly in ways that allowed us to engage shared concerns. This presence provided evidence of an ongoing commitment, which in both interviews and meeting notes many participants indicated they appreciated. They viewed our work as having potential for positive change and thus were willing to engage. As one respondent indicated, "There is potential to bring people together through the collaboration of ideas and working strategically." In addition, given the IHE researchers' role as evaluators, we were able to be transparent with participants and encourage them to share their needs, as well as challenges they had met, without concern of recourse. Our transparency encouraged open, candid exchanges, which we perceived as fostering trust, or at least comfortable familiarity, and the possibility for ongoing relationships. One participant noted that because of these conversations, "Real issues emerged, and difficult discussions were conducted with mutual respect." The relationships we developed meant we were considered for other projects that were driven by both parties. In addition, the work that we engaged in served as an overall way to make clear connections and demonstrated the potential value of university researchers to the local community.

Resources

The IHE–community evaluation offered the opportunity to seriously consider community resources and assets. As mentioned previously, part of the evaluation included developing a useable asset map and directory for the school district, school, and community organizations to use. This literal acknowledgement of resources proved to be critical for both the project and the relationships we built. We approached the community with an understanding of their strengths and the components that were already in place. Together, we developed a document that respondents indicated was of value because organizations, and in particular the school, could use it to identify resources that were already there, as well as acknowledge gaps they might be able to fill and ways to avoid engaging in redundant, duplicative work.

The process of the evaluation itself allowed us to better understand the varying stakeholders' perceptions of the role of the university's resources and our resources as individual researchers in completing this (and other) work. For instance, when talking with the school's leadership team, the principal indicated that once he realized City University was part of the work, he hoped to be able to draw from some of the university's resources, such as tickets to City University sporting events, gift cards, or university gear to incentivize students and support some of his programming. Similarly, a few parents brought up university programming occurring at the school and the resources it afforded their children. Others indicated that they were dismayed they did not know about this programming or felt it should be more readily provided from the university to more children in the school. During a SWOT (strengths, weaknesses, opportunities, threats) analysis that we noted in one of our meeting observations, respondents deepened their awareness that the support of the university and associated research was both a strength and an opportunity.

The financial, intellectual, and other resources of City University are undeniable, and many respondents indicated that they appreciated these. Some felt that City University should be doing much more. They further indicated that they hoped or saw this as a sign that the university would consider greater investment—including meeting both basic student needs and offering financial support for university attendance in the community and in particular in the school. This process thus allowed the research team to see our work as embedded in a larger system that might be able to extend resources beyond the offerings of individual researchers. This was particularly salient as we considered the stark racial and economic differences between Westmont, a majority African American neighborhood, and City University, a primarily White institution—in particular because City University professes interest in and forwards initiatives focused on diversifying its student population and engaging more African American students from the local area. Connections such as those fostered through participant evaluation might support pathways for local students of color to attend City University.

Reciprocity

Finally, engaging in the work allowed us to be part of a reciprocal relationship creating programming and systems that would have never occurred in the absence of these collaborations. This generative reciprocity occurred through the process itself, as well as our ability to not only evaluate but also participate. Our participation allowed us to experience the importance of the community in real-world application; the need for a clear linkage of prekindergarten through Grade 12 to higher education systems, including through college and high school activities; and the value of seeing the community as a true partner in this work, not just the beneficiary of IHE and other resources. Similarly, the end products—summary brief, report, and PowerPoint slide deck—were concrete items that were shared with all community participants and available for use. Although this was rather straightforward, it differed from the products sometimes associated with research, such as journal articles, conference presentations, and research briefs, to which there is often limited access and limited use value for community participants.

Through our role as evaluators, we were able to engage in some of the valuable work that connects IHE and communities. In reflecting on this work, we highlighted the importance of relationships, resources, and reciprocity. In particular, we were able to establish relationships based on both ongoing commitment and shared purpose.

Through explicit tasks and outcomes, this work acknowledged the assets in the community and offered some of the assets that our IHE roles afford (research skills). We were also able to support the school and community in making further connections between the resources of City University and Westmont to benefit the school. Finally, we were able to do this work in ways that bordered on the kind of generative reciprocity discussed by Dostilio et al. (2012) because this process created new pathways and understandings across parties. Engagement along these lines was particularly critical given the racial differences between the broader City University and Westmont.

CHALLENGES TO THIS WORK

Despite the favorable outcomes discussed, this work also faced challenges. These challenges further give us an opportunity to reflect on the value of the relationships, resources, and reciprocity embedded in IHE work in and with diverse communities.

Relationships

One of the primary challenges to this work that became apparent early in the evaluation was our affiliation with both City University and the school district; this was sometimes viewed with suspicion, depending on community members' prior experiences. Researchers are, of course, associated with their institutions—in many cases, this provides credibility but also bears the weight of prior initiatives and university engagement with the community. Indeed, past relationships—and negative aspects of these—came up across our work. In this case, this meant prior work in the community that a community member felt was not completed or outcomes were not sufficiently shared in ways to improve the community.

Similarly, confusion about our role and a limited understanding of the project process meant that our work and affiliations were not always initially clear to project participants. This fact became abundantly clear when the process was being explained, and we were part of those meetings. Because we were unknown to some community members, but had an apparent relationship with the school district, participants often assumed we worked there or were forwarding what they saw as the district's agenda. Past experiences with City University and a confusion about our purpose in being there challenged our ability to build relationships.

Resources

An additional challenge was the actual work of evaluation and the way it yields or does not yield tangible resources for the work being undertaken in communities. Evaluation is not an intervention—even when done in a participatory way—and when communities want problems addressed, or at least specific support, there may be frustration or confusion. In our role as evaluators, we had limited ability to influence who was involved in the process or what actions and activities would occur. However, participants' frustration with the process sometimes led to or carried over to frustration with evaluators. Concerns were also transferred to the evaluators—in particular around sustainability, City University's involvement, and City University's programming at the school.

Reciprocity

In terms of establishing truly reciprocal processes and outcomes, the limitations of timelines, as well as the project-specified and limited activities of evaluation, meant that while there might be reciprocal aspects of the work, it did not reach the generative reciprocity that Dostilio et al. (2012) described. The project itself was designated and funded to occur for one year, and the activities for that year were primarily dictated in advance; this looks different from Dostilio et al.'s vision of generative reciprocity, in which activities, exchanges, structures, and engagement may change, evolve, and transform to be reflective of the relationships and jointly produced knowledge coming from IHE–community relationships. And while it may be a stretch to think that one evaluation project or even a series of such projects will yield such generative reciprocity, they may offer one piece of such an exchange and allow for concrete opportunities to honor multiple ways of meaning making, tying back to both the relationships and the resources that are at the core of IHE–community engagement. In addition, through our role as evaluators, while we were connected to City University, we were not the representatives connected to ongoing exchange and realignment of understanding or ways of knowing and engagement that are hallmarks of generative reciprocity.

CONCLUSION

Our study's findings are valuable to faculty and graduate students, as current training and professional development infrequently address community evaluation research. Having these insights can help university researchers better understand the potential for asset-based evaluation to engage with diverse and often marginalized communities. Organizing evaluations in ways that acknowledge building and maintaining relationships, understanding and connecting resources, and engaging in ways that offer reciprocal processes and outcomes offers the possibility for outcomes and products that are valued by and valuable to both communities and IHEs. This is particularly critical, given the potential for tense or negative relationships between minoritized communities and IHEs, as well as the often competing interests between researchers' professional demands and community needs (Bruning et al., 2006; Evans et al., 2009; Mitchell et al., 2012; Uehling, 2009). We found that taking an asset-based approach to the community—in terms of both what it has and what an IHE can offer—may be facilitated with evaluation. IHEs and researchers must consider the historical relationships, as well as the community's history, and draw from these experiences. Participant valuation is one asset-based approach that faculty and graduate students should consider as a means to expand relationships, understand the resources of diverse communities, and identify together some clear needs that they can work on reciprocally.

NOTE

1. All place names are pseudonyms.

REFERENCES

Adams, K. A. (2002). *What colleges and universities want in new faculty. Preparing future faculty occasional paper series.* Washington, DC: Association of American Colleges & Universities.

Ahmed, S. M., & Palermo, A. G. (2010). Community engagement in research: Frameworks for education and peer review. *American Journal of Public Health, 100*(8), 1380–1387.

Asghar, M., & Rowe, N. (2017). Reciprocity and critical reflection as the key to social justice in service learning: A case study. *Innovations in Education and Teaching International, 54*(2), 117–125.

Bringle, R. G., & Hatcher, J. A. (2002). Campus-community partnerships: The terms of engagement. *Journal of Social Issues, 58*(3), 503–516.

Bruning, S. D., McGrew, S., & Cooper, M. (2006). Town–gown relationships: Exploring university–community engagement from the perspective of community members. *Public Relations Review, 32*(2), 125–130.

Buys, N., & Bursnall, S. (2007). Establishing university–community partnerships: Processes and benefits. *Journal of Higher Education Policy and Management, 29*(1), 73–86.

Cherry, D. J., & Shefner, J. (2004). Addressing barriers to university-community collaboration: Organizing by experts or organizing the experts? *Journal of Community Practice, 12*(3–4), 219–233.

Collins, D. E., Weinbaum, A. T., Ramón, G., & Vaughan, D. (2009). Laying the groundwork: The constant gardening of community—university—school partnerships for postsecondary access and success. *Journal of Hispanic Higher Education, 8*(4), 394–417.

Cotter, J. J., Welleford, E. A., Vesley-Massey, K., & Thurston, M. O. (2003). Town and gown: Collaborative community-based research and innovation. *Family & Community Health, 26*(4), 329–337.

Cousins, J. B., & Whitmore, E. (1998). Framing participatory evaluation. *New Directions for Evaluation, 1998*(80), 5–23.

Cox, D. N. (2000). Developing a framework for understanding university–community partnerships. *Cityscape, 5*(1), 9–26.

Cruz, N. I., & Giles, D. E., Jr. (2000). Where's the community in service-learning research? *Michigan Journal of Community Service Learning, 7*, 28–34.

Davis, K. L., Kliewer, B. W., & Nicolaides, A. (2017). Power and reciprocity in partnerships: Deliberative civic engagement and transformative learning in community-engaged scholarship. *Journal of Higher Education Outreach and Engagement, 21*(1), 30–54.

Dempsey, S. E. (2010). Critiquing community engagement. *Management Communication Quarterly, 24*(3), 359–390.

Donaldson, L. P., & Daughtery, L. (2011). Introducing asset-based models of social justice into service learning: A social work approach. *Journal of Community Practice, 19*(1), 80–99.

Dostilio, L. (2015). Faculty roles and faculty-related topics. *International Journal of Research on Service-Learning and Community Engagement, 3*(1), 1.

Dostilio, L. D. (2014). Democratically engaged community–university partnerships: Reciprocal determinants of democratically oriented roles and processes. *Journal of Higher Education Outreach and Engagement, 18*(4), 235–244.

Dostilio, L. D., Harrison, B., Brackmann, S. M., Kliewer, B. W., Edwards, K. E., & Clayton, P. H. (2012). Reciprocity: Saying what we mean and meaning what we say. *Michigan Journal of Community Service Learning, 19*(1), 17–33.

El Ansari, W., & Weiss, E. S. (2005). Quality of research on community partnerships: Developing the evidence base. *Health Education Research, 21*(2), 175–180.

Evans, S. Y., Taylor, C. M., Dunlap, M. R., & Miller, D. S. (Eds.). (2009). *African Americans and community engagement in higher education: Community service, service-learning, and community-based research.* Albany: State University of New York Press.

Fisher, R., Fabricant, M., & Simmons, L. (2004). Understanding contemporary university-community connections: Context, practice, and challenges. *Journal of Community Practice, 12*(3–4), 13–34.

Freire, P. (1982). Creating alternative research methods: Learning to do it by doing it. In B. Hall, A. Gillette, & R. Tandon (Eds.), *Creating knowledge: A monopoly? Participatory research in development* (pp. 29–37). New Delhi, India: Society for Participatory Research in Asia.

Henry, S. E., & Breyfogle, M. L. (2006). Toward a new framework of "server" and "served": De(and re)constructing reciprocity in service-learning pedagogy. *International Journal of Teaching and Learning in Higher Education, 18*(1), 27–35.

Holland, B. A., & Gelmon, S. B. (1998). The state of the "engaged campus": What have we learned about building and sustaining university-community partnerships? *AAHE Bulletin, 51*, 3–6.

Howarth, J., Currie, M. A., Morrell, E., Sorensen, J., & Bengle, T. (2017). Challenges of building community-university partnerships in new poverty landscapes. *Community Development, 48*(1), 48–66.

Martin, L. L., Smith, H., & Phillips, W. (2005). Bridging 'town & gown' through innovative university-community partnerships. *Innovation Journal, 10*(2), 1–16.

Mayfield, L. (2001). Town and gown in America: Some historical and institutional issues of the engaged university. *Education for Health, 14*(2), 231–240.

McGirr, D., Kull, R., & Enns, K. S. (2003). Town and gown. *Economic Development Journal, 2*(2), 16–23.

Minkler, M. (2004). Ethical challenges for the "outside" researcher in community-based participatory research. *Health Education & Behavior, 31*(6), 684–697.

Mitchell, T. D., Donahue, D. M., & Young-Law, C. (2012). Service learning as a pedagogy of Whiteness. *Equity & Excellence in Education, 45*(4), 612–629.

O'Mara, M. P. (2012). Beyond town and gown: University economic engagement and the legacy of the urban crisis. *Journal of Technology Transfer, 37*(2), 234–250.

Ostrander, N., & Chapin-Hogue, S. (2011). Learning from our mistakes: An autopsy of an unsuccessful university–community collaboration. *Social Work Education, 30*(4), 454–464.

Strier, R. (2011). The construction of university-community partnerships: Entangled perspectives. *Higher Education, 62*(1), 81–97.

Uehling, K. (2009). *Building a relationship between a university and its surrounding community: The Community Remembrance Project revisited* (Unpublished doctoral dissertation). University of Delaware, Newark, DE.

U.S. Department of Housing and Urban Development. (2011). Collaborating for change: Partnerships to transform our local communities. Washington, DC: Author. Retrieved from https://www.huduser.gov/portal//publications/pdf/collaboratingforchangev2.pdf

Walsh, D. (2006). Best practices in university–community partnerships: Lessons learned from a physical-activity-based program. *Journal of Physical Education, Recreation, & Dance, 77*(4), 45–56.

Weerts, D. J., & Sandmann, L. R. (2010). Community engagement and boundary-spanning roles at research universities. *Journal of Higher Education, 81*(6), 632–657.

Weinberg, A. S. (1999). The university and the hamlets: Revitalizing low-income communities through university outreach and community visioning exercises. *American Behavioral Scientist, 42*(5), 800–813.

Williamson, H. J., Young, B.-R., Murray, N., Burton, D. L., Levin, B. L., Massey, O. T., & Baldwin, J. A. (2016). Community–university partnerships for research and practice: Application of an interactive and contextual model of collaboration. *Journal of Higher Education Outreach and Engagement, 20*(2), 55–84.

CHAPTER 7

EXPLORING THEMES OF CULTURE IN A MEDICAL SCHOOL CULTURAL COMPETENCE COURSE

Abdesalam Soudi
University of Pittsburgh

Leyan deBorja
University of Pittsburgh

Jeannette E. South-Paul
University of Pittsburgh

ABSTRACT

This chapter examines the impact of cultural competency training on clinicians and the care they provide. This chapter analyzes over 70 reflection essays from a teaching course on cultural competence in medical education and practice collected over the past 12 years. This chapter first describes the structure, materials, and teaching methods of the course in which students were instructed to analyze a problem in their field that relates to cultural

Diversity Across the Disciplines, pages 101–118
Copyright © 2020 by Information Age Publishing
All rights of reproduction in any form reserved.

competency in medicine; then suggests strategies for solutions. Secondly, this chapter reports a meta-analysis of the data summarizing and explaining important themes relevant to instructing cultural competence in medical education including race, ethnicity, language, age, nationality, gender, socioeconomics, and discrimination.

The rapidly increasing diversity in the general population as well as the substantially slower diversification of the healthcare workforce has driven newer curricular requirements for cultural competence education in medical schools (prescribed by the Liaison Committee on Medical Education [LCME], accreditor of allopathic medical schools) beginning in the late 1990s. Soon thereafter, state licensing boards also recognized the need for this training among clinicians practicing in their states. New Jersey first passed legislation in 2002 requiring medical school curricula to include at least one required cultural competency course "designed to address the problem of race and gender-based disparities in medical treatment decisions" and mandating that out-of-state physicians and those applying for relicensure document at least 16 hours of cultural competency training (U.S. Department of Health and Human Services, Office of Minority Health, 2016). Subsequently, other states, including Arizona, New York, California, and Illinois, began requiring similar training ("States Increasingly Requiring Cultural Competency Courses," 2006).

This increased attention to cultural competency education and training resulted in more scrutiny of specifically what was being offered in this curricular category. One of the authors, Jeannette South-Paul (JS), chaired the committee of the Association of American Medical Colleges that developed the Tool for Assessing Cultural Competence Training (TACCT), to assist schools in developing and evaluating cultural competency curricula to meet these new LCME requirements. Research has demonstrated that systematic cultural competency training can improve the knowledge, skills, and attitudes of medical trainees, but there is a wide variation in the content and evaluations of such programs (Jernigan, Hearod, Tran, Norris, & Buchwald, 2016).

In 2003, JS developed an elective cultural competency course for fourth-year medical students and physicians completing a master's degree in medical education at the University of Pittsburgh School of Medicine. This course had a core curriculum that was modified to address the dynamic events in both the local and national environments, as well as to reflect the increasing number and diversity of cultural groups entering American society. Five years after the creation of the course, the first author Abdesalam Soudi (AS) was invited to codirect the course and to introduce a linguistic perspective on culture as well as to enhance other curricular material. Personal reflection papers were a part of this course from the very beginning.

AS directed a process and framework for discussing these papers within the course itself. These papers form the data drawn upon in this work.

This chapter builds on this collaborative work between the Department of Family Medicine in the School of Medicine and the Department of Linguistics in the School of Arts and Sciences, both at the University of Pittsburgh; this work aims to integrate humanities into health and medicine. The aforementioned master's course for students in medicine and the health sciences (Soudi & South-Paul, 2017) is one of several initiatives for strengthening humanities and health connections at Pitt (Soudi et al., 2018; Soudi, Gooden, Chang, Kiesling, & South-Paul, 2017). A major component of the course is the aforementioned reflection work that trainees are required to do: Students must write an essay on a personal clinical experience that highlights the impact of cultural determinants (a key one of which is language). Students are asked to apply models of intercultural sensitivity (Bennett, 1986) to these issues. This class exercise, which leads to a term paper at the end of the course, allows trainees to examine their experiences in clinical practice and engage in self-dialogue. More than 70 papers have been submitted during the past 12 years of the course. Below is the first meta-analysis of these papers; we summarize the concepts, examine how trainees' attitudes have changed, and observe trends in how they applied the course concepts. This project is supported by a grant from the provost and from the David Berg Center for Ethics and Leadership at the University of Pittsburgh. The results of this study will help inform subsequent teaching and target needs.

STRUCTURE, MATERIALS, AND DIVERSITY OF TEACHING METHODS

The didactics of this course is based on presentations by the interdisciplinary team (a family physician [JS] and a sociolinguist [AS]), class presentations by the trainees, and group discussion facilitated by the two instructors. Much of the content of these discussions is triggered by the shared readings, videotapes, and personal reflections on events experienced by the trainees in their clinical practice or as patients themselves. The focus of these projects is on exploring some aspect of becoming a doctor, the patient's illness experience, or the interaction between doctor and patient.

Advancing diversity in the health disciplines requires us to approach teaching from diverse perspectives. Both instructors work together collaboratively to design lessons and deliver content for most sessions. Occasionally, the instructors will lead different parts of the course depending on their expertise. Table 7.1 is adapted from previous work (Soudi & South-Paul, 2017) and summarizes the major topics and goals of the course.

TABLE 7.1 Cultural Competence Course Outline

Topic	Student Outcomes
1. Culture and history	Define cultural determinants; recount historical events that shape how diverse populations interact with the healthcare system.
2. Patient-centeredness versus cultural competence	Recognize how personal worldview shapes relationships and encounters; describe and use Bennett's model of intercultural sensitivity.
3. Working with communities	Recognize changes in family structure, racial/ethnic distribution, socioeconomic status, and national origin in the past 20 years and their influence on health.
4. Social determinants of health	List the behavioral and social factors that influence population health; list differing status for diverse groups.
5. Immigrant and refugee health	Describe the predominant immigrant groups, the impact of their journey on how they interface with the healthcare system, and common health issues they face.
6. Appreciating language/ linguistic competency	Recognize how the patient's language of origin and fluency, as well as literacy and technology, impact clinical encounters.
7. Identifying and addressing discrimination	Understand the many faces of discrimination and how they influence health (e.g., racial/ethnic, age, gender, religious, national origin, sexual orientation, disability).
8. Assessing your organization's response to diverse populations	Describe indicators of organizational cultural competence; outline the representation of diverse groups at the faculty and student levels and describe the influence of public and legislative initiatives.

MATERIALS AND TRAINEES

As discussed, the authors of the papers are medical students enrolled in a cultural competence fourth-year elective course at the University of Pittsburgh School of Medicine or practicing academic clinicians (largely physicians, but also one physical therapist and one dentist). The authors come from different cultural backgrounds. Some were born and raised in the United States, while others identify as international medical graduates. Other students were brought up within two different cultures (e.g., the children of immigrants). At times, the authors' cultural backgrounds and sociocultural identities played a crucial role in the events depicted in the narratives, but at other times did not seem to influence the clinical encounters.

To apply the class content, the trainees are asked to write a reflection paper of 8–10 single-spaced pages on an experience related to a cultural and linguistic competency issue within the course framework. The exercise is designed to force students to apply the course material and stimulate its ongoing applicability. The trainees must identify an event, analyze the problem, and suggest strategies for solutions. They also must address how to teach it to others or note if they would approach the situation differently today. The assignment can focus on any of the course sessions or topics discussed in class. Students then reflect on the event by describing the challenge or learning point(s) from the encounter. The essay should provide a framework to explore cultural or linguistic determinants impacting the health of their patients or affecting the authors as healthcare professionals/educators.

This final reflective assignment generates responses from various points of view and contexts. Authors described events in which they were the protagonists of experiences that illustrated cultural insensitivity or raised issues of cultural awareness and competence. Others described events to which they were observers, interns, or attending physicians; they also detailed events that potentially involved family members. Some students focused on the literature to demonstrate how culture impacts specific populations and their interactions with the healthcare system.

In general, trainees focused on how a lack of awareness of cultural and sociocultural factors impacted communication and relationships in a clinical setting and how that lack of cultural competence impacted patient care. Other experiences related in the reflection papers stemmed from a sense of injustice that the authors felt was present in the described interactions. The injustice varied by the environment, hospital setting, nature of the encounter, participants, and power dynamics.

SOCIOECOLOGICAL MODEL

The papers were written to focus on the principles taught in the course. Initially, each paper centered around one of the cultural determinants introduced in the earliest coursework but rapidly revealed the overlay of multiple cultural, socioeconomic, and even political factors on the course and on the management of acute and chronic disease encounters. Although beyond the scope of this chapter, the topics on which the students chose to focus developed in an interesting fashion over the years of the course, reflecting political, economic, and social changes within our society. For example, in the early years of the course, the papers focused more on race and language, whereas in more recent years, students reflected their experiences, conflicts, and concerns regarding care of the uninsured, of refugees, and of the disabled. Examples of recurring themes can be illustrated in excerpts from individual papers.

Race/Ethnicity

> I realized in that moment that I would have to be his voice if his story was to be heard. I convinced the team to, at a minimum, get a psych consult in the vain hope that someone could help manage the underlying issues that led to his alcoholism... However, the resident who saw him did not put much effort in the interaction... Once the [delirium tremens, a dangerous form of alcohol withdrawal] passed, our team discharged him back to his apartment, with my attending making the comment that, "He is just going to start drinking again," with the implication that it was not worth our time to continue worrying about him.

This student observed a case that she interpreted as racial discrimination against a patient and was unable to successfully advocate for resources and care due to the dismissive attitude of the senior members of the healthcare team. This asymmetry in power and authority was clearly apparent to the student. This incident stimulated a discussion of the complicated overlapping situation of a racial minority presenting with a chronic condition that has extremely high recidivism rates. The student was challenged to determine whether the resultant disengagement and apathy of the medical team toward the patient suggested discrimination or a fundamental lack of faith in the patient's potential for sobriety, given the chronicity of the disease. Nevertheless, the student felt unable to advocate for a patient she felt was receiving substandard care.

Language

> As I questioned my first patient and her family with my attending about what brought them into the clinic that day, we followed what we thought were the appropriate techniques for using an interpreter. We established triangle-shaped spacing between us, the patient and parents, and the interpreter... I ultimately felt comfortable that the patient's parents agreed to follow our recommended treatment and understood how to properly take the medications recommended in each of the two cases. However, I also felt that both families were robbed of an opportunity to have truly informed consent about the care their children were receiving. The experience felt more paternalistic than the other patient encounters that I had that day, which did not require an interpreter.

The presence of multiple participants, such as a patient's family members, is crucial to understanding how and why clinical interactions flow as they do. Family members are important participants in clinical interactions, especially when the patient is a minor, as they provide support, clarifying information or, in some cases, advocating for addressing the patient's cultural practices or beliefs. Language discordance presents a barrier to providing a culturally sensitive encounter in health care. Interpreters insert an additional level of complexity because they have various levels or an absence of training. Standards pertaining to language barriers in healthcare were introduced formally through the National CLAS (Culturally and Linguistically Appropriate Services) Standards in 2000 but have been unevenly implemented nationwide resulting in an uncontrolled, spontaneous use of a variety of qualified and unqualified individuals, the presence of whom changes the patient–provider dynamic.

Nationality

> I was able to observe that many of my patient's symptoms developed or worsened at the time of her immigration from Nepal to the U.S. A native of Bhutan, she had spent the last few years of her life in a refugee camp in Nepal. Although her life in the refugee camp was one of devastatingly limited resources, her family described that she had friends and social support at the camp and was respected for her cooking skills. On their transition to the U.S., they noted she became more withdrawn and showed a lack of interest in her previous activities. I wondered if depression might be at least contributing to, if not the primary driver of her failure to thrive in the U.S.

Recognizing the commonalities among individuals of a shared cultural identity helps to frame how new immigrants access health care. Those of a different nationality present with unique concerns that differ depending on whether they arrive as immigrants, who bring particular resources to their new lives, versus refugees, who may have been stranded for years in a temporary stateless status, with little access to education, nutrition, or health care. The narratives highlighted how having a greater understanding of environmental and background factors may change how patients and providers interact. The patient's immigration status, the major changes to her life, and social setting had a great impact on her health.

Age

> She said she was ashamed. Her oncologist told her HPV is something you get from sexual activities, and she was embarrassed to talk about her cancer, which was HPV positive, because she was afraid people will think she was promiscuous, despite the fact that she has only been with two men in her life. The only person in her family or community she even told about the cancer was her daughter due to this embarrassment.

One student's interaction with a patient with cancer demonstrated the impact of generational differences when communicating with patients and addressing diagnoses. The patient was an older adult Hispanic woman who was diagnosed with anal squamous cell carcinoma. Her oncologist had communicated the fact that this form of cancer could have resulted from a sexually transmitted infection, specifically HPV, or human papillomavirus. The oncologist was unaware of the patient's cultural background that resulted in her feelings of shame regarding her diagnosis and her reluctance to seek support from her community. Thus, she kept her health complications a secret because of an unwillingness to reveal an illness originating from a sexually transmitted infection. This also led the patient to ignore her diagnosis.

Gender

> Some physicians flat out refuse to look at data about gender differences. Thus, they conclude that women are the same as men, possibly just a little smaller in size...Still other physicians think that the literature and media attention is a reflection of our sensationalistic society, which is using the issue of gender to increase ratings and create controversy. And finally, the most common belief from my experience, is that women's heart disease has been created to be a "new and different" disease so that it can be used as a marketing tool to attract more patients and do unnecessary tests.

Attitudes toward certain populations, specifically women, was the focus of one paper. In the case of women's health, particularly in terms of cardiovascular health, one student found that some of her colleagues refused to recognize differences in how cardiovascular disease presents and is treated in men as opposed to women.

Socioeconomic

> Occasionally a stray patient will end up in the "wrong hospital." An African American homeless man who was schizophrenic with diabetes and not truly able to care for himself presented to the private hospital...The staff as a whole is uncomfortable with him due to his state of uncleanliness, disarray, stench, and behavior...This hospital is not used to this patient. At the city hospital, this is every other patient that is cared for—it is their norm—but here it is a gross anomaly that no one truly understands.

This encounter emphasized the stark differences in the quality of care provided to a patient not because of availability of services, but because the patient clearly presented from a resource-poor environment with a lack of ability for self-care. His minority racial/ethnic status further complicated his quest for care.

Discrimination

Mistrust of the healthcare system among the African American community influences how members of this community interact with healthcare providers (Jacobs, Rolle, Ferrans, Whitaker, & Wernecke, 2006; Kennedy, Mathis, & Woods, 2007).

> Mrs. B's distrust of nearly all medical professionals was shaped not only by her personal history of discrimination in health care but also by the experiences of her neighbors in the medical system. Her experience with discrimination and disparate treatment because of her race is much broader than the healthcare setting.

Other narratives illustrated a clear sequence that began with assumptions and preconceived notions held by the authors toward a certain person or patient based on a single description, such as a diagnosis or medical record.

> I was taught early on in my medical education to approach each patient with an open mind and to refrain from looking at charts and notes by other staff until after seeing the patient. This being a high-volume service, I disregarded this advice immediately and opened up her chart and read all about her before she reached the floor... She had hepatitis C and was coming in with abdominal pain. I had seen this before and went into pain medication denial mode, as I suspected that she had probably been here a number of times before. She was almost certainly an intravenous drug user. As it turned out, in 1977, Ms. H was involved in a head-on collision with an 18-wheeler while sitting in the passenger seat. Her best friend was driving and was killed instantly. Due to her massive blood loss, she received multiple blood transfusions, one of which was contaminated with hepatitis C... In actuality, she would not have arrived at our hospital and become my responsibility were it not for her car crash 36 years ago.

The clear contrast of the authors' thoughts before and after meeting these patients offers an important learning tool for healthcare providers. The sequence of events leading to the realization that patients are complex, multifaceted, and much more than their medical record or diagnosis is a central aspect of this narrative. Reflexive biases based on perceived patient behaviors can negatively impact the entire encounter, causing the clinician to overlook key elements of the patient's history and resulting in substandard care.

GENERAL THEMES AND DISCUSSION

The papers dealt not only with issues directly related to cultural competency issues but also to a variety of sociocultural factors, such as social climate, historical context, generalizations versus patient-centered care, institutional culture, and communication.

Sociocultural Context and Historical Context

The social context has a great bearing on general perceptions and normal behaviors and beliefs (McLeroy, Bibeau, Steckler, & Glanz, 1988; Schultz, Nolan, Cialdini, Goldstein, & Griskevicius, 2007). Student papers have demonstrated that social context and norms have a cascading effect on the culture of medicine and an impact on patient care. One student narrative chronicled the historical and current relationship between persons with disabilities and American society, and illustrated how this relationship has impacted the treatment and experiences of persons with disabilities.

> From the founding of the United States and for almost the next two centuries, children, men and women who suffered handicaps were deemed unfit for society.

The language used to describe this population had set a precedent long before the first schools or first nationally known advocates arose. Being viewed as intrinsically odd, defective, or even evil created barriers for the disabled.

Societal norms influence how people perceive the world and how they interact with others (McLeroy et al., 1988; Schultz et al., 2007). For example, the beauty standards of a given society can impact how people perceive and act toward others who do not fit into a particular mold. Obesity carries a very negative connotation, and many people project negative attitudes toward individuals who are obese (Puhl & Heuer, 2009). A student narrative demonstrated that these societal norms can and do infiltrate the walls of the healthcare system.

> As demonstrated in pop culture mediums such as contemporary literature ... there is a real concept of the "ideal" body type and that some people simply have "too much meat on [their] bones." We live in a culture that values thinness, and those who do not embody thinness are often presumed to be "defective" in some way. Whether it be "lazy" or "overindulgent" or, very relevant to us as healthcare providers, "noncompliant," we assign value judgements to individuals who are obese.

This indicates that patients' health can be impacted when these norms become integrated into the institutional culture of the healthcare system. This attitude toward individuals who do not fit the socially accepted model of beauty, specifically in terms of weight, can affect the way healthcare providers treat these patients and the quality of care that is provided.

> I hope to show that our attitudes as healthcare professionals can negatively impact the care of obese patients beyond the clinical comorbidities they have as a result of obesity, and that awareness of the cultural determinants on which those attitudes are formed supports the provision of culturally and clinically competent patient care.

Relationships are not formed in a vacuum and are not spontaneously generated. They are built over time through interaction. On a broad social scale, there are clear relationships between different populations and societal institutions that have a basis in historical context. A prime example is the relationship between the African American community and the healthcare system. This relationship is mired in conflict and tension based on negative interactions that span generations (Jacobs et al., 2006; Kennedy et al., 2007). Historically, those in the U.S. healthcare system have taken advantage of the power they have held over minority groups, such as the African American community. Unethical experiments, mistreatment, and the provision of substandard health care create skepticism and mistrust among many African American individuals (Jacobs et al., 2006; Kennedy et al., 2007). One student experienced this mistrust and utilized the experience to

> reflect on the effects of racial disparities, the perception of racial discrimination, and mistrust of the medical system on the communication between patients and physicians.... [The patient] noted that only medical students had taken care of her and her friends at community hospital [and] that they didn't ever see a doctor while they were there. She felt that the student and residents were doing experimental treatments on them and noted that her experience with pain after her first surgery for her rectal cancer at that hospital had been horrific, with terrible pain after the surgery.

The context of interactions is important, as seen in the impact of setting on narrative development. The examples discussed and the topics they bring forth illustrate how the physical and social settings play a role in how the participating individuals react and how the discourse develops. These examples also highlight how social norms have an influence on interactions between individuals, specifically in a clinical setting. These social norms or attitudes play a role in how the participants of an interaction will act toward other individuals and how they will communicate (McLeroy et al., 1988;

Schultz et al., 2007). Therefore, these social norms have a bearing on the outcomes of social interactions and events, such as those presented in the student papers.

Generalizations and Patient-Centered Care

Overall, the student papers indicated that although generalizations can be useful in some instances, in order to be aware of differences that one may encounter while working with a diverse patient population, reliance on generalizations of cultural tenets and other aspects of a group may lead to negative interactions and outcomes between patients and the healthcare system. The students recognized that although it was useful to learn about general cultural tenets, cultural competence education must go beyond the teaching of different aspects of minority cultures based on stratifying factors such as race or ethnicity. They also made it clear that cultural competence skills do not emerge purely out of the knowledge of different cultural tenets; rather these skills are developed through awareness, listening, and constant learning from experiences and interactions with people who identify with those cultures. The application of generalizations to interactions with patients of diverse backgrounds can mislead a healthcare provider in diagnosing and treating a patient (Epner & Baile, 2012).

Negative stereotypes and generalizations are utilized and perpetuated in our society. Racial stereotypes are still present today; the presence of this negative force in society infiltrates the medical culture as well (Hardeman, Medina, & Kozhimannil, 2016). Student experiences illustrated that even in this modern age, stereotypes, such as those based on race, are used to assess and judge a patient.

> My attending dismissed him from the beginning. On round, before my attending had met the patient, the following conversation ensued:
>
> **Attending:** "Well, why do you think he was shot?"
> **Me:** "I am not sure. I can ask him after rounds."
> **Attending:** "It was drugs. He is a young Black man—it's always drugs."
> **Attending:** [turning to the patient's nurse] "Why do you think he was shot?"
> **Nurse:** "It was probably drugs."

The student who witnessed this conversation was working with a patient who was a young Black man dealing with alcoholism due to a gunshot injury that left him with chronic health issues. In addition, the patient had suffered personal tragedy, which prompted him to use alcohol as a coping mechanism. The attending physician's assumption that the gunshot wound was a result of dealing drugs proved to be untrue. Although this fact should not have affected the patient's care, the negative label placed on this patient led to substandard care and lack of compassion from the healthcare providers.

> I learned that the inequality demonstrated every day in the justice system extends deep within the sacred area of medicine. It may be as simple as referring to two mid-20-something Black sickle cell patients as the same person because, "I can't tell them apart—they are identical." Or it may be a much deeper problem that ends with patients not [receiving] the level of care they deserve.

The author's role as a student left her in a powerless position compared to the other participants, specifically her superiors. Although the student advocated for better care and treatment of the patient, the power disparity between her and her attending physician was not conducive to being successful. As in previous examples, the perpetuation of attitudes toward certain patient populations sets a precedent that becomes ingrained within medical culture and the healthcare system. In one instance, a student discusses the interaction between the healthcare system and patients with substance abuse issues.

> Stigma associated with substance dependence remains deeply ingrained in medical culture. These biases are evidenced in the labels that are commonly assigned to these individuals in healthcare settings (e.g., referring to a patient as an "addict," a "drug-seeker," or an "alcoholic," not as being a substance-dependent) and the method in which these patients are framed during presentations (e.g., including substance-dependence information when clearly non pertinent).

The author highlights the use of terms or labels with a negative connotation in relation to such patients and how this perpetuates judgment within the medical community; this negative attitude also impacts the interactions and relationships these patients have with the healthcare system.

> These patients are more likely to develop difficult relationships with the U.S. healthcare system. These difficult relationships can manifest in the patient as distant behavior...defensive behavior.... These behaviors, then, can be reasoned to cause increasing tension on this relationship.

Applying cultural generalizations to an individual patient may cause misunderstanding and unnecessary conflict (Epner & Baile, 2012). Individuals may present aspects of the culture to which they belong in a manner different than others in the group with which they identify (Epner & Baile, 2012). In the student papers, there was significant emphasis placed on considering an individual's culture in addition to the cultural tenets and values put forth by the cultural community to which the individual may belong.

> One of the major themes of health care, even more prominently in children, is the balance between patient-centered and culturally competent care.... Patient-centered care refers to health care that meets the individual needs of a patient. Culturally competent care describes the practice of assessing an individual's needs based on the culture from which they come. Together, they can provide an exquisite model for holistic health care if used in an appropriate balance.... In this case, though, TT was never described as Caucasian or African American; he was unimmunized. The term brought with it such stigma to an 8-month-old with literally no say in the matter. Immediately, preconceptions of radical parents breastfeeding their children through kindergarten or cosleeping came to mind.

This student recognized that the healthcare team interacting with this family made assumptions based on individual decisions of the patient's parents—in this case, not to vaccinate. These assumptions led to conflict in the relationship and judgments on the part of the healthcare providers, which did not contribute to a successful relationship between the providers and patient's caretakers.

> If we had only looked at my patient from the angle of an unimmunized child, we would have missed the effort that this mom had put into making sure her child remains healthy. She trusted the healthcare system, but she had been put in a position where her own beliefs did not align with her pediatrician.... [She was] eventually dismissed from the practice due to conflict between her goals and those of the [primary care provider]."

Members of the healthcare team treating the patient and working with the patient's parents based their approach to the interaction on preconceived notions. These ideas were based on how they viewed those who chose not to vaccinate their children; they assumed that the parents of this particular child had a certain lifestyle and various beliefs that were contributing to a problem with the pediatric patient's development and that would cause conflict when deciding on a treatment plan.

Institutional Culture

Institutions carry their own sets of norms and cultural tenets that are accepted and experienced by those working and interacting within them (Davies, Nutley, & Mannion, 2000; Scott, Mannion, Davies, & Marshall, 2003). The institution of medicine is no different, and the norms and cultural tenets that are accepted and practiced have an impact on clinical care (Davies et al., 2000; Scott et al., 2003).

The institutional culture of medicine can also be seen through the concept of the "hidden curriculum," which refers to the gap that exists between what students learn from formally taught concepts or lessons and what students learn from the social and cultural environment of an institution (Giroux & Penna, 1979; Hafferty & Gaufberg, 2013). One example is when medical students and trainees learn about the concepts of professionalism and collaboration in their classes and from formal educational settings, but then observe an attending speaking negatively about physicians practicing a different specialty of medicine. As one student experienced, this hidden social norm or culture influences the interactions between healthcare professionals and, in turn, determines the quality of care that patients receive:

> We make...broad and sometimes unflattering generalizations about surgeons, specialist[s], "just primary care docs," nurses, students... but then talk extensively about professionalism and respect.

The student highlights how the teachings from lectures and other academic settings are not necessarily put into practice. This demonstrates the institutional culture and the normal behaviors that, although contradictory with common teachings, are accepted by the system and by those who work and interact within it. In order to address the issue of the "hidden curriculum," which is found in the common culture of the medical profession, it must first be identified. This student's reflection provided a clear example of the issues with this accepted norm and how it impacts patient care and outcomes.

Communication and Cultural Awareness

The students recognized the importance of communication in its influence on dialogue and in the overall relationship between patients and providers. Encouraging dialogue and effective communication allows a physician not only to learn crucial information about a patient but also may create and strengthen a bond of trust between patient and provider (Jacobs et al., 2006). The importance of communication in encouraging dialogue and impacting the patient–provider relationship was recognized by the students and was clearly illustrated throughout the narratives:

> By eliciting patients' beliefs and then engaging in open, respectful dialogue, I was able to have productive clinical encounters with patients from a variety of backgrounds.

Without communication between the provider and patient, physicians may not be able to extract the necessary information from patient interviews to diagnose and treat a patient effectively (Hafferty & Gaufberg, 2013). As demonstrated by one student's experience working with an Amish family, a lack of communication may force a healthcare provider to base decisions on preconceived notions of a patient's culture and how that culture impacts the patient's healthcare-related decisions. A student treating an Amish pediatric patient decided not to inquire about the parents' thoughts on vaccinations for the child, based solely on preconceived ideas about the Amish culture. The belief that the child's parents would not want the child vaccinated was incorrect. Once the student realized his error, he understood how preconceived perceptions could be detrimental in a clinical setting.

> My preconceived notion was formed based on media portrayal and social biases, and I have never personally had any contact with any Amish people in person. As a healthcare provider, the assumption and stereotype could lead me to misdiagnose the patient or provide [the patient] with wrong type[s] of services and treatment.

These examples demonstrate the importance of being aware of the components of interaction, recognizing cultural norms, and understanding personal characteristics in patient–provider encounters; all are crucial to providing effective and quality care.

CONCLUSION

The papers compiled during the 12 years that this cultural competency course has been offered reveal both the strengths and failings of clinical interactions across the many cultures in the United States today. Some common overarching themes identified using this model included social climate and historical context, generalizations versus patient-centered care, institutional culture, cultural awareness, and communication. The students reflected on the historical failings and/or microaggressions perpetuated by medical practitioners, as well as the distrust of the medical system in many communities of color. They also described the difficulty of balancing what they understood (or thought they understood) about a patient from his or her culture or background with the individual attributes of each patient's story. They identified institutional and specialty biases and the impact these had on the care of patients. Lastly, the need for polite and respectful, but ultimately frank, communication regarding the impact of culture within the healthcare team and between the team members and patients was a common theme among the narratives.

The themes from student papers emphasize the importance of interdisciplinary teaching methods for medical students, trainees, and professionals. Disease-oriented medical knowledge alone does not provide healthcare professionals with sufficient skills to interact and effectively communicate with patients. Communication is key to providing high-quality care and producing positive outcomes for patients. A firm understanding and awareness of how culture and sociocultural factors impact patients' lives, their interactions with providers, and, ultimately, their adherence to physicians' advice and decisions is crucial for delivering quality patient care.

Future analysis can result in additional correlations and potentially the creation of predictive models for analyzing the impact of culture on health care. It will be valuable to explore the formation of a database of common cultural competence issues faced by clinicians. This could lead to better training of clinicians across the spectrum of health care. In addition to teaching students to be open to other cultures and avoid bias, we could provide examples that illustrate their own internalized biases, giving students a chance to consciously work to overcome these and improving their ability to deliver health care to all patients.

REFERENCES

Bennett, M. J. (1986). A developmental approach to training for intercultural sensitivity. *International Journal of Intercultural Relations, 10*(2), 179–196.

Davies, H. T. O., Nutley, S. M., & Mannion, R. (2000). Organizational culture and quality of health care. *BMJ Quality & Safety, 9*(2), 111–119.

Epner, D. E., & Baile, W. F. (2012). Patient-centered care: The key to cultural competence. *Annals of Oncology, 23*(3), 33–42.

Giroux, H. A., & Penna, A. N. (1979). Social education in the classroom: The dynamics of the hidden curriculum. *Theory & Research in Social Education, 7*(1), 21–42.

Hafferty, F. W., & Gaufberg, E. (2013). The hidden curriculum. In J. A. Dent & R. M. Harden (Eds.), *A practical guide for medical teachers* (4th ed., pp. 52–60). London, England: Churchill Livingstone Elsevier.

Hardeman, R. R., Medina, E. M., & Kozhimannil, K. B. (2016). Structural racism and supporting Black lives—The role of health professionals. *New England Journal of Medicine, 375*, 2113–2115.

Jacobs, E. A., Rolle, I., Ferrans, C. E., Whitaker, E. E., & Warnecke, R. B. (2006). Understanding African Americans' views of the trustworthiness of physicians. *Journal of General Internal Medicine, 21*, 642–647.

Jernigan, V. B., Hearod, J. B., Tran, K., Norris, K. C., & Buchwald, D. (2016). An examination of cultural competence training in US medical education guided by the tool for assessing cultural competence training. *Journal of Health Disparities Research and Practice, 9*(3), 150–167.

Kennedy, B. R., Mathis, C. C., & Woods, A. K. (2007). African Americans and their distrust of the health care system: Healthcare for diverse populations. *Journal of Cultural Diversity, 14*(2), 56–60.

McLeroy, K. R., Bibeau, D., Steckler, A., & Glanz, K. (1988). An ecological perspective on health promotion programs. *Health Education Quarterly, 15*(4), 351–377.

Puhl, R. M., & Heuer, C. A. (2009). The stigma of obesity: A review and update. *Obesity, 17*(5), 941–964.

Schultz, P. W., Nolan, J. M., Cialdini, R. B., Goldstein, N. J., & Griskevicius, V. (2007). The constructive, destructive, and reconstructive power of social norms. *Psychological Science, 18*(5), 429–434.

Scott, T., Mannion, R., Davies, H. T., & Marshall, M. N. (2003). Implementing culture change in health care: Theory and practice. *International Journal for Quality in Health Care, 15*(2), 111–118.

Soudi, A., South-Paul, J., Gooden, S., Kinloch, V., Murrell, A., Chang, J., Malone, C., & Kiesling, S. (2018) Cross-disciplinary conference on Family and Healthy U, The Year of Healthy U, University of Pittsburgh. Retrieved from https://www .linguistics.pitt.edu/sites/default/files/Family%20and%20Healthy%20U%20 Conference%20Booklet%20.pdf

Soudi, A., Gooden, S., Chang, J., Kiesling, S., & South-Paul, J. (2017). Humanities in health editorial. *European Journal for Person Centered Healthcare, 5*, 506–512.

Soudi, A., & South-Paul, J. (2017). An interdisciplinary approach to cultural competence education in an academic health center. *European Journal for Person Centered Healthcare, 5*(4), 516–521.

States Increasingly Requiring Cultural Competency Courses to Improve Patient Care. (2006, March). Retrieved from https://www.healio.com/orthopedics/ business-of-orthopedics/news/print/orthopedics-today/%7b942941ff-b9d8 -4c36-8805-4d0770b33bcd%7D/states-increasingly-requiring-cultural -competency-courses-to-improve-patient-care

U.S. Department of Health and Human Services, Office of Minority Health. (2016). National standards for culturally and linguistically appropriate services in health and health care: Compendium of state-sponsored national CLAS standards implementation activities. Washington, DC: Author. Retrieved from https://thinkculturalhealth.hhs.gov/assets/pdfs/CLASCompendium.pdf

CHAPTER 8

INTERGROUP DIALOGUE

Transformation From the Inside Out

Mario C. Browne
University of Pittsburgh

Erika Gold Kestenberg
University of Pittsburgh

ABSTRACT

This chapter examines the use of Intergroup Dialogue (IGD) to develop awareness and understanding of diverse social identities in the context of higher education and at the University of Pittsburgh. The process of Intergroup Dialogue pedagogy encourages participants to discuss openly intergroup identities, social identities, and inequalities to deepen awareness and understanding of diversity in our current society. This chapter reports on the process of IGD, the challenges and benefits of IGD, and the implementation of IGD in higher education through a stakeholder analysis framework.

In a multicultural society, meaningful dialogue about issues of conflict and community are needed to facilitate a deeper understanding between and among people with varying intersecting social identities, including race,

Diversity Across the Disciplines, pages 119–130

ethnicity, gender, religion, socioeconomic status, sexual orientation, ability status, and nationality. Through intergroup dialogue (IGD) pedagogy, participants discuss relevant issues and explore personal and group experiences in various social and institutional contexts. Participants also examine historical, political, psychological, and sociological materials and lived experiences. The goal is to create a setting in which faculty, staff, and students engage in open and constructive dialogue, in the hope of increasing understanding and equity while alleviating the macro- and microaggressions and biases affecting our campuses and broader society. Intergroup dialogues, according to Gurin, Nagda, and Zúñiga (2013) "aim to increase participants' knowledge of intergroup issues, especially group-based social identities and inequalities; improve and deepen intergroup communication and relationships; and develop skills in and commitment to intergroup collaboration" (p. viii). Through both qualitative and quantitative research approaches, Gurin et al. (2013) found that IGD pedagogy can be more effective than other forms of diversity, inclusion, and equity-based efforts, such as anti-bias training or one-off diversity workshops. This chapter will delve into what is meant by IGD, the benefits and challenges of incorporating it into the classroom, and considerations in growing IGD across the University of Pittsburgh. The institutional development process will be discussed through a stakeholder analysis framework using Mendelow's (1981) approach of environmental scanning to understand this adaptive challenge in working to grow IGD in a higher education institution, specifically the University of Pittsburgh.

WHAT IS INTERGROUP DIALOGUE?

Intergroup dialogues are "face-to-face meetings between members of two (or more) social groups that have a history of conflict or potential conflict" (Zúñiga, Nagda, Chesler, & Cytron-Walker, 2007, p. vii). The groups are broadly defined by race, ethnicity, gender identity, sexual orientation, ability, religion, socioeconomic status, and other social group identities. According to Zúñiga et al. (2007), IGDs are structured, sequenced, and sustained; are experiential and intimate; focus on process and content; are safe, yet brave, spaces, where honesty and conflict can be utilized for learning; are democratic; and challenge traditional distributions of power and legitimacy.

The overarching mission of IGD is grounded in social justice. It is hoped that IGD will contribute to this goal by helping participants do the following:

- Increase their understanding of one another.
- Use this understanding to honestly and deeply explore differences in power, privilege, and discrimination between groups.

- To ask themselves what next steps, if any, they wish to take to promote equity and justice.

In IGD, participants dialogue about controversial issues regarding group equity and experience while learning to stay in dialogue mode, even during disagreement with one another. Dialogue mode means that students remain open and committed to learning from and with one another, seeking to understand and explore thoughts and feelings, challenging assumptions, and working through conflict, collectively. The Michigan model of IGD, as developed by Zúñiga et al. (2007) is one of the most well-known and established approaches to this work, especially in institutions of higher education. The work of Zúñiga et al. (2007) builds on a number of theories, including the following:

- *Sociological theories of conflict:* This is the assumption that conflict between social groups is predictable and should not be repressed, but instead should be expressed constructively; that constructive processing of conflict can lead to learning, empowerment of marginalized groups, and increased social justice; and that conflict avoidance often serves to perpetuate the status quo regarding social privilege and disadvantage.
- *Contact theory within psychology:* This is the assumption that contact between groups can lead to decreased prejudice and stereotyping, but only if conditions of good contact are met, which include superordinate goals, alternatives to normative roles and power distributions, and sustained interaction that embraces issues of group.

Intergroup dialogue is a powerful tool to bridge the divide among people and address the injustice often seen in society. Gurin et al.'s (2013) research using multilevel linear modeling, two psychological indices, and the critical-dialogic theoretical framework of IGD with a comparative control group showed that the students who participated in IGD courses showed statically significant increases in three key indicators related to IGD, namely, an increase in the areas of IG understanding, IG relationship, and IG action. There was a statistically significant difference in IGD participants' understanding of structural inequity, IG empathy, and actions (Gurin et al., 2013).

WHY THE NEED FOR INTERGROUP DIALOGUE?

In the current polarized climate in the United States, it is common for challenging conversations to arise as people, including students in our higher education classrooms, delve into various societal and political topics and issues. During this moment in history, we are increasingly finding that social media and its algorithms are providing people with content in a vacuum, seemingly only exposing us to viewpoints similar to our own. As a result, our country has become increasingly divided in terms of people's positions related to politics, as well as perspectives of social identities and the dynamics of power and privilege that are enacted in this country, both inside and outside of the classroom. Divisive examples include the rise of White nationalism, Islamophobia, and anti-Semitism; the criminalization and police killings of unarmed Black people and the Black Lives Matter movement; the growing wealth gap; the Me Too movement; and LGBTQIA rights. Considering the dynamic of growing polarization, it is common for challenging conversations to arise in our classrooms. Many faculty and staff have not been trained in how to support students with varying viewpoints and lived experiences to have these conversations in ways that provide rich opportunities for learning. IGD provides a framework for doing just that. By offering an approach and a structure for deep, connected dialogue, this pedagogy has been extraordinarily valuable in offering the opportunity to design safe and brave spaces for people to come together to deeply share and learn from one another in respectful and enriching ways that build bridges where there were previously chasms.

Most individuals, especially those with dominant or agent identities (e.g., White, male, Christian, heterosexual, cisgender, able-bodied, United States born), often avoid discussions about social identities for fear that they will offend someone and mistakenly be seen as racist, sexist, homophobic, or the like. Considering that it is not commonplace to have such discussions, people growing up in the United States and within its culture tend to fear such conversations that are often seen as taboo. Examining White individuals' reactions to dialogues around race, DiAngelo (2018) found that for White individuals, "the smallest amount of racial stress is intolerable—the mere suggestion that being white has meaning often triggers a range of defensive responses" (p. 2). DiAngelo (2018) named this White fragility. When we do not talk about our social identities, we do not develop the competency to do so. Just like with many things in life, our skills related to competency and agency in these conversations grow along with our experience. The challenge is creating spaces where people feel safe to be brave and dive into such dialogues in ways that nurture their courage and curiosity as well as add to their knowledge, skills, and ability.

WHAT HAPPENS IN INTERGROUP DIALOGUE?

One of the greatest challenges, especially in our often conflict-averse culture, is to hold space for and learn how to navigate conflict in the classroom and even to welcome it as an opportunity for learning. Intergroup dialogue provides a roadmap to learning productive, nurturing ways to create a space where people are encouraged to speak their truth, where differing opinions are invited, and where space is designed to hold conflict as appropriate and necessary for learning and growth to occur. Deep, meaningful learning occurs when we are brave enough to step outside of our comfort zone. Most IGD experiences begin with stating and even co-creating ground rules for the participants to agree to as a foundation for maintaining a space where everyone feels safe enough to be brave together.

There are many approaches to incorporating IGD into the classroom and campus experience (Gurin et al., 2013). The University of Michigan's (https://igr.umich.edu/about) nationally renowned Program on IG Relations has an effective approach to this work. The Michigan model involves the following characteristics:

- has a structured (but flexible) process;
- is sustained over an extended period of time;
- is graded utilizing class participation, readings, journals, and assignments;
- is distinct from traditional classroom formats;
- is balanced to represent identity groups; and
- is co-facilitated by undergraduate students (co-facilitators represent dialogue identities).

The Michigan model is commonly delivered through credit-bearing courses with semester-long curricula that include readings, group activities, dialogic experiences, and opportunities for critical reflection (Gurin et al., 2013). The Program on IG Relations at the University of Michigan has other formats for carrying out IGD efforts as well, including the CommonGround workshop program and community outreach initiatives like the Youth Dialogues on Race and Ethnicity program (University of Michigan, 2018).

The experience of IGD with the Michigan model occurs through a four-stage process:

- Stage 1: group beginnings: creating a shared meaning of dialogue;
- Stage 2: identity, social relations, and conflict;
- Stage 3: issues of social justice ("hot topics"); and
- Stage 4: empowerment, alliances, and action.

The process is sustained over an extended period, such as a semester or term. Numerous activities guide the participants as they progress through the stages. Activities revolve around topics including identity, stereotyping, power, and privilege. Participants engage in critical reflection and dialogues through a variety of experiences and exercises, such as social identity formation exploration, fishbowl exercises that allow participants to observe and participate in dialogue, pair and small group dialogic dynamics, and gallery walks.

In addition to the Michigan model of IGD, there are other models used at universities nationally and globally, including courageous conversations (Singleton, 2014) and transformative social therapy (Rojzman, Bibrowska, Pillods, & Liddelow, 1999); both are typically used outside of university contexts and in conflict mediation situations.

DIFFUSION OF INTERGROUP DIALOGUE AT THE UNIVERSITY OF PITTSBURGH: AN ADAPTIVE CHALLENGE

The University of Pittsburgh is one of the many institutions of higher education across the United States and beyond that recognizes the value of IGDs. Because there exists a constant cacophony of staff and faculty voices asking for ways and spaces to discuss difficult but pertinent issues, the University of Pittsburgh dedicated a full year to diversity and established the Office of Diversity and Inclusion (ODI) to institutionalize those efforts and continue them beyond that year. ODI, along with the Office of the Provost and other University of Pittsburgh units and entities, have hosted multiple diversity retreats and initiatives where one- or two-hour workshops have been marketed as "dialogue" opportunities. On a macro level, this aligns nicely with the *Plan for Pitt*'s strategic Goal 4 to promote diversity and inclusion: "We aspire to be a university community that embodies diversity and inclusion as core values that enrich learning, scholarship, and the communities we serve" (University of Pittsburgh, 2016, p. 12). Strategies articulated in this goal include transforming the campus climate to reinforce diversity and inclusion and enriching the student experience through engagement with diverse perspectives. This has given individuals the opportunity to engage in authentic dialogue, questioning, and listening, with many asking for more time, training, and places to engage. Over the course of 3 years, the Pitt IGD Collaborative, a group of faculty and staff interested in the pedagogy of IGD, were meeting, learning, and sharing. Outputs of the Pitt IGD Collaborative include the following:

- a 3-day workshop on the Michigan model of IGD, hosted by the Provost's Diversity Institute for Faculty Development in partnership with the Pitt IGD Collaborative; and
- an IGD workshop led by Pitt IGD Collaborative organizers (who were invited by the vice chancellor for diversity and inclusion) at the ODI University Wide Diversity Retreat.

However, an adaptive challenge to the adoption of IGD by various stakeholders at the University of Pittsburgh exists. For example, students may experience a conflation of safety and comfort (Arao & Clemens, 2013), whereas faculty may experience a loss of power in the dual role of learner–educator (Maxwell, Nagda, & Thompson, 2011). In this section, we attempt to elucidate some adaptive and technical challenges, as well as analyze stakeholders and gaps in adoption.

One of the challenges that continues to surface on campus is how to address sociopolitical issues that affect individuals and the campus community. Whether listening to individual students and colleagues in informal conversations or conducting diversity or cultural competency workshops, one hears repeatedly about the need to create spaces, places, and opportunities for genuine dialogue to take place between peers and students across the university. Faculty members desire the skills to introduce difficult societal issues in the context of the subject matter they are teaching in the classrooms. As human beings, they recognize that they and their students embody these issues. As educators, they want to provide their students with the opportunities to discuss and explore the issues in the context of their developing personal and academic identities. As mentioned previously, salient issues involving as race, sexual orientation, gender identity, religion, and nationality have divisive power and are polarizing our country. University campuses reflect the tensions of the larger society, and faculty, staff, and students are embodying these dynamics as well. Teaching and encouraging people to enact the art of dialoging across difference can be a major part of the solution. Institutionalizing IGD, in all of its simplicity and complexity, is no small task, though. There are three challenges facing higher education in general and the University of Pittsburgh, specifically:

- There is a need to help faculty adopt IGD as pedagogy.
- There is a need to create a learning community of practice to facilitate the adoption of IGD as pedagogy.
- There is a need to change the institutional culture from one focused solely on safe spaces to one that encourages brave spaces, such that engaging in difficult dialogues across difference is the standard (Arao & Clemens, 2013).

As with anything that seeks to challenge the status quo, there is resistance to change. What is promising is that there is a growing trend happening among institutions of higher learning adopting this pedagogy of change (Zúñiga et al., 2007). Recognizing both the scientific validity and the transformational power of IGD (Dessel & Rogge, 2008), campuses across the country are adopting curricula to teach faculty and students how to facilitate IGD or how to use IGD techniques to get their students to think and act critically on social issues. Initial projects across the University of Pittsburgh's campus have been a catalyst for change and include:

- creating partnerships with staff and faculty who have an interest in learning to facilitate IGD groups;
- providing workshops across campus for staff and faculty to experience participation in an IGD group; and
- initiating small tests of concept, such as piloting IGD noncredit classes in the Graduate School of Public Health, adding a one-credit IGD course to an existing course in the political science department, and creating and leading a group of early adopters to create a community of learning and practice.

The Pitt IGD Collaborative is helping to create an inclusive space for dialogue that offers individual and institutional transformational possibilities.

ADOPTING INTERGROUP DIALOGUE: LESSONS FROM STAKEHOLDER ANALYSIS

If IGD is a promising pedagogical approach, how do we address issues like the conflation of safety and comfort among students and the dual roles imposed on faculty as learner-educators? Here we focus on faculty as stakeholders and their adaptive challenges to adopting IGD. However, it is important to see and diagnose the system that we are operating in (Heifetz, Grashow, & Linsky, 2009). Issues of race, class, and other sociopolitical challenges are not new to higher education, and institutions address these issues from a status quo perspective, meaning that out-of-class learning is usually in the form of one-off workshops, such as anti-bias training or multiculturalism. In the classroom, rote knowledge about race, gender, and class taught by a race, gender, or class expert is typically the standard. To be fair, the University of Pittsburgh has been providing innovative experiential learning opportunities for students, such as service- and project-based learning, for some time now. Although these pedagogical approaches may offer a more democratic way of teaching and learning, they are not necessarily social justice frameworks and therefore do not seek to challenge issues of power and hegemony. What happens when the usual way of doing things is not enough and we, as a campus community, begin to stretch and adopt new ideas? Here we examine the stakeholders and the structures that facilitate or impede the adoption of IGD.

STAKEHOLDER ANALYSIS AND THEORETICAL CONSTRUCTS

Mendelow's (1981) model of environmental scanning was adopted to catalog the level of power and interest of university stakeholders to prioritize efforts. Mendelow (1981) describes a stakeholder taxonomy of sorts, where the position that you allocate to a stakeholder reveals the actions you need to take with them:

- *High power, highly interested people; this is the group to "manage closely":* You must fully engage these people and make the greatest effort to satisfy them. This group includes people in places and spaces of authority, such as the Office of the Provost, the vice chancellor for diversity and inclusion, Pitt IGD Collaborative members, diversity and inclusion staff, faculty and experts across the university, deans and department chairs, and students.
- *High power, less interested people; this is the "keep satisfied" group:* Put enough work in with these people to keep them satisfied, but not so much that they become bored with your message. This group includes some tenured faculty, for example.
- *Low power, highly interested people; this is the "keep informed" group:* Adequately inform these people and talk to them to ensure that no major issues are arising. People in this category can often be very helpful with the details of your project and may include the University Center for Teaching and Learning, junior faculty, graduate and professional students, and other staff doing similar types of trainings in other units and with students. Here we consider stakeholders who may be doing similar diversity, inclusion, or social justice teaching or initiatives but may see IGD as competition.
- *Low power, less interested people; this is the "monitor" group:* Again, monitor these people, but do not bore them with excessive communication. This group are the late adopters or laggards in diffusion of innovation theory (Lundblad, 2003). They may include stakeholders who are ambivalent to issues of social justice or far removed from teaching or student engagement, depending on their roles at the institution. This group may include research-focused faculty, staff members, and members of the board or upper management.

DISCUSSION

Theories like diffusion of innovation enhance a stakeholder analysis and offer a value add to diagnoses of a system and an adaptive challenge, such as the effort to develop capacity for doing IGD work across a university. Heifetz et al. (2009) note that "adaptive leadership is the practice of mobilizing people" and that "adaptive challenges can only be addressed through challenges in people's beliefs, habits, and loyalties" (p. 14). A bird's eye view reveals whether the system is risk averse and whether the status quo encourages teachers to act only as experts and disseminators of knowledge and not as co-creators of new knowledge. This way of operating can be challenging in IGD, as this approach can position students as co-teachers, experts, and creators of new knowledge in the classroom as well. Furthermore, incentive among and between faculty to be recognized as experts in their fields encourages a certain elitism and even angst toward anything that may challenge their status. However, faculty can be the greatest allies if they can find personal and professional value in the approach. Professionally, this may connect to the larger institutional mission on one level, and commitment to the growth and education of their students on another. Indeed, many tenured faculty have seen the need for a different approach and have the freedom to test new approaches—something that less senior faculty may not be able to do. As for staff and administrators, depending on their roles and positions or levels of power, there is an inherent competitiveness regarding who is recognized as the innovator, who gets credit, and where the formal and informal alliances are. Ultimately, it is not the change or the innovation that people resist or shy away from—it is, as Heifetz et al. state, a resistance to loss.

The adoption of IGD as an adaptive challenge cuts across many dimensions of adaptive leadership. The model itself challenges innovators and early adopters to diagnose the system of the institution and the system of the self while simultaneously participating in the work that is IGD.

Facilitators must be experienced in ongoing processes of exploring their own attitudes and behaviors regarding diversity, inclusion, equity, and justice. Training should enable them to create safe environments where participants can discuss difficult topics with honesty. They should know how to share power and create democratic, nonauthoritarian environments, and they should be trained in expert listening skills and in empathy skills (Regents of the University of Michigan, n.d.).

Other critical traits of a facilitator are the ability to hold the environment and resist the urge to offer fixes or solutions. Facilitation encourages participants to press their learning edges, which is synonymous to dancing on the edge of authority into leadership. In other words, the question is how to push people to move beyond inclusive excellence, the new buzzword for diversity and inclusion, and code for operational excellence (Heifetz et al., 2009). Another challenge is to move people away from a culture rooted primarily in technical problem-solving to one that values and promotes adaptive inquiry. The former often offers a quicker fix, which human beings tend to gravitate toward, yet that approach rarely gets to the root of the issue. The latter, however, may have greater opportunity for systemic and effective change, but also often requires greater time, honesty, and accountability with all involved parties; it also requires a courage and vulnerability that human beings tend to avoid.

As noted, IGD requires teaching university community stakeholders—including administrators, faculty, staff, and students—how to surface conflict, hold the tension that is created when people authentically share experiences, seek understanding of others' views and experiences, and, ultimately, move into some form of collective action. One could overlay this description with what Heifetz et al. (2009) refer to as the "productive zone of disequilibrium" defined as "the optimal range of distress within which the urgency in the system motivates people to engage in adaptive work" (p. 29). As discussed, we want administrators, faculty, staff, and students to "dance on the edge" of the authority circle into leadership territory (Heifetz et al., 2009, p. 25). This can be daunting when the institution rewards stakeholders for maintaining status quo through the authority given to them. Administrators and staff have asked how individuals can give voice to their authentic selves while protecting themselves at the same time. In other words, "I have it pretty good towing the company line, so why should I disrupt?" This is a real tension between the ideal goals of stakeholders and reality.

Delving into this tension and working through it together is exactly what IGD encourages us to do. Now seems like a critical time for us all to find our courage to engage in IGDs. Our universities, including the University of Pittsburgh, have and will continue to be spaces to shape the minds and hearts of students who we send out into the world with our university name attached to them—and all that they have learned and experienced integrated as an integral part of their identities, perspectives, and lives. IGDs provide an extraordinary opportunity for us to play an impactful role in who our graduates are in the world, how they use their power, and the impact they will have on individuals and systems with that power. IGDs have been shown to have a meaningful impact on participants in ways that challenge the status quo and produce more justice-minded people in the world. Imagine what would be possible if we all engaged in IGDs regularly. IGD can be a powerful bridge across societal divides, both in our nation and on our university campuses. One of the beautiful things about IGD is that, through mindful creativity, it is adaptable to any space and place throughout the institution to connect all of us through our collective humanity across discipline and difference.

IGD requires that we be vulnerable and courageous in ways not widely experienced in university classrooms and campuses. It challenges us to look into ourselves and beyond ourselves to create spaces where we grow, expand, and connect with one another far beyond the content of usual courses or collective experiences. The University of Pittsburgh is on a bold journey to join other campuses and spaces in having difficult dialogues by believing that pushing against the status quo and constructing spaces for challenging yet critical dialogues will increase the possibility of creating a more just world.

REFERENCES

Arao, B., & Clemens, K. (2013). From safe spaces to brave spaces: A new way to frame dialogue around diversity and social justice. In L. M. Landreman (Ed.), *The art of effective facilitation* (pp. 135–150). Sterling, VA: Stylus.

Dessel, A., & Rogge, M. E. (2008). Evaluation of intergroup dialogue: A review of the empirical literature. *Conflict Resolution Quarterly, 26*(2), 199–238.

DiAngelo, R. (2018). *White fragility: Why it's so hard for White people to talk about racism.* Boston, MA: Beacon Press.

Gurin, P., Nagda, B. R. A., & Zúñiga, X. (2013). *Dialogue across difference: Practice, theory, and research on intergroup dialogue.* New York, NY: Russell Sage Foundation.

Heifetz, R., Grashow, A., & Linsky, M. (2009). *The practice of adaptive leadership: Tools and tactics for changing your organization and the world.* Boston, MA: Harvard Business Press.

Lundblad, J. P. (2003). A review and critique of Rogers' diffusion of innovation theory as it applies to organizations. *Organization Development Journal, 21*(4), 50–64.

Maxwell, K. E., Nagda, B. R. A., & Thompson, M. C. (Eds.). (2011). *Facilitating intergroup dialogues: Bridging differences, catalyzing change.* Sterling, VA: Stylus.

Mendelow, A. L. (1981). Environmental scanning—The impact of the stakeholder concept. *ICIS 1981 Proceedings.* Retrieved from https://aisel.aisnet.org/icis1981/20

Regents of the University of Michigan. (n.d.). *The program on intergroup relations at the University of Michigan.* Retrieved from https://igr.umich.edu

Rojzman, C., Bibrowska, S., Pillods, S., & Liddelow, E. (1999). *How to live together: A new way of dealing with racism and violence.* Melbourne, Australia: Acland Press.

Singleton, G. E. (2014). *Courageous conversations about race: A field guide for achieving equity in schools* (2nd ed.). Thousand Oaks, CA: Corwin.

University of Michigan. (2018). *The program on intergroup relations at the University of Michigan.* Retrieved from https://igr.umich.edu/about

University of Pittsburgh. (2016). *The plan for Pitt: Making a difference together: Academic years 2016–2020.* Retrieved from https://www.pitt.edu/sites/default/files/Strategic-Plan-Presentation.pdf

Zúñiga, X., Nagda, B. R. A., Chesler, M., & Cytron-Walker, A. (2007). *Intergroup dialogue in higher education: Meaningful learning about social justice.* Hoboken, NJ: Wiley.

CHAPTER 9

CULTURAL AND LINGUISTIC DIVERSITY

A Multifaceted Approach

Shelome Gooden
University of Pittsburgh

Abdesalam Soudi
University of Pittsburgh

Karen Park
University of Pittsburgh

Valerie Kinloch
University of Pittsburgh

ABSTRACT

This chapter focuses on the ways in which cultural and linguistic diversity impact working and living together with attention to how higher education can foster cultural and linguistic diversity across the disciplines. We describe some ways by which cultural and linguistic diversity benefits the higher education

Diversity Across the Disciplines, pages 131–144
Copyright © 2020 by Information Age Publishing
All rights of reproduction in any form reserved.

classroom, medical practice, and biocultural diversity. We examine how cultural and linguistic diversity broadens perspectives, enhances trust and communication, and is vital to an informed and engaged society. Implications for future research across disciplines in higher education are also discussed.

The Committee on Ethnic Diversity in Linguistics, a subcommittee of the Linguistic Society of America, states that "it is in the interest of the field of linguistics and of American society to be enriched by the participation of all its ethnic groups" (Linguistic Society of America, n.d., para. 3). This statement explicitly recognizes the United States as a diverse, multicultural, multiethnic, and multilingual nation, a recognition that is in contrast with the metaphor of the American melting pot (i.e., the idea that American culture is an amalgam of different cultures, nationalities, and ethnicities). On a global level, linguistic diversity is undergoing significant reduction hand in hand with an increase in the number of speakers of hegemonic languages (Brezinger, 2011). In this chapter, we give an overview of examples from our own research and experiences in higher education, medical practice, and biocultural diversity, through which we underscore the importance of cultural and linguistic diversity in cultivating and promoting an informed and engaged society, broadening perspectives, and enhancing trust and communication across different groups of people both within and beyond the United States.

BACKGROUND

Language and Culture

Language and culture are intimately intertwined. Language serves as a spoken expression of culture and, in turn, influences our social attitudes and ideological perspectives. It is thus a social practice through which people channel or construct cultural and social identities (Eckert, 2000) or racial and ethnic identities (Fought, 2012). For instance, accent, word choice, identity, race, ethnicity, conversational style, gender, and social status, among many other factors come into play. As speakers hear and interpret language, they create or index social meaning by connecting linguistic information (e.g., accent, word choice) to macro-level social information, such as age, region, level of education, gender, and social status, or by connecting to micro-social information, such as stance (joint engagement of participants in evaluative activity of their talk and/or of one another; Kiesling, 2009; Silverstein, 2003).

A thoughtful examination of language allows us to develop an intricate understanding of how and why speakers make one linguistic choice or another, consciously or subconsciously and thereby better appreciate linguistic diversity. It allows us to describe the social meaning(s) of language and the impact of linguistic choices on our interactions and engagements with one another. That is, we can inquire into what allows one style of speaking (formal versus casual), choice of language variety (French versus Arabic, Standard English versus African American Language [AAL]), or other verbal practices (sentence composition or tone of voice) to be evaluated as building solidarity and inclusivity, while another is evaluated as sounding authoritative and alienating. We can inquire into why overlap in conversation for some speakers signals high involvement or engagement, while the same approach would be considered rude for others (Gumperz, 1982; Kiesling & Paulston, 2008; Tannen, 1984). These variations in language use underlie human attitudes toward language and engagement with others and may sometimes lead to serious miscommunication problems in the classroom, the workplace, and elsewhere (Soudi, Gooden, Chang, Kiesling, & South-Paul, 2017).

Culture is multifaceted and includes behavior, way of life, religion, background, social norms, patterns, assumptions, values, and language, among other factors. Similar to language, culture is crucial to delivering appropriate health and educational services because it can influence worldview, belief, and trust. It is now commonplace for organizations and institutions to have culturally and linguistically appropriate programs that adequately respond to diverse communities and that provide access to high-quality services. The process entailing the development of understanding how to effectively and respectfully interact with diverse populations is known as cultural competency. This is a set of congruent behaviors, attitudes, and policies that come together in a system or agency or among professionals, enabling these entities to work effectively in cross-cultural, or culturally diverse, situations (Cross, Bazron, Dennis, & Isaacs, 1989). Thus, to understand culture as multifaceted is to understand the need for increasing levels of cultural competence within systems and how it can lead to positive outcomes and improved understanding of key population needs.

Ecology and Language

Studying language in its cultural context necessarily involves a variety of perspectives. The discussions presented in this chapter lean heavily on ecological approaches to language variation and change, which consider the complex relationships among the environment, languages, and their speakers (Wendel, 2005), where "environment" is intended to cover physical, biological, and social environments. Language functions only in relating users to one another and to their social, psychological, and natural environments. The concept of language ecology or linguistic ecology (Haugen, 1972) therefore also considers a psychological and a sociological component to the environment. The psychological aspect of ecology considers its interaction with other languages in the minds of monolingual, bilingual, and multilingual speakers and how that affects speakers' attitudes and language ideologies. The other part of language ecology is sociological, having to do with the interaction of language with the society in which it functions as a medium of communication by the people who learn it, use it, and transmit it to others. This is a more encompassing perspective than traditional studies of language and social interaction, and combines speakers' ideological and ethnographic perspectives as well (Eckert, 2012). We believe that this expanded approach is important since, the true environments of a language include members of a given society who use it and simultaneously the cognitive reality of that language in the minds of its users.

Linguistic outcomes of contact between speakers of different languages, for example, are determined largely by the history of social relations among populations, including economic, political, and demographic factors (see Gooden, 2020). Language ecology influences speakers' social motivations for making linguistic choices in these and other situations of language (or dialect) and cultural contact. Moreover, speakers' attitudes toward particular languages help to shape the contexts (social and ideological) in which these languages exist and are simultaneously shaped. For example, in North American societies, English is valorized at the expense of other languages. Therefore, we must treat the individual speaker as an active agent who is influenced by and who can, in turn, influence his or her own linguistic ecology.

In an effort to seriously embrace diversity, we must also acknowledge that speakers of nondominant languages, as well as multilingual and multiethnic communities and cultures, are challenged when they are situated within the context of dominant, or hegemonic, cultures. In many cases, these speakers face grave socioeconomic disparities and threats to both their linguistic and cultural vitality. Speakers must often choose between economic gain and affinity to their mother-tongue languages or native cultural practices (Lai, 2018; Ramírez-Cruz, 2017). Thus, the perceived social or economic dominance of one social group over another influences people's language choices (cf. van Coetsem, 1988) and are therefore very much a part of the linguistic ecology.

The second conceptualization of ecology that frames our discussion of the functions of language in society considers the physical environment. Language use occurs in a definable space, which can include speakers' geographical location and the more abstract spaces given form by both the written word and our ever-increasing digital landscapes (Danet & Herring,

2007; Scollon & Scollon, 2003). The physical context in which language is used provides the parameters and context within which contact among speakers occurs: "We speak and listen, write and read not only *about the world* but *in the world*, and much of what we understand depends on exactly where we and the language are located in the world" (Scollon & Scollon, 2003, p. ix). The physical environment can also play a direct role in inspiring acts of linguistic creativity. Neologisms rarely arise fully formed and original from the ether of human consciousness. More frequently, context, both linguistic and environmental, provides a template by which new words and expressions enter our lexicons. Linguistic context engages the mental linguistic landscape of the speaker and can result in the formation of new words through processes such as compounding, borrowing, amalgamations, and use of place names and personal names. The impact of environmental context on linguistic creativity is most readily seen in onomatopoeic words such as "buzz," "tweet," and "woof" (Campbell, 2004).

Praxis

This praxis of (socio)linguistics (Gooden, 2020) makes explicit connections between (socio)linguistics and other disciplines to shed light on common problems and applies linguistic research to craft workable and effective solutions that will be beneficial to the communities we work with. In particular, the examples that will be highlighted demonstrate how attention to issues concerning cultural and linguistic diversity broadens perspectives and enhances trust and communication across different groups of people. One aspect of practicality has to do with the teaching of sociolinguistic courses, through which we emphasize the importance of embracing cultural and linguistic diversity in higher education. Another common aspect of praxis relates to the importance of cultural and linguistic diversity to medicine and working with culturally and linguistically diverse patient populations (Soudi & South-Paul, 2017). Finally, there is growing interest in cross-disciplinary studies of biocultural diversity. This includes linguistic, cultural, and biological perspectives as multifaceted manifestations of diversity, applied to practices of engagement with traditional ecological knowledge and conservation of linguistic and biological diversity (Maffi, 2001). This trifecta of diversity touches on all aspects related to our existence as humans. When mapped on a global scale, however, these kinds of diversity are in some ways being threatened by analogous forces. In other words, the loss of diversity at all levels translates into dramatic consequences for humanity on a much broader multidisciplinary scale (Maffi, 2005).

LANGUAGE EQUALITY AND EQUITY IN EDUCATION

Vernacular language education has the potential to contribute to the social equity of speakers of these linguistic varieties. Awareness of social, cultural, and linguistic differences goes a long way in advancing cultural and linguistic self-determination of speakers. Education systems that persist in hegemonic languages and cultures are at best destructive to minority languages and cultures. We might reimagine curricula in light of linguistic and cultural diversity with a view toward enhancing student outcomes and redirecting teacher perspectives. Additionally, we might capitalize on cultural differences and use this as a resource to enhance learning, rather than see these differences as obstacles.

Linguistics courses, for example, offer an opportunity to include content on diverse cultures and languages, especially with respect to minority or underrepresented populations (Mallinson & Charity Hudley, 2014). Through these courses, students can better understand that all languages are naturally systematic and rule-governed. They can better understand, for instance, that some language varieties can be the object of negative or pejorative evaluations (Rickford, Sweetland, Rickford, & Grano, 2013). For example, the Pittsburgh dialect (aka Pittsburghese) was selected as the ugliest U.S. accent in popular media (Evans, 2014), and AAL has been widely stigmatized (Smitherman, 1975, 1977). Thus, the focus is not just on languages of traditional power and prestige, but also on those languages that have been long marginalized and considered illegitimate. Equally important, however, is the reality that we ought to ensure that underrepresented students see themselves in the texts, research, assigned readings, and themes of courses. In addition, students who are speakers of majority language varieties are exposed to some of the many ways in which linguistic diversity and cultural differences impact speakers of minority language varieties, thereby facilitating a broadening of their perspectives and the value and authenticity of these language varieties (see Di Paolo & Spears, 2014; Wolfram & Schilling, 2015). The results of a nationwide survey of faculty who teach about AAL (Weldon, 2012) underscores the importance of these courses in the college or university curriculum. Weldon (2012) finds that race plays a role in the teaching of AAL, especially in terms of how instructors approach teaching and how students respond to these courses. Both are affected by the racial and/or ethnic backgrounds of instructors and students. The greatest challenge in teaching about AAL is getting students to overcome their own prejudices against the language variety. Weldon notes further that while such prejudices are likely to be encountered by any instructor teaching a course or unit on a nonstandard or nonmainstream language variety, instructors of AAL "must be prepared to address how racial biases, in particular, feed into observed linguistic prejudices" (p. 243).

In an undergraduate course titled Language and the Black Experience, Gooden (co-author on this chapter) focuses on two minority languages, Jamaican Creole and AAL. The different topics engages students in discussions on interactions among race, ethnicity, and language and on how these impact and shape people's everyday lives. Topics include language and music (hip-hop, dancehall) as well as language and religion (Rastafarianism, African American churches in the United States). One activity engages students in using variationist sociolinguistic methods to analyze language data in musical lyrics and to discover systematicity in variation. In another undergraduate course titled Sociolinguistics of Arabic, Soudi (co-author on this chapter) focuses on the interaction of language and society in the Arab world and the Arabic diaspora in North America, but with particular attention to Pittsburgh. Using various sociolinguistic models, such as social networks, communities of practice, and speech communities, students discuss major sociolinguistic issues pertaining to language status, diglossia; language change and variation in Arabic; place, time, accent, language, and gender; language contact; language planning; and language policy. Building on his own personal experience as an Arab American linguist living in Pittsburgh, and father of two children who are exposed to Arabic and English, Soudi encourages his class to investigate other sociolinguistic issues, such as dialect leveling, code-switching, language attitudes, linguistic accommodation, power and solidarity, and ethnic identity among speakers of different dialects of Arabic. As part of a sociolinguistic interview session, the class also invites members of the Arab American community in Pittsburgh to the class to share their linguistic experiences and discuss the issues raised during the course of the class directly with students.

However, pedagogical engagement with, and a curricular focus on, diversity must also address the inequities facing speakers of minority or minoritized languages in higher education classrooms, which range from perceived levels of linguistic incompetence to unfair treatment and evaluations of these speakers. Weldon's (2012) study suggests that inequities exist and are experienced by student populations and faculty members who are members of minoritized groups. Thus, it becomes extremely important that engagements with diversity within higher education contexts are both intentional and purposeful, and that such engagements are experienced in ways that afford minority language speakers access to what Kinloch (2017), borrowing the words of songstress Solange, refers to as "a seat at the table" through education and advocacy. This latter point is significant to note, as countless education and language scholars (Alim & Baugh, 2007; Kinloch, 2010; Richardson, 2003; Smitherman, 2000) assert the crucial role played by the explicit utility of multiple languages inside classroom spaces. When speakers of minority languages—and their linguistic practices; language uses; and cultural, racial, and ethnic identities—are centered in higher education classrooms, then necessary critiques of the language of power, prestige, and social and educational advancement can be explicitly examined. They can come to better understand that the perceived language of power, often popularly referred to as the dominant language variety, is both limiting and exclusionary for too many people whose language is often "othered" in educational and sociopolitical spaces. Those who are often perceived to not be able to adequately command this language can then better reject such perceptions as they come to rely on their own linguistic registers, varieties, and language forms inside and beyond classroom contexts.

Minority language varieties such as AAL play a significant and often unrecognized role in the reading achievement of millions of children in the United States (Washington, Terry, & Seidenberg, 2013). Negative perceptions of such language varieties very likely contribute to the persistence of socio-educational inequities and the Black–White gap with regard to standardized test scores (Rickford, 1999, 2005; Wolfram, 1998). Researchers have shown that, in many cases, teachers have negative and even prejudicial attitudes toward minority language varieties (see Mallinson & Charity Hudley, 2014). Perhaps the most debated case is the Oakland school board resolution of 1996, which placed AAL in the crosshairs of national ridicule (Wolfram, 1998). Nevertheless, and as realized by the Oakland school district, AAL speakers still often lag behind their peers who do not speak AAL, primarily because of the stigmatization directed toward AAL speakers from teachers and adults who harbor deficit perspectives (Mallinson & Charity Hudley, 2014; Rickford, 2005). Rickford (1999, 2005) suggests, for example, that teachers can become more linguistically informed about language and dialect differences for their students. In this way, they can be better equipped to distinguish between what many consider to be language errors and what others know to be dialect features. This necessary distinction can help students better understand the importance of language varieties and linguistic registers.

CULTURAL COMPETENCY IN MEDICAL CARE

For decades, the biomedical approach has dominated the medical system, and the focus on the physician–patient relationship has diminished (Roter, 2002). However, more recently, medicine has started to value the patient's psychosocial status and the behavioral dimensions of illness in the medical interview (Engel, 1977). Doctors have begun to access useful information about the culture of their patient population, leading to increased rapport between doctors and their patients (Soudi et al., 2017; Soudi & South-Paul, 2017).

Deloge (2017) investigates pathways to better healthcare access for indigenous populations in Bolivia. This work intends to show that linguistic considerations are of critical importance to positive health outcomes among indigenous Quechua-speaking populations in Bolivia, as these are also intimately tied to identity and ethnicity issues. While the Bolivian healthcare system operates predominantly in Spanish and adheres doggedly to biomedical practices, the indigenous population, who speak Quechua, instead access ethnomedical resources, which remain largely invisible to biomedical traditions.

The United States, like many developed nations, is becoming more diverse and multicultural, and we must be prepared to serve an increasingly diverse population of students by continuing to explore ways to infuse knowledge and appreciation of other cultures into medical curricula and treatment plans. This can be done by adapting our research, educational practices, and programs to better reflect the values and needs of culturally and linguistically diverse populations (Soudi & South-Paul, 2017). In light of the fact that cultural competency emphasizes acceptance of and respect for differences, it is clearly also connected to diversity.

LINGUISTIC AND BIOLOGICAL DIVERSITY

The third avenue of praxis that we explore is the connection between linguistic and biological diversity, which was originally popularized and recognized in the mid-1990s. Although this has been of interest to biologists and anthropologists, the subject has yet to be examined much in the field of linguistics. Research on biocultural diversity has led to scholarly and practical outputs that include mapping of language and species groups (Loh & Harmon, 2005), investigation into the traditional ecological knowledge of indigenous peoples (Singh, Pretty, & Pilgrim, 2010), and correlations between linguistic and biological diversity (Sutherland, 2003).

These observed correlations have a certain logic in the fact that both species and languages evolve in a defined place. Geographical barriers that lead to speciation can (though not always) also lead to linguistic diversification. Moreover, since language encodes the values and knowledge of its community of speakers, where livelihood and identity are closely linked to place, this knowledge has strong geographical biases. In both research and practice, therefore, biocultural diversity has most commonly been invoked within the context of indigenous and minority languages in biologically diverse landscapes threatened by external forces of development and change (Maffi, 2005; Posey & Dutfield, 1996). This is also clearly connected to issues of ethnolinguistic vitality since, in these multilinguial and multiethnic spaces, language is an important resource for the expression of ethnic and cultural identity (Gooden, Ramirez-Cruz, Lai, & Deloge, 2018). Recent work, has also begun to explore this theme within urban contexts and majority languages (Elands et al., 2018).

The Creative Multilingualism research group (https://www.creativeml.ox.ac.uk), in which Park (co-author on this chapter) is involved, has made efforts to take a holistic approach to the subject of biocultural diversity, bringing together scholars and practitioners with multidisciplinary expertise. The team, comprised of specialists from ornithology,[1] linguistics, anthropology, and conservation practice, investigates current approaches to the documentation and maintenance of linguistic diversity on a global scale. The research goals include mapping of ornithological and linguistic data; large-scale on-the-ground testing and investigation of assumed correlations; and exploration of how the links between language and environment change alongside cultural values (especially with respect to technology and urbanization), as well as how these changes impact the health and well-being of people and environments.

A postulate underlying this research is that "linguistic diversity protects biodiversity," with one core practical outcome of the work being the recognition and integration of languages and linguistic diversity in biological conservation practice. On the flip side of this, with respect to language maintenance and documentation, the work also has the potential to contribute more directly to our understanding of the number and diversity of the world's languages. Two other significant projects include the development of the Ethno-Ornithology World Atlas (EWA) (https://ewatlas.net), an online citizen science database of linguistic, geographic, cultural, and ornithological knowledge, and the creation of an international and interinstitutional network of scholars and practitioners, including individuals at the University of Oxford, the Smithsonian National Museum of Natural History, and BirdLife International.

With respect to documentation, a long-term desired outcome involves employing EWA and global networks to realize a citizen science language documentation program that has parallels to citizen science work in ornithology (eBird, https://ebird.org/home). Documentation projects would greatly encourage public participation, potentially through a Great Language Count (analogous to the Great Backyard Bird Count, an online citizen science project that collects data on wild birds and displays results online almost simultaneously). EWA is also working on the development of databases that can contribute to digital interactive maps illustrating linguistic, biological, cultural, and historical intersections while also encouraging users to share their own biocultural knowledge, thereby advancing agency and self-advocacy.

SUMMARY AND DISCUSSION

It is perhaps the case that outside of academia there is a deeply rooted perspective that would argue against the importance of cultural and linguistic diversity. This is particularly true when we examine the world at the level of the nation state that equates one language with one nation (May, 2012). It is possible that there is something within this narrow concept of nation that is antagonistic to multilingualism. We believe that this gives us even more reason to argue that we have a responsibility to demonstrate how cultural and linguistic diversity is important on multiple levels. To the best of our understanding the majority of the human race is multilingual (Romaine 2003). Linguists and cognitive scientists are increasingly recognizing the cognitive benefits of bi- and multilingualism (Bak & Mehmedbegovic, 2017).

But beyond this, cultural and linguistic diversity grants us new ways of understanding our world, ourselves, and one another. Embracing rather than erasing cultural and linguistic diversity is also important for advancing trust and communication across diverse groups and countering dominant, hegemonic ideologies. Recognizing that humanity is naturally multicultural and multilingual should sharpen our desire for a better understanding of variation and difference. Equally, there is an argument for highlighting the multilingualism hidden in our own languages, which would likely tell a story of cultural contact, linguistic borrowing, and processes of change that stem both from our unique cultural histories and our evolving identities.

As we have discussed, language evolves within communities and within the places where people live, gather, and interact. These environments impact knowledge systems, linguistic creativity, and interpersonal as well as intergroup communication. There is much work to be done with respect to research that supports praxis, especially because this work has real-world applications that tangibly affect the lives of people beyond the reaches of academia. This kind of focus is not only vital but also gratifying to an informed and engaged society. This collaborative engagement with nonacademic and cross-disciplinary audiences is just the kind of multifaceted approach to linguistic and cultural diversity that is needed, one that offers a far more nuanced perspective than a unary approach. In this way, we yield both research and praxis efforts that are well equipped to serve culturally and linguistically diverse communities.

NOTE

1. This is the branch of zoology concerned with the study of birds.

REFERENCES

Alim, H. S., & Baugh, J. (Eds.). (2007). *Talking Black talk: Language, education, and social change.* New York, NY: Teachers College Press.

Bak, T. H., & Mehmedbegovic, D. (2017). Healthy linguistic diet: The value of linguistic diversity and language learning across the lifespan. *Languages, Society, and Policy.* Retrieved from https://www.repository.cam.ac.uk/bitstream/handle/1810/264363/Bak%20Mehmedbegovic%C2%A0%20JLSP%202017.pdf?sequence=6

Brezinger, M. (Ed.). (2011). *Language diversity endangered.* New York, NY: Mouton de Gruyter.

Campbell, L. (2004). *Historical linguistics: An introduction.* Boston, MA: MIT Press.

Cross, T., Bazron, B., Dennis, K. W., & Isaacs, M. R. (1989). *Towards a culturally competent system of care: A monograph on effective services for minority children who are severely emotionally disturbed* (vol. 1). Washington, DC: CASSP Technical Assistance Center.

Danet, B., & Herring, S. C. (2007). *The multilingual Internet: Language, culture, and communication online.* Oxford, England: Oxford University Press.

Deloge, A. (2017). *Ethnolinguistic vitality of Quechua: Biomedicine and ethnomedicine.* Dissertation in preparation, University of Pittsburgh, Pittsburgh, PA.

Di Paolo, M., & Spears, A. K. (Eds.). (2014). *Languages and dialects in the US: Focus on diversity and linguistics.* New York, NY: Routledge.

Eckert, P. (2000). *Linguistic variation as social practice: The linguistic construction of identity in Belten High.* Malden, MA: Blackwell Publishers.

Eckert, P. (2012). Three waves of variation study: The emergence of meaning in the study of sociolinguistic variation. Annual Review of Anthropology, 41, 87–100.

Elands, B. H. M., Vierikko, K., Andersson, E., Fischer, L. K., Gonçalves, P., Haase, D., ... Wiersum, K. F. (2018). Biocultural diversity: A novel concept to assess human-nature interrelations, nature conservation and stewardship in cities. *Urban Forestry & Urban Greening. 40*, 29–34. https://doi.org/10.1016/j.ufug.2018.04.006

Engel, G. L. (1977). The need for a new medical model: A challenge for biomedicine. *Science, 196*(4286), 129–136.

Evans, D. (2014, October 15). America's ugliest accent has come down to Pittsburgh vs. Scranton. *Gawker.* Retrieved from https://gawker.com/americas-ugliest-accent-has-come-down-to-pittsburgh-vs-1646594002

Fought, C. (2012). Ethnic identity and language contact. In R. Hickey (Ed.), *The handbook of language contact* (pp. 282–298). Malden, MA: Wiley-Blackwell.

Gooden, S. (2020). In the fisherman's net: Language contact in a sociolinguistics context. In R. Blake & Isabelle Buchstaller (Eds.), *The Routledge Companion to the work of John R. Rickford* (pp. 17–25). New York, NY: Taylor Francis.

Gooden, S., Ramirez-Cruz, H., Lai, L., & Deloge, A. (2018, August). *Ethnolinguistic vitality in hybrid ecologies.* Paper presented at the Society for Caribbean Linguistics, Heredia, Costa Rica.

Gumperz, J. J. (1982). *Discourse strategies.* Cambridge, England: Cambridge University Press.

Haugen, E. (1972). The ecology of language. In A. S. Dil (Ed.), *The ecology of language: Essays by Einar Haugen* (pp. 325–339). Stanford, CA: Stanford University Press.

Kiesling, S. F. (2009). Style as stance: Stance as the explanation for patterns of sociolinguistic variation (pp. 171–194). In A. Jaffe (Ed.), *Stance: Sociolinguistic Perspectives.* Oxford, England: Oxford University Press.

Kiesling, S. F., & Paulston, C. B. (Eds). (2008). *Intercultural discourse and communication: The essential readings.* Malden, MA: Blackwell Publishing.

Kinloch, V. (2010). "To not be a traitor of Black English": Youth perceptions of language rights in an urban context. *Teachers College Record, 112*(1), 103–141.

Kinloch, V. (2017, March 29). "A seat at the table": Cultural and linguistic diversities in times of unrest. Presentation presented at the *Cultural and Linguistic Diversity Conference: Living and working together,* Pittsburgh, PA.

Lai, L.-F. (2018). *Intonation and contact: Prosodic transfer and innovation among Yami-Mandarin bilinguals* (Unpublished doctoral dissertation). University of Pittsburgh, Pittsburgh, PA.

Linguistic Society of America. (n.d.). *Committee on ethnic diversity in linguistics (CEDL).* Retrieved from https://www.linguisticsociety.org/about/who-we-are/committees/ethnic-diversity-linguistics-cedl

Loh, J., & Harmon, D. (2005). A global index of biocultural diversity. *Ecological Indicators, 5*(3), 231–241.

Maffi, L. (Ed.). (2001). *On biocultural diversity: Linking language knowledge and the environment.* Washington, DC: Smithsonian Institution Press.

Maffi, L. (2005). Linguistic, cultural, and biological diversity. *Annual Review of Anthropology, 34,* 599–617.

Mallinson, C., & Charity Hudley, A. H. (2014). Partnering through science: Developing linguistic insight to address educational inequality for culturally and linguistically diverse students in U.S. STEM education. *Language and Linguistics Compass, 8*(1),11–23.

May, S. (2012). *Language and minority rights: Ethnicity, nationalism and the politics of language.* New York, NY: Routledge.

Posey, D. A., & Dutfield, G. (1996). *Beyond intellectual property: Toward traditional resource rights for indigenous peoples and local communities.* Ottawa, Canada: International Development Research Centre.

Ramírez-Cruz, H. (2017). *Ethnolinguistic vitality in a Creole ecology: San Andrés and Providencia* (Unpublished doctoral dissertation). University of Pittsburgh, Pittsburgh, PA.

Richardson, E. (2003). *African American literacies.* New York, NY: Routledge.

Rickford, J. R. (1999). Language diversity and academic achievement in the education of African American students: An overview of the issues. In C. Adger, D. Christian, & O. Taylor (Eds.), *Making the connection: Language and academic achievement among African American students* (pp. 1–29). Washington DC: Center for Applied Linguistics.

Rickford, J. R. (2005). Using the vernacular to teach the standard. In J. D. Ramirez, T. G. Wiley, G. de Klerk, E. Lee, & W. E. Wright (Eds.), *Ebonics: The urban education debate* (pp. 18–40). Toronto, Buffalo: Multilingual Matters.

Rickford, J., Sweetland, J., Rickford, A. E., & Grano, T. (2013). *African American, Creole, and other vernacular Englishes in education: A bibliographic resource*. New York, NY: Routledge.

Romaine, S. (2003). Multilingualism. In M. Aronoff & J. Ress-Miller (Eds.), *The handbook of linguistics* (pp. 512–532). Oxford, England: Blackwell.

Roter, D. (2000). The enduring and evolving nature of the patient-physician relationship. *Patient Education and Counseling, 39*(1), 5–15.

Scollon, R., & Scollon, S. W. (2003). *Discourses in place: Language in the material world*. New York, NY: Routledge.

Silverstein, M. (2003). Indexical order and the dialectics of sociolinguistic life. *Language & Communication, 23*(3–4), 193–229.

Singh, R. K., Pretty, J., & Pilgrim, S. (2010). Traditional knowledge and biocultural diversity: Learning from tribal communities for sustainable development in northeast India. *Journal of Environmental Planning and Management, 53*(4), 511–533.

Smitherman, G. (1975). *Black language and culture: Sounds of soul*. New York, NY: Harper and Row.

Smitherman, G. (1977). *Talkin and testifyin: The language of Black America*. Detroit, MI: Wayne State University Press.

Smitherman, G. (2000). *Talkin that talk: Language, culture, and education in African America*. New York, NY: Routledge.

Soudi, A., Gooden, S., Chang, J., Kiesling, S., & South-Paul, J. (2017). Humanities in health editorial. *European Journal for Person Centered Healthcare, 5*, 506–512.

Soudi, A., & South-Paul, J. (2017). An interdisciplinary approach to cultural competence education in an academic health. *European Journal for Person Centered Healthcare, 5*(4), 516–521.

Sutherland, W. J. (2003). Parallel extinction risk and global distribution of languages and species. *Nature, 423*, 276–279.

Tannen, D. (1984). *Conversational style: Analyzing talk among friends*. Oxford, England: Oxford University Press.

van Coetsem, F. (1988). *Loan phonology and the two transfer types in language contact*. Dordrecht, The Netherlands: Foris.

Washington, J. A., Terry, N. P., & Seidenberg, M. S. (2013). Language variation and literacy learning: The case of African American English. In C. A. Stone, E. R. Silliman, B. J. Ehren, & G. P. Wallach (Eds.), *Handbook of language and literacy: Development and disorders* (pp. 204–221). New York, NY: Guilford Press.

Weldon, T. L. (2012). Teaching African American English to college students: Ideological and pedagogical challenges and solutions. *American Speech, 87*(2), 232–247.

Wendel, J. N. (2005). Notes on the ecology of language. *Bunkyo Gakuin University Academic Journal, 5*, 51–76.

Wolfram, W. (1998). Language ideology and dialect: Understanding the Oakland Ebonics controversy. *Journal of English Linguistics, 26*(2), 108–121.

Wolfram, W., & Schilling, N. (2015). *American English: Dialects and variation*. New York, NY: Wiley Blackwell.

CHAPTER 10

DIVERSITY IN THE CLASSROOM

Microaggressions and Their Impact

Nisha Nair
University of Pittsburgh

Deborah C. Good
University of Pittsburgh

ABSTRACT

This chapter calls to attention the need to investigate exclusionary practices that inhibit diversity and inclusion, with particular attention to the role of microaggressions and their negative impact on higher education classrooms. Through an examination of theory and literature, we analyze the nature and significance of microaggressions in university classrooms, which are tasked with upholding inclusionary practices. We also report on our research findings indicating microaggressions impede the process of diversity and inclusion through the use of incorrect pronouns, by fueling invisibility and visibility, and by producing unintentional messaging. Implications for practice and future research are also discussed.

Diversity Across the Disciplines, pages 145–158
Copyright © 2020 by Information Age Publishing
145

Increasingly, diversity discourse has moved to incorporate the notion of inclusion (Hays-Thomas & Bendick, 2013; Roberson, 2006). While diversity and inclusion tend to go hand in hand, a focus on the other side of inclusion—exclusion (Mor Barak, 2011) and the processes by which it happens—has typically received somewhat less attention in diversity studies (Abrams, Hogg, & Marques, 2005). Research suggests that prejudice and discrimination operate as psychological processes that influence the exclusion of employees (Mor Barak, 2008). While most of the work on inclusion and exclusion has typically focused on organizational settings and outcomes, the same processes of exclusion also operate in the classroom.

One of the ways in which exclusion happens is through subtle forms of expression, such as microaggressions. In recent years, there has been much attention directed at the concept of microaggressions, which refers to subtle forms of bias and discrimination, such as slights, snubs, or insults directed toward minorities, studied predominantly through the lens of race (Sue, 2010). The term was first introduced in the 1970s, with microaggressions defined as "subtle, stunning, often automatic, and non-verbal exchanges which are 'put downs'" (Pierce, Carew, Pierce-Gonzalez, & Willis, 1978, p. 66). More recently, the concept of microaggressions has been popularized and mainstreamed largely through the work of Sue and others (Sue, Bucceri, Lin, Nadal, & Torino, 2007; Sue, Capodilupo, et al., 2007; Sue, Capodilupo, & Holder, 2008; Sue, Capodilupo, Nadal, & Torino, 2008; Sue, 2010, 2017). Microaggressions are defined by Sue, Capodilupo, et al. (2007) as "brief and commonplace daily verbal, behavioral, and environmental indignities, whether intentional or unintentional, that communicate hostile, derogatory, or negative racial slights and insults to the target person or group" (p. 273). Research on microaggressions has focused on different marginalized groups and identities, studied in terms of race (Sue, Bucceri, et al., 2007; Sue, Capodilupo, et al., 2007; Sue, Capodilupo, & Holder, 2008; Sue, Capodilupo, Nadal, et al., 2008); gender (Basford, Offermann, & Behrend, 2014; Gartner & Sterzing, 2016); ethnic minorities and people of color (Balsam, Molina, Beadnell, Simoni, & Walters, 2011; Clark, Kleiman, Spanierman, Isaac, & Poolokasingham, 2014; Nadal, 2011); sexual orientation (Shelton & Delgado-Romero, 2011; Woodford, Howell, Kulick, & Silverschanz, 2013); religion (Husain and Howard, 2017); and intersectional identities, such as microaggressions at the confluence of sexual orientation and gender (McClelland, Rubin, & Bauermeister, 2016; Sterzing, Gartner, Woodford, & Fisher, 2017).

Whatever the nature of microaggressions, some argue that they are potentially more damaging than active forms of discrimination (Sue, Capodilupo, Nadal, et al., 2008), particularly to those with minority identities. With increasing diversity in the classroom and on college campuses (Milner, 2010), it becomes imperative to have a conversation and dialogue around the particular kind of exclusion that happens in the form of microaggressions. In this chapter, we focus attention on understanding microaggressions, including their varying forms and expressions, and unpack some of the subtle ways in which microaggressions can play out either intentionally or inadvertently in the classroom.

FORMS AND TYPES OF MICROAGGRESSIONS

By definition, microaggressions are subtle put-downs, expressed either directly through verbal communication or indirectly via nonverbal messaging; they may also be relayed through environmental indignities (Sue, 2010). Microaggressions are broadly thought to appear in the form of microinsults, microassaults, or microinvalidations (Sue, Capodilupo, et al., 2007). Microinsults are subtle forms of messaging, communicated either knowingly or unknowingly, that signal a slight, denigration, or insult as perceived by the receiver of the microaggression. For instance, when African American employees are asked how they got a job, this can be perceived as rude and insensitive, implying that they got the job through affirmative action and might not be otherwise qualified for the job. These are usually communicated in the form of rude, demeaning, or insensitive comments and utterances that may be conscious or unconscious in their delivery. Microinvalidations are the many ways in which a person may be made to feel invisible or that his or her identity is invalidated in some way. For example, when someone comments with surprise at the good English of an ethnic minority member, such as an Asian American, this can be received as both a microinsult and a microinvalidation because it denotes exceptionalism and carries a slight to the individual's ascribed identity. While the slight may be unintentional and may even potentially be intended as a compliment, it nevertheless can sting the individual and be viewed as an insult or an invalidation of one's identity, as perceived by the recipient of the microaggression. Microassaults, however, are purposeful denigrations or exclusions that can be viewed as attacks; these communicate some kind of explicit censuring, rebuke, or discrimination, with examples including using racial slurs and referring to people as "Oriental" or "colored" (Sue, Capodilupo, et al., 2007). Microassaults tend to express underlying racism, sexism, or homophobia and are deliberate attempts to undermine the other, although they are expressed in a "micro" kind of way. Alternatively, when people of color are perceived as dangerous and avoided in social interactions, such environmental indignities connote both insults and assaults on the individual being avoided.

Research on microaggressions has focused on the different types of microaggressions affecting various marginalized groups or identities, predominantly centering on racial minority- and ethnic minority-related microaggressions, gender-based microaggressions, and microaggressions directed at people with nonconforming sexual orientations (Sue, 2010). Racial microaggressions are subtle and commonplace snubs, slights, or environmental indignities aimed toward racial minorities or people of color that communicate hostile, derogatory, or negative attitudes. Similarly, research on gender microaggressions has focused on the slights, snubs, put-downs, and insults directed at women, either willfully or unknowingly. Some, like Gartner and Sterzing (2016), have referred to gender microaggressions as low-severity forms of violence toward women that potentially serve as a gateway to more problematic offenses if left unchecked. Microaggressions directed at LGBTQ people have also been studied separately, with various taxonomies and themes emerging from this research (Sue, 2010; Woodford, Chonody, Kulick, Brennan, & Renn, 2015). Other kinds of microaggressions, like those experienced by immigrants (Shenoy-Packer, 2015) and religious minorities, are also beginning to be studied (Husain & Howard, 2017). Another evolving strand of research involves intersectional identities and their experiences with microaggressions. For example, Caraves (2018) offers an intersectional look at the Latina lesbian at the intersection of race and sexual orientation marginalization.

Much of the racial microaggression literature has focused on the experiences of Black Americans and the microaggressive behaviors that White Americans may direct at them (Sue, 2010; Sue, Capodilupo, Torino, et al., 2007). Nadal (2011) developed a scale to measure racial and ethnic microaggressions, with six factors that focus on themes such as exoticization, assumptions of inferiority, and assumptions of criminality. Verbal and nonverbal actions—including behaviors that project some kind of racial unworthiness or invisibility (e.g., when Black Americans do not receive money placed back into their hands but placed on the counter while shopping; when Black Americans are avoided in public spaces or experience others' refusal to sit next to them)—may connote microinsults and invalidations at the racial level (Sue, Capodilupo, & Holder, 2008). Other forms of racial microaggressions, such as those directed at Asian Americans, have also been studied (Ong, Burrow, Fuller-Rowell, Ja, & Sue, 2013), with a common theme of ascriptions of intelligence directed at Asian Americans (Sue, Bucceri, Lin, Nadal, & Torino, 2007). Comments indicating that Asian Americans should be good at math or questions concerning where the individual is from (even if native born), are also subtle forms of microaggression directed at racial minorities. Clark et al. (2014) highlighted some themes of racial microaggressions experienced by aboriginal people in Canada, such as encountering expectations of primitiveness, enduring voyeurism, and experiencing elimination or misrepresentation in the curriculum. More recently, a Black female shopper at a Walmart store in New York complained of having to wait for a store associate to unlock a hair care product she was shopping for but that was kept in a glass case labeled "multicultural hair care"; this particular product could not be accessed from a typical shelf, unlike most other products in the store (Griffith, 2019). Such acts of exclusion and behavior denoting assumptions of criminality can also be viewed as microaggressions toward all Black Americans.

A common microaggression toward people with nonconforming sexual orientations is the expression "That's so gay," which conveys a put-down or a slight. In their study, Woodford et al. (2013) found that this particular microaggression correlated with holding negative perceptions of people who identify as gay. A scale for evaluating microaggressions pertaining to sexual orientation was offered by Sue (2010), with themes such as the use of heterosexist language, assumptions of abnormality and sinfulness, and denial of the sexuality of people with nonheterosexual identities.

Individuals usually have multiple bases for their identities, and while microaggression research has focused primarily on singular identities, increasingly more attention is being paid to the intersectional space (Sterzing et al., 2017). Researchers like Endo (2015) also note that while racial microaggressions are complex and multilayered, they become more so when analyzing identity intersections among subgroups, such as Asian American women. In a study considering the intersection of race and gender, Lewis, Mendenhall, Harwood, and Huntt (2016) examined microaggressions experienced by Black women at a predominantly White university, reporting themes including the projection of the angry Black woman stereotype, marginalization and silencing of voices and opinions, and incorrect assumptions about Black women's style and beauty; all of these emerged from stereotypes about this particular gendered racial group.

ATTENTION TO MICROAGGRESSIONS: WHY IS IT IMPORTANT?

While microaggressions are not typically active forms of discrimination, and their classification carries an indication of being "micro" in nature, they are by no means trivial in the scope or damage they can potentially incur. Microaggressions can affect the well-being and psychological health of those subject to them. Some have argued that microaggressions are a form of subtle racism or another act of discrimination; however, what may seemingly be innocuous can nonetheless sting (Wang, Leu, & Shoda, 2011).

Racial microaggressions has been associated with a negative impact on the affected individual's physical and mental health (Nadal, Griffin, Wong, Davidoff, & Davis, 2017). Such microaggressions have also been linked to lower job satisfaction (DeCuir-Gunby & Gunby, 2016) and to significant psychological and emotional distress among Black Americans (Sue, Capodilupo, & Holder, 2008); this is because of the implicit signals that Black Americans may carry of not belonging or being intellectually inferior. A study by Isom (2016) found that microaggressions and injustices independently predict serious and violent offenses among African Americans. A study by Ong et al. (2013) focusing on the racial microaggression experience of Asian Americans revealed that elevations in microaggressions were seen as predicting somatic symptoms and heightened negative affect.

Wang et al. (2011) found that Asian Americans reported high negative emotional intensity and lower emotional well-being when they experienced microaggressions of a positive kind, even when the aggressor intended the comments to be seen as praise or a compliment. Thus, ascriptions of intelligence attributed to Asian Americans, for example, can be perceived negatively, still stinging the recipient and signaling ethnic discrimination.

Some resultant feelings associated with microaggressions were powerlessness, invisibility, and perceived pressure to be the representative of one's group (Sue, Capodilupo, & Holder, 2008). Considering what can influence or mitigate the impact of microaggressions, Offermann, Basford, Graebner, DeGraaf, and Jaffer (2013) found that microaggressions were less intense when the supervisor had a reputation for equity and fairness, regardless of the severity of the microaggression. Ways of dealing with microaggressions also vary, with mechanisms such as turning to spirituality and seeking support networks and mentorship being noted (Holder, Jackson, & Ponterotto, 2015).

Given the subtle and complex nature of microaggressions, as well as the potentially detrimental effects on the physical and mental health of those who experience these microaggressions, it is imperative to draw attention to these seemingly innocuous but nonetheless harmful and pervasive forms of under-the-radar aggression. Highlighting microaggressions may be the first step toward stemming the tide of what could become fatal and damaging to the psyches and self-images of marginalized identities still being shaped in the classroom.

MICROAGGRESSIONS IN THE CLASSROOM

Given the pervasive nature of the microaggression experience and the varied marginalized minority identities that are susceptible to it, can the college classroom be bereft of its expression and impact? Although most of the microaggression research has not located itself in the classroom, there has still been some prior research exploring the microaggression experience, albeit from a singular identity lens, in relation to students and the classroom.

Considering the microaggressions experienced by students of color, Harwood, Huntt, Mendenhall, and Lewis (2012) abstract four broad themes related to microaggressions experienced by students in residence halls: (a) racial jokes and verbal comments, (b) racial slurs written in shared spaces, (c) segregated spaces and unequal treatment, and (d) denial and minimization of racism. With regard to the K–12 classroom, Kohli and Solórzano (2012) observe that many students of color experience cultural disrespect within the classroom in relation to their names, internalizing a cultural hierarchy and notions of minority inferiority. Kohli and Solórzano (2012) also caution that having to endure disrespect linked to the pronunciation or mockery of one's name can have a lasting impact on the self-perception of a child. In a study focused on nonheterosexual college students, Platt and Lenzen (2013), who use focus group methodology to explore the microaggression experiences of college students based on their sexuality, offer support for Sue's (2010) typology of microaggression themes related to sexual orientation, even adding other themes, such as the undersexualization of people with nonconforming sexual identities. A scale to evaluate microaggressions targeting LGBT in everyday life—with themes such as the use of heterosexist and transphobic terminology, endorsement of heteronormative or gender normative culture/behaviors, assumptions of universal LGBT experience, and assumptions of sexual pathology or abnormality—was developed by Woodford et al. (2015). Not all of the microaggressions experienced by students in the classroom have to be verbal. Sometimes seemingly innocuous things, like a White teacher failing to acknowledge (knowingly or unknowingly) students of color in the classroom (Sue, Capodilupo, et al., 2007), can be interpreted as microaggressions.

In our own study (which was part of a larger study on the microaggression experience for marginalized identities), we interviewed a total of 25 students who participated in focus groups on microaggressions relating to gender, race, religion, and sexual orientation. All participants were students at a large midwestern university in North America. The majority were graduate students (76%), with the remaining 24% representing undergraduate students. We used a semistructured interview protocol for our study, with both the authors taking turns leading the focus groups and interviewing participants about their microaggression experiences. While our original study focused on understanding the microaggression experience across different identity groups, in this chapter we identify and report on the different ways in which microaggressions play out in the classroom. Based on interviews with students and focus groups with different identity group members, we offer here some excerpts from participants that highlight how these microaggressions emerge in the classroom or on college campuses via exchanges with fellow students or as perpetuated by teachers, staff, or administrators.

Use of Incorrect Pronouns

Many students reported feeling uncomfortable when the incorrect pronoun relating to their gender identity was used for them in the classroom. As one student with a nonconforming gender identity observed,

> "We shouldn't be . . . assuming. It's good to ask people what pronouns they prefer. It's awkward, if you're just in a casual situation. Like, "Hi, my name is so and so—. What pronouns do you prefer?" It seems forced at first. So, it's understandable if you get it wrong, but being aware and paying attention, and noticing how people refer to themselves and then respecting that."

While a teacher or professor may not be aware that an incorrect pronoun was used in a particular exchange, it can still be perceived as an invalidation of the particular identity for the student who experiences a rejection of their chosen identity, even though it may emerge from a place of ignorance. Being mindful of the pronouns that students use for themselves, or asking students to indicate which pronouns they prefer, may be a way to address this concern.

Perpetuating Stereotypes

When teachers and fellow students make attributions based on group categorizations, such as ascribing intelligence in math and science to Asian American students or exhibiting surprise at the high performance of African American students, it not only serves to perpetuate existing stereotypes but also translates to the experience of exclusion for those who do not fit the stereotype. Such characterizations expressed verbally or nonverbally can signal an invalidation of the student's unique identity and feel like a microassault.

Sometimes, stereotypical assumptions are portrayed in everyday exchanges between students. For example, one gay student commented on the stereotypical assumptions that exist concerning gay couples, which did not apply to him:

> Some of my friends who know my orientation, actually when I talk to them about my relationship with my boyfriend, they always treat us like one is a man and one is a woman in the relationship. Which means the stereotype about a gay couple—one takes on a man's role and the other the woman. But, hey, we both think we are all man.

Exchanges such as this can appear belittling, with a caricaturizing of one's identity when stereotypes are applied without accounting for individual differences. Another student commented on how the stereotype that Asian Americans are intelligent and proficient in math was actually limiting:

> Sometimes I feel like maybe because I'm Asian, people would be more likely to think I have, like, a good mathematical ability. Like, when we are required to work in a team, and my team member will say to me, "Hey, [name], how about you be responsible for the calculations?" And uh, yeah, I'm super cool with doing that, but if you ask me to do it like 100 times, so it's, like, you know, I feel like I'm also capable of doing other things, instead of only the mathematical calculations.

A few women in our study also noted stereotypes that emerged in relation to task assignments on a group project, in which the work among team members was assigned along gendered lines: Women were relegated to cleaning up and making presentations look nice, while men got to work on the content. This implied that men were able to shoulder more important responsibilities, whereas women played supporting roles. Snubs like this are often based on stereotypes that operate at the subconscious level but nevertheless connote a put-down and may be perceived as a microaggression.

Unintentional Messaging

Microaggressions do not always come in derisory forms where they are directly expressed as put-downs or slights. Sometimes even intended compliments (such as ascriptions of intelligence to Asian Americans or surprise at good academic performance of African Americans) can be interpreted as microaggressions and slights, even when the issuers of these microaggressions might intend them otherwise. One study participant discussed a conversation in which an intended compliment translated into a microaggression:

> I had this consulting field project, and I had an all-female team, which I was really proud of. This one girl, her boyfriend said to her, "[It] doesn't really matter what you say [be]cause you're so cute." And she's very smart, and I was, like, highly offended by it, but I didn't say anything. I was like, "He shouldn't say that to you, [be]cause you're very smart and a very good student." He actually meant it as comforting. He was actually trying to help her, but the words and the comment came out the wrong way.

This is an example of how unintentional messaging is perceived as devaluing one's worth, as observed by a third party. An exchange between two students, where one individual is probably only seeking to boost the other's confidence, appears as a gendered microaggression that reduces a woman's worth to her appearance when perceived by a third party. Thus, even compliments or words of encouragement that can potentially belittle a less salient identity, either directly or by import, can also become a microaggression.

Fueling Invisibility and Visibility

As mentioned earlier, it is sometimes the acts of omission that can be perceived as slights, such as a teacher not making eye contact with, or failing to acknowledge, particular students in a class who may attribute this (correctly or incorrectly) to a slight directed at their minority identity. Alternatively, sometimes microaggressions emerge in the form of verbal slipups, where the teacher fails to use gender-neutral language. One student actually reported an instance where a particular professor kept addressing only the male members in class during the lecture, ignoring the significant female population present in class via language that was exclusionary of the female gender. As another example of experiencing invisibility, one student commented on feeling left out through the lack of attention provided to their racial identity by school administration and staff during their initial orientation to the program:

> Speaking of our orientation, we learned different things, like learn-to-love-everybody kind of stuff. We talked about international students; we talked about religion; we learned all about how certain cultures work, women are viewed this way and such; we talked about just all sorts of things, except for Black people. We never talked about Black people! And I don't know if it's because there's just so few of us.

Perceived omissions in the socialization process can lead to certain students feeling invisible or as though their identities have been deemed irrelevant by those in authority, perpetuating a sense of invalidation and invisibility.

While invisibility of one's identity can fuel a sense of invalidation, sometimes it is the process of drawing attention to the minority identity of a student in the classroom that can take the form of a microaggression. For example, one of the participants in our study spoke of the sense of discomfort she felt when a professor commented on her wearing of a religious artifact:

> A professor who is a known atheist commented once to me that, "Oh! You have a cross!" And he said something along the lines of, "That's weird." That little microaggression made me think—should I not wear my cross around here? In that instance, it felt like he was judging me for wearing my cross.

In this case, highlighting and making visible the Catholic identity of the student by a professor, with a comment that appeared to denigrate that particular identity, appeared as a microassault. Thus, microaggressions in the classroom can be driven by those in authority, such as teachers, when they either render student identities invisible and invalidate their relevance to the discourse at hand or when they make visible minority identities by drawing attention to markers, such as religious symbols (e.g., cross, turban, veil, skullcap). In both instances, the exhibition of insensitivities by a person in power (the teacher) via comments or conversations that are selective or disparaging of certain marginalized identities and directed at those less powerful (students) in the classroom can go down as microaggressions.

DISCUSSION AND A WAY FORWARD

If microaggressions are the subtle forms of bias and discrimination directed at minorities that occur in everyday actions and comments that denote slights, insults, or snubs, then the classroom is as much a place as any other where these can potentially play out. Any conversation on diversity and inclusion in the classroom would thus be incomplete without focusing attention on microaggressions. Understanding what they mean, their various forms of expression, and the potential damage that they can inflict on those who perceive them are all pertinent to promoting diversity and inclusion.

Sometimes microaggressions emerge in conversations between students—at other times, it is the teacher or the professor who is the aggressor. They may be intended as aggression, couched as a microaggression, or projected innocuously but still be received or read as an affront. Since, by their very definition, microaggressions are subtle, they operate in ways that are often invisible, making them that much harder to point out as active forms of discrimination. If we begin addressing the issue of microaggressions in the classroom, we have to start with an awareness of what they are and the varied forms they can take, coupled with a sensitivity to our own role as educators in perpetuating and enabling their expression.

In this chapter, we highlight the relevant literature on microaggressions and, based on our qualitative study that involved interviewing students who have experienced microaggressions in the classroom, we offer some insights into how microaggressions tend to play out in the classroom. We classify these microaggressions as emergent in the use of incorrect pronouns; the perpetuation of stereotypes; unintentional messaging where seemingly positive attributions or compliments have somehow gone wrong; and the process of making marginalized identities become less salient and invisible, or more salient and visible, thereby invalidating or discomfiting particular minority identities.

The classroom can be a place where everyday conversations between participants perpetuate certain stereotypes or myths about certain identities.

It is immaterial whether those stereotypes are positive or negative, correct or incorrect; instead, the reductionism that such stereotyping entails can leave individuals feeling typecast and shorn of their full identities. It also becomes important to be mindful of language to ensure that minority identities are not being excluded or invalidated. Inadvertently or knowingly drawing attention to minority identities can be perceived negatively by minority students, as would be rendering them invisible in our comments and everyday actions and behaviors. Enabling a healthy and safe space for nonjudgmental and inclusive dialogue and participation among diverse students is a responsibility of all educators, even if it entails walking a tightrope between invisibility and visibility of minority identities. The least we can do is become mindful of our own roles in enabling or engaging in the expression of microaggressions in our classrooms.

REFERENCES

Abrams, D., Hogg, M. A., & Marques, J. M. (2005). A social psychological framework for understanding social inclusion and exclusion. In D. Abrams, M. A. Hogg, & J. M. Marques (Eds.), *The social psychology of inclusion and exclusion* (pp. 1–24). New York, NY: Psychology Press.

Balsam, K. F., Molina, Y., Beadnell, B., Simoni, J., & Walters, K. (2011). Measuring multiple minority stress: The LGBT people of color. *Cultural Diversity and Ethnic Minority Psychology, 17*(2), 163–174.

Basford, T. E., Offermann, L. R., & Behrend, T. S. (2014). Do you see what I see? Perceptions of gender microaggressions in the workplace. *Psychology of Women Quarterly, 38*(3), 340–349.

Caraves, J. (2018). Straddling the school-to-prison pipeline and gender non-conforming microaggressions as a Latina Lesbian. *Journal of LGBT Youth, 15*(1), 52–69.

Clark, D. A., Kleiman, S., Spanierman, L. B., Isaac, P., & Poolokasingham, G. (2014). "Do you live in a teepee?" Aboriginal students' experiences with racial microaggressions in Canada. *Journal of Diversity in Higher Education, 7*(2), 112–125.

DeCuir-Gunby, J., & Gunby, N. W., Jr. (2016). Racial microaggressions in the workplace: A critical race analysis of the experiences of African American educators. *Urban Education, 51*(4), 390–414.

Endo, R. (2015). How Asian American female teachers experience racial microaggressions from pre-service preparation to their professional careers. *Urban Review, 47*(4), 601–625.

Gartner, R. E., & Sterzing, P. R. (2016). Gender microaggressions as a gateway to sexual harassment and sexual assault: Expanding the conceptualization of youth sexual violence. *Journal of Women and Social Work, 31*(4), 491–503.

Griffith, J. (2019, February 5). Black beauty products kept under lock and key at some Walmart stores, raising complaints. *NBC News.* Retrieved from https://www.nbcnews.com/news/us-news/walmart-s-practice-locking-black -beauty-products-some-stores-raises-n967206

Harwood, S. A., Huntt, M. B., Mendenhall, R., & Lewis, J. A. (2012). Racial microaggressions in the residence halls: Experiences of students of color at a predominantly White university. *Journal of Diversity in Higher Education, 5*(3), 159–173.

Hays-Thomas, R., & Bendick, M., Jr. (2013). Professionalizing diversity and inclusion practice: Should voluntary standards be the chicken or the egg? *Industrial & Organizational Psychology, 6*(3), 193–205.

Holder, A. M. B., Jackson, M. A., & Ponterotto, J. G. (2015). Racial microaggression experiences and coping strategies of Black women in corporate leadership. *Qualitative Psychology, 2*(2), 164–180.

Husain, A., & Howard, S. (2017). Religious microaggressions: A case study of Muslim Americans. *Journal of Ethnic & Cultural Diversity in Social Work, 26*(1–2), 139–152.

Isom, D. (2016). Microaggressions, injustices, and racial identity. An empirical assessment of the theory of African American offending. *Journal of Contemporary Criminal Justice, 32*(1), 27–59.

Kohli, R., & Solórzano, D. G. (2012). Teachers, please learn our names!: Racial microaggressions and the K–12 classroom. *Race Ethnicity and Education, 15*(4), 441–462.

Lewis, J. A., Mendenhall, R., Harwood, S. A., & Huntt, M. B. (2016). "Ain't I a woman?" Perceived gendered racial microaggressions experienced by Black women. *Counseling Psychologist, 44*(5), 758–780.

McClelland, S. I., Rubin, J. D., & Bauermeister, J. A. (2016). Adapting to injustice: Young bisexual women's interpretations of microaggressions. *Psychology of Women Quarterly, 40*(4), 532–550.

Milner, H. R., IV. (2010). *Start where you are, but don't stay there: Understanding diversity, opportunity gaps, and teaching in today's classrooms.* Cambridge, MA: Harvard Education Press.

Mor Barak, M. E. (2008). Social psychological perspectives of workforce diversity and inclusion in national and global contexts. In R. J. Patti (Ed.), *Handbook of human service management* (pp. 239–254). Thousand Oaks, CA: SAGE.

Mor Barak, M. E. (2011). *Managing diversity: Toward a globally inclusive workplace.* Thousand Oaks, CA: SAGE.

Nadal, K. L. (2011). The Racial and Ethnic Microaggressions Scale (REMS): Construction, reliability, and validity. *Journal of Counseling Psychology, 58*(4), 470–480.

Nadal, K. L., Griffin, K. E., Wong, Y., Davidoff, K. C., & Davis, L. S. (2017). The injurious relationship between racial microaggressions and physical health: Implications for social work. *Journal of Ethnic & Cultural Diversity in Social Work, 26*(1–2), 6–17.

Offermann, L. R., Basford, T. E., Graebner, R., DeGraaf, S. B., & Jaffer, S. (2013). Slights, snubs, and slurs: Leader equity and microaggressions. *Equality, Diversity & Inclusion, 32*, 374–393.

Ong, A. D., Burrow, A. L., Fuller-Rowell, T. E., Ja, N. M., & Sue, D. W. (2013). Racial microaggressions and daily well-being among Asian Americans. *Journal of Counseling Psychology, 60*(2), 188–199.

Pierce, C. M., Carew, J., Pierce-Gonzalez, D., & Willis, D. (1978). An experiment in racism: TV commercials. In C. M. Pierce (Ed.), *Television and education* (pp. 62–88). Beverly Hills, CA: SAGE.

Platt, L. F., & Lenzen, A. L. (2013). Sexual orientation microaggressions and the experience of sexual minorities. *Journal of Homosexuality, 60*(7), 1011–1034.

Roberson, Q. M. (2006). Disentangling the meanings of diversity and inclusion in organizations. *Group & Organization Management, 31*(2), 212–236.

Shelton, K., & Delgado-Romero, E. A. (2011). Sexual orientation microaggressions: The experience of lesbian, gay, bisexual, and queer clients in psychotherapy. *Journal of Counseling Psychology, 58*(2), 210–221.

Shenoy-Packer, S. (2015). Immigrant professionals, microaggressions, and critical sensemaking in the U.S. workplace. *Management Communication Quarterly, 29*(2), 257–275.

Sterzing, P. R., Gartner, R. E., Woodford, M. R., & Fisher, C. M. (2017). Sexual orientation, gender, and gender identity microaggressions: Toward an intersectional framework for social work research. *Journal of Ethnic & Cultural Diversity in Social Work, 26*(1–2), 81–94.

Sue, D. W. (2010). *Microaggressions in everyday life: Race, gender, and sexual orientation.* Hoboken, NJ: Wiley.

Sue, D. W. (2017). Microaggressions and "evidence": Empirical or experiential reality? *Perspectives on Psychological Science, 12*(1), 170–172.

Sue, D. W., Bucceri, J. M., Lin, A. I., Nadal, K. L., & Torino, G. C. (2007). Racial microaggressions and the Asian American experience. *Cultural Diversity and Ethnic Minority Psychology, 13*(1), 72–81.

Sue, D. W., Capodilupo, C. M., & Holder, A. M. B. (2008). Racial microaggressions in the life experience of Black Americans. *Professional Psychology: Research and Practice, 39*(3), 329–336.

Sue, D. W., Capodilupo, C. M., Nadal, K. L., & Torino, G. (2008). Racial microaggressions and the power to define reality. *American Psychologist, 63*(4), 277–279.

Sue, D. W., Capodilupo, C. M., Torino, G. C., Bucceri, J. M., Holder, A. M., Nadal, K. L., & Esquilin, M. (2007). Racial microaggressions in everyday life: Implications for clinical practice. *American Psychologist, 62*(4), 271–286.

Wang, J., Leu, J., & Shoda, Y. (2011). When the seemingly innocuous "stings": Racial microaggressions and their emotional consequences. *Personality & Social Psychology Bulletin, 37*(12), 1666–1678.

Woodford, M. R., Chonody, J. M., Kulick, A., Brennan, D. J., & Renn, K. (2015). The LGBQ microaggressions on campus scale: A scale development and validation study. *Journal of Homosexuality, 62*(12), 1660–1687.

Woodford, M. R., Howell, M. L., Kulick, A., & Silverschanz, P. (2013). "That's so gay": Heterosexual male undergraduates and the perpetuation of sexual orientation microaggressions on campus. *Journal of Interpersonal Violence, 28*(2), 416–435.

PART III

POLICIES

CHAPTER 11

COMPARATIVE POLITICAL SCIENCE RESEARCH ON DIVERSITY

Scott Morgenstern
University of Pittsburgh

Kelly Morrison
University of Pittsburgh

ABSTRACT

This comparative chapter asks why ethnic groups in some countries, even if they are large, fail to win local or national political representation. Here we are concerned with how different electoral institutions (e.g., proportional representation) affect minority representation including fair representation for Latinos in the United States and indigenous minority groups in Latin America. We also examine how different political institutions can contribute to (or ameliorate) ethnic conflict in Latin America.

A key concern in political science research, for studies of U.S. domestic politics and comparisons among countries, is representation. In studies of the United States, political scientists seek to understand variation in the rates at

Diversity Across the Disciplines, pages 161–177
Copyright © 2020 by Information Age Publishing
All rights of reproduction in any form reserved.

which different ethnic or minority groups vote or participate in the political process, the determinants of the participation rates, and the responsiveness of the political system to the groups' demands. Studies of different countries, including comparisons among countries, have similar questions.

A first goal of this chapter is to provide a short background on how comparative political science has addressed the question of minority representation around the world. Like research on minority representation and voting behavior in the United States, research in comparative politics is concerned with descriptive representation. A second goal is to address the research question about why representation is often poor. Political science answers this question by looking at institutions (e.g., the Constitution, the electoral system) but also societal factors (e.g., discrimination) and informal practices (e.g., clientelism). The third goal is to report on our ongoing project engaging these issues, which examines (the lack of) national political representation for indigenous communities in Latin America.

Political science uses the term "descriptive representation" to consider the degree to which elected officials are similar in terms of ascriptive characteristics—gender, ethnicity, religion—as the people that they represent (Mansbridge, 1999; Pitkin, 1967). This is contrasted with policy-oriented or sympathetic representation, in which, for example, a man could support feminist themes. To an important degree, these ideas emanate from discussions in political science that trace their roots to early writings about representation. Irish legislator Edmund Burke (1774/1906) defined representation in terms of "delegates" and "trustees" in the late 1700s. For Burke, a delegate carried to the legislature the wishes of the group that he (seldom "she" in those days) represented. By contrast, the expectation of a trustee was that he would study the issues and make the best decision possible, even if members of the group were (wrongly) opposed.

In the political science literature on U.S. politics, there are discussions of both types of representation. To what degree men support women's rights has been a question at least since the suffrage movements, and a serious concern has long been the ability and willingness of Whites to support civil rights. While of course based on racism, the ability of Southern legislators to block civil rights laws for generations after the Civil War has formal institutional roots (e.g., the overrepresentation of small states in the Senate). Political science is particularly interested in institutions because, at least ostensibly, they can be changed more easily than can culture or geography. How might politics have changed if the South had not had the power to block civil rights initiatives in the period from the 1860s to the 1960s?

Perhaps because minority groups have so often lacked delegates, they have pushed their concerns through social movements. Political scientists study such movements in an effort to understand their impacts on political outcomes, such as civil rights or suffrage in the United States or the recognition of indigenous rights and electoral quotas in other countries. While social mobilizations have had an undisputedly central role in bringing about large political changes, political science frequently focuses on the interaction of the movements with the political system. They might ask, for example, how political pressures are processed or transmitted through the formal institutions of government. Other questions include the following: What are the roadblocks? What coalitions are necessary for change? With respect to civil rights in the United States, the role of a Southerner (Texan) president in corralling the necessary support for change also takes a role in the theoretical discussions. As such, this example highlights not only the interplay of institutions and social mobilization in determining a political outcome relevant to diversity but also provides an example of trustee-style representation.

Gender provides another diversity-related issue that highlights concerns about delegate- and trustee-style representation. This issue, pertinent to studies focusing on the United States as well as the wider world is of interest both in terms of policy outcomes and the degree to which women have obtained delegate representation. It also can highlight the role of social mobilization in pressing for change in nondiverse institutions.

While gender and some other themes are pertinent in both the United States and elsewhere, the comparative politics literature often has other concerns that it can analyze using the delegate and trustee points of view. One particular interest to the discipline is ethnic conflict and whether it results from minority groups' exclusion from national politics. In these worst-case scenarios, a lack of representation can lead to civil war and irredentism. In analyzing these processes, the role of movements takes central stage, but such discussions must also address context and political institutions. From a policy perspective, the goal is to understand whether particular constitutional, electoral, or other rules can help to improve representation and thus prevent conflict.

In what follows, we review both classic and newer literature on representation around the world. We first note the very poor representation of ethnic minorities in the halls of many governments, but then focus on the literature about ethnic conflict. There we emphasize the interesting debate about how different political institutions can contribute to (or ameliorate) these conflicts. Our goal is not to be comprehensive, but to simply provide a flavor of a very large and broad literature.

COMPARATIVE LITERATURE

A first focus of the classical comparative literature on representation focuses on how ideology shapes voters' decisions and how that choice affects the number and type of political parties in a system. This work, based on the work of Duverger (1954) and Downs (1957), assumed voters would choose the parties that represented positions closest to their own ideological preferences. Political science research typically classifies electoral systems—which define the processes that translate votes into seats in the legislature—into two basic categories: majoritarian and proportional representation (PR) systems. Majoritarian systems are marked by districts that elect only one candidate, meaning that the candidate with the largest number of votes takes office and the voters for the losing candidate(s) are unrepresented (Lijphart, 1999). This single-member district system, which is used for elections to both the U.S. House of Representatives and the U.S. Senate, typically generates fewer (often two) parties. As Duverger (1954) taught, this would be the result of voters not wanting to waste their votes on parties that could not win, and alternative parties not forming for the same reason. In contrast, because PR systems allocate more than one seat to each district and parties win seats in proportion to the number of votes that they win in each district, it takes fewer votes to win a spot in the legislature. Thus, PR systems typically yield a multiplicity of parties, especially in diverse or divided societies where multiple groups clamor for representation.

While this voting literature often focused on the relation of ideology to representation, later discussions, often concerned with violence and irredentism, turned to the questions of how well minority, ethnic, and regional groups were represented. Some of this literature used a society's fragmentation to explain the high number of parties in a society (see Chhibber & Kollman, 2004). Other authors (Madrid, 2012, 2016; Van Cott, 2003, 2005) turned the question around and asked why some ethnic groups were unsuccessful in gaining significant representation. This has been a particularly important issue in developing democracies where minority groups have faced generations of suppression and degradation. In some of these countries, even after democracy brought formal voting rights to all, small minorities of Whites ruled over large majorities of indigenous populations. As an example, while over 60% of Bolivians identify as indigenous, until 2002, indigenous parties never gained even 5% of the vote (Van Cott, 2003). Why has it been so difficult for minority groups to gain representation?

As we discuss later with reference to many Latin American cases, part of the answer is based on the groups' actualized identity and their interests and abilities in attaining political representation. In order to create political parties, minority groups must overcome internal divisions and use ethnic or regional identities as the basis for organization. Forming parties and winning votes also requires these groups to overcome a number of barriers, which frequently include poverty and low literacy. Another barrier is clientelism, under which "patrons" use multiple pressures, ranging from persuasion and vote-buying to incentives to violence, to induce particular voting patterns. They advance their electoral goals using a variety of tools. First, party leaders across the region have traditionally organized buses to take groups to the polls. They then ensure voting for their preferred candidates, as Lyne (2008) describes with reference to Brazil and Venezuela, by designing ingenious methods to subvert the secrecy of the vote (see Corstange, 2018, on similar practices in Lebanon; and Healy, 1987, on Bolivia). Thus, in combination with control over who gets on their own party ballots, plus barriers for other parties to form, traditional parties have been able to limit representation of indigenous groups (see Auyero, 2000; Kitschelt & Altamirano, 2015).

Another area of the comparative literature on ethnic representation has focused on conflict. Historically, scholars took for granted that diverse societies would face division and conflict in politics, in the worst cases leading to violence between groups and irredentism. With this backdrop in mind, later researchers asked whether certain institutions could mitigate the potential for conflict in diverse polities. In a series of tomes, for instance, Arendt Lijphart (1969, 1977, 1985, 2004), Donald Horowitz (1985, 1991, 1993), and their followers debated the merits of "consociationalism." Lijphart defined this term as a form of government that empowered regional (often ethnic) groups in order to ensure coalition building and avoid imposition by central powers on regions. These institutions, Lijphart argued, would assuage the potential grievances of minority groups and ensure political peace. Horowitz took the other side, arguing that these models would enshrine divisions in society, leading to continuing conflicts.

A key to this debate was how to elect representatives. Lijphart (1977, 1999) focused on PR to ensure that ethnic or regional groups would have a fair share of seats in the legislature. Horowitz (2004), in contrast, supported systems such as the alternative vote, which privilege centrist politicians. One way that they do this is by asking voters to rank candidates and then counting the second or third place votes as part of the selection method. Because extremists are likely to pick less-extreme candidates as their second choice, centrists sit in a privileged position.

While driving a tremendous part of the comparative politics literature, this institutional approach failed to significantly deal with the voter repression or clientelism that has led to such poor representation of ethnic groups in many countries. It further ignores discrimination, active campaigns to hamper ethnic parties, and socioeconomic conditions that have clearly hindered the formation of minority parties. Yet, in spite of all of these factors, minority ethnic groups have gained significant representation and even participated in governing coalitions in countries like Spain, Hungary, and Romania (Birnir, 2007). Minority ethnic groups in Ecuador and Bolivia have also gained representation or even control over the executive office. How were minority groups able to overcome so many barriers in order to achieve representation? In what follows, we discuss the literature answering this question for the Latin American context. We then discuss our own research addressing this issue.

REPRESENTATION OF INDIGENOUS COMMUNITIES IN LATIN AMERICA

Why are indigenous groups poorly represented in Latin American governments? Only once has an indigenous leader been elected to a Latin American presidency (Evo Morales in Bolivia in 2005), and indigenous populations are underrepresented across Latin American legislatures. Consider, for instance, the three countries with the largest indigenous populations: Bolivia, Guatemala, and Peru. In Bolivia, 41% of the population but only 22.9% of the legislature identifies as indigenous, while the mismatch is 41% to 12.7% in Guatemala and 24% to 0.8% in Peru. In countries with lower populations of indigenous people, the ratio is even worse (Cabrero, Pop, Morales, Chuji, & Mamani, 2013; Comisión Económica para América Latina y el Caribe, 2014; Htun, 2016; World Bank, 2018). Though data on the ethnic makeup of governments is mostly nonexistent, even a cursory glance across the region shows that indigenous citizens are mostly absent from positions of power.

Of course, oppression and racism play a major role in the exclusion of minority groups throughout history. Political science also points to more subtle factors, including institutional rules and voting behavior, that prevent indigenous groups from organizing, competing, and winning votes in mainstream politics. There are many barriers on the long path toward representation. Indigenous groups must first overcome a number of collective action problems to organize as a cohesive group with a political voice. Subsequently, they must decide whether to pursue self-government and regional autonomy or participate in mainstream politics. For those groups opting to pursue power in national offices, they must further decide whether to ally with existing parties (which may fail to nominate indigenous candidates) or create their own parties (which often face high barriers to entry). In recent years, political science research has begun to address the challenges at each of these stages on the path to representation. We next discuss some of these main contributions and, later, relate how our own work addresses the last hurdle to representation: winning votes.

To gain a foothold in national politics, indigenous communities often must first craft a cohesive political identity as a group. Research across the fields of political science, anthropology, and sociology has emphasized the difficulty of this process, given the fluid and constructed nature of social identities, particularly for members of indigenous communities (see

Lucero, 2008). This is especially true in Latin America, where many indigenous individuals identify as *mestizo*, which means of mixed European and native American descent. Even those who speak an indigenous language may eschew partisan ethnic appeals in favor of other group-based means of representation (Madrid, 2016). As might be expected in this context, there is a wide variety in the extent to which indigenous communities seek representation along ethnic lines. As sociologist Tanya Murray Li (2000) explains,

> A group's self-identification as tribal or indigenous is not natural or inevitable, but neither is it invited, adopted, or imposed. It is, rather, a *positioning* that draws upon historically sedimented practices, landscapes, and repertoires of meaning, and emerges through particular patterns of engagement and struggle. (p. 151)

Thus, although there has been a growing desire for national representation among indigenous communities across Latin America since the late 20th century, many indigenous communities have instead sought local sovereignty or representation through existing political parties.

Why then do some communities form political identities while others do not? One condition is the degree of homogeneity between indigenous groups within national boundaries. As Lucero (2008) explains, "Though there is the assumption that ethnically and racially defined communities have an advantage in acting collectively, indigenous movements have a host of divisions and internal differences that complicate efforts to forge larger 'imagined communities'" (p. 3). In his studies of indigenous movements in Bolivia and Ecuador, Lucero (2008) argues that it was the process by which "supralocal indigenous units were constructed" that determined the success of indigenous movements at the national level (p. 178). While Bolivia's indigenous movement was dominated by the class-based concerns of indigenous leaders in the highlands, Ecuador's movement featured a conglomeration of highland and lowland interests, the latter of which stressed local issues that were not necessarily class based. For this reason, the Bolivian indigenous movement had an easier time fielding legislative and executive candidates at the national level.

Yet the Bolivian case also points to the difficulty of mobilizing along political lines for indigenous concerns. Evo Morales's work to transform the Bolivian coca growers' movement into a political party, for instance, was quite contentious at the time (Alcántara Sáez & Marenghi 2007; Korovkin, 2006). Lucero's (2008) argument explains how indigenous movements' ability to gain national traction first depends on the power dynamics between different groups at the subnational level. To the extent that some subnational groups may block nationalistic appeals, intergroup struggles can prevent the incorporation of indigenous voices in national politics.

Other research points to temporal trends to explain changes in indigenous representation, given that mobilization along ethnic lines seemed to come in a wave at the close of the 20th century. One factor to explain this cross-country trend is the adoption of neoliberal economic policies in a range of Latin American countries during this period (Alcántara Sáez & Marenghi, 2007; Jackson & Warren, 2005; Van Cott, 2010; Yashar, 1998, 1999). Neoliberal reforms often resulted in the privatization of natural resources, increased cultural individualism, and a lack of social services for the poor. These changes left many indigenous communities isolated and impoverished, and spurred them to mobilize in favor of changes to national policies. Because of the extent that the neoliberal reforms had a disproportionate effect on indigenous communities, they fomented mobilization. Given that this period was also marked by a weakening of the mainstream political left (Van Cott, 2005), indigenous communities filled the vacuum by clarifying their own unique political interests.[1]

International advocacy efforts were a final factor that explains the mobilization of ethnic groups. The International Labor Organization's Indigenous and Tribal Peoples Convention, 1989 (No. 169), for instance, was adopted in 1989 and had far-reaching effects in articulating a cohesive agenda for indigenous activists across Latin America. Transnational efforts from nongovernmental organizations also played a role in the formation of national political identities during this time period (Jackson & Warren, 2005).

The previous discussion delineates the first necessary condition for indigenous communities to gain national representation: The group must overcome divisions and use their ethnic identity to organize with the intention of gaining political representation. Yet this complex internal process is only a first necessary condition for attaining representation. Indigenous movements must also be able to compete for political power, either through existing party labels or through the formation of their own parties. The first option is often out of reach due to outright racism against indigenous candidates and structural sources of inequality. Existing parties may be unwilling to allow indigenous leaders to run under their party labels even when they share political values. Poverty and lack of education in indigenous communities may mean that few indigenous leaders have the capacity to compete. Yet, given that many Latin American countries utilize PR electoral systems, newer, smaller parties made up of indigenous leaders may still have a chance to gain office. This raises the question of why some indigenous movements are able to form political parties but others are not.

In foundational work on this subject, Van Cott (2005) traces the process by which indigenous movements in Bolivia, Ecuador, Peru, Colombia, Venezuela, and Argentina formed viable parties in the 1990s.[2] As mentioned previously, not all indigenous movements achieve this threshold of viability. This is especially surprising given that indigenous communities often comprise the majority of some districts or even regions in many Latin American countries. In spite of their numbers, movements are rarely viable. Both internal and external factors play a role.

Regarding internal characteristics, Korovkin (2006) emphasizes the organizational structure of indigenous pueblos as determining whether they can nominate and unite behind one candidate for national office. Similarly, Van Cott (2003) argues that party formation required taking advantage of a "political opportunity structure" and two decades of sustained mobilization, which succeeded in generating a solid and deep organization that put indigenous rights onto the political agenda (p. 753). However, most work points to the institutional features of each country as determining how and when movements can compete as political parties.

Van Cott and others have outlined several of these institutional characteristics. One commonly cited factor is the requirements for new parties to register to compete in national elections (Birnir, 2007; Rice & Van Cott, 2006; Van Cott, 2003, 2005). In her case study on Bolivia, for instance, Van Cott (2005) points to requirements, such as fees and signatures, that kept fringe indigenous parties from gaining a foothold in national politics. These requirements were one of the driving forces behind several indigenous groups' decision to unify under the label of the Movement towards Socialism (MAS) so that they could pool resources and signatures. Other important institutions include each country's district magnitude (defined as the number of seats available in a given (usually legislative) electoral district and other aspects of the electoral system. Though some point to PR systems with high district magnitudes as favoring minority groups (because fewer votes are needed to win seats in the legislature), Van Cott (2005) argues that indigenous communities can gain representation in the federal legislature in single-member districts if they are the majority in at least some districts. It is the interaction between the geographic dispersion of indigenous communities and electoral institutions that determines whether groups will be able to win (Lublin, 2014; Rice & Van Cott, 2006).

The level of decentralization and the presence of reserved seats are other important institutions. Van Cott (2005) points to decentralization as one way that indigenous movements can gain popularity among voters before running for national office. Local representatives gain political experience that will make them more competitive in national races. Van Cott (2003) references Bolivia's municipal decentralization of 1994 as playing a role in the rise of indigenous parties around this time as they gained more political experience. However, Madrid (2012) notes that MAS did not gain votes from the departments where it controlled municipal governments. So, while decentralization may explain the formation and viability of MAS, it cannot fully explain how MAS was able to become electorally successful.

Another institutional factor that facilitates the viability of indigenous parties is the reservation of seats for indigenous (or other) representatives. So-called reserve seats, which guarantee a very small number of legislative seats for ethnic minorities, have been adopted in Colombia, Venezuela, and Bolivia, although there is a debate over their effectiveness. One benefit of reserved seats is that they can pave the way for indigenous representation by spurring mobilization along ethnic lines (Van Cott, 2005). However, reserved seats could also cause the fractionalization of indigenous movements that compete for a limited number of seats.[3] The presence of reserved seats may also deter indigenous candidates from running under mainstream party labels.

A final institution that facilitates inclusion of underrepresented groups is the existence of quotas for women or minority candidates on panethnic party lists (Bird, 2014). Unlike reserved seats, which mandate inclusion of minority groups in the legislature, candidate quotas aim to increase the number of minority candidates competing for political office. Quotas stipulate that parties must include a certain number of individuals from an underrepresented group on their lists. This institution can therefore be subject to manipulation by party leaders seeking to maintain the status quo: If the rules are not clearly specified, parties can comply with quotas by including minority candidates at the bottom of their lists where they are unlikely to win office. Although quotas are commonly used to improve representation of women in Latin America, they are rarely used to facilitate the representation of minority ethnic groups; there are some exceptions, however (Bird, 2014).[4] For example, Peru requires that parties include minority candidates on their lists for local elections, and Brazil has adopted quotas for its university system (Htun, 2016).

Indigenous movements that have articulated a national political identity and formed a viable political party must still win enough votes to hold office. At this level, success depends on both the actions of the party itself and the behavior of voters. Existing literature suggests that alliances between indigenous and mainstream parties are one key to success (Alcántara Sáez & Marenghi, 2007; Madrid, 2005, 2012). Doing so may gain indigenous movements local partnerships and additional resources. Relatedly, Madrid (2012) argues that indigenous candidates are more successful when they appeal to broader electorates beyond their own indigenous communities. Indigenous candidates can highlight issues that span the political spectrum, including poverty alleviation, social programs, and environmental protection. Indigenous parties that spurn radial rhetoric are typically more successful at winning national office. This may also explain why the rise of indigenous parties followed a decline of the political left. By appealing to broader leftist values, indigenous candidates could fill a vacuum in national politics and gain voters of various ethnicities (Alcántara Sáez & Marenghi, 2007; Madrid, 2012; Van Cott, 2003, 2008).[5]

Success ultimately depends on the willingness of individual voters to put indigenous candidates into office. Some point to ethnicity as a reliable heuristic for coethnics to choose candidates that represent their own values (Chandra, 2004; Kelly, 2016). Yet, nonindigenous voters may also cast votes for indigenous parties. For instance, Htun (2016) explains how left-leaning Colombian citizens at times opted to cast their votes for indigenous parties, as these candidates ran on platforms further to the left than many mainstream competitors. In such cases, the urban poor may make natural allies of indigenous communities, both of which want increased social protection. On the other hand, some indigenous communities prefer to remain loyal to mainstream party machines that can reliably provide them with clientelistic benefits. These dynamics might also help to explain why there is only mixed evidence that indigenous candidates are more likely to win votes from poorer districts (Madrid, 2012).

ONGOING RESEARCH AND DATA LIMITATIONS

In spite of the robust literature that has developed around these issues, there are still many unanswered questions. For instance, to our knowledge, there are no data that systematically track the number of representatives in each legislature who identify as members of indigenous communities. Some research instead analyzes the number of legislators who belong to indigenous parties, an easier figure to track. Still, this is an imperfect proxy, given that some indigenous candidates inevitably choose to run under the banner of mainstream parties. Another weakness is that these data are subject to selection bias. Data on national legislators track only those candidates who won national elections; there is very little information on candidates who participated in elections but were defeated. The data, therefore, do not permit us to assess participation of ethnic minorities, and thus we cannot study the factors that determine their competitiveness.

One reason that such data do not yet exist is the difficulty in categorizing individuals by their ethnic identity using archival sources. Recent efforts have begun to survey citizens for their self-identification as members of minority groups (Telles, 2014). However, it is difficult to attain data on the self-identification of political leaders, and even more so to attain data on the historical identification of leaders and candidates. Archival sources might provide names or even photos of officials, but these indicators are of little use for most Latin American countries that are predominantly *mestizo*. Because ethnic identification is so fluid across the continent, self-identification may have as much to do with personal experiences as family history, language, and skin tone.

Another difficulty in using archival materials is that candidates and leaders may have had strategic reasons to either advertise or conceal their connections to indigenous communities. Facing racist electorates, some candidates may have had to distance themselves from their indigenous roots in order to have a better chance at winning office or to appeal to broader swaths of the electorate. On the other side of the issue, we know that nonindigenous candidates at times try to appeal to indigenous communities by speaking in indigenous languages or by referencing indigenous culture and customs. Such strategic behavior is unlikely to be a good indicator of actual representation.

In our own research, we have used several strategies to bypass these empirical challenges. We have begun to collect data on ethnic identification of presidential candidates in Colombia and Bolivia dating back to the mid-20th century. We have consulted newspapers, journals, and encyclopedias of elections to find any references that indicate whether candidates self-identify with indigenous communities or speak an indigenous language. We began this work by choosing two cases that represent opposite ends of the spectrum of ethnic diversity in Latin America. The most recent census data indicate that Colombia is 3.3% indigenous, whereas Bolivia is 41% indigenous (World Bank, 2018), but which both have reserved seats for indigenous legislators, indicating some level of mobilization along ethnic lines.

Although we were initially interested in determining where candidates for reserved seats actually won votes, we were quickly overwhelmed with the difficulty of establishing the ethnic identity of all legislative candidates. We were also disappointed with the lack of data on the geographic dispersal of votes cast for reserved seats. Because we were interested in tracking variation in voting patterns over time, we decided to collect data on the self-identification of presidential and vice presidential candidates, with the hope that historical sources would be more available for these high-profile candidates. Our initial findings suggest that there were more indigenous candidates in both countries than we had initially assumed, further highlighting the importance of obtaining comparable data across countries rather than relying on impressionistic accounts.

However, the elite-level data provided only one piece of the puzzle. In order to link the ethnic identification of candidates to voting patterns, we also had to gather data on the ethnic identification of citizens at the subnational level. Again, this process proved to be more of a challenge than we anticipated. Although most Latin American censuses have tracked ethnic identification over time, their methods of ascertaining individuals' ethnicities are inconsistent. The Colombian case presents one example.

Colombia first began tracking ethnic identification of citizens in 1912, when citizens could identify with broad-based racial categories (Romero, 2008). In 1918, the process changed, such that the census administrators indicated the ethnic identity of the people they were interviewing. By 1938, citizens could specify their maternal tongue, but administrators used the location of respondents (whether in urban or rural communities) to identify their membership in indigenous groups. Later, censuses in 1973, 1985, and 1993 asked respondents whether they self-identified as belonging to a specific racial community and whether they spoke an indigenous language. Finally, in 2005, the census asked respondents whether, in accordance with their culture, *pueblo*, or physical characteristics, they identified with a particular ethnic group and whether they spoke the language of this *pueblo*. Though certainly similar, the variation in questions over time has prevented political scientists from tracking where indigenous populations live and how they vote with reliable consistency. This may explain why the percentage of each country that is identified as indigenous tends to fluctuate over time, not simply because of population changes but also because of changes in census questions and procedures.

In spite of these limitations, we hope to further analyze the correlation between ethnic identification and votes for minority candidates over time with statistical analysis of Bolivia and Colombia at the district level from 1950 to the most recent elections. We are working to identify whether there is a positive correlation between the percentage of citizens in each district who identify as indigenous and the vote share for candidates who also identify as indigenous. Is it the case that districts with higher populations of indigenous civilians are likely to have higher vote shares for minority candidates? We also want to know how this relationship relates to party politics. We have two theories for the potential relationship between these variables. It could be the case that ethnicity is highly correlated with left-leaning party politics, and that it is impossible to distinguish between these two identities. It could also be the case that districts with high concentrations of indigenous voters prefer to vote for mainstream parties, which are better at guaranteeing patronage, than minority parties that typically run on ideological grounds. These theories may also interact with economic conditions and levels of poverty at the district level. Do variations in economic conditions influence the propensity of voters (indigenous-identifying or otherwise) who vote for minority candidates? The next step in our research agenda is to finish gathering data and conduct exploratory analysis to see how these important variables interact over time. Though seemingly simple, such correlational foundations are still lacking in the literature on patterns of indigenous representation and voting in Latin America.

DIRECTIONS FOR FUTURE RESEARCH

We discuss these challenges not to suggest that research on ethnic voting is impossible, but to highlight some of the challenges that political scientists face in their attempts to gain leverage on the causal relationships among institutions, structural characteristics, voting, and representation. In our own work, we utilize statistics on elections, plus censuses, archives, and other sources that review elections, to paint with broad strokes the trends in representation. Other work zooms in to look at specific communities, years, or groups of legislators to get fine-grained data on ethnic interests and identification. New survey research has also attempted to use a standardized metric (skin tone) to assess ethnicity across countries throughout the region (Telles & the Project on Ethnicity and Race in Latin America [PERLA], 2014). In the end, these difficulties point to opportunities for new research and data collection, with which we will hopefully develop a clearer picture of minority representation in Latin America over time.

Our focus on the representation of diverse groups in Latin America also speaks to broader research agendas on diversity across disciplines, tying together all issues central to this book: people, processes, policies, and paradigms. The policies and processes that we examine in our study of representation of indigenous groups in Latin America have parallels not only for representation in other world legislatures but also in organizations, including universities and corporations. Because we share concerns with other fields, such as history, anthropology, psychology, sociology, and organizational theory, we can all gain by sharing insights about factors that limit minority representation.[6] Moreover, our disciplinary (or intradisciplinary) diversity, which encompasses distinctive quantitative and qualitative research methodologies, should be a strength in addressing crucial questions related to representation of diverse groups.

NOTES

1. Certainly, indigenous citizens need not necessarily identify with left wing politics. In practice, however, indigenous parties have focused on policies to increase social equality, provide social programs, and protect the environment that more align with leftist values.
2. Van Cott (2005) defines a movement as politically viable when it is legally registered as a political party and has attained a sufficient level of consolidation and voter support to be competitive.
3. See, for instance, Htun's (2016) description of the Colombian case, in which 14 indigenous parties competed for two reserved seats in 2014.
4. It should be noted that in Latin America, quotas are more often used to increase the representation of women in mainstream parties (Htun, 2016). For various reasons, the mobilization and inclusion process discussed here is quite different from the experience of women who seek better representation. Although space constraints prevent a more extensive discussion of these dynamics, we recommend that interested readers see Htun (2004).

5. See Przeworski and Sprague (1986) for an explanation of why it is difficult to hold together a purely socialist (class-based) coalition.
6. Lucero (2008), Van Cott (2005), and Yashar (1999), for instance, are all excellent examples of integration of research agendas in anthropology and political science.

REFERENCES

Alcántara Sáez, M., & Marenghi, P. (2007). Los partidos étnicos de América del Sur: Algunos factores que explican su rendimiento electoral [The ethnic parties of South America: Some factors that explain their electoral performance]. In S. Martí & I. Puig (Eds.), *Pueblos indígenas y política en América Latina [Indigenous communities and politics in Latin America]* (pp. 57–102). Barcelona, Spain: Fundació CIDOB.

Auyero, J. (2000). The logic of clientelism in Argentina: An ethnographic account. *Latin American Research Review, 35*(3), 55–81.

Bird, K. (2014). Ethnic quotas and ethnic representation worldwide. *International Political Science Review, 35*(1), 12–26.

Birnir, J. K. (2007). *Ethnicity and electoral politics.* Cambridge, England: Cambridge University Press.

Burke, E. (1906). *Speech to the electors of Bristol in the works of the right honorable Edmund Burke 1774* (Vol. 2). New York, NY: Oxford University Press.

Cabrero, F., Pop, A., Morales, Z., Chuji, M., & Mamani, C. (2013). *Ciudadanía intercultural: Aportes desde la participación política de los pueblos indígenas en Latinoamérica [Intercultural citizenship: Contributions from the political participation of indigenous communities in Latin America].* New York, NY: United Nations Development Programme.

Chandra, K. (2004). *Why ethnic parties succeed: Patronage and ethnic headcounts in India.* Cambridge, England: Cambridge University Press.

Chhibber, P., & Kollman, K. (2004). *The formation of national party systems: Federalism and party competition in Canada, Great Britain, India, and the United States.* Princeton, NJ: Princeton University Press.

Comisión Económica para América Latina y el Caribe. (2014). *Los pueblos indígenas en América Latina: Avances en el último decenio y retos pendientes para la garantía de sus derechos [The indigenous communities of Latin America: Advances in the last decade and pending challenges for the guarantee of their rights].* Santiago, Chile: United Nations.

Corstange, D. (2018). Clientelism in competitive and uncompetitive elections. *Comparative Political Studies, 51*(1), 76–104.

Downs, A. (1957). *An economic theory of democracy.* New York, NY: Harper and Row.

Duverger, M. (1954). *Political parties, their organization and activity in the modern state.* New York, NY: Wiley.

Healy, K. (1987). *Caciques y patrones: Una Experiencia de Desarrollo Rural en el Sud de Bolivia [Chiefs and patterns: An experience of rural development in southern Bolivia].* Cochabamba, Bolivia: Center for the Study of Economic and Social Reality.

Horowitz, D. L. (1985). *Ethnic groups in conflict.* Berkeley, CA: University of California Press.

Horowitz, D. L. (1991). *A democratic South Africa? Constitutional engineering in a divided society.* Berkeley, CA: University of California Press.

Horowitz, D. L. (1993). Democracy in divided societies. *Journal of Democracy, 4*(4), 18–38.

Horowitz, D. L. (2004). The alternative vote and interethnic moderation: A reply to Fraenkel and Grofman. *Public Choice, 121*(3–4), 507–516.

Htun, M. (2004). Is gender like ethnicity? The political representation of identity groups. *Perspectives on Politics, 2*(3), 439–458.

Htun, M. (2016). *Inclusion without representation in Latin America: Gender quotas and ethnic reservations.* Cambridge, England: Cambridge University Press.

Jackson, J. E., & Warren, K. B. (2005). Indigenous movements in Latin America, 1992–2004: Controversies, ironies, new directions. *Annual Review of Anthropology, 34,* 549–573.

Kelly, S. G. W. (2016). *Ethnic voting in the Andes: How ethnicity and ethnic attitudes shape voters' presidential vote choice* (Unpublished doctoral dissertation). University College London, London, England.

Kitschelt, H., & Altamirano, M. (2015). Clientelism in Latin America: Effort and effectiveness. In R. E. Carlin, M. M. Singer, & E. J. Zechmeister (Eds.), *The Latin American voter: Pursuing representation and accountability in challenging contexts* (pp. 246–274). Ann Arbor, MI: University of Michigan Press.

Korovkin, T. (2006). The indigenous movement in the Central Andes: Community, class, and ethnic politics. *Latin American and Caribbean Ethnic Studies, 1*(2), 143–163.

Li, T. M. (2000). Articulating indigenous identity in Indonesia: Resource politics and the tribal slot. *Comparative Studies in Society and History, 42*(1), 149–179.

Lijphart, A. (1969). Consociational democracy. *World Politics, 21*(2), 207–225.

Lijphart, A. (1977). *Democracy in plural societies: A comparative exploration.* New Haven, CT: Yale University Press.

Lijphart, A. (1985). *Power-sharing in South Africa.* Berkeley, CA: Institute of International Studies.

Lijphart, A. (1999). *Patterns of democracy: Government forms and performance in thirty-six countries.* New Haven, CT: Yale University Press.

Lijphart, A. (2004). Constitutional design for divided societies. *Journal of Democracy, 15*(2), 96–109.

Lublin, D. (2014). *Minority rules: Electoral systems, decentralization, and ethnoregional party success.* Oxford, England: Oxford University Press.

Lyne, M. M. (2008). *The voter's dilemma and democratic accountability: Latin America and beyond.* University Park, PA: Penn State University Press.

Lucero, J. A. (2008). *Struggles of voice: The politics of indigenous representation in the Andes.* Pittsburgh, PA: University of Pittsburgh Press.

Madrid, R. L. (2005). Indigenous parties and democracy in Latin America. *Latin American Politics and Society, 47*(4), 161–179.

Madrid, R. L. (2012). *The rise of ethnic politics in Latin America.* New York, NY: Cambridge University Press.

Madrid, R. L. (2016). Obstacles to ethnic parties in Latin America. In S. Levitsky, J. Loxton, B. Van Dyck, & J. I. Domínguez (Eds.), *Challenges of party-building in Latin America* (pp. 305–330). New York, NY: Cambridge University Press.

Mansbridge, J. (1999). Should Blacks represent Blacks and women represent women? A contingent "yes." *Journal of Politics, 61*(3), 628–657.

Pitkin, H. F. (1967). *The concept of representation.* Berkeley: University of California Press.

Przeworski, A., & Sprague, J. (1986). *Paper stones: A history of electoral socialism.* Chicago, IL: University of Chicago Press.

Rice, R., & Van Cott, D. L. (2006). The emergence and performance of indigenous peoples' parties in South America. *Comparative Political Studies, 39*(6), 709–732.

Romero, A. H. (2008). La experiencia de la identificación étnica en los censos de población de Colombia: Los retos para el próximo censo [The experience of ethnic identification in the Colombian population census: Challenges for the next census]. In *Censos 2010 y la Inclusión del Enfoque Étnico: Hacia una Construcción Participativa con Pueblos Indígenas y Afrodescendientes de América Latina [Census 2010 and the inclusion of an ethnic focus: Toward a participatory structure with indigenous communities and afro-descendents in Latin America].* Santiago, Chile: Economic Commission for Latin America and the Caribbean.

Telles, E. E., & The Project on Ethnicity and Race in Latin America. (2014). *Pigmentocracies: Ethnicity, race, and color in Latin America.* Chapel Hill: The University of North Carolina Press.

Van Cott, D. L. (2003). From exclusion to inclusion: Bolivia's 2002 elections. *Journal of Latin American Studies, 35*(4), 751–775.

Van Cott, D. L. (2005). *From movements to parties in Latin America: The evolution of ethnic politics.* New York, NY: Cambridge University Press.

Van Cott, D. L. (2008). *Radical democracy in the Andes.* New York, NY: Cambridge University Press.

Van Cott, D. L. (2010). Indigenous peoples' politics in Latin America. *Annual Review of Political Science, 13*, 385–405.

Yashar, D. J. (1998). Contesting citizenship: Indigenous movements and democracy in Latin America. *Comparative Politics, 31*(1), 23–42.

Yashar, D. J. (1999). Democracy, indigenous movements, and the postliberal challenge in Latin America. *World Politics, 52*(1), 76–104.

World Bank. (2018). *Indigenous Latin American in the twenty-first century: The first decade.* Washington, DC: World Bank.

CHAPTER 12

USING DIVERSITY RESEARCH TO CHANGE SOCIAL POLICY

The Case of Racial Discrimination in Local Government Contracting

Ralph Bangs
University of Pittsburgh

Audrey J. Murrell
University of Pittsburgh

ABSTRACT

This chapter examines the ways in which the practice of critical participatory action research (CPAR) can contribute to policy development providing greater equity for minority business enterprises (MBE). The chapter first provides background on racial discrimination with local government contracting in the city of Pittsburgh. Second, this chapter identifies persistent disparities in the utilization of local MBEs in existing evidence and literature. Third, the chapter examines the use of CPAR in discovering explanatory factors for persistent disparities and creating a social change policy to develop greater equity for MBEs. The chapter also discusses lessons learned and the future development of CPAR in social change policy.

Diversity Across the Disciplines, pages 179–194
Copyright © 2020 by Information Age Publishing
179

The practice of critical participatory action research (CPAR) focuses on the use of university research in collaboration with community-based organizations in order to impact and change social policy (Sandwick et al., 2018). Our chapter provides a specific illustration of CPAR that aims to influence social policy surrounding the utilization and inclusion of minority business enterprises (MBEs) in local government public contracting. Our application of CPAR within the current context is warranted, given that this research approach has a long history of examining social issues related to diversity, such as work on racial differences in urban policing (Stoudt et al., 2019); disparities in severity of disciplinary actions based on race, gender, and sexuality (Chmielewski, Belmonte, Stoudt, & Fine, 2016); disparities in education access and feelings of psychological safety based on sexual orientation (Birkett, Russell, & Corliss, 2014); and minority youth activism (Stoudt et al., 2016).

Scholars in this field argue that the use of CPAR as a research methodology in the areas of diversity and inclusion is critical in order to address issues of power, privilege, hierarchy, and academic biases that can impact the formation, content, and interpretation of academic research (Torre, 2009). A core tenet of CPAR relevant to examining minority contractors is giving traditionally marginalized communities the right to both participate in and shape research and policy formation that impacts their lives (Appadurai, 2006). Thus, we argue that diversity research seeking to inform, impact, and change social policy must attend to the ethical necessity of inclusion among those diverse voices most affected by the outcomes of their research.

Our work focuses on reducing disparities in MBEs in relation to contracting opportunities with public or governmental organizations. This research seeks to not only document the issues of race discrimination that produce disparities in access and utilization of minority contractors, but also to put in place policies and processes that reduce this well-documented negative impact. The use of CPAR as a methodological framework is a good fit for this research because it helps to clarify the complex nature of racial disparities by including the perspective of minority entrepreneurs who are most impacted by persistent discrimination while engaging community partners to ensure impact validity that is essential for meaningful policy change (Massey & Barreras, 2013). It also means that our conclusions and recommendations are structured in order to shape evidence-based policy by utilizing inclusive research methodologies for producing transformative social change (Nelson, 2013).

Our chapter first provides background on the issue of disparities in minority business utilization in public contracting work. We examine existing evidence and documentation on the persistent disparities in utilization of MBEs, as well as some of the factors that have been identified as key variables to account for these disparities. We then outline a series of CPAR projects that examine potential explanatory factors for these persistent disparities, along with community–academic collaborative efforts to bring about policy changes toward greater equity. This work, along with some of the outcomes of these efforts, are reviewed over a 12-year period. Insights and recommendations on how to utilize CPAR to impact social policy in the area of contracting discrimination are discussed, as are areas for future research.

DISPARITIES FOR MINORITY AND WOMEN BUSINESSES IN PUBLIC CONTRACTS

The Minority Business Development Agency (MBDA, 2016), in a review of 100 disparity studies, found that the median share of local and state government contract dollars awarded to MBEs was just 19% of the amount expected based on the availability of MBEs in the relevant product and geographic markets.[1] Disparity studies for local governments provide compelling information on the disparities and underutilization of MBEs of dollars awarded relative to overall MBE availability. For example, recent disparity studies found the following:

- MBEs were substantially underutilized on City of Charlotte contracts (Charlotte Management & Financial Services, 2018).
- MBEs and women business enterprises (WBEs) were substantially underutilized as subcontractors in Atlanta Housing Authority contracts (Holland & Knight LLP, 2017).
- MBEs and WBEs received just 60% of contract dollars awarded by Hennepin County (Minneapolis) compared to their availability for contracts (Keen Independent Research LLC, 2018).
- Statistically significant and substantial underutilization of Caucasian WBEs occurred in all procurement categories in Nashville (Griffin & Strong, P.C., 2018).

The MBDA (2016) report points to additional key factors that have been observed and/or require additional research. Some of these factors include:

- Federal court decisions that determine which types of evidence can be used to support local contracting programs;
- Race-neutral and race-conscious contracting policies in a particular local government;
- MBE and WBE utilization (i.e., shares of dollars awarded [or dollars spent] to businesses through prime contracts and subcontracts);
- MBE and WBE availability (i.e., shares of actual and potential bidders for prime and subcontract opportunities);

- Disparity ratios (i.e., MBE and WBE shares of dollars awarded divided by MBE and WBE shares of available firms, and the statistical significance of the disparities);
- Regression analysis to determine whether race and gender discrimination in business formation, business earnings, and loan denials in the private sector was a cause of the contracting disparities;
- Anecdotal evidence from MBEs, WBEs, and other firms to determine discriminatory and nondiscriminatory barriers to contracting opportunities;
- Evaluation of the effectiveness of a local government's MBE and WBE programs and which policies and practices contribute to success or failure; and
- Recommended race-neutral and race-conscious actions for improving MBE and WBE participation in contracting.

While disparity studies document that a problem exists, clear evidence of discrimination is needed to justify race-conscious social policy change efforts. Thus, what is often missing from these well-publicized disparity studies is clear and convincing evidence that these targeted groups may be justifiably given preferential treatment in order to alter detrimental outcomes (*City of Richmond v. J. A. Croson Co.*, 1989). Additional inferential research is required to provide actual proof of discrimination causing economic harm. For example, reports by credible witnesses can serve as powerful evidence (*Concrete Works of Colorado, Inc. v. City and County of Denver*, 1994).

Discrimination can be by local government, financial institutions, and prime contractors. Local government discrimination can include insufficient information and time for MBEs to bid while favored firms (sometimes referred to as "good ole boy" networks) have advance or timely notice, racial bias in prequalification processes and reviews of bids, and harassment of MBEs after receiving prime contracts. Examples of discrimination by financial firms include unfair denial and terms for loans and lines of credit. Discrimination by prime contractors can involve (a) excluding MBEs for racist or sexist reasons, (b) denying MBEs access to subcontracts by late bid notifications, (c) shopping for lower subcontractor bids by sharing MBE bids with White male firms, (d) including MBEs as subcontractors in prime contract bids but not using them after receiving contracts, (e) expecting higher performance for MBEs than for others, and (f) providing late payment or nonpayment for MBE work.

Nondiscriminatory barriers are factors that could apply to all firms but tend to impact MBEs disproportionately because these firms are smaller, have less experience, and have fewer resources. Local governments create these barriers when they do not break large contracts into smaller sizes, require excessive amounts of bonding and insurance, and have late bid notifications and late payments. Race-neutral policies recommended by local disparity studies usually include unbundling large contracts, providing faster payments, and improving data collection. Race-conscious remedies often include improved goal setting and better monitoring (MBDA, 2016). Despite local government spending of hundreds of thousands of dollars on each disparity study, the high quality of many studies, and the repetition of studies by individual local governments, substantial contracting disparities for MBEs continue to exist (MBDA, 2016). Examining specific examples may help explain why. After spending $500,000 on a disparity study and receiving nine volumes of reports in 2000, the City of Pittsburgh's elected officials rejected the study's findings. City Council members appeared to have enough political power to get the study funded but did not have sufficient engagement by community partners or other key stakeholders to support their efforts and advocate for any major recommendations or policy reforms (USCCR, 2002).

Based on these disparity studies and the resulting lack of transformative and sustainable social change, we undertook our first CPAR effort in 2004–2005 in order to better understand why qualified and available MBEs were not bidding on prime contracts from local governments in Pittsburgh. We conducted our work in collaboration with several community, MBE-serving, and legal partners in order to move beyond documenting the problems and toward advancing corrective social policy changes based on the key principles of the CPAR methodology.

EXAMINING FACTORS UNDERLYING LACK OF BIDDING ON LOCAL GOVERNMENT CONTRACTS

It was unclear from prior studies to what extent lack of bidding was a reason why MBEs were not obtaining local government contracts. In 2004, we decided to study this issue in relation to MBEs in the Pittsburgh area and prime contracts awarded by the City of Pittsburgh and Allegheny County governments (Bangs, Murrell, & Constance-Huggins, 2004). We shaped our action research around three key questions based on our discussions with community-based partners:

- To what extent are certified MBEs qualified for local government prime contracts of $25,000 or more?
- To what extent do certified MBEs submit bids for these prime contracts?
- Why don't certified MBEs submit bids for these prime contracts?

Our methodology was structured to help answer these three key questions in a manner that provided valid evidence of discrimination, collected meaningful first-person experiences from minority business owners who are both qualified and willing to engage in public contracting work, and utilized key community, nonprofit, and legal experts in the shaping of our survey questions, recruitment of participants, and review of research findings. Thus, in our initial study, we did the following:

- identified 131 prime contract opportunities of $25,000 or more at the City of Pittsburgh, Allegheny County, and their authorities from January to April 2004;
- identified 91 certified MBEs in the county in the same industry as one or more of the 131 contract opportunities;
- made 384 matches between 65 contract opportunities and 91 local MBEs;
- provided information on the contract opportunities to the matched MBEs;
- tracked 108 bid openings with at least one bid submitted, 376 bids submitted, and 101 prime contracts awarded; and
- surveyed certified MBEs and 102 (55%) of 184 reported reasons for not bidding.

Our initial findings were that 123 MBEs had completed contracts of $25,000 in the past 3 years and that 91 were in the same procurement category as at least one of the local government prime contract opportunities. Further, MBEs submitted 3.2% (12) of the 376 bids, submitted 3 of the 101 low bids, received 3% of the contracts (3 of 101), and received 2.3% of the dollars awarded.

In addition to capturing data on overall submits and participation levels, we also were advised to collect survey data to provide more details on what experiences and factors were seen by the minority contractors as the most significant barriers that they faced. The 72 minority business owners completing our survey gave these reasons for not submitting bids:

- 55% do not have the right contacts (contracting opportunities "wired" for some firms who get early information);
- 49% have difficulty getting information (e.g., bid information is sent too late or not at all);
- 46% have difficulty getting bonding;
- 44% find it too expensive to prepare bids;
- 38% were unsuccessful in the past;
- 31% perceive the process to be unfair;
- 17% lack technical knowledge to submit bids; and
- 16% were not paid from previous contracts.

Other reasons for not bidding were lack of working capital; slow pay; lack of time and resources; and changing supplier prices, which resulted in losing money on the contract and White firms being awarded more than their low bids. Based on discussions with our research partners, we concluded:

- Lack of MBE bidding is a major reason for lack of MBE prime contracts with local government.
- No support exists for the notion that there are no "qualified" MBE firms for prime contracts.
- Perceived and actual access to bidding information and key social networks are important.
- Determining a pattern of discrimination in prime contract decisions by local government will require increasing bidding by qualified MBEs so there are sufficient cases to study.

After additional discussion of our findings with our community partners, we outlined several policy implications of this study for local government, including the need to do the following:

- Focus on prime contracts in addition to subcontracting participation.
- Focus on the size of prime contracts where there is low MBE participation.
- Focus on increasing bidding by qualified MBEs.
- Monitor MBE shares of prime contract bids and awards and use both measures to determine program effectiveness.
- Ensure that discrimination in prime contracting is not occurring.
- Expand networking so that MBEs have access to important information and contacts.
- Convince and help qualified and "willing" MBEs and WBEs to submit competitive bids.
- Avoid using censuses of all firms or only firms that bid to measure MBE availability because both data sources underestimate MBE availability rates for local government contracts.

We shared our findings, methodology, and recommendations in several meetings with our community partners. Our report was also disseminated publicly to stimulate further dialogue, as well as to honor our commitment to the research participants that our findings would be widely shared. Based on their feedback and input from our interactions with the MBEs, the need to look not only at contract awards but also at change orders was identified. Thus, we undertook a second participatory research study to look more deeply into change orders in one public contracting agency within Pittsburgh. Our use of CPAR identified this as a necessary next step.

PRIME CONTRACTS AND CHANGE ORDERS
AWARDED BY PITTSBURGH PUBLIC SCHOOLS

In the first 9 months of 2005, we gathered data on prime contracts of $10,000 or more awarded by one local government entity, Pittsburgh Public Schools (PPS). The purpose was to determine MBE shares of contracts and contract dollars. We collected this information by examining school board minutes, including committee reports and board resolutions, on the PPS website. We organized the data according to department (e.g., Facilities, General Services) and whether the approvals were for original contracts or for change orders. We identified firms certified as MBEs among the approved firms by checking listings provided by our community partners (Pennsylvania Unified Disadvantaged Business Enterprise Directory, Allegheny County Minority Business Office, and the Pittsburgh Regional Minority Purchasing Council. The resulting list of MBEs with board-approved prime contracts was then cross-checked against the list of PPS contracts awarded, as provided by the PPS Minority/Women Business Department.

We found that PPS awarded initial prime contracts of $47.0 million, of which MBEs received $2.15 million (4.6%). In the first nine months of 2005, PPS also used change orders to increase awards to non-MBEs by $7.3 million and reduce awards to MBEs by $435,000. After accounting for change orders, MBEs received 3.2% of prime contract dollars awarded by PPS.

We also reported that the MBE share of prime contract dollars awarded by PPS in 2005 was much smaller than MBE shares of available firms. A prior disparity study for the City of Pittsburgh (Mason Tillman, 2000) found that MBEs made up 15.9% of available firms in the city for construction prime contracts, 12.7% for architecture and engineering prime contracts, and 16.5% for other professional services prime contracts. Thus, the inclusion of an examination of change orders as identified by our community-based partners yielded important differences in the results of overall MBE underutilization.

We then interviewed contracting officials of PPS and 20 certified MBEs that the PPS Minority/Women Business coordinator wanted to get to know better or have submit more bids. We asked the following questions of the MBEs during our engagement interviews:

- Could you tell us about the strengths of your company and your vision for the company?
- What work have you done in recent years with PPS? In what ways has the experience been positive or negative?
- Are you interested in obtaining prime contracts with PPS? Why or why not?

- In what ways have you tried to find out about prime contract opportunities with PPS? What were the results of these efforts?
- What would help you to increase your bidding for prime contracts with PPS?

Examining the content of these interviews revealed that most of the MBEs had many contracts in the public and private sectors but were doing business outside of the local area because of lack of access to opportunity. Of the MBEs interviewed, eight had received prime contracts from PPS, seven had tried but not received prime contracts from PPS, and five had not tried. Thus, there was evidence of underutilization of minority contractors who were qualified by PPS. Lastly, a majority of the MBEs (19 of the 20) indicated a desire to have prime contracts or more prime contracts with PPS. This provided evidence that there were qualified MBEs who were available and interested in more work with PPS, especially involving prime contracts. This contradicts the feedback we received from PPS during our meetings with community partners in which the lack of availability of qualified, available, and interested MBEs was frequently cited as the reason for the lack of minority participation in contracting work.

In addition, we found that the MBEs were proactively looking for business and used a variety of methods to try to find out about PPS prime contract opportunities, including the following:

- looking for public announcements by PPS, such as in newspapers and on the PPS website/BidNet;
- calling PPS officials;
- asking PPS department staff to place the firm on bidders lists and becoming part of the approved pool of vendors so that announcements are sent directly to the firm;
- meeting with PPS department staff;
- receiving information from the PPS Minority/Women Business Department; and
- receiving announcements through the Pittsburgh Builders Exchange, Black Contractors Association, and Bid Sheet.

Despite these proactive efforts, MBEs reported that they had difficulty obtaining prime contract opportunities. When we discussed these obstacles, MBEs reported a range of issues that could be addressed by changes in policy and process for PPS. The difficulties MBEs encountered included that PPS often does not publicize or list prime contract opportunities, awards noncompetitive or partially competitive contracts, or excludes MBEs from bidders lists so that information on opportunities is not readily available. One MBE shared an experience in which a major PPS department did not list specific staff to contact for opportunities so that only those with inside knowledge or existing relationships with the staff point of contact had access to upcoming contract work. In addition, MBEs frequently commented on lack of responsiveness from some staff (e.g., not returning phone calls from MBEs).

As part of the CPAR methodology, we asked our MBE participants to provide their input and insight into areas for improvement to both policy and the business process. In order for them to submit more bids, MBEs indicated that PPS staff needed to be less opposed to supplier diversity and that bid and proposal specifications needed to be more accurate. They also strongly advised that large contracts needed to be broken into smaller parts and, consistent with our research findings, that excessive change orders needed to be curtailed, especially for work involving small contractors and MBEs.

Based on our work with community partners, collection of data, and inclusive feedback from our MBEs, we then constructed a set of recommendations that would be used to shape policy and process locally in Pittsburgh. Our findings recommended the following changes in PPS policies concerning utilization of MBEs for public contracting work:

Policy Change 1: Notify Firms About Prime Contract Opportunities

- PPS should follow current policy that all prime contracts for products and services of $10,000 or more, except in rare emergency circumstances, will be awarded through an open and competitive process.
- All prime contract opportunities of $10,000 or more should be publicly announced in newspapers according to current policy. For example, current policy for the General Services Department is that these contract opportunities will be announced in two newspapers each week during the 3 weeks prior to the bid or proposal due date. The school board should require that newspaper announcement dates and bid due dates be reported with each contract proposed for board approval, and the board should not approve any contracts where bid announcements did not follow current policy. The work should be rebid when current policy on public notice was not followed.
- PPS should list on one webpage all prime contract opportunities of $10,000 or more.
- All prime contract opportunities of $10,000 or more should be publicly announced on the PPS website at least 3 weeks prior to the bid or proposal due date.

- PPS staff should inform the PPS Minority/Women Business coordinator of all prime contract opportunities well in advance of publicly announcing the opportunities.
- PPS bid lists should contain vendors and firms that have not previously been a PPS vendor but are interested in bidding.
- A complete listing of staff to contact for information on contract opportunities should be available and easily accessible on one webpage.
- If phone calls to staff about contract opportunities are not returned or if staff do not provide needed information, MBEs and WBEs should complain to the appropriate department head and, if not satisfied, to the Minority/Women Business coordinator and the superintendent.

Policy Change 2: Provide and Use Accurate Specifications

- PPS staff should review all bid and proposal specifications for prime contracts to ensure that the specifications are accurate, up-to-date, and complete.
- Contract awarding officials and the PPS Minority/Women Business coordinator should ensure that only the publicly announced bid and proposal specifications are used to review bids and proposals and award contracts.

Policy Change 3: Break Contracts Into Smaller Sizes

- PPS staff should break some large prime contracts into smaller parts, especially when qualified MBEs and WBEs are available to perform these parts, so that PPS does not limit access to primarily large, majority firms.

Policy Change 4: Reduce Change Orders

- PPS should improve project design and management to reduce change orders (which will result in more honest bid prices for prime contracts and will increase access by minority businesses).
- The PPS Minority/Women Business coordinator should review each proposed change order to determine whether minority business participation is satisfactory before change orders are submitted to the board for approval.

Policy Change 5: Oversee Prime Contracting

- The superintendent should make management of contracting processes a high priority since the current system unfairly diminishes access to contract opportunities for many minority firms, reduces competition, raises contract costs, and creates a situation for possible legal action against PPS.
- The school board should receive information on the amount of minority business participation in each proposed contract or change order presented to the board.
- The school board should receive information on whether an open and competitive process has been followed for each proposed prime contract of $10,000 or more, including whether public notice policies were followed.
- The PPS Minority/Women Business coordinator should set quarterly goals for minority business participation as prime contractors, assess PPS performance on these goals, and report goals and performance to the board.

IMPACT OF OUR CRITICAL PARTICIPATORY ACTION RESEARCH ON MINORITY BUSINESS ENTERPRISES

Our research findings, together with advocacy by our legal and political partners, resulted in the adoption of a number of changes in policies by the PPS school board in 2008 (which are still in place today). The leadership directed the creation of a strategic plan supported by administrative rules and procedures to ensure that emerging business enterprises (EBEs) have full access to and equal opportunity to participate in the school district's public contracting. The strategic plan shall contain at a minimum a mission statement, goals, strategies, and performance measures. Thus, PPS created a strategic plan for contracting, which they call a business opportunity plan.[2] This plan included several administrative rules and procedures that were required to be addressed. The changes encompassed two main categories: supporting MBE firm capacity building and strengthening the contracting process. Several specific recommendations were included (but not limited to) in each of these categories.

Supporting Minority Business Enterprise Firm Capacity-Building

- Provide or refer MBEs to appropriate resources as needed for technical and financial assistance.

- Conduct outreach to encourage new MBEs to bid on public contracting.
- Advertise in newspapers to ensure appropriate reach and frequency of potential MBEs per specific public contracting opportunities.
- Encourage mentoring and joint ventures with other majority or minority firms.
- Provide a dedicated resource to manage the promotion, development, and growth of MBEs for the school district's public contracting opportunities.

Strengthening Contracting Processes

- Determine which government certifications reliably identify minority, women, and socially and economically disadvantaged business ownership and control so participation can be accurately counted.
- Design bid packages in such a way to promote rather than discourage participation.
- Accelerate contract awards as well as payments to prime contractors and subcontractors.
- Include language in bid solicitations that clearly sets forth the objective of the policy and includes the school district's antidiscrimination clause.
- Provide quarterly reports of MBE participation that can be readily accessed on the school district's website.
- Maintain a searchable MBE database that can be readily accessed on the school district's website.
- Establish an advisory committee to provide feedback and support of the school district's efforts.
- Ensure that the job descriptions of leadership and managers within the school district include a responsibility for understanding and adhering to the school district's MBE policy.

LESSONS LEARNED FOR CONDUCTING CRITICAL PARTICIPATORY ACTION DIVERSITY RESEARCH

Our work provides a number of insights on how to engage community-based partners in producing meaningful change in social and organizational policy concerning diversity and inclusion. Conducting interdisciplinary research means that the researchers are from different disciplines. To be successful, the researchers need to respect one another's capabilities and ideas and have a good working relationship. This can come from knowing and valuing one another's past work and spending time working together. Conducting diversity research means focusing on historically disadvantaged populations (e.g., minority racial and ethnic groups; women; LGBT community). This requires that researchers have expertise in diversity.

LESSONS FOR HAVING AN IMPACT ON POLICIES

Our studies had an impact on local government policies in the case of PPS because the research produced definitive evidence of racial discrimination and our legal and community partners were able to use the research to pressure PPS to change policies. However, policy change does not mean that all of our recommended policies were adopted or implemented. Further, the recommended policies may not be effective in reducing a diversity problem even if adopted and implemented. A key lesson is that doing a one-off study is never enough. Researchers need to make sure that new and appropriate policies were adopted and implemented and that the policies were effective in improving conditions.

LESSONS FOR RESEARCH ON DIVERSITY IN LOCAL GOVERNMENT CONTRACTING

Disparity studies can provide all of the information that local governments need to set goals for MBE and WBE participation in contracts, determine why goals are not being met, and identify policy changes for achieving these goals. However, these studies are expensive and should be done only if the political will exists to enact recommended policies. Further, disparity studies need to be repeated every 3 to 5 years to find out if policy changes were made and if the policies were effective.

If disparity studies are not done, then local researchers can conduct relatively low-cost studies that gather some important information and have an impact. These studies need to be ongoing to determine whether new policies were adopted and implemented, whether diverse owners of businesses increased their participation in contracting, and what additional policy changes are needed. Our efforts are consistent with previous scholars in this field, who argue that the use of CPAR as a research methodology in the areas of diversity and inclusion is critical in order to address issues of power, privilege, hierarchy, and academic biases that can impact the formation, content, and interpretation of academic research (Torre, 2009). Using CPAR within the area of increasing utilization of MBEs in contracting work has provided additional support for this approach within diversity research. Thus, we provide the current research as another illustration of how this powerful technique can be used to enhance diversity research as a tool for informing as well as shaping social policy in a manner that is inclusive of those diverse voices most impacted by the outcomes of diversity research.

NOTES

1. The MBDA reported only on MBEs, although disparity studies usually cover MBEs and WBEs. The MBDA did not report separately on local government, although 59 of the 100 disparity studies were on local governments (41 were on states). Ninety-six of the 100 studies were released from 2004 to 2016; the other four were from 1994 to 2001.
2. To date, this plan has not been released to the public.

REFERENCES

Appadurai, A. (2006). The right to research. *Globalisation, Societies and Education, 4*(2), 167–177.

Bangs, R., Murrell, A. J., & Constance-Huggins, M. (2004). *Why minority firms are underrepresented in local government prime contracts: Pilot study summary, University of Pittsburgh*. Pittsburgh, PA: University of Pittsburgh Center on Race and Social Problems.

Birkett, M., Russell, S. T., & Corliss, H. L. (2014). Sexual-orientation disparities in school: The mediational role of indicatory of victimization in achievement and truancy because of feeling unsafe. *American Journal of Public Health, 104*(6), 1124–1128.

Charlotte Management & Financial Services. (2018, February 20). *Disparity study: Phase II update*. Retrieved from https://charlottenc.gov/finance/procurement/cbi/Documents/2017_Disparity%20Study_City%20of%20Charlotte_FINAL.PDF

Chmielewski, J. F., Belmonte, K. M., Stoudt, B. G., & Fine, M. (2016). Intersectional inquiries with LGBTQ and gender nonconforming youth of color: Participator research on discipline disparities at the race/sexuality/gender nexus. In R. J. Skiba, K. Mediratta, & M. K. Rausch (Eds.), *Inequality in school discipline: Research and practice to reduce disparities* (pp. 171–188). New York, NY: Palgrave Macmillan.

City of Richmond v. J. A. Croson Co., 488 U.S. 469 (1989)

Concrete Works of Colorado, Inc. v. City and County of Denver, 36 F.3d 1513 (10th Cir. 1994)

Griffin & Strong, P. C. (2018). *Metro Nashville government, TN: 2018 disparity study*. Retrieved from https://media.bizj.us/view/img/11048965/metro-nashville-disparity-study-findings-and-recommendations-180917-copy.pdf

Holland & Knight LLP. (2017). *2017 Atlanta Housing Authority disparity study*. Retrieved from https://www.atlantahousing.org/wp-content/uploads/2018/03/atlanta-housing-authority-disparity-study-1.pdf

Keen Independent Research LLC. (2018). *2017 Minnesota joint disparity study: Hennepin County executive summary.* Retrieved from https://mn.gov/admin/assets/KeenIndependentHennepinCountyDisparityStudyExecutiveSummary03122018_tcm36-331964.pdf

Massey, S. G., & Barreras, R. E. (2013). Introducing "impact validity." *Journal of Social Issues, 69*(4), 615–632.

Mason Tillman Associates. (2000). *City of Pittsburgh contracting and procurement study.* Oakland, CA: Authors.

Minority Business Development Agency. (2016). *Contracting barriers and factors affecting minority business enterprises: A review of existing disparity studies.* Retrieved from https://www.mbda.gov/sites/mbda.gov/files/migrated/files-attachments/ContractingBarriers_AReviewofExistingDisparityStudies.pdf

Nelson, G. (2013). Community psychology and transformative policy change in the neo-liberal area. *American Journal of Community Psychology, 52*(3–4), 211–223.

Sandwick, T., Fine, M., Green, A. C., Stoudt, B. G., Torre, M. E., & Patel, L. (2018). Promise and provocation: Humble reflections on critical participatory action research for social policy. *Urban Education, 53*(4), 473–502.

Stoudt, B. G., Cahill, C. X. D., Belmonte, K., Djokovic, S., Lopez, J., . . . Torres, M. E. (2016). Participatory action research as youth activism. In J. Conner & S. M. Rosen (Eds.), *Contemporary youth activism: Advancing social justice in the United States* (pp. 327–346). Santa Barbara, CA: ABC-CLIO.

Stoudt, B. G., Torre, M. E., Bartley, P., Bissell, E., Bracy, F., Caldwell, H., . . . , Yates, J. (2019). Researching at the community–university borderlands: Using public science to study policing in the South Bronx. *Education Policy Analysis Archives, 27*(56). http://dx.doi.org/10.14507/epaa.27.2623

Torre, M. E. (2009). Participatory action research and critical race theory: Fueling spaces for *nos-otras* to research. *Urban Review, 41*(1), 106–120.

U.S. Commission on Civil Rights (UCCR), Pennsylvania Advisory Committee (2002). *Barriers facing minority- and women-owned businesses in Pennsylvania.* Chapter 5. Retrieved from: https://www.usccr.gov/pubs/sac/pa0802/pa0802.pdf

CHAPTER 13

CROSS-DISCIPLINARY EFFECTS OF URBANIZATION IN AFRICA

The Case of Family, Culture, and Health in Ghana

Jennifer L. Petrie-Wyman
University of Pittsburgh

ABSTRACT

As the urban population continues to rise across Africa, family health burdens unique to the urban environment are also increasingly necessitating critical and inclusive policy research. This chapter investigates the effects of urbanization in Ghana through a cross-disciplinary approach. Rather than viewing family, culture, and health in isolation, this chapter explores sociocultural and health effects as an interconnected network. This cross-disciplinary approach to urban development research provides space for the discussion of intervention policies inclusive of local conditions and diverse cultural perspectives. This chapter first analyzes the effects of urbanization on Ghanaian family, culture, and health. Secondly, this chapter examines three cultural

Diversity Across the Disciplines, pages 195–212
Copyright © 2020 by Information Age Publishing

interventions aiming to improve the health outcomes for Ghanaian families and discusses future implications on research, practice, and urban policy-development.

Increased urbanization has impacted the family composition in Ghana. Between 1984 and 2013, Ghana's population doubled, with urban population growth outpacing rural growth (The World Bank, 2015). As of the 2010 census, 50.9% of Ghanaians live in urban areas (Ghana Statistical Service, 2012). While the increased urban population growth has coincided with economic growth, a stable democracy since 1992, poverty reduction, and wider access to education, the urban expansion has also altered the sociocultural and health dynamics of Ghanaian families (Ardayfio-Schandorf, 2006; Epstein et al., 1967; Kpoor, 2015; Wahab, Odunsi, & Ajiboye, 2012). This chapter analyzes the effects of urbanization on Ghanaian family, culture, and health from a cross-disciplinary perspective and examines three cultural interventions aiming to improve health outcomes for Ghanaian families: (a) the Agoro International Symposium on Arts, Health, and Wellness; (b) music and dance in the Ghanaian classroom; and (c) the National Festival of Arts and Culture (NAFAC). This cross-disciplinary interplay among family, culture, and health is critical to understanding development challenges broadly and envisioning sustainable solutions. This chapter supports this book's consideration of diversity research across the disciplines and calls for additional cross-disciplinary research on development across Africa and globally.

The erosion of extended family networks due to urbanization is producing profound sociocultural changes and health challenges in Ghana (Ardayfio-Schandorf, 2006; Kpoor, 2015). Urban Ghanaian children are socialized with less influence of extended kin and traditional culture (Kpoor, 2015). With reduced access to time spent with elders and village community members, urban children are growing up with limited knowledge of their traditional customs, morals, music, dance, and food (Cho, 2010; Dei, 2004; Jukes, Zuilkowski, & Grigorenko, 2018; Kpoor, 2015; Wahab et al., 2012). Urban families are removed from the traditional social and emotional support previously available in the extended family (Kpoor, 2015). At the same time, urban families, especially poor families, confront urban challenges that place strain on family cohesion and health. Increased pollution, inadequate water and sewage systems, diminished access to affordable housing, urban food consumption, and sedentary urban lifestyles negatively impact the health and well-being of urban families in Ghana (The World Bank, 2015). The sociocultural transitions confronting urban families require close attention and more robust cross-disciplinary research.

Rather than examine family, culture, and health in isolation, this chapter investigates culture as an interconnected network affecting social and health outcomes. This cross-disciplinary interplay among family, culture, and health has been undervalued in recent research concerning urbanization and family change in Africa (Ardayfio-Schandorf, 2006; Goody, 1989; Kpoor, 2015; Oheneba-Sakyi & Takyi, 2006; Twumasi, 1983). In examining the urban social structure of Africa in the 1960s, Epstein et al. (1967) called for a cross-disciplinary approach, noting that "urbanization cannot be treated as a uni-dimensional phenomenon: it has demographic, social structural, and cultural aspects, each of which poses separate analytical problems, but which also have to be studied in their inter-relations" (p. 276). Epstein's (1967) early demand for cross-disciplinary analysis of urbanization has not been fully actualized. While current public health interventions throughout Africa analyze health, demographic, and social variables, specific consideration for cultural effects across these variables occurs less (Lall, Henderson, & Venables, 2017; The World Bank, 2015). This chapter contends that more cross-disciplinary discourse is still needed when researching urbanization and social change in Ghana and other postcolonial contexts.

This chapter uses postcolonial theory and sustainable development frameworks to guide analysis of the impact of urbanization. Three public intervention cases—(a) the Agoro International Symposium on Arts, Health, and Wellness; (b) music and dance in the Ghanaian classroom; and (c) the NAFAC—highlight the benefits of leveraging traditional and local cultures to improve family culture and health outcomes. Next steps are also proposed concerning research and public policy aiming to improve family culture and health outcomes in Ghana.

THE CHANGING GHANAIAN FAMILY

Since the acceleration of urbanization began in the 1980s, researchers have documented significant changes occurring in Ghanaian families (Ardayfio-Schandorf, 1996, 2006; Goody, 1989; Kpoor, 2015; Oheneba-Sakyi & Takyi, 2006; Twumasi, 1983). The percentage of households comprised of extended family has declined drastically from 21.7% in 2000 to 11.9% in 2010 (Ghana Statistical Service, 2012; Kpoor, 2015). An extended family consists of close and immediate relatives living together in one household, including children, parents, grandparents, aunts, uncles, and cousins, and can also be made up of an extended group of people related by blood or marriage who consider themselves to be part of a large family ("Extended Family," n.d.). More Ghanaian families are becoming nuclear in structure, comprised of two-parent families, single-headed families, or polygamous families (Kpoor, 2015).

While Ghanaian cities have expanded rapidly in recent times, it is important to acknowledge that urban living is not a new phenomenon in

Ghana. Urban centers existed in Ghana prior to the arrival of Europeans (Davidson, 1998). Kumasi served as the center of the Ashanti kingdom with commercial enterprise, diverse technologies, organized social and political systems, and spiritual centers (Otiso & Owusu, 2008). Kumasi and other coastal cities, such as Cape Coast and Accra, expanded during the colonial and postcolonial periods (Otiso & Owusu, 2008; Yankson & Bertrand, 2012). The growth of urban populations throughout the colonial and postcolonial periods influenced Ghanaian families, transformed religious and cultural values, and altered labor markets (Davidson, 1998; Otiso & Owusu, 2008). While urbanization has occurred in Ghana over many centuries, the recent growth in cities is distinctive due to the rapid pace of population growth occurring amidst high-speed technological innovations and its consequences on extended families.

The decline in extended families is relevant to Ghana's development due to the traditional significance of this structure in families across ethnic groups in Ghana. Ghana is comprised of almost 50 different ethnic groups, each with its own distinct customs and lineage traditions (Younge, 2011). Major ethnic groups include the Akan, making up 47.5% of the population; Mole-Dagbon (16.6%); Ewe (13.9%); Ga-Dangme (7.4%); Gurma (5.7%); Guan (3.7%); Grusi (2.5%); Mande (1.1%); and other (1.4%; Central Intelligence Agency, 2019). While cultural customs and lineage differ across ethnic groups, the significance of extended family relations, including parents, siblings, grandparents, aunts, uncles, cousins, and other important relatives, is a common characteristic (Kpoor, 2015). Although the most populous ethnic group, Akan, follows matrilineal descent, Ghana's third largest ethnic group, Ewe, follows patrilineal descent. Within both matrilineal and patrilineal structures, the extended family holds relevance (Kpoor, 2015; Twumasi, 1983).

In the traditional extended family, relatives live together in communal household compounds. They work together, share in household and community responsibilities, and mutually help in the upbringing of children and caring for family members in need (Ardayfio-Schandorf, 2006). Traditionally, the extended family imparts vital knowledge to children across generations (Ardayfio-Schandorf, 2006; Kpoor, 2015). Cognitive thinking skills, creativity, rituals, and sociocultural values are transferred to children through socialization with an extended family (Badu-Younge, 2002; Twumasi, 1983; Younge, 2011). Community beliefs, responsibilities, and values tend to be instructed through community elders and cultural activities, including music and dance (Badu-Younge, 2002; Younge, 2011).

Twumasi (1983) emphasizes the vital educational role that extended families provide children:

The family (extended family) is a very important social institution to the Ghanaian. It is an indispensable unit for social organisation, and for social reckoning. Functionally it socialises the child, it helps in educating the child. It anchors the child, so to speak, in an insurance system, especially when the individual is faced with risk and uncertainties of life. (p. 4)

Twumasi (1983) further remarks that the nighttime was of particular significance when elders would tell meaningful stories and oral histories to the young, passing on sociocultural values and relevant knowledge across the generations. The urbanization of families has diminished access to this vital intergenerational knowledge.

Previous literature has marginally discussed the cultural implications of diminished intergenerational family relationships due to urbanization (Ardayfio-Schandorf, 2006; Goody, 1989; Kpoor, 2015; Oheneba-Sakyi & Takyi, 2006; Twumasi, 1983). Much of Ghanaian family research and African family research focuses on changes occurring in marriage patterns (rising single female households); labor markets; housing; gender roles in the family; inheritance, such as the intestate law; financial responsibilities to family; elderly care; childbearing; and religious morals (Ardayfio-Schandorf, 1996; Kpoor, 2015; Oheneba-Sakyi & Takyi, 2006). Less attention has been given to the changes in sociocultural behaviors, attitudes, and knowledge as a consequence of reduced time spent with extended family.

THE IMPACT OF URBANIZATION
ON GHANAIAN FAMILIES' CULTURE

The influence of urban population growth on soft factors, including social, cultural, and family health dimensions, are less examined in the literature. The economic, environmental, and public health consequences of rapid urbanization are commonly considered in global surveys and reports (Lall et al., 2017; Otiso & Owusu, 2008; Owusu & Yankson, 2017; The World Bank, 2015). Increased pollution, strain on water and sewage systems, diminished access to housing, worsening traffic congestion, and unregulated constructions are topics frequently researched and reported through governmental agencies and international organizations, with family culture and health given less attention (The World Bank, 2015). These soft factors are often analyzed within academic and disciplinary boundaries. A cross-disciplinary dialogue concerning the influence of urbanization is needed in Ghana and other similar contexts in the developing world.

As extended families have diminished in Ghanaian cities, certain cultural customs are being lost, and new urban and Western traditions are being acquired. Intergenerational knowledge concerning history, culture, nature, and morals has been reduced (Ardayfio-Schandorf, 2006; Kpoor, 2015).

For example, instead of learning traditional performing arts practices from relatives and village community members, children watch Westernized versions of traditional dances on the television. Children also watch and listen to nontraditional popular music and dance trends of Afropop and hiplife (Shipley, 2013a, 2013b). The practice of the performing arts being a vessel for communicating important community knowledge and history to the next generation is being eroded (Petrie, 2015).

The custom of eating fresh traditional food is also diminishing in urban centers due to time and geographic constraints (Laryea, Akoto, Oduro, & Appaw, 2016). Fast food and processed foods are increasingly common in urban households, limiting children's knowledge of traditional cultural cooking practices and contributing to diets that are low in nutritional value (Laryea et al., 2016; Ofori-Asenso, Agyeman, Laar, & Boateng, 2016; Searcey & Richtel, 2017). The traditional pounding of fufu, a mixed cassava and plantain starch, often prepared with the help of extended family, is becoming less feasible to make in the city. Instead, prepackaged instant fufu, where the maker just adds water, is becoming more common.

The urban space also diminishes the family's connection to the natural world. Children spend less time learning morals that teach respect for the natural environment, farming, and animal husbandry. In cities, children are learning less about the origins of their food. The consumer culture of food replaces traditional sociocultural values concerning food, which uphold the value of the environment (Dei, 2004). Consumer values also privilege individuality over communal values, including sharing and respect for others.

The erosion of intergenerational sociocultural connections is compounded by an educational system that marginally instructs cultural education (Dei, 2004; Petrie, 2015). In Petrie's (2015) study, educational administrators, teachers, and students frequently emphasized that students receive inadequate access to cultural performing arts education at the basic, junior high school, and senior high school levels in Ghana. As increased urbanization detaches students from their traditional culture, educators and students indicate a greater need for schools to instruct traditional music and dance (Petrie, 2015). The absence of music and dance in schools results in negative consequences including (a) a public less educated about the music and dance and cultural traditions of Ghana; (b) students entering the university level unprepared; and (c) a lack of world-class musicians in Ghana (Petrie, 2015). Jukes et al. (2018) also document how students' travel experiences to cities decreases their degree of social responsibility in West Africa.

The urban digital world is also reshaping the socialization process of Ghanaian families. Children gain instant access to media displaying urban, American, and other global cultures. Mobile technology is widening children's exposure to the popular music styles of Afropop and hiplife, reducing their engagement with traditional culture (Cho, 2010; Shipley, 2013a, 2013b). Although cultural change is an unavoidable force of globalization, the erosion of traditional culture from a child's socialization is not inevitable. Rather than harnessing digital, global, and popular trends as an interactive engagement with traditional culture, digital, global, and popular culture is expanding with limited connection to traditional cultural roots in Ghana (Petrie, 2015, 2018).

THE IMPACT OF URBANIZATION
ON GHANAIAN FAMILIES' HEALTH

Urbanization and the reduction of extended families are contributing to negative health outcomes for urban Ghanaian families. Sedentary careers and increased transportation via cars, trotros (a shared minibus taxi), and public buses have limited the time families spend walking and being physically active in their urban communities (Laryea et al., 2016). Traditional music and dance practice have diminished in urban environments, further reducing families' physical activity. Cheap food imports and fast food are becoming more common and are contributing to unhealthy food consumption, where more foods with less nutritional value are consumed (Searcey & Richtel, 2017). The compounding factors of poor nutritional diets and reduced physical activity are contributing to increased rates of obesity, cardiovascular disease, and other chronic disease (Agyei-Mensah & De-Graft Aikins, 2010).

The increased rates of chronic disease are particularly problematic for Ghana because the country is already confronted with high rates of infectious disease (Agyei-Mensah & De-Graft Aikins, 2010). The co-occurrence of chronic disease with infectious disease is creating a double disease burden in Ghana's urban centers, contributing to increased rates of morbidity and mortality (Agyei-Mensah & De-Graft Aikins, 2010). The increased rates of noncommunicable diseases are made worse by the fact that Ghana's healthcare system is underprepared to treat these conditions (Komla Kushitor & Boatemaa, 2018). In a survey of 220 health facilities in Ghana, Komla Kushitor and Boatemma (2018) documented that 78% and 87% of the health facilities had two essential malaria drugs on hand, while less than 35% of the facilities had necessary drugs for diabetes and hypertension. The double disease burden is a growing concern in developing countries, confronting both an increase in fast and processed foods and a decrease in spaces available for physical activity (Searcey & Richtel, 2017).

Indicators of risk for double disease are showing up in children in Ghana. According to the Active Healthy Kids Report Card, a global assessment of child and adolescent physical activity levels, Ghana received a failing grade of D in 2014 and F in 2016 (Ocansey et al., 2016). The decrease in score indicates that low levels of physical activity are only worsening in Ghana. This is particularly worrisome because limited childhood physical activity can also negatively impact cognitive, emotional, and educational outcomes, as well as the long-term physical health of adults (Reilly, 2015). According to a pilot study, female senior high school students were more likely to be obese and engage less frequently in high levels of physical activity than male students (Nyawornota, Aryeetey, Bosomprah, & Aikins, 2013). Ghanaian women also conceived of physical activity differently for men and women, indicating a need to further study the gender dynamic of physical activity interventions in Ghana (Tuakli-Wosornu, Rowan, & Gittelsohn, 2014). These studies indicate a need to develop interventions aimed at improving the physical activity level of youth in Ghana, with attention paid to the role of gender.

In 2011, the First Global Ministerial Conference on Healthy Lifestyles and Noncommunicable Disease Control stressed the growing concern of the double disease burden in the developing world, but there has been limited large-scale and multisector policy implementation addressing these challenges ("UN-Backed Conference Adopts Declaration," 2011). Several articles have considered Western solutions to the double disease burden, including increased access to health resources, nutritional education, and an increase in Westernized physical education programs (Nyawornota et al., 2013; Ocansey et al., 2016). One article suggests strengthening local community engagement to find effective long-term solutions to the chronic disease burden confronting Africa (de-Graft Aikins et al., 2010). Although these current interventions are important first steps, this paper suggests that local cultural solutions already exist in Ghana that could help to reduce the double disease burden even more. Many of these local solutions are also inexpensive, making their implementation sustainable. A revitalization of traditional cultural practices could help to alleviate some of the urban health problems. However, combating negative health outcomes through local cultural practices has received limited academic and public policy consideration.

THE NEED FOR TRADITIONAL LOCAL SOLUTIONS TO IMPROVE GHANAIAN FAMILY CULTURE AND HEALTH

Applying traditional and local solutions to improve urban Ghanaian family culture and health is rooted in postcolonial and sustainable development theory. Postcolonial theory critically examines the consequences of colonization on cultural, economic, educational, and sociopolitical systems (Wa Thiong'o, 1986; Young, 1990). Postcolonial theorists support incorporating indigenous cultural knowledge into development solutions, such as education and community partnerships (Dei, 2004; Freire, 2005). Rather than looking to Western power structures, postcolonial theorists posit attention to indigenous and integrated solutions that respect the specific needs of the local community (Wa Thiong'o, 1986; Young, 1990). In line with postcolonial theory, this study seeks to give voice to the "Other," the colonized, by dismantling the power of the "Subject," the colonizer (Young, 1990).

In the past decade, sustainable development has become a guiding development assistance model for nonprofits and international organizations in Africa. There has been a deep acknowledgement in the international development and business communities that solutions to Africa's development and public health problems must engage a long-term and locally conscious agenda. According to the United Nation's 2030 Agenda for Sustainable Development,

> Sustainable development has been defined as development that meets the needs of the present without compromising the ability of future generations to meet their own needs. Sustainable development calls for concerted efforts towards building an inclusive, sustainable and resilient future for people and planet. (The United Nations, 2019)

The roots of sustainable development lie in both the critiques of Western progress and indigenous cultural values and customs respecting nature and community consensus (Du Pisani, 2006). The green movement of the 1960s, encouraged by Rachel Carson's (1962) *Silent Spring* and other environmental critiques, brought the need for sustainability to public attention (Du Pisani, 2006). Kenyan Wangari Maathai (2004) and Nigerian Ken Saro-Wiwa (1992) advocated that environmental sustainability can foster the political rights of African women and ethnic minorities (Okome, 1999). Sustainable development is now driving locally engaged development projects throughout Africa. Drawing from sustainable development with postcolonial theory, the next three intervention cases describe the ways indigenous culture can create solutions for challenges confronted by urbanization in Ghana.

CASE 1: THE AGORO INTERNATIONAL SYMPOSIUM ON ARTS, HEALTH, AND WELLNESS

The Agoro International Symposium on Arts, Health, and Wellness is an example of public discourse concerning leveraging cultural and arts resources to improve health outcomes. The symposium engaged cross-disciplinary research, practice, and performance to impact public awareness regarding family culture and health ("Ohio University Will Join Agoro," 2018).

In June 2018, the Agoro International Symposium on Arts, Health, and Wellness, titled the Transformative Nature of the Arts, premiered at the National Theatre of Ghana in Accra, Ghana. The symposium was organized by Paschal Younge and Zelma Badu-Younge, in collaboration with Azaguno, Ohio University, and the National Theatre of Ghana, which had support from Ghana's Ministry of Tourism, Arts and Culture; Ministry of Health; Ministry of Education; Ministry of Youth and Sports; and Ministry of Gender, Child and Social Protection ("Performing Africa," n.d.).[1] In celebration of the National Theatre of Ghana's 25th anniversary, this international symposium brought together practitioners, academics, and educators across the disciplines for a 3-day dialogue concerning the impact of the arts on health and wellness in Ghana, Africa, and other postcolonial contexts (Agoro: National Theatre of Ghana, n.d.).

This symposium was the first of its kind in Ghana and marked an influential public discussion on the contributions the arts provide to health and wellness in individuals, families, and communities in Ghana. In order to improve health and well-being outcomes for Ghanaian families, this conference proposed that the arts, including traditional, popular, and global forms, must be utilized to create broader positive outcomes ("Performing Africa," n.d.).

The Agoro International Symposium on Arts, Health, and Wellness organized paper presentations, panel discussions, workshops, demonstrations, and performances to build community and institutional knowledge across the disciplines concerning the effect of the arts on health and wellness. Presentations covered the following topics: contributions of the arts to health and wellness; the role of sport in a healthy society; whole-person wellness and the transformation of health and health care; celebrating national and personal wellness; music, dance, and drama therapy; the role of arts in community health; storytelling and speech; the arts in traditional herbal and healing practices; and taking care of the artist. Ghanaian and international participants provided deep discourse on improving health and wellness through attention to local cultures ("Performing Africa," n.d.). Participants also participated in workshops where they practiced dance, recuperative stretching, injury care, and physical exercises for healthy living. Through lectures and experiential practice, participants learned how to better incorporate physical activity into their lives, with specific attention paid to the indigenous practices available.

The symposium also actively celebrated and promoted the cultural and creative arts through its headline artistic production, *Agoro*, with Paschal Younge (composer), Zelma Badu-Younge (choreographer), Mawuli Semevo (director of drama), Isaac Annor (conductor), and Nii Tete Yartey (artistic director; Owoo, 2018). The production received outstanding reviews highlighting the cross-cultural exploration of traditional and contemporary arts and the value of the interdisciplinary nature of the arts in Ghana

(Owoo, 2018). The performance created a wide platform to celebrate and engage the public in dialogues about art, health, and wellness. The conference was an effective first step in expanding research, practice, advocacy, and public policy concerning the role of traditional culture and the arts in improving health and well-being in Ghana and other postcolonial contexts (Agoro: National Theatre of Ghana, n.d.).

CASE 2: MUSIC AND DANCE IN THE GHANAIAN CLASSROOM

As traditional avenues to learn music and dance have diminished with rising rates of urbanization, teaching music and dance in schooling can be an effective remedy to instruct children about their traditional cultural outcomes, while also providing children with increased physical activity. In Ghanaian education policy, music and dance are taught in senior high schools through the music elective, which teaches music and dance and emphasizes music to prepare students for the West African Senior School Certificate Examination (West Africa Examination Council, 2013). Music and dance are also taught as non-examinable subjects in creative arts classes at the basic and junior high school levels (Arthur, 2015; Republic of Ghana Ministry of Education, Science, and Sports, 2007). A comparative analysis of performing arts education policies across Africa indicates that Ghana has one of the most progressive performing arts education policies on the continent (Petrie, 2015, 2018).

Although music and dance are included in national education policy in Ghana, policy implementation is limited (Arthur, 2015; Petrie, 2015). Current Ghanaian educational objectives emphasize science, technology, engineering, and math; reading proficiency; and economic development, pushing aside the arts and cultural education (Ghana Statistical Service, Ghana Health Service, & ICF Macro, 2009). Consequently, education about music and dance occupies a narrow portion of the curriculum. Despite these shortcomings, some schools still teach music and dance, providing children with important exposure to their cultural traditions and vital exercise through drumming and dance.

Ghanaian educators suggest expanding teachers and resources to instruct more music and dance classes at all grade levels. Teachers also suggest tapping into local community resources to further develop music and dance education (Petrie, 2015). Ahuma Bosco Ocansey, the director of communications and special projects at the Musicians Union of Ghana, recommended community-based solutions, including using the musical instruments of local community musician groups and recruiting community elders to instruct music and dance classes in schools to carry on intergenerational customs and dialogues (Petrie, 2015).

Expanding access to music and dance in schools is necessary because music and dance have been shown to improve students cultural knowledge, academic achievement, and well-being (Petrie, 2018). As traditional avenues to learn music and dance decline for urban students, music and dance classes allow senior high school students to learn their culture and pass it on to the next generation. A male student at Winneba Senior High School acknowledged the cultural outcomes of music and dance: "Because of the traditional music and things, it has helped me to know about our society and our country" (Petrie, 2015, p. 236). Education about music and dance conveys core cultural values essential to Ghanaians and Africans, including respect for the community and local environment. Music and dance develop critical cultural awareness, as a female student at Aggrey Memorial A.M.E. Zion Senior High School discussed:

> I think that the traditional music and dance should be encouraged because now the youth of today, most of us are losing our morals due to Western music and their dances. So they need to encourage the African music. And just sometimes you don't understand why this is done, so we tend to do things that the White people do because we don't understand. But through music and dances they are able to explain to us the reason why these should be done and not be done the other way around so that we will be able to contain and preserve our culture because it is actually fading away. (Petrie, 2015, p. 236)

According to administrators, teachers, and students, music and dance education provided space for cultural exposure, reflection, and discussion, which is especially relevant for urban students confronting diminished access to their traditional culture (Petrie, 2015).

Music and dance also advance students' success in senior high school (Petrie, 2018). Improved educational outcomes are significant, as higher educational attainment has been linked to higher health outcomes (Reilly, 2015). Music and dance education reportedly fostered learning across subjects, improved discipline and focus, and improved grades (Petrie, 2018). Exposure to music and dance also improves students' well-being by reducing stress, promoting emotional wellness, and improving social engagement with classmates (Petrie, 2018). Music and dance provide an accessible space for women to feel comfortable physically moving in Ghana, which is necessary as girls are physically moving less than boys and hold different perspectives about physical education (Nyawornota et al., 2013). Music and dance in Ghanaian classrooms facilitate a critical educational role in providing access to traditional cultural knowledge and physical activity that are less available in the urban household and social environment (Petrie, 2015).

CASE 3: THE NATIONAL FESTIVAL OF ARTS AND CULTURE

The NAFAC is an educational initiative aimed at promoting community and cultural engagement in Ghanaian schools. The initiative is organized with the assistance of the Ghana Education Service, the National Commission of Culture, and the Ministry of Tourism, Arts and Culture. The NAFAC aims to get students in diverse regions of Ghana involved in learning about culture, dance, drama, and music through an annual school competition and community festival (Petrie, 2015). The festival represents a significant avenue in which students gain exposure to traditional culture, which is especially important for students who lack access to extended family networks and do not have access to music and dance classes in school. According to Freeman A. Aguri, director of cultural education at the Ghana Education Service, the NAFAC involves the whole community to bolster understanding of the vital role that the cultural arts play in Ghana. A new part of the festival called the Traditional Way brings the community together by having students and community members eat traditional foods and learn about traditional cultural practices (Petrie, 2015).

Additionally, the festival has been moved to large outdoor public spaces to enhance the visibility of the cultural activities the festival promotes. The festival often happens in jubilee parks, which are public squares built in Ghana's major cities at the time of the country's independence that are used to host public gatherings and celebrations. The largest jubilee park, Independence Square, also known as Black Star Square, is located in Accra and is used to host Ghana's Independence Day celebrations (Petrie, 2015). The NAFAC used the jubilee parks to give the festival more visibility at a low cost. The large outdoor spaces also provide an excellent opportunity for children and adults to move physically through dance, performance, and cultural games. By increasing involvement of the community in the festival, Aguri hoped to improve the perceptions of parents and community members regarding the value of cultural education for youth and community development:

> We want parents, stakeholders, community leaders, people from all walks of life to come and see what we teach the kids in the classroom and they apply it practically outside, where it is beneficial to those kids and to the communities and to Ghana as a whole. (Petrie, 2015, p. 366)

While the NAFAC appears to be an effective program for community engagement, Aguri indicated that a related challenge was implementation of the program being reliant on decisions made outside of his office; implementation of the festival is ultimately dependent on governmental financial decisions. Additional cultural programs for community engagement that are initiated and financed via local communities are further suggested for sustainable progress.

DISCUSSION AND NEXT STEPS

The three cases described represent initial steps in revitalizing cultural practices for health benefits to Ghanaian families. Engaging children, parents, and community members in dialogue and cultural experiences is a common mission throughout the interventions. As intergenerational cultural ties have declined, greater public awareness and discussion is proposed in the Agoro International Symposium for Arts, Health, and Wellness. Both music and dance classes in schools and the NAFAC aim to reinvigorate cultural education for youth and communities.

Private, public, and community partnerships could also provide additional resources and opportunities for adults to participate in cultural experiences beneficial to their health, including music classes, traditional cooking experiences, and activities supporting cultural family health. State and public policy can also increase budgetary allocations and resources supporting cultural education for children and community members through the arts. The public and private sectors, parents, and communities should reconsider the value of traditional cultural education to family health. The increase in traditional cultural practices will not only contribute to alleviating the double burden of disease but also will also allow Ghanaian families to regain access to traditional cultural activities.

The literature review and current case studies indicate a need for more attention to improving Ghanaian family culture and health. A vital next step for intervention includes greater attention to traditional cultural practices as solutions to declining family culture and health in public discourse, programs, and policy. Annual symposiums and robust research concerning the connections between culture and family health and wellness are recommended. Research and program development should also be attentive to the ways family culture and health vary across gender and socioeconomics. Additionally, academics, professionals, and community groups should expand public advocacy to government officials. These interventions also showcase that there has been limited private sector involvement in leveraging the cultural arts and traditions to improve urban families' health. For example, there is ample room for growth in the private sector related to providing convenient, healthy, and locally sourced food for urban families. This research recommends a need to build community engagement through private and public partnerships to improve cultural and health outcomes.

In order to achieve sustainable development in Ghana, more research is needed to address the sociocultural transitions occurring in Ghanaian urban families. The author recommends expanding interdisciplinary research on family culture and health in Ghana, Africa, and other postcolonial and development contexts. Because the entire continent of Africa is confronting a growing double disease burden, best practices should be shared and discussed. International dialogue concerning the interplay between family culture and health is further proposed.

CONCLUSION

Increasing exposure to cultural experiences for youth and parents provides needed cultural education that has diminished due to urbanization in Ghana. As the double disease burden continues to rise in urban Ghana and Africa, critical and creative interventions using family culture to improve health offer potential solutions to reverse negative health trends. This chapter proposes greater attention to this culture and health exchange to promote better health and wellness in urban families in Ghana and other postcolonial contexts. Rather than duplicate conventional Western development interventions to improve health outcomes, the interventions in this chapter highlight the additional benefits of including indigenous and local cultural solutions to improve family health. The cross-disciplinary interplay among family, culture, and health in Ghana illustrates the critical need of this research methodology in development and international studies. The cross-disciplinary connection between cultural and development challenges requires the support of additional cross-disciplinary diversity research projects in developmental organizations, governments, and academia. This book project, *Diversity Across Disciplines*, is a strong initial step in breaking down the disciplinary barriers to permit broader examination of dynamic global social phenomena and developmental challenges.

NOTE

1. Azaguno, directed by Paschal Younge and Zelma Badu-Younge, is a multicultural ensemble focusing on the research, preservation, education, and performance of African music and dance and performing arts traditions of the African diaspora. Visit www.azaguno.com for more information.

REFERENCES

Agoro: National Theatre of Ghana. (n.d.). *Performing Africa*. Retrieved from https://performingafrica.com/

Agyei-Mensah, S., & De-Graft Aikins, A. (2010). Epidemiological transition and the double burden of disease in Accra, Ghana. *Journal of Urban Health, 87*(5), 879–897. https://doi.org/10.1007/s11524-010-9492-y

Ardayfio-Schandorf, E. (Ed.). (1996). *The changing family in Ghana.* Accra, Ghana: Ghana Universities Press.

Ardayfio-Schandorf, E. (2006). The family in Ghana: Past and present perspectives. In Y. Oheneba-Sakyi & B. K. Takyi (Eds.), *African families at the turn of the 21st century* (pp. 129–152). Westport, CT: Praeger.

Arthur, K. K. (2015). The performing arts in Ghanaian education: Junior high school and beyond. *Globus, 3*, 119–132.

Badu-Younge, Z. C. M. (2002). *Ewe culture as expressed in Ghana West Africa through Adzogbo dance ceremony: A foundation for the development of interactive multimedia* (Unpublished doctoral dissertation). McGill University, Montreal, Canada.

Carson, R. (1962). *Silent spring.* New York, NY: Houghton Mifflin.

Central Intelligence Agency. (2019). *Ghana.* Retrieved from https://www.cia.gov/library/publications/the-world-factbook/geos/gh.html

Cho, G. (2010). Hiplife, cultural agency and the youth counter-public in the Ghanaian public sphere. *Journal of Asian and African Studies, 45*(4), 406–423. https://doi.org/10.1177/0021909610373888

Davidson, B. (1998). *West Africa before the colonial era: A history to 1850.* New York, NY: Routledge.

de-Graft Aikins, A., Unwin, N., Agyemang, C., Allotey, P., Campbell, C., & Arhinful, D. (2010). Tackling Africa's chronic disease burden: From the local to the global. *Globalization and Health, 6*(5), 1–7.

Dei, G. J. S. (2004). *Schooling and education in Africa: The case of Ghana.* Trenton, NJ: Africa World Press.

Du Pisani, J. A. (2006). Sustainable development—Historical roots of the concept. *Environmental Sciences, 3*(2), 83–96. https://doi.org/10.1080/15693430600688831

Epstein, A. L., Bruner, E. M., Gutkind, P. C. W., Horowitz, M. M., Little, K. L., McCall, D. F., . . . Schack, W. A. (1967). Urbanization and social change in Africa. *Current Anthropology, 8*(4), 275–295.

Extended Family. (n.d.). In *Merriam-Webster* online dictionary. Retrieved from https://www.merriam-webster.com/dictionary/extendedfamily

Freire, P. (2005). *Pedagogy of the oppressed.* New York, NY: Continuum.

Ghana Statistical Service. (2012). *2010 population and housing census: Summary report of final results.* Retrieved from http://www.statsghana.gov.gh/gssmain/storage/img/marqueeupdater/Census2010_Summary_report_of_final_results.pdf

Ghana Statistical Service, Ghana Health Service, & ICF Macro. (2009). *Ghana demographic and health survey 2008.* Retrieved from http://dhsprogram.com/pubs/pdf/FR221/FR221%5B13Aug2012%5D.pdf

Goody, J. (1989). Futures of the family in rural Africa. *Population and Development Review, 15*, 119–144.

Jukes, M. C. H., Zuilkowski, S. S., & Grigorenko, E. L. (2018). Do schooling and urban residence develop cognitive skills at the expense of social responsibility? A study of adolescents in the Gambia, West Africa. *Journal of Cross-Cultural Psychology, 49*(1), 82–98. https://doi.org/10.1177/0022022117741989

Komla Kushitor, M. K., & Boatemaa, S. (2018). The double burden of disease and the challenge of health access: Evidence from access, bottlenecks, cost and equity facility survey in Ghana. *PLOS ONE, 13*(3), e0194677. https://doi .org/10.1371/journal.pone.0194677

Kpoor, A. (2015). The nuclearization of Ghanaian families. *Current Politics and Economics of Africa, 8*(3), 435–458.

Lall, S. V., Henderson, J. V., & Venables, A. J. (2017). *Africa's cities: Opening doors to the world.* Washington, DC: World Bank.

Laryea, D., Akoto, E. Y., Oduro, I., & Appaw, W. O. (2016). Consumer perception of traditional foods in Ghana: A case-study in Kumasi and Sekondi. *Nutrition & Food Science, 46*(1), 96–107. https://doi.org/10.1108/NFS-05-2015-0051

Maathai, W. (2004). *The Green Belt movement: Sharing the approach and experience.* New York, NY: Lantern Books.

Nyawornota, V. K., Aryeetey, R., Bosomprah, S., & Aikins, M. (2013). An exploratory study of physical activity and over-weight in two senior high schools in the Accra Metropolis. *Ghana Medical Journal, 47*(4), 197–203.

Ocansey, R., Aryeetey, R., Sofo, S., Zazzar, A., Delali, M., Pambo, P., . . . Sarkwa, R. (2016). Results from Ghana's 2016 report card on physical activity for children and youth. *Journal of Physical Activity & Health, 13*(Suppl. 2), S165–S168.

Ofori-Asenso, R., Agyeman, A. A., Laar, A., & Boateng, D. (2016). Overweight and obesity epidemic in Ghana—A systematic review and meta-analysis. *BMC Public Health, 16*, 1239. https://doi.org/10.1186/s12889-016-3901-4

Oheneba-Sakyi, Y., & Takyi, B. K. (Eds.). (2006). *African families at the turn of the 21st century.* Westport, CT: Praeger.

Ohio University Will Join Agoro. (2018, April 23). Retrieved from https://www. ohio.edu/compass/stories/17-18/04/fine-arts-health-sciences-ghana-national-theatre.cfm

Okome, O. (Ed.). (1999). *Before I am hanged: Ken Saro-Wiwa, literature, politics, and dissent.* Trenton, NJ: Africa World Press.

Otiso, K. M., & Owusu, G. (2008). Comparative urbanization in Ghana and Kenya in time and space. *GeoJournal, 71*(2–3), 143–157. https://doi.org/10.1007/s10708-008-9152-x

Owoo, J. (2018, July 6). Brilliant fusion of artistic creativity buzz audience. *ArtsGhana.* Retrieved from http://artsghana.org/brilliant-fusion-of-artistic-creativity -buzz-audience

Owusu, G., & Yankson, P. W. K. (2017). Urbanization in Ghana. In E. Aryeetey & R. Kanbur (Eds.), *The economy of Ghana sixty years after independence* (pp. 207–222). Oxford, England: Oxford University Press.

Performing Africa. (n.d.). Retrieved from https://performingafrica.com/

Petrie, J. L. (2015). *Music and dance education in senior high schools in Ghana: A multiple case study* (Doctoral dissertation). Ohio University, Athens, OH.

Petrie, J. L. (2018). Advancing student success: Assessing the educational outcomes of music and dance education in Ghanaian senior high schools. *Compare: A Journal of Comparative and International Education.* Advance online publication. https://doi.org/10.1080/03057925.2018.1513319

Reilly, J. (2015). The pandemic of low physical activity in children and adolescents. *Aspetar Sports Medicine Journal, 4*, 234–238.

Republic of Ghana Ministry of Education, Science and Sports. (2007). *Teaching syllabus for creative arts: Primary school 1–3*. Retrieved from https://www.google .com/search?client=firefox-b-1-d&q=Republic+of+Ghana+Ministry+of+ Education%2C+Science+and+Sports.+%282007%29.+Teaching+syllabus+for+ creative+arts%3A+Primary+school+1%E2%80%933

Saro-Wiwa, K. (1992). *Genocide in Nigeria: The Ogoni tragedy*. Nigeria: Saros International.

Searcey, D., & Richtel, M. (2017, October 2). Obesity was rising as Ghana embraced fast food. Then came KFC. *The New York Times*. Retrieved from https://www. nytimes.com/2017/10/02/health/ghana-kfc-obesity.html

Shipley, J. W. (2013a). *Living the hiplife: Celebrity and entrepreneurship in Ghanaian popular music*. Durham, NC: Duke University Press.

Shipley, J. W. (2013b). Transnational circulation and digital fatigue in Ghana's Azonto dance craze. *American Ethnologist, 40*(2), 362–381.

Tuakli-Wosornu, Y. A., Rowan, M., & Gittelsohn, J. (2014). Perceptions of physical activity, activity preferences and health among a group of adult women in urban Ghana: A pilot study. *Ghana Medical Journal, 48*(1), 3–13. https://doi .org/10.4314/gmj.v48i1.1

Twumasi, P. A. (1983). *The changing family in the Ghanaian context*. Retrieved from https://unesdoc.unesco.org/ark:/48223/pf0000058928

UN-backed conference adopts declaration on non-communicable diseases. (2011, April 29). *UN News*. Retrieved from https://news.un.org/en/story/2011/ 04/373662-un-backed-conference-adopts-declaration-non-communicable -diseases

United Nations. (2019). *What is sustainable development?* Retrieved from https:// www.un.org/sustainabledevelopment/development-agenda/

Wahab, E. O., Odunsi, S. O., & Ajiboye, O. E. (2012). Causes and consequences of rapid erosion of cultural values in a traditional African society. *Journal of Anthropology, 2012*, e327061. https://doi.org/10.1155/2012/327061

Wa Thiong'o, N. (1986). *Decolonising the mind: The politics of language in African literature*. Nairobi, Kenya: East African Educational.

West Africa Examination Council. (2013). West African Senior School Certificate Examination. Retrieved from http://www.waecgh.org/wassce

The World Bank. (2015). *Rising through cities in Ghana: Ghana urbanization review overview report*. Retrieved from http://www-wds.worldbank.org/external/default/WDSContentServer/WDSP/IB/2015/05/13/090224b082e7 6e98/1_0/Rendered/PDF/Ghana000Rising0view0overview0report.pdf

Yankson, P. W. K., & Bertrand, M. (2012). Challenges of urbanization in Ghana. In E. Ardayfio-Schandorf, P. W. K. Yankson, & M. Bertrand (Eds.), *The mobile city of Accra: Urban families, housing and residential practices* (pp. 25–46). Dakar, Senegal: CODESRIA.

Young, R. (1990). *White mythologies: Writing history and the West*. New York, NY: Routledge.

Younge, P. (2011). *Music and dance traditions of Ghana: History, performance and teaching*. Jefferson, NC: McFarland & Company.

CHAPTER 14

FROM DISRUPTIVE TO FRUGAL INNOVATION

Meeting the Personalized Healthcare Needs of Diverse Patient Populations

Rose E. Constantino
University of Pittsburgh School of Nursing

Margarete L. Zalon
University of Scranton Department of Nursing

ABSTRACT

The purpose of this chapter is to understand how disruptive innovation (DI) and frugal innovation, as a global phenomenon, can be used to promote health and transform health care through new models of delivery systems. The evolution of disruptive innovation theory within the healthcare context is described with attention to the ways disruptive and frugal innovation can meet the needs of diverse patient populations. As global healthcare needs become more complex and diverse, disruptive and frugal innovation can provide a paradigm shift needed to provide healthcare systems that accommodate change, build bridges, foster collaboration and diversity, and improve healthcare delivery and outcomes globally.

Diversity Across the Disciplines, pages 213–223
Copyright © 2020 by Information Age Publishing
213

Disruptive innovation is a global phenomenon that can be harnessed for multidisciplinary diversity research to promote health and transform health care through new models of delivery systems. Our changing world and the increasing demands for improvements in health care across the globe require dramatic strategies that change how we design and deliver health care to achieve quality health outcomes. The emerging issues of diversity within health care—ranging from issues of care to diversity in the workforce to changes in leadership—all point to the need for rapid change and thus set the stage for disruptive innovation (Dotson & Nuru-Jeter, 2012). For example, in the United States, the confluence of an aging population, an increase in chronic disease, and a shortage of healthcare professionals creates a need for innovative models and the application of technology to provide health services. Across the globe, the rise of noncommunicable chronic diseases, associated mental health problems, and the transmission of new diseases will require new ways of thinking and responding to address these challenges and provide access to healthcare solutions. Thus, theories, models, and frameworks for disruptive innovation can provide a valuable perspective for issues related to diversity and the changing landscape within health care.

Health care has evolved differently across the globe, resulting in opportunities for innovation, collaboration, and practice. Disruptive innovation can be thought of as a product, service performance, or process that enables users to shift a paradigm in the way they think, interact with one another, engage with emerging technology, and adopt a worldview (Christensen, Raynor, & McDonald, 2015). Understanding how disruptive innovation can be applied to health care can facilitate substantial improvement in the quality of care as well as access to care, particularly among increasingly diverse patient populations. A brief overview of disruptive innovation illustrates its potential impact in creating a much-needed paradigm change within health care. The evolution of the theory of disruptive innovation is examined, along with examples that highlight the potential of innovation in accelerating change and promoting improvements in healthcare systems. Challenges to innovation are described, as are strategies to accelerate the process using multidisciplinary teams and engagement of communities of interest. Finally, moving from disruptive to frugal innovation is discussed to illustrate the potential for creating dramatic change in healthcare systems and processes that have lasting beneficial impacts on diverse communities.

DISRUPTIVE INNOVATION

Innovation may involve creativity, changes in products, or changes that radically transform ways of doing things. Very often, small, incremental improvements to existing products or services involve some degree of creativity. For example, MP3 players, like the Apple iPod, have largely been replaced with smartphones. Commercial innovation is seen most commonly with new products or substantial improvements in existing products and processes. Innovation that disrupts existing processes, markets, or sectors from the common and ordinary into extraordinary and diverse is disruptive innovation.

Innovation can be also classified with regard to how it impacts change: incremental, breakthrough, disruptive, and game-changing. Incremental innovations are small changes that improve a product or service; breakthrough innovations are those that dramatically advance products or services; disruptive innovations involve a more dramatic paradigmatic change in the way a product is used; and game-changing innovations are when a societal need is met, or an entire industry is displaced. Fostering and harnessing innovation across all types of innovation at each level has the potential to impact changes of the design and delivery of health care in ways that range from the incremental to the game-changing (sometimes referred to radical change).

Healthcare practitioners have a history of developing innovations that have transformed history. For example, Johnson & Johnson released an advertisement highlighting nurses' historical contributions to improvements in health care, including Florence Nightingale's introduction of sanitary practices and a student nurse's use of plastic bags and duct tape to protect against Ebola transmission in Africa. A phenomenon known as the Maker Movement, which is a participatory model for healthcare professionals working with end users of products, has given rise to novel and transformative innovations to address specific healthcare problems (Awori & Lee, 2017). Although this movement has provided creative solutions, it has come under criticism because it is perceived as a vehicle to expand American cultural influence (Turner, 2018). The emerging use of telehealth provides a more substantial or radical innovation to meet the needs of rural populations who have traditionally been left out of access to medical care. Thus, general innovation within health care ranges from the need to address diverse populations to large-scale changes in the process and delivery of healthcare services.

Disruptive innovation takes a distinctly different process and pace than traditional ways of thinking about innovation. The theory of disruptive innovation developed by Christensen et al. (2015) describes how an innovation introduces simplicity, convenience, accessibility, and affordability but ultimately displaces the established competitors, perspectives, or processes. Thus, disruptive innovation does not merely create incremental change in process or services but can also transform or interrupt them. In fact, when disruptive innovation is first introduced, it is often not widely embraced or is viewed as unattractive to the established businesses or processes.

Typically, disruptive innovation gains an initial foothold within an underserved market, less attractive service area, or a previously ignored arena. However, because it fulfills a need, has discovered a gap, or uncovers a new product or service, the innovation spreads further. Eventually, the adoption of this innovation completely changes the way business is done. For example, retail clinics have significantly increased across the United States as a lower-cost model for convenient healthcare services that are outside of the conventional physician offices. However, these clinics also serve to provide access to healthcare services in areas where access to physicians has been historically limited by geographic location or income barriers (Pollack & Armstrong, 2009). New products or ideas within health care are disruptive innovations because they redefine practice, research, education, and business processes by gaining a foothold within previously untapped or ignored markets that gradually displace established behaviors, procedures, and practices, particularly for underserved populations.

Christensen et al.'s (2015) theory of disruptive innovation has evolved over time since its introduction in 1995; initially, it focused on the role of traditional business models. Later, it was modified to the theory of hybrids, which centers on sustaining innovation through the combination of existing and disruptive technologies. Sustaining innovations are those that make improvements that allow a company or organization to continue to be competitive over time. In contrast to traditional or disruptive innovations, hybrid innovations have elements that include sustaining and disrupting features and are characterized by (a) including old and new technology, (b) targeting existing customers, (c) providing the existing service or product, and (d) not significantly reducing cost or expertise (Christensen, Horn, & Staker, 2013). Hybrid and disruptive models of innovation are not necessarily mutually exclusive, but disruptive innovation has the potential to achieve greater impact, which we find is especially the case within health care. In fact, both can coexist and even develop concurrently in ways that can benefit and provide needed change for healthcare systems.

For example, disruptive innovations, particularly those that are focused on technology, will not necessarily replace healthcare providers, but they have the potential to radically transform what healthcare providers do and how they use their time. Disruptive innovations do not always involve a new product or idea, but they can entail an application being different or novel in a way that meets diverse consumer needs. For example, a smartphone application may include a wireless attachment that allows for the completion of a medical-grade electrocardiogram, point-of-care diagnostic testing, or an ultrasound. Miniaturization and reductions in cost make it easier for primary care practices to provide such services at a lower cost, make them more accessible to the general public, and meet the unique needs of underserved or diverse communities. In some cases, these products will become available to emerging consumer segments who will be the end users, changing the way healthcare diagnostic services are delivered and used, especially among different patient populations.

While the concept of disruptive innovation has been typically applied to traditional business endeavors, it has received increased attention within the realms of health care and medical education. As with business, disruptive innovation in these arenas can create turmoil in established institutions and processes. For example, distance education, which had its origins in the correspondence schools of 60 to 70 years ago, has moved to an online environment and has greater flexibility with not only the establishment of formal degree programs but also massive open online courses. Disruptive innovations have also obtained a foothold in healthcare delivery across the globe. For example, smartphones have been used to collect public health data in low-income countries, which has created different processes and ways of collecting healthcare information in these areas (Raza et al., 2017), as well as the need to develop different methods to provide preventive health services among rural and low-income communities (Benski et al., 2017). Examining different instances of how disruptive innovation takes place in health care can outline ways in which we can better serve the needs of diverse communities in terms of both the content and processes involved in healthcare delivery.

DISRUPTIVE INNOVATION AND PERSONALIZED HEALTH TECHNOLOGY

Challenges and opportunities for disruptive innovation include resources, processes, leadership, values, culture, diversity, reduction of costs, and delivery of evidence-based practices (Friedberg et al., 2018). Every person has the potential to be a part of forces that drive a disruptive innovation to the forefront, whether they are a healthcare professional or a recipient of care. Healthcare professions have evolved differently across the globe, resulting in differences in roles and potential opportunities for collaboration. Such is the case for the emergence of personalized health technology and its impact on health literacy within diverse patient populations. Not only is this a disruption in the development of technological innovations, such as wearable devices, and personalized medicine, but it is also reflective of a larger paradigm shift in health care. Moerenhout, Devisch, and Cornelis (2018) indicate that our world is changing from a focus on health care provided in response to a situation to one with a greater focus on preventive health care.

Given that innovation can occur through a change in processes such as delivery models, the development of novel treatments can be targeted to the individual characteristics of patients and the delivery of care for unmet needs. The application of technology in advancing diagnostic and treatment options has made a new level of personalized medicine possible. The use of personalized health technology includes a wide arrange of tools, technologies, and equipment that seek to monitor and provide information to help individuals track and improve their health behaviors and outcomes (Allen & Christie, 2016). Smartwatches, sensors, health applications, and other user-oriented technologies offer a range of different options for individuals to monitor and receive feedback on health status, lifestyle choices, and overall health conditions. These technologies are also linked to the overall need for health literacy, which targets the personal, social, and relational factors that impact an individual's ability to acquire, understand, and apply health-related information in order to improve health outcomes (Batterham, Hawkins, Collins, Buchbinder, & Osborne, 2016). Understanding and increasing health literacy is particularly important for diverse populations, and many argue that this is a critical pathway to reducing health inequities based on income, race, ethnicity, and geographic location (Batterham et al., 2016).

The connection between personalized health technology and improved health literacy is a strong illustration of how disruptive innovation takes place, especially in reducing historical inequities in healthcare outcomes. One of the key issues that is driving the need for innovation is the well-documented finding that the use of technology to improve the impact of health literacy typically focuses only on patient groups that already have access to healthcare services and products. Issues such as educational attainment, rural location, low economic position, and minority status are well-documented barriers to accessing healthcare services as well as new options and technologies (Berkman, Sheridan, Donahue, Halpern, & Crotty, 2011). Improvements in technology may target the improvements in health outcomes. However, if limited access to these new technologies or low health literacy exists, then some populations will be left out of the benefits of these innovative technologies (Chang & Kelly, 2007).

Some of the innovations related to personalized health technologies have produced a range of options for wearable devices that help consumers and healthcare professionals receive a large amount of data on health conditions and outcomes. Research shows that these technologies help to reduce a wide range of risk factors that have demonstrable effects on individual health outcomes and can decrease the healthcare costs for treatable conditions (Allen & Christie, 2016). These devices provide a continuous stream of information so that an individual can be constantly informed about his or her health status, thus creating a subtle shift toward taking responsibility for one's health (Moerenhout et al., 2018). Unfortunately, some of these devices continue to be out of the financial reach of many patient populations, and many lack the technological knowledge to take advantage of their functionality. Consequently, some argue that instead of improving access to health information and outcomes, these innovative personalized technologies are actually exacerbating inequities based on race, culture, and economic status (Groeneveld, Sonnad, Lee, Asch, & Shea, 2006). This means that addressing issues of access, affordability, and literacy across diverse populations is essential, or else the widening disparities in health care will continue despite the availability of these innovative personalized technologies (McAuley, 2014). Ironically, the inverse care law (also known as Hart's Law) states that the benefits of healthcare products and services are always better utilized by those patient segments who have a range of different options and thus need them less (Hart, 1971). The relevance of Hart's Law is echoed in today's world, with persistent inequities in care and access to care among the neediest (Marmot, 2018). Unless different methods of use, distribution, and education are put into place, disruptive innovation in healthcare technologies will continue to only benefit the privileged and economically advantaged (Weiss & Eikemo, 2017). Variations in the use of technology and unequal access to technology influence social inequalities; therefore, it is important to understand how people not only access technology but also how they use it (Weiss et al., 2018).

THE MOVE TOWARD FRUGAL INNOVATION

Achieving global health objectives presents particular challenges because of diversity in approaches to health care. As we have discussed, inadequate use of information and technology; lack of comprehensive workforce development; and inconsistent data access, analysis, use, and management hinder progress in the equitable access to healthcare innovations (Shaikh, Ferland, Hood-Cree, Shaffer, & McNabb, 2015). As advances are being made in the use of technologies in new ways, considerable additional work is needed to address unforeseen issues with their implementation. Disruptive innovation, while necessary and beneficial, can be costly and out of reach for key segments of diverse populations. This is especially true in the increasing marketplace of personalized health technology. Clearly, we have a global problem and a critical need that requires a solution.

Nambisan and Nambisan (2017) draw from research on co-creation and digitalization to focus on the need to educate, evolve, and engage to ensure that innovations benefit all target populations, including communities and individuals with limited resources. Education is seen as a reciprocal process, with healthcare organizations providing knowledge to consumers about an innovation and consumers communicating to healthcare organizations about their use of this innovation. The use of technologies evolves over time, which, in turn, impacts various associated practices and improvements. Consumers need to be engaged in providing ongoing feedback about issues and ideas for potential solutions to those problems (Nambisan & Nambisan, 2017).

However, it has been argued that products, services, and technologies need to be designed, innovated, and distributed in a manner that targets those at the "bottom of the pyramid," the four billion poorest people in the world (Prahalad & Hart, 2002, para. 6). This has led to a new perspective known as "frugal innovation," or producing high-quality products and services that target previously marginalized consumers (Radjou & Prabhu, 2015). The focus is on creating high-quality products with limited resources; these products are effective but limited in complexity so that they are not out of the reach of consumers with low technology skills. There is also an emphasis on producing products that can have a longer use cycle, thus having low replacement costs. Disruptive innovation can be more effective if it is also frugal, taking into account users at the bottom of the traditional economic pyramid. The notion of frugal innovation cannot only impact how personalized health technologies are priced and distributed, but also how overall healthcare services can be more cost effective and scalable. In fact, one medical technology for monitoring patients' vital signs that was developed in Asia outperformed more expensive competitors both inside and outside of the U.S. major market (El-Amrawy & Nounou, 2015). This example illustrates the potential for frugal disruption.

In matters of global health and literacy, the role of frugal innovation in personalized health and other types of technologies is limitless. Examples include digital tools for electronic-based surveillance, online training programs, and applications of information and other communication technologies. However, challenges do arise at the institutional, professional, national, and international levels. At the institutional level, challenges may stem from a lack of resources, time, or staff; leadership turnover; a lack of systemic focus on innovation; and a short-term focus on the operation. At the professional level, challenges may be attributable to costly and time-consuming licensing, accrediting, certification, and continuing education standards for new innovators, along with a lack of reimbursement from insurance companies. At the national level, challenges may be linked to a lack of established policies and uniform standards of practice, as well as a restrictive reimbursement policies. At the international level, differences in healthcare systems and resources impact the adoption of innovation, as do political issues related to product distribution and global regulatory requirements.

Innovation (both disruptive and frugal), especially in health care, requires strong communication and coordination. The continuous nature of learning within healthcare systems requires the capture and dissemination of knowledge from patient encounters, research, and diagnostics. Real-time feedback and data analytics is the new basis for change within the healthcare system, requiring a heightened responsibility from all those involved. For example, Chang and Kelly (2007) issue a call for both provider education and patient health literacy, especially related to cultural competence, to ensure that all types of innovation produce the desired health outcomes across diverse patient segments. They point to the specific impact that nurses have as healthcare providers who assess the critical needs of diverse patients at intake and at discharge. This means that nurses and other first-line health professionals are an essential part of the implementation of any frugal innovation.

Innovation has the potential to accelerate change and improve health globally, but the best way to provide innovation is to include and develop members from a variety of healthcare professions in the innovation process. Those who are impacted by care and those who might use products designed to assist with the delivery of care should be included as partners in innovation development groups. Healthcare leaders need to actively engage in fostering innovation to harness the potential of solutions to real-world problems. Thus, the willingness to accommodate change, build bridges, collaborate, and foster diversity have the potential to create innovations that can disrupt existing paradigms in a manner that improves healthcare outcomes across the diverse spectrum of patient populations both locally and globally.

REFERENCES

Allen, L. N., & Christie, G. P. (2016). The emergence of personalized health technology. *Journal of Medical Internet Research, 18*(5), e99. https://doi.org/10.2196/jmir.5357

Awori, J., & Lee, J. M. (2017). A maker movement for health: A new paradigm for health innovation. *JAMA Pediatrics, 171*(2), 107–108. https://doi.org/10.1001/jamapediatrics.2016.3747

Batterham, R. W., Hawkins, M., Collins, P. A., Buchbinder, R., & Osborne, R. H. (2016). Health literacy: Applying current concepts to improve health services and reduce health inequalities. *Public Health, 132*, 3–12. https://doi.org/10.1016/j.puhe.2016.01.001

Benski, A. C., Stancanelli, G., Scaringella, S., Herinainasolo, J. L., Jinoro, J., Vassilakos, P., . . . Schmidt, N. C. (2017). Usability and feasibility of a mobile health system to provide comprehensive antenatal care in low-income countries: PANDA mHealth pilot study in Madagascar. *Journal of Telemedicine and Telecare, 23*(5), 536–543. https://doi.org/10.1177/1357633X16653540

Berkman, N. D., Sheridan, S. L., Donahue, K. E., Halpern, D. J., & Crotty, K. (2011). Low health literacy and health outcomes: An updated systematic review. *Annals of Internal Medicine, 155*, 97–107. https://doi.org/10.7326/0003-4819-155-2-201107190-00005

Chang, M., & Kelly, A. E. (2007). Patient education: Addressing cultural diversity and health literacy issues. *Urologic Nursing, 27*(5), 411–417.

Christensen, C. M., Horn, M. B., & Staker, H. (2013). *Is K–12 blended learning disruptive? An introduction to the theory of hybrids.* Retrieved from https://files.eric .ed.gov/fulltext/ED566878.pdf

Christensen, C. M., Raynor, M. E., & McDonald, R. (2015, December). What is disruptive innovation? *Harvard Business Review.* Retrieved from https://hbr .org/2015/12/what-is-disruptive-innovation

Dotson, E., & Nuru-Jeter, A. (2012). Setting the stage for a business case for leadership diversity in healthcare: History, research, and leverage. *Journal of Healthcare Management, 57*(1), 35–46.

El-Amrawy, F., & Nounou, M. I. (2015). Are currently available wearable devices for activity tracking and heart rate monitoring accurate, precise, and medically beneficial? *Healthcare Informatics Research, 21*(4), 315–320. http://doi .org/10.4258/hir.2015.21.4.315

Friedberg, R. D., Nakamura, B. J., Winkelspect, C., Tebben, E., Miller, A., & Beidas, R. S. (2018). Disruptive innovations to facilitate better dissemination and delivery of evidence-based practices: Leaping over the tar pit. *Evidence-Based Practice in Child and Adolescent Health, 3*(2), 57–69. https://doi.org/10.1080/23794925.2018.1427009

Groeneveld, P. W., Sonnad, S. S., Lee, A. K., Asch, D. A., & Shea, J. E. (2006). Racial differences in attitudes toward innovative medical technology. *Journal of General Internal Medicine, 21*(6), 559–563.

Hart, J. T. (1971). The inverse care law. *Lancet, 297*(7696), 405–412.

Marmot, M. (2018). An inverse care law for our time. *BMJ, 362*, k3216. https://doi .org/10.1136/bmj.k3216

McAuley, A. (2014). Digital health interventions: Widening access or widening inequalities? *Public Health, 128*(12), 1118–1120. https://doi.org/10.1016/j.puhe .2014.10.008

Moerenhout, T., Devisch, I., & Cornelis, G. C. (2018). E-health beyond technology: Analyzing the paradigm shift that lies beneath. *Medicine, Health Care and Philosophy, 21*(1), 31–41. https://doi.org/10.1007/s11019-017-9780-3

Nambisan, S., & Nambisan, P. (2017). How should organizations promote equitable distribution of benefits from technological innovation in health care? *AMA Journal of Ethics, 19*(11), 1106–1115. https://doi.org/10.1001/journalofethics .2017.19.11.stas1-1711

Pollack, C. E., & Armstrong, K. (2009). The geographic accessibility of retail clinics for underserved populations. *Archives of Internal Medicine, 169*(10), 945–949. https://doi.org/10.1001/archinternmed.2009.69

Prahalad, C. K., & Hart, S. L. (2002, January 10). The fortune at the bottom of the pyramid. *strategy+business.* Retrieved from https://www.strategy-business .com/article/11518?gko=9b3b4

Radjou, N., & Prabhu, J. (2015). *Frugal innovation: How to do more with less.* New York, NY: PublicAffairs.

Raza, A., Raza, I., Drake, T. M., Sadar, A. B., Adil, M., Baluch, F., . . . Harrison, E. M. (2017). The efficiency, accuracy and acceptability of smartphone-delivered data collection in a low-resource setting—A prospective study. *International Journal of Surgery, 44,* 252–254. https://doi.org/10.1016/j.ijsu.2017.06.081

Shaikh, A. T., Ferland, L., Hood-Cree, R., Shaffer, L., & McNabb, S. J. N. (2015). Disruptive innovation can prevent the next pandemic. *Frontiers in Public Health, 3,* 215. https://doi.org/10.3389/fpubh.2015.00215

Turner, F. (2018). Millenarian tinkering: The Puritan roots of the Maker Movement. *Technology and Culture, 59*(Suppl. 4), S160–S182. https://doi.org/10.1353/tech.2018.0153

Weiss, D., & Eikemo, T. A. (2017). Technological innovations and the rise of social inequalities in health. *Scandinavian Journal of Public Health, 45*(7), 714–719. https://doi.org/10.1177/1403494817711371

Weiss, D., Rydland, H. T., Øversveen, E., Jensen, M. R., Solhaug, S., & Krokstad, S. (2018). Innovative technologies and social inequalities in health: A scoping review of the literature. *PLOS ONE, 13*(4), e0195447. https://doi.org/10.1371/journal.pone.0195447

CHAPTER 15

THE INTERSECTION OF DIVERSITY AND BUSINESS ETHICS RESEARCH

Examining the Special Case of Predatory Affinity Fraud

Ray Jones
University of Pittsburgh

Jennifer Petrie-Wyman
University of Pittsburgh

Audrey J. Murrell
University of Pittsburgh

ABSTRACT

One of the most challenging aspects of an attention to diversity is that some of the underlying processes that make an attention to diversity a valuable approach in organizations have the potential to have negative impacts and

Diversity Across the Disciplines, pages 225–243
Copyright © 2020 by Information Age Publishing
All rights of reproduction in any form reserved.

can even be willfully misused for the detriment of organizations and various stakeholder groups. One of the most interesting examples of this is the social psychology of affinity fraud. Our chapter examines the nature of social group phenomenon in relation to affinity fraud and social identity theory. We describe cases of affinity fraud targeting diverse groups, including (a) affinity fraud as in-group favoritism through an at-risk youth sports program, (b) affinity fraud as outgroup derogation through the case of notarios publicos and scams targeting immigrants, and (c) affinity fraud as positive distinctiveness through the religious affiliation and the American pension services scam. We conclude with an ethical business analysis of affinity fraud and the implications for teaching business ethics to prevent unethical business practices including affinity fraud.

The topic of affinity fraud represents the intersection of fraud and diversity research as a critical topic that has been examined by academic scholars and business professionals in recent decades. Perri and Brody (2011) define affinity fraud as "investment scams that prey upon members of identifiable groups, such as racial, religious and ethnic communities, the elderly, professional groups, or other types of identifiable groups (p. 34). Previous work shows that affinity fraud disproportionately targets diverse groups, such as African Americans, Hispanics, and religious minority groups based on community and ethnic connections (Austin, 2004; Federal Trade Commission, 2016; Khasru, 2001). Within the affinity fraud literature, there is an attempt to draw a clear distinction between individual- versus group-level factors in cases of unethical behavior, such as fraud (Treviño, Weaver, & Reynolds, 2006). Examining fraud at these distinct levels of analysis challenges the traditional view of fraud as conceptualized only at the individual level of analysis, which typically focuses primarily on personality attributes, values dimensions, or individual decision-making (Morales, Gendron, & Guénin-Paracini, 2014). However, an alternate line of work looks at group-level factors that influence or predict fraud, with a special emphasis on the impact of social groups, group affiliation, and other group-level processes (Sutherland, Cressey, & Luckenbill, 1992). This expands the notions of fraud and challenges existing models to look beyond traditional individual levels of analyses, which is particularly relevant for the interface between fraud and diversity research (Anand, Dacin, & Murphy, 2015). Thus, our chapter looks at the unique case of affinity fraud as the intersection between diversity and fraud, an unethical social group behavior based on race or ethnicity. We examine several specific cases of affinity fraud as a group-level phenomenon within the context of diversity and provide insights and ideas for effective teaching of business ethics.

EXAMINING FRAUD AS A SOCIAL GROUP PHENOMENON

There is little doubt that fraud poses significant economic, ethical, and leadership challenges for organizations. The accounting profession has focused considerable attention on better understanding the complex issue of fraud. Central to examining fraud as a social phenomenon is the extensive work on the concept of "co-offending." This idea of co-offending shifts our attention in cases of fraud toward a specific group of perpetrators involved in deliberate criminal cooperation or collusion (Free & Murphy, 2015). This moves away from looking at fraud as only an individual-level phenomenon and toward examining the social group processes that may also predict fraud behavior. Research on co-offending points to different risks, vulnerabilities, and agendas compared to individual cases of fraud, yet a paucity of research examines why and how individuals decide to co-offend (Morales et al., 2014).

The notion of co-offending is important in cases of affinity fraud because group cohesion, intergroup dynamics, and social identity processes play key roles that are unique to group fraud. This means shifting away from traditional approaches that seek to identify and prevent the one "bad apple" and moving toward a better understanding of social processes that influence group behavior and co-offending acts (Power, 2012). This is consistent with emerging models that focus on group-level factors, such as organizational identification, to better understand and predict unethical behavior (Umphress, Bingham, & Mitchell, 2010). Free and Murphy (2015) identify three archetypes that outline the social bond or affinity that exists in cases of co-offending: individual-serving functional bonds, organization-serving functional bonds, and affective bonds. Most relevant to the current context are affective bonds, which are a function of deep, familiar friendships and social ties that are defined by strong psychological attachment; thus, the experience of affinity is embedded within affective bonds. Examples of affective bonds include friendship, family, social affiliation, and ethnicity. Research by Free and Murphy showed that affective bonds in actual cases of fraud are different than the other archetypes because group-level affiliation and psychological attachment are central to understanding the decision to co-offend. Factors such as identification, mistrust of outsiders, and group sanctions for potential acts of betrayals means that affective bonds operate in a manner that is very distinct from other fraud archetypes. Thus, we must acknowledge and more extensively examine the unique impact of social group processes, especially in the unique case of affective bonds in co-offending cases of fraud. This is central to cases of affinity fraud, which involves co-offending that is targeted toward social group members with a strong affective or identity bond (Anderson, 2013).

THE UNIQUE CASE OF AFFINITY FRAUD

In affinity fraud, perpetrators frequently use distinct social characteristics to gain ingroup trust (Perri & Brody, 2012). The effects of fraud also vary widely, resulting in heavier consequences for marginalized social groups (Austin, 2004; Federal Trade Commission, 2016; Khasru, 2001). Affinity fraud is the process of exploiting group trust based on shared affiliations or common social characteristics, such as race, religion, ethnicity, age, and professional designation, for the purpose of financial advantage or gain (Perri & Brody, 2012). In affinity fraud, an offender uses identification with a specific targeted group to gain the trust of group members. Because social identity plays a central role, fraudulent or unethical practices can spread quickly due to positive feelings of affinity among individuals.

Some argue that the impact of affinity-based fraud can be more devastating than non-affinity fraud or schemes. For example, one estimate over a 10-year period is that there were more than 300 sizeable affinity fraud schemes with combined losses for investors of more than $23 billion. It is estimated that over half of these were cases of affinity fraud (Perri & Brody, 2012). One of the largest Ponzi scheme offenders in history, Bernie Madoff, relied on his affinity with Jewish clients and wealthy investor circles to scam an estimated $20 billion from clients (Marquet International, 2011). Affinity fraud continues to have detrimental effects on the American consumer, with the Federal Trade Commission indicating that an estimated 10.8% of all U.S. adults are victims of fraud, with many crimes relying on group trust (Anderson, 2013).

The interface between fraud and diversity is clearly evident in cases of co-offending affinity fraud. However, previous work does not address the role that diversity plays in the unique case of affinity fraud. A better understanding of how affinity fraud reflects the negative use of kinship or social identity—that is, how it exploits dimensions of diversity (e.g., race, ethnicity, religion, gender, social class)—is an important contribution to existing research. Looking at the intersection between affinity fraud and affective bonds that are based on dimensions of diversity is important for understanding and, ultimately, preventing this type of predatory unethical behavior in the future.

Thus, we examine several cases of diversity-based affinity fraud targeting marginalized social groups to better understand the processes and impact of co-offending in affinity fraud cases. Researchers indicate that marginalized groups such as African Americans, Hispanics, immigrants, and senior citizens experience more harm from affinity fraud, necessitating more proactive investigation and intervention (Austin, 2004; Federal Trade Commission, 2016). To better understand diversity-based affinity fraud, we describe three specific case examples of affinity fraud and link them to key social identity processes within the literature on diverse groups: (a) ingroup favoritism, (b) outgroup derogation, and (c) positive distinctiveness. We then discuss the potential impact of ethical business leadership as a critical intervening factor that can help address the devastating impact of diversity-based identity affinity fraud. This perspective is based on previous literature that documents the necessity for statutory change, enforcement, consumer education, and individual behavioral change to combat affinity fraud (Austin, 2004; Bosley & Knorr, 2018; Fairfax, 2003; Federal Trade Commission, 2016; Kramer, 2009). We argue that principles of ethical business leadership can serve to influence individual, group, and organizational behavior in such a manner as to help reduce predatory biases, such as identity-based affinity fraud, which negatively affects diverse groups. We conclude by providing implications for future research and practice.

PRINCIPLES OF SOCIAL IDENTITY THEORY

Developed by Tajfel and Turner (1979), social identity theory (SIT) outlines the process and consequences of categorizations of individuals into various social groups. This social categorization significantly influences how individuals evaluate the self and others in terms of either ingroup or outgroup membership. A key motivating factor is the individual's effort to maintain a positive social identity that is reinforced by positive self-esteem and group distinctiveness. These processes drive how group membership is both defined and valued, as well as the nature of intergroup behaviors and interactions within an organizational context (Ashforth & Mael, 1989).

There are a number of psychological principles that underlie SIT in terms of processes and outcomes. Three of these principles are relevant to our discussion of identity-based affinity fraud: ingroup favoritism, outgroup derogation, and positive distinctiveness. These key principles are important because they help to explain how and why individual information processing, judgment, and decision-making systems are often flawed and ineffective in the case of identity-based affinity fraud. Social categorization (the underlying process within SIT) asserts that socially constructed categories, such as race, gender, age, religion, nationality, income, and culture, are powerful structures that shape, direct, and alter perceptions and decision-making far beyond what would otherwise be labeled as normal or rational (Turner, 1999).

First, social identity leads to category accentuation in that people often exaggerate or enhance the similarities of people within their ingroup in positive or beneficial ways. This is often labeled as a preference for characteristics of one's own group or ingroup favoritism. Some argue that rather than a negative perception of nongroup members, ingroup favoritism is an enhancement of positive group-based self-esteem (Hogg & Abrams, 1990). This means that ingroup advancement, worth, and validation function somewhat independently of evaluations or perceptions of other social groups. The need for maintaining a positive sense of ingroup membership is often driven by the permeability of the individual's social category—that is, whether one's category is changeable (e.g., social class) versus permanent (e.g., race). The less permeable the social category, the greater the motivation to engage in favoritism towards one's own group.

Second, when social identity is salient, social comparison processes naturally occur. This means that when outgroups are visible and relevant within the context, people naturally make social comparisons between their own group and other social groups. The notion of the salience of social identity is a key factor in triggering social comparison processes (Oakes, 1987). Salience can be triggered by the presence of other group members or by a threat to identity based on status differences, failures, or negative social group image (Steele, Spencer, & Aronson, 2002). A threat to identity creates a need to regain positive ingroup status, which can often be achieved through devaluing other social groups, a process known as outgroup derogation (Turner, 1975). Since outgroup derogation is purely a social process, the criteria for comparison, evaluation of relative status, and overall outcome of the comparison process is driven by the individual's subjective belief systems and the strength of his or her own social group identification.

Third, when individuals categorize themselves and others into social groups, there are cognitive processes that enhance the differences between social groups in a manner that both defines and maintains their own positive group identity (Brewer & Gardner, 1996). This positive distinctiveness is a social comparison process in which features and dimensions that define one's ingroup are evaluated more positively than those of others within the outgroup (Tajfel & Turner, 1979). In extreme cases, positive distinctiveness can drive intergroup discrimination by establishing, maintaining, and maximizing differences between social groups. Positive distinctiveness is a motivated process that leads to bias in information processing, attributions, and preferential behaviors that favor one's own group. This notion is further developed by Brewer's (1991) optimal distinctiveness theory that describes the need for validation, with similarity to one's own group being driven by the dual need to maintain uniqueness and differentiation from other groups. Preserving these two processes involves biased perceptions of positive ingroup members relative to outgroup members and biased attributions that maintain a balance between uniqueness and social belongingness (Pickett, Bonner, & Coleman, 2002). Behavioral outcomes of positive or optimal distinctiveness include intense ingroup loyalty, assumptions of ingroup trustworthiness, and strong incentives toward cooperation and consensus (Brewer, 2007).

These three key principles of SIT are relevant for helping to explain race-based affinity fraud. Ingroup favoritism, outgroup derogation, and positive distinctiveness can arguably play a role in better understanding how affinity fraud can intensify historic racial barriers that are salient and impermeable within an U.S. context. For example, research on the impact of media in making racial categories salient shows that movies with African American leading actors frequently fail in their appeal to larger, mixed-race audiences (Weaver, 2011). Weaver's research explains the impact of media as a function of the combined effects of identity salience, ingroup bias, outgroup derogation, and the need to maintain positive distinctiveness associated with racial group status. Thus, it makes sense to explore the ways in which affinity fraud are understood as a function of social identity processes that lead to predatory biases and outcomes based on social category, specifically race.

AFFINITY FRAUD AS PREDATORY SOCIAL IDENTITY BIAS

Our discussion attempts to reconceptualize affinity fraud as a function of predatory bias that targets members of identifiable or vulnerable social identity groups, such as those based on race, ethnicity, religion, or social class, as victims of deliberate deception to secure unfair or unlawful financial gain. The perpetrators who commit affinity fraud can be members of the same identity group as the victims, and they can use social identity to engender support and compliance from members of the target group. Perpetrators who are outgroup members can enlist respected or trusted ingroup members as key influencers who convince individuals that the opportunity is legitimate or worthy of advancing identity-relevant interests (Perri & Brody, 2012). For example, perpetrators of affinity fraud often design their investment opportunities to appeal to specific demographic groups through appeals that emphasize shared identity, common heritage, or social connections based on group factors, such as race or religion. Using principles of SIT, we attempt to explain the processes and potential outcomes of affinity-based fraud that targets vulnerable groups based on social affiliations, such as race or social class (Brown, 2017; Pearce, 2013). Identity-based processes may help explain how in the case of affinity fraud, individuals frequently overlook contradictory evidence or their own personal knowledge and interests in favor of biased decision-making based on group affiliation, loyalty, and mistrust of the "other" group (Free & Murphy, 2015). With SIT as our conceptual framework, we can also attempt to counter the assumption that victims of affinity fraud are somehow financially unsophisticated or uneducated to these types of co-offending predatory schemes (Deason, Rajgopal, Waymire, & White, 2015).

Principles of SIT would also suggest that otherwise constructive attributes, such as positive social exchange relationships and organizational identification, can lead individuals to neutralize their moral assessments of unethical actions (Umphress & Bingham, 2011). This is how the perpetrators of affinity fraud explain, justify, or reframe unethical behavior. For example, people who know or share a social group affinity with the perpetrator often claim that their offense is out of character (Free & Murphy, 2015). A 2007 survey of imprisoned white-collar criminals found that many of the convicted offenders indicated that they believe that they should not be in prison and that their behavior was noncriminal or unbiased (Dhami, 2007). Particularly with respect to co-offenders who work in business, they are not likely to consider their conduct as criminal or racially motivated, and they can even view specific fraudulent activities as acceptable and as common practices that are necessary to overcome financial difficulties or to make a profit for the organization (Moohr, 2007). This aspect of ingroup bias may explain why perpetrators or co-offenders and some victims of affinity fraud often engage in rationalizing their actions as part of so-called business practice and often ignore the differential impact or targeting of their actions based on factors such as race, ethnicity, religion, or social class. In addition, co-offenders often either stereotype or deny the existence of a victim, particularly if these co-offenders are a member of an affinity-based organization, as a way of protecting and preserving identity group status (Fairfax, 2003).

CASES OF AFFINITY FRAUD TARGETING DIVERSE GROUPS

Previous work shows that affinity fraud disproportionately targets marginalized groups, such as African Americans, Hispanics, and religious minority groups, based on community and ethnic connections (Austin, 2004; Federal Trade Commission, 2016; Khasru, 2001). African Americans are more likely to be fraud victims (17.3%) compared to Hispanics (13.4%) and non-Hispanic Whites (9%; Anderson, 2013; Federal Trade Commission, 2016). Affinity fraud exacerbates financial obstacles for African Americans and Hispanics, as they already encounter higher rates of fraudulent practices, such as predatory subprime loans, even when controlling for income and risk factors, such as credit score (Fisher, 2009). African Americans and Latinos, including undocumented immigrants, are also less likely to report being a victim of affinity fraud due to the bonds of ingroup trust and a proclivity to distrust law enforcement and government as the outgroup. The reluctance to report affinity fraud frequently hinders investigation, prosecution, and prevention (Austin, 2004; Bosley & Knorr, 2016; Federal Trade Commission, 2016; Perri & Brody, 2011).

Marginalized groups are the targets of predatory investment schemes by those who leverage a common group identity within the community. For example, Cambodian immigrants were targeted based on their shared oppression encountered under the Pol Pot regime and their desire to have a fulfilling, peaceful, and prosperous life in the United States (Perri & Brody, 2011). Unethical individuals frequently commit fraud by tapping into shared religious beliefs. African American Christians, Mormons, and people of Jewish faith have all been targeted based on shared religious and cultural beliefs (Austin, 2004).

On a macro level, affinity fraud renders more harm for marginalized groups than for mainstream White populations. The negative financial and psychological effects of fraud and betrayal, which all victims experience, are compounded by detrimental and stigmatizing effects (Austin, 2004; Fink, 2009). For example, fraud targeting African Americans often erodes trust and hinders community resource development (Austin, 2004). The effects of affinity fraud on senior citizens depletes fixed income resources, leaving seniors feeling vulnerable, isolated, and ashamed when they should be living out their happiest retirement days. The switch from pension funds to defined contribution plans also leaves aging baby boomers more vulnerable than previous generations to fraud targeting the financial assets of seniors (Mears, Reisig, Scaggs, & Holtfreter, 2014).

The high prevalence of fraud among African Americans, Latinos, and Mormons has recently prompted the Federal Trade Commission (2016) to enhance the prevention and recording of affinity-based fraud cases. In addition, analyses from the Federal Trade Commission and academic research called for additional research on fraud across race and ethnic groups (Austin, 2004; Federal Trade Commission, 2016; Marlowe & Atiles, 2005). Thus, it is essential for us to explore key factors that influence predatory biases, such as co-offending affinity fraud targeting diverse social groups. In order to accomplish this, we describe three real cases of affinity fraud and examine how social identity processes operate.

AFFINITY FRAUD AS IN-GROUP FAVORITISM: THE AT-RISK YOUTH SPORTS PROGRAM

James Brown and Darnell Jones targeted African-American athletes in high schools in Aiken, South Carolina (Keating, 2011). These co-offenders gained credibility within communities with a strong sports culture because of their reputation and fame as professional athletes. In addition, they used stories of previous professional players who were either bankrupt or under financial stress after retirement to provide credibility and appeal to their youth sports program. These co-offenders especially targeted young athletes and their families, seeing them as highly trusting and most likely to form a common bond since Brown and Jones came out of disadvantaged communities yet achieved success in the sports arena. Thus, they positioned their company, Summit Management, as a financial services company that targeted African American athletes, mostly in high school and all from low-income areas (Keating, 2011).

Brown and Jones attended high school sporting events while wearing expensive suits and driving Lexus automobiles, and they talked openly about using sports to change their social and economic situations, taking their own families out of economic hardship. Their own financial wealth made these appeals very attractive. As such, the co-offenders in this case singled out high school athletes who came from low-income homes and approached each athlete with expensive athletic shoes, tracksuits, and gifts to family members. After gaining their trust, they then promised to help the athlete through the process of turning professional, signing contracts, and managing finances. They also stayed in contact with each of the athletes and talked with them through the ups and downs of their attempts to play at a high level in professional sports (Keating, 2011). Ingroup favoritism was leveraged by using current clients' families to connect with future athletes and their families so the pipeline of victims was maintained.

All the while, Brown and Jones were using the money from the various professional contracts that they negotiated, as well as the subsequent bonus and contract money that they controlled for the athletes, to fund their expensive lifestyles (Keating, 2011). They charged exorbitant fees to clients and moved funds around, often draining the accounts of their young clients. There were no financial accountability measures in place, and many of their victims described their actions as nothing more than a pyramid scheme, which is an illegal investment scam based on a hierarchical setup. The power of their scheme was based on the strength of young athletes' identification with Brown and Jones as African American athletes from poor backgrounds who became successful. However, the devastating impact of their schemes on these athletes and their families soon became visible. When one victim received notice that his mother's home was in foreclosure, it was explained away by Brown and Jones as simply an accounting error. However, the reality was that her mortgage had not been paid and the money that had been earned playing sports was laundered through bogus credit lines, leaving the athlete and his family bankrupt. When this was reported to the Federal Bureau of Investigation, Brown and Jones went into hiding, and it took several years before they were found, charged, and convicted. Brown and Jones were convicted in federal court on 56 counts of fraud and money laundering but cut a deal and served 21 and 41 months in prison, respectively. However, the damage done to reputations and to financial histories could not be reversed. Most victims received only meager financial payments because the money they entrusted to Brown and Jones was already gone. Jones was ordered to pay a total of $1,817,537.50 in financial restitution at monthly payments of $250—this means that he would pay off all penalties in the year 2609 (Keating, 2011).

AFFINITY FRAUD AS OUTGROUP DEROGATION: NOTARIOS PUBLICOS AND SCAMS TARGETING IMMIGRANTS

Manuel and Lola Alban were co-offenders for immigrant groups; their Baltimore-based company, the Loma International Business Group, Inc., scammed Spanish-speaking immigrants out of $616,000 by playing on their trust, cultural ties, and common language (Federal Trade Commission, 2014). The Albans marketed themselves as notarios publicos, which directly translates to notaries public. In English, a notary public is a state-sanctioned public officer capable of signing legal documents. In Spanish, the phrase means a specially trained legal professional. While the language connotes a legal and ethical service, in reality, those posing as notaries publicos were unlicensed to practice law (Kieler, 2015; Kudialis & Todd, 2018) and posed as attorneys in order to scam clients out of thousands of dollars (Choi, 2014; Kieler, 2015).

Many notarios publicos claim to know how to easily navigate immigration documents and laws because of their common language and culture with clients (Neuhauser, 2017). They market themselves as being a safer alternative to federal, state, and U.S. legal resources (Federal Trade Commission, n.d.). The Albans and other notarios publicos accomplish their fraud by creating a climate where the outgroup (government, law enforcement, and U.S. attorneys) is perceived as threatening to the ingroup (Spanish-speaking immigrants). The Albans as co-offenders preyed on the historic and well-documented mistrust within immigrant communities of the government and especially law enforcement. They took advantage of immigrants' fear of deportations to scam them (Federal Trade Commission, n.d., 2014; Kieler, 2015). John Breyault, vice president of public policy for the National Consumers League, describes the role of fear and outgroup derogation in affinity fraud: "Whether it's fear of deportation, fear of a loved one being detained or in trouble, scammers feed off fear" (Neuhauser, 2017, para. 14). When distrust of "others" is high, affinity fraud is more effective in creating barriers between victims of predatory practices and the very systems and individuals designed to be protective resources.

What is unique about the case of the Loma International Business Group, Inc. is that it was successfully prosecuted by a federal court (Federal Trade Commission, 2014). Most of the time, victims fear wider reprisal or deportation and are reluctant to contact law enforcement or attorneys (Federal Trade Commission, 2016). Ironically, services provided by notarios publicos often result in legal sanctions and deportation of immigrants due to the failure to submit necessary documentation or incorrect filing of such documentation (Federal Trade Commission, 2016). As efforts toward deportations are on the rise due to President Donald Trump's crackdown on illegal immigration, cases of affinity-based fraud against immigrants through notarios publicos are also increasing, demanding additional attention and resources.

AFFINITY FRAUD AS POSITIVE DISTINCTIVENESS: RELIGIOUS AFFILIATION AND THE AMERICAN PENSION SERVICES SCAM

The notion of positive distinctiveness suggests that when social identity is salient within the content, individuals will exaggerate the differences between their social group and others in a manner that favors ingroup membership. In essence, this is the combination or the processes of ingroup favoritism and outgroup derogation. Individuals will selectively attend to and value information that helps to maintain this positive distinctiveness. For example, prior research shows that national identity is maintained through positive distinctiveness when readers from the United States versus Germany positively read articles and news accounts of their country or culture (Trepte, Schmitt, & Dienlin, 2016).

Curtis DeYoung and his then-wife, Michelle, were co-offenders who took $25 million from the cash deposits in some 5,500 accounts administered by his American Pension Services over about a 10-year period (Green, 2015). The DeYoungs used their religious affiliation to target members of the Church of Jesus Christ of Latter-Day Saints, or the Mormon Church, for high-risk investments. The couple made loans to friends that were not repaid and gave themselves high yearly salaries (Harvey, 2008, 2016).

The DeYoungs wired $24 million from client accounts to ill-conceived investments or other purposes. From 2001 to 2010, Curtis DeYoung's salary inflated from $100,000 to $250,000, and Michelle DeYoung's salary grew from $24,000 to $250,000. In total, Curtis DeYoung made $1.9 million, while Michelle DeYoung made $1 million (Romboy, 2016). These co-offending criminal actions were made possible due to their high level of legitimacy with their victims as members of the Mormon Church. In this case, the co-offenders used faith-based affiliation to build bonds of trust in their victims. The strong affiliation with the Mormon Church was exploited to create a sense of positive distinctiveness by exaggerating the differences between those inside of and outside of the church in a manner that leveraged group affiliation in support of their bogus fund. The co-offenders also served to increase the religious-based affinity dimensions and social bonds connected to their religious affiliation. This is not an isolated incident in this area, as the rates of affinity fraud in Utah have continued to rise, prompting the state legislature to create the first ever white-collar crime registry (Lam, 2016). Similar to the sex offender registry, the online database requires a recent photograph of second-degree felony criminals involved in fraud in the past 10 years (Lam, 2016). While the registry is an important first step in fraud prevention, interventions should also aim at educating the public about the socially distinctive nature of affinity fraud scams.

PREDATORY AFFINITY FRAUD: AN ETHICAL BUSINESS ANALYSIS

There is a need for businesses offering legitimate, legal, and ethical investment opportunities to improve their identity salience within marginalized social groups (Marin, Ruiz, & Rubio, 2009). This is especially important given that distrust in the investment banking systems and of majority groups is high among minority groups. This distrust of legitimate banking systems could make these diverse groups more vulnerable to affinity-based fraud (Austin, 2004). Some also argue that this distrust is warranted as many minority groups have been disenfranchised by mainstream banking and, therefore, have few alternatives other than falling prey to affinity fraud and other investment schemes (Austin, 2004).

Thus, community, public, and religious leaders have an ethical responsibility to warn their members of affinity-based fraud scams and provide ethical financial and legal education. Local banks can work in partnership with these diverse social groups to provide legal and financial education and to secure investment opportunities. It is the responsibility of victims and wider business and civil leadership to prevent unethical business practices, such as affinity fraud.

IMPLICATIONS FOR TEACHING BUSINESS ETHICS

Business schools can work to expand their business education to include topics of affinity fraud and the complexity of diversity in business ethics and leadership. Service-learning can help provide students with firsthand experience in navigating the dynamics of social identities and ethics within businesses and community partnerships. Grounded in experiential and social learning theory, service-learning is an effective pedagogy for teaching business ethics and leadership. In service-learning, students actively participate in organizational projects aimed at building community capacity. Course objectives are learned through dynamic real-world experience and critical reflection (Bryant, Schonemann, & Karpa, 2011; Eyler & Giles, 1999; Kenworthy-U'Ren & Peterson, 2005; Martin, 2015; Papamarcos, 2005). What makes service-learning distinct from community service is that the service experience is tied to course learning objectives (Eyler & Giles, 1999; Rama, 2007). Service-learning projects frequently work with nonprofit organizations but are also applied to for-profit companies seeking to expand their corporate social responsibility and sustainability agendas (Kenworthy-U'Ren & Peterson, 2005; Martin, 2015; Pless & Borecká, 2014).

For example, the University of Pittsburgh's College of Business Administration developed a unique 16-credit Certificate Program in Leadership and Ethics (CPLE) that places emphasis on teaching leadership and ethical competencies through service-learning. The interface between leadership and ethics is the distinctive content feature of the CPLE: Each of the five required courses has an experience-based learning component. In their service-learning projects, students work for clients including businesses, alumni, university offices, and community organizations involved in various communities throughout Pittsburgh. The program is based on the assumption that an emphasis on leadership without proper consideration of ethics will not generate leaders who approach their roles with a sense of responsibility and accountability. Similarly, an emphasis on ethics without proper consideration of leadership will not produce leaders with the necessary tools to develop and implement their vision and understanding of ethics.

One CPLE service-learning project entailed students researching the outcomes of an inner-city high school financial literacy program. Through this project, students and community partners learned more about the distinct challenges of providing financial literacy to diverse student populations. Additional projects involving local restaurants and organizations attempting to address the lack of access to affordable and healthy food within urban areas in Pittsburgh have actively exposed students to the food needs of consumers across diverse socioeconomic groups. By investigating a real-world business problem involving diverse stakeholders, students learn transferable skills, such as ethical decision-making, interpersonal communication, service to community, and attention to diversity and inclusion. These skills are necessary to confront complex unethical business practices that they will encounter in their professional lives.

CONCLUSION

This chapter examines the dynamics of diversity as embedded within cases of affinity fraud, which must be seen as the exploitation of group trust based on common social demographic characteristics, such as race, religion, ethnicity, age, and social class, for the purpose of financial advantage (Perri & Brody, 2012). In affinity fraud, co-offenders use identification with a specific targeted identity group to gain the trust of group members. Because social group membership plays a central role, we use principles of SIT perspectives to examine three key factors: ingroup favoritism, outgroup bias, and positive distinctiveness. Each of these factors is used to explain an actual case of diversity-based affinity fraud. We also add to the existing literature on co-offending fraud by focusing on the role that social identity plays in creating a strong social bond that can be exploited in cases of affinity fraud. This points to the need for ethical business leaders and business education to address the distinctive needs of diverse social groups to combat unethical business practices, including affinity fraud. We discuss one approach that uses service-learning as an experiential educational tool to place business students in complex situations to help develop ethical decision-making and other skills that will prepare them to address these complex issues in their future workplaces. Placing affinity fraud within the context of diversity and business ethics in an important contribution to the research, policy discussion, and preventive measures that seek to offset the negative impact of this predatory behavior in society.

REFERENCES

Anand, V., Dacin, M. T., & Murphy, P. R. (2015). The continued need for diversity in fraud research. *Journal of Business Ethics, 131*(4), 751–755.

Anderson, K. B. (2013). *Consumer fraud in the United States, 2011: The third FTC Survey.* Retrieved from https://www.ftc.gov/sites/default/files/documents/reports/consumer-fraud-united-states-2011-third-ftc-survey/130419fraudsurvey_0.pdf

Ashforth, B. E., & Mael, F. (1989). Social identity theory and the organization. *Academy of Management Review, 14*(1), 20–39.

Austin, D. E. (2004). "In God we trust": The cultural and social impact of affinity fraud in the African American church. *University of Maryland Law Journal of Race, Religion, Gender & Class, 4*, 365–410.

Bosley, S., & Knorr, M. (2018). Pyramids, Ponzis and fraud prevention: Lessons from a case study. *Journal of Financial Crime, 25*(1), 81–94.

Brewer, M. B. (1991). The social self: On being the same and different at the same time. *Personality and Social Psychology Bulletin, 17*(5), 475–482.

Brewer, M. B. (2007). The importance of being we: Human nature and intergroup relations. *American Psychologist, 62*(8), 726–738.

Brewer, M. B., & Gardner, W. (1996). Who is this "we"? Levels of collective identity and self representations. *Journal of Personality and Social Psychology, 71*(1), 83–93. http://dx.doi.org/10.1037/0022-3514.71.1.83

Brown, D. A. (2007). Pensions and risk aversion: The influence of race, ethnicity, and class on investor behavior. *Lewis and Clark Law Review, 11*, 385–406.

Bryant, J. A., Schonemann, N., & Karpa, D. (2011). *Integrating service-learning into the university classroom.* Sudbury, MA: Jones and Bartlett.

Choi, D. S. (2014). *Health care scams on immigrants in the age of the Affordable Care Act.* Retrieved from http://povertylaw.org/clearinghouse/articles/scams

Deason, S., Rajgopal, S., Waymire, G., & White, R. (2015). *Who gets swindled in Ponzi schemes?* Retrieved from https://www0.gsb.columbia.edu/mygsb/faculty/research/pubfiles/12962/ponzi%20draft%20may%2013%202015.pdf

Dhami, M. K. (2007). White-collar prisoners' perceptions of audience reaction. *Deviant Behavior, 28*(1), 57–77. https://doi.org/10.1080/01639620600987475

Eyler, J., & Giles, D. E., Jr. (1999). *Where's the learning in service-learning?* San Francisco, CA: Jossey-Bass.

Fairfax, L. M. (2003). The thin line between love and hate: Why affinity-based securities and investment fraud constitutes a hate crime. *U.C. Davis Law Review, 36,* 1073–1143.

Federal Trade Commission. (n.d.). *Scams against immigrants.* Retrieved from https://www.consumer.ftc.gov/media/video-0053-scams-against-immigrants

Federal Trade Commission. (2014, April 11). *FTC wins court judgment against immigration services scam* [Press release]. Retrieved from https://www.ftc.gov/news-events/press-releases/2014/04/ftc-wins-court-judgment-against-immigration-services-scam

Federal Trade Commission. (2016). *Combating fraud in African American & Latino communities: The FTC's comprehensive strategic plan.* Retrieved from https://www.ftc.gov/system/files/documents/reports/combating-fraud-african-american-latino-communities-ftcs-comprehensive-strategic-plan-federal-trade/160615fraudreport.pdf

Fink, P. J. (2009). Fink! Still at large: People who suffer losses as a result of affinity fraud often struggle with the psychological ripple effects of such betrayal. What strategies can we use to help victims move forward? *Clinical Psychiatry News, 37*(2), 6–6.

Fisher, L. E. (2009). Target marketing of subprime loans: Racialized consumer fraud & reverse redlining. *Journal of Law and Policy, 18,* 121–155.

Free, C., & Murphy, P. R. (2015). The ties that bind: The decision to co-offend in fraud. *Contemporary Accounting Research, 32*(1), 18–54. https://doi.org/10.1111/1911-3846.12063

Green, T. (2015, February 26). Draper man indicted for 15 counts of mail fraud after allegedly misappropriating $24 million. *Fox 13.* Retrieved from https://fox13now.com/2015/02/26/draper-man-indicted-for-15-counts-of-mail-fraud-after-allegedly-misappropriating-24-million

Harvey, T. (2008, June 14). Swindler duped Mormon faithful, others in $180m investment scam. *The Salt Lake Tribune.* Retrieved from http://archive.sltrib.com/article.php?id=9587492&itype=NGPSID

Harvey, T. (2016, September 13). Utah man pleads guilty in $25 million theft from retirement accounts. *The Salt Lake Tribune.* Retrieved from https://archive.sltrib.com/article.php?id=4344515&itype=CMSID

Hogg, M. A., & Abrams, D. (1990). Social motivation, self-esteem and social identity. In D. Abrams & M. A. Hogg (Eds.), *Social identity theory: Construction and critical advances* (pp. 28–47). New York, NY: Harvester Wheatsheaf.

Keating, P. (2011, April 22). How to scam an athlete. *ESPN*. Retrieved from http://www.espn.com/espn/news/story?id=6408849

Kenworthy-U'Ren, A. L., & Peterson, T. O. (2005). Service-learning and management education: Introducing the "WE CARE" approach. *Academy of Management Learning & Education, 4*(3), 272–277.

Khasru, B. Z. (2001). Affinity scams target religious, ethnic investors. *Fairfield County Business Journal, 36*(17), 1–20.

Kieler, A. (2015, April 2). How 'notario' fraud preys on language differences & can result in unfair deportation. *Consumerist*. Retrieved from https://consumerist.com/2015/04/02/how-notario-fraud-preys-on-language-differences-can-result-in-unfair-deportation

Kramer, R. M. (2009). Rethinking trust. *Harvard Business Review*. Retrieved from https://hbr.org/2009/06/rethinking-trust

Kudialis, C., & Todd, C. (2018, April 13). Notary scams a grave danger for immigrant community. *U.S. News & World Report*. Retrieved from https://www.usnews.com/news/best-states/nevada/articles/2018-04-13/notary-scams-a-grave-danger-for-immigrant-community

Lam, B. (2016, March 29). Why is Utah the first state to have a white-collar crime registry? *The Atlantic*. Retrieved from https://www.theatlantic.com/business/archive/2016/03/utah-white-collar-crime/475896

Marin, L., Ruiz, S., & Rubio, A. (2009). The role of identity salience in the effects of corporate social responsibility on consumer behavior. *Journal of Business Ethics, 84*(1), 65–78. https://doi.org/10.1007/s10551-008-9673-8

Marlowe, J., & Atiles, J. H. (2005). Consumer fraud and Latino immigrant consumers in the United States. *International Journal of Consumer Studies, 29*(5), 391–400. https://doi.org/10.1111/j.1470-6431.2005.00463.x

Marquet International. (2011). *The Marquet report on Ponzi schemes*. Retrieved from https://fraudtalk.blogspot.com/2011/06/marquet-international-issues-report-on.html

Martin, M. C. (2015). Service learning as marketing pedagogy: Practical, theoretical, and institutional perspectives. *Academy of Educational Leadership Journal, 19*(2), 109–127.

Mears, D. P., Reisig, M. D., Scaggs, S., & Holtfreter, K. (2016). Efforts to reduce consumer fraud victimization among the elderly: The effect of information access on program awareness and contact. *Crime & Delinquency, 62*(9), 1235–1259.

Moohr, G. S. (2007). On the prospects of deterring corporate crime. *Journal of Business & Technology Law, 2*, 25–41.

Morales, J., Gendron, Y., & Guénin-Paracini, H. (2014). The construction of the risky individual and vigilant organization: A genealogy of the fraud triangle. *Accounting, Organizations and Society, 39*(3), 170–194.

Neuhauser, A. (2017, March 16). As ICE cracks down, scams ramp up. *U.S. News & World Report*. Retrieved from https://www.usnews.com/news/national-news/articles/2017-03-16/as-ice-cracks-down-scams-ramp-up

Oakes, P. J. (1987). The salience of social categories. In J. C. Turner, M. A. Hogg, P. J. Oakes, S. D. Rieche, & M. S. Wetherell (Eds.), *Rediscovering the social group: A self-categorization theory* (pp. 117–141). Oxford, England: Blackwell.

Papamarcos, S. D. (2005). Giving traction to management theory: Today's service-learning. *Academy of Management Learning & Education, 4*(3), 325–335. https://doi.org/10.5465/AMLE.2005.18122422

Pearce, J. A. (2013). Using social identity theory to predict managers' emphases on ethical and legal values in judging business issues. *Journal of Business Ethics, 112*(3), 497–514.

Perri, F. S., & Brody, R. G. (2011). Birds of the same feather: The dangers of affinity fraud. *Journal of Forensic Studies in Accounting and Business, 3*(1), 33–46.

Perri, F. S., & Brody, R. G. (2012). The optics of fraud: Affiliations that enhance offender credibility. *Journal of Financial Crime, 19*(4), 355–370. https://doi.org/10.1108/13590791211266359

Pickett, C. L., Bonner, B. L., & Coleman, J. M. (2002). Motivated self-stereotyping: Heightened assimilation and differentiation needs result in increased levels of positive and negative self-stereotyping. *Journal of Personality and Social Psychology, 82*(4), 543–562. https://doi.org/10.1037//0022-3514.82.4.543

Pless, N. M., & Borecká, M. (2014). Comparative analysis of International Service Learning Programs. *Journal of Management Development, 33*(6), 526–550. https://doi.org/10.1108/JMD-04-2014-0034

Power, M. (2012). The apparatus of fraud risk. *Accounting, Organizations and Society, 38*(6–7), 525–543.

Rama, D. V. (Ed.). (2007). *Learning by doing: Concepts and models for service-learning in accounting.* Sterling, VA: Stylus.

Romboy, D. (2016, November 22). Victims decry 10-year sentence for Draper man who stole $25M in retirement funds. *Deseret News.* Retrieved from https://www.deseretnews.com/article/865667795/Victims-decry-10-year-sentence-for-Draper-man-who-stole-25M-in-retirement-funds.html

Steele, C. M., Spencer, S. J., & Aronson, J. (2002). Contending with group image: The psychology of stereotype and social identity threat. *Advances in Experimental Social Psychology, 34*, 379–440.

Sutherland, E. H., Cressey, D. R., & Luckenbill, D. F. (1992). *Principles of criminology* (11th ed.). Lanham, MD: General Hall.

Tajfel, H., & Turner, J. C. (1979). An integrative theory of intergroup conflict. In W. G. Austin & S. Worchel (Eds.), *The social psychology of intergroup relations* (pp. 33–47). Monterey, CA: Brooks/Cole.

Trepte, S., Schmitt, J. B., & Dienlin, T. (2016). Good news! How reading valenced news articles influences positive distinctiveness and learning from news. *Journal of Media Psychology, 30*, 66–78. https://doi.org/10.1027/1864-1105/a000182

Treviño, L. K., Weaver, G. R., & Reynolds, S. J. (2006). Behavioral ethics in organizations: A review. *Journal of Management, 32*(6), 951–990.

Turner, J. C. (1975). Social comparison and social identity: Some prospects for intergroup behaviour. *European Journal of Social Psychology, 5*(1), 5–34.

Turner, J. C. (1999). Some current issues in research on social identity and self-categorization theories. In N. Ellemers, R. Spears, & D. Doosje (Eds.), *Social identity: Context, commitment, content* (pp. 6–34). Oxford, England: Blackwell.

Umphress, E. E., & Bingham, J. B. (2011). When employees do bad things for good reasons: Examining unethical pro-organizational behaviors. *Organization Science, 22*(3), 621–640.

Umphress, E. E., Bingham, J. E., & Mitchell, M. (2010). Unethical behavior in the name of the company: The moderating effect of organizational identification and positive reciprocity beliefs on unethical pro-organizational behavior. *Journal of Applied Psychology, 95*(4), 769–780.

Weaver, A. J. (2011). The role of actors' race in White audiences' selective exposure to movies. *Journal of Communication, 61*(2), 369–385. https://doi.org/10.1111/j.1460-2466.2011.01544.x

PART IV

PARADIGMS

CHAPTER 16

ENCOUNTERING DIVERSITY THROUGH COMMUNITY-ENGAGED SCHOLARSHIP

Lina Dee Dostilio
University of Pittsburgh

ABSTRACT

This chapter surfaces a number of ways diversity and inclusion are encountered through community-engaged scholarship across the disciplines. The first objective of the chapter is to familiarize readers with the practice of community-engaged scholarship and the multiple instances of diversity within community-engaged scholarship. I describe how community engagement, particularly community-engaged research, calls forward greater inclusion of diverse participants and community-generated inquiry agendas. The second objective is to describe the ways in which community-engaged scholarship fosters inclusion, collaboration, and attention to the value of diversity within partnerships.

Research universities embrace their civic purposes when they combine their research and teaching activities with community collaboration in a rigorous way (Campus Compact, n.d.). This chapter lays bare a number

Diversity Across the Disciplines, pages 247–260

of ways diversity is encountered through community-engaged scholarship (CES) across the disciplines. The first objective of the chapter is to familiarize readers with the practice of CES. The second objective is to explicate multiple instances of diversity, be it demographic, geographic, disciplinary, or epistemological, that are encountered within CES. The third objective is to explain how CES calls forward greater inclusion of diverse expertise, collaborators, and research agendas that include those identified by community collaborators. The fourth and final objective is to offer reflections on how cultivating awareness of bias, conducting critical analysis, and employing cultural and intellectual humility within CES may promote effective work within a diverse ecosystem of partners and problem-solvers.

COMMUNITY ENGAGEMENT IN HIGHER EDUCATION

This chapter is focused on CES as characterized by Gordon da Cruz (2018), who defines CES as "mutually beneficial partnerships between universities and communities designed with the intention to collaboratively develop and apply knowledge to address consequential public issues" (p. 148). Gordon da Cruz (2018) provides the example of a graduate-level class on community organizing and research methods—"in which students, faculty, and community organizing groups collaboratively investigate and publish successful strategies of community organizing groups working for education reform"—to show "how community engagement can simultaneously bolster research, scholarship, and teaching and be of service to the public good" (p. 151).

Gordon da Cruz (2018) details six components of CES that recurred thematically within the literature: (a) a focus on real-life social problems defined with or by the community, (b) scholarly inquiry into the problems or issues, (c) collaborative and reciprocal community–university partnerships in which community partners share authority for defining success, (d) production of collaboratively developed knowledge that addresses and improves the issues, (e) redress of the issues through institutional knowledge and resources, and (f) production of scholarship that is relevant to university research and teaching.

There are varied motivations for undertaking CES. In some instances, the motivation is primarily technical improvement (Butin, 2007): By involving members of the public in research activities, the outcomes of research may be improved. In other cases, the motivation might be to introduce cultural or political change (Butin, 2007), in that involving academic work in public problem-solving helps the institution to realize its civic mission and intervene in social problems. This chapter promotes a practice of CES that spans technical, cultural, and political goals.

The nature of involvement between academic and nonacademic stakeholders also varies widely. There are a number of spectrums or continuums (Arnstein, 1969; Biggs, 1989; "Clinical and Translational Science Awards," 2011; International Association for Public Participation, n.d.) that portray community involvement as ranging from outreach or information-sharing (on the low end of community or lay involvement) to engagement/collaboration and partnership/colleagueship (on the higher ends of community or lay involvement, which often involves mutual benefit and shared decision-making). This chapter advocates a form of CES that prioritizes collaboration and partnership, which puts it on the higher end of most participation spectrums. In addition, it is the presence of collaborative work between academic and nonacademic partners, the coproduction of knowledge, and public problem solving within CES that intensifies its possible encounters with diversity, be it demographic, geographic, cultural, organizational, or epistemological. Thus, engagement with CES necessitates encounters with diversity in both teaching and research scholarship within the academy.

ENCOUNTERING DIVERSITY WITHIN THE ACADEMY AND WITHIN THE COMMUNITY

Practitioners and scholars of higher education community engagement often refer to the joining of academicians and persons not associated with higher education as community–campus partnership or community–campus collaboration. Community is typically construed as including residents, community organization staff, members of for-profit entities, and governmental offices or legislators. Campus includes a range of diversity of higher education stakeholders (faculty, staff, students, administrators) and institutions (associate degree–granting, comprehensive, research-intensive, and liberal arts institutions; community colleges). Despite the naming convention providing a conceptual umbrella for a broad range of entities and stakeholders, it also paints each—campus and community—as respectively homogeneous, thereby minimizing the diversity within each.

Dempsey (2010) bristles at how this essentializes community, invoking the work of Lorde (1984) and Moraga and Anzaldúa (1983) to explain that casting all members of a community as having a unified experience denies and neutralizes their diversity. Whether we are referring to a community of geography or a community of interest, Dempsey (2010) explains that portraying a community as homogenous obscures distinctions of class, race, education, and religion. Doing so ignores the dynamics of competing interests among members of a community and glosses over multiple cultural expectations coexisting within the same community. Cornwall and Jewkes (1995) similarly describe a community as actually being "a heterogenous group of people with multiple interrelated axes of difference" (p. 1673). This means that encounters within and collaborations between community and campus must be equipped to navigate these cultural expectations.

A similar situation arises when we cast all members of the academy as homogenous. Silver (2003) argues that: "The university is a 'collection' of groups, all with their own touchstones of academic and professional behaviour, scholarly values and critical endeavours, which are capable of opening up rifts with its real or perceived values and behaviours" (p. 166). Diversity in methodologies, theories, and problem-solving approaches, often undergirded by distinct disciplinary traditions, can create friction when unseen or ignored (Sutton & Kemp, 2006). For example, in their work doing interdisciplinary, community-engaged design charrettes, Sutton and Kemp (2006) found that the methods, theories, and problem-solving approaches used by participants coming from a social science discipline differed from those used by participants coming from the arts and design disciplines.

Another phenomenon exists when we dichotomize community and university, making invisible those who might share degrees of membership in both groups. Banks (1998) outlines a number of positionalities that blur distinctions between scholars and particular ethnic, racial, and cultural groups: indigenous-insider, indigenous-outsider, external-insider, and external-outsider. To these we can add "insider-outsider" (Merton, 1972) for minoritized scholars working within their own communities but for whom their educational or professional identities create a degree of separation and an "outsider-within" status (Collins, 2000) when minoritized scholars have membership within the academy but a degree of exclusion because of their social identities. The concept of shared membership complicates the construction of community residents being "town," whereas faculty, staff, and students are "gown." Shared membership in both community and university, through employment, enrollment, partnership (e.g., long-term collaborator with a higher education institution), and patronage (business owners and vendors who have an economic relationship with the institution), is discounted when we rigidly categorize and assign allegiances to where someone fits in relation to community versus campus.

The invisibility of intersectionality is also a concern for students. In many instances where CES involves students, there is an explicit cultural goal (Butin, 2007) of providing students with cross-sector experiences so that they can exercise civic skills "across difference" and "with diverse partners" (National Task Force on Civic Learning and Democratic Engagement, 2012, p. 4). These experiences frequently occur in and with minoritized communities and often in communities of color. For example, Mitchell, Donahue, and Young-Law (2012) explain that these experiences, when void of significant critical race analysis, promote a pedagogy of Whiteness, or "strategies of instruction that consciously or unconsciously reinforce norms and privileges developed by, and for the benefit of, White people in the United States" (p. 613). Though Mitchell et al.'s (2012) work explicitly addresses race, their explanation that activities that may be "border-crossing" or unique for some students are actually "returning home" or familiar for others (p. 620) can also be applied to other aspects of social identity: the aspects of one's identity that come from the groups to which they belong, such as country of origin (Tajfel & Turner, 1979). When we ignore the multidimensional and intersectional positionalities of scholars and students, we may be led to marginalize or exaggerate the access that minoritized scholars and students may have to their matched racial, religious, sexual identity, or gender expression communities. In addition, we may dismiss the complexities of power and trust within these diversity encounters and reify a socially dominant construction of the scholar and student as straight, White, and middle class.

EPISTEMOLOGICAL AND PERSPECTIVAL DIVERSITY

Even as we appreciate the diversity found within and between university stakeholder and community stakeholder groups, we must still recognize there is a predominant approach to public problem-solving that is not only found within Western higher education, but actively reproduced through the ways we educate students and evaluate the rigor and merit of scholarship (Hollander & Hartley, 2009; Mathews, 1996; Sullivan, 2000). Saltmarsh, Hartley, and Clayton (2009) explain this approach as being "grounded in an institutional epistemology that privileges the expertise in the university and applies it externally, through activities in the community...creating a division between knowledge producers (in the university) and knowledge consumers (in the community)" (pp. 7–8). Our epistemological assumptions dictate how we think knowledge is created, acquired, and communicated (Scotland, 2012, p. 9). Within Western higher education, knowledge is predominantly produced within a scientific paradigm through objective, positivistic science done by credentialed experts. This approach assumes and asserts that knowledge is both the right and the possession of those within the academy rather than those within the community. In CES, the creation of knowledge is shared between academic and community members. Such collaborations involve participants who bring a diversity of epistemological assumptions and perspectives.

Sutton and Kemp (2006) share an example of the epistemological and perspectival diversity present in collaborative knowledge production. Within their case of collaborative design charrettes, Sutton and Kemp (2006) characterize the problem-solving and knowledge building approach of community members (or laypeople) as coming from practical experience gained in particular places in particular moments in time (in context) that accounts for social and political complexities. Sutton and Kemp (2006) contrasted this with the knowledge-building approaches of social science participants in the charrettes, who framed problems with theory and prior evidence. Community problem-solving can involve community-based professionals. Sometimes, professionals can have a technocratic epistemology that involves specific technical knowledge gained through formal study and credentialing and that is conveyed in technical language and practice (Mathews, 1996). As a result, when we do the work of CES, we have to recognize the particular epistemological orientation from which we originate and acknowledge the ways it may differ from the diversity of perspectival and epistemological orientations of our collaborators.

Encounters with epistemological and perspectival diversity are intensified as members of Western higher education consider working with people who identify as part of non-Western and indigenous cultures. In her work on indigenous identity within North America, Weaver (2001) uses the terms "native" and "indigenous" interchangeably to denote the descendants of the original inhabitants of North America. Likewise, the term "indigenous" has been used to describe the people inhabiting lands uncolonized by the West or prior to colonization. It has also been used to refer to minoritized communities within the United States (Miller, Wilder, Stillman, & Becker, 1997) self-identifying apart from a White, Western identification. Dei, Hall, and Rosenberg (2000) differentiate indigenous knowledge as "a body of knowledge associated with the long-term occupancy of a certain place" (p. 6) and provide examples of knowledge contained within many indigenous worldviews accrued over time, such as

> seeing the individual as part of nature; respecting and reviving the wisdom of elders; giving consideration to the living, the dead, and future generations; sharing responsibility, wealth, and resources within the community; and embracing spiritual values, traditions, and practices reflecting connections to a higher order, to the culture, and to the earth. (p. 6)

Thus, caution is necessary when a scholar who may be an outsider to a non-Western or indigenous community assumes to fully understand and represent that community's knowledge. Generating knowledge about communities and practices without engaging the people of those communities in the development of that knowledge privileges one epistemological approach over others and interjects the researcher's biases and assumptions into the framing of questions, judgement of appropriate data collection methods, decisions about who and what might be representative of the community (and, thus, who might become key informants), and interpretation of findings. Not only is this approach bad science, it is a form of colonization:

> It galls us that Western researchers and intellectuals can assume to know all that is possible to know of us, on the basis of their brief encounters with some of us. It appalls us that the West can desire, extract, and claim ownership of our ways of knowing, our imagery, the things we create and produce, and then simultaneously reject the people who created and developed those ideas and seek to deny them further opportunities to be creators of their own culture and own nations. (Smith, 1999, p. 1)

Decolonization moves past valuing diversity and orients scholarship toward relinquishing domination perspectives and approaches developed by traditional Western scholarship in favor of indigenous perspectives rooted within the communities being studied.

COMMUNITY-ENGAGED SCHOLARSHIP: INCLUSION AND COLLABORATION

Because CES must include a diversity of stakeholders' perspectives, it ensures that the diversity of perspectives and knowledges within the community of interest are not rendered invisible or silenced by the researcher's epistemological biases (Van de Ven, Meyer, & Jing, 2018). On the contrary, it both seeks out and attributes knowledge creation to those of that community. It is insufficient for higher education to apply its knowledge work to community settings without collaboration with and engagement of community stakeholders. Doing so risks essentializing communities, neutralizing the diversity found within community and campus audiences, constructing research that is not valid in the community setting, obscuring competing interests, and appropriating cultural knowledge based on privilege. What is required is a collaborative stance that cocreates knowledge with community stakeholders. Saltmarsh et al. (2009) compare a normative approach to community engagement, where the expertise and epistemology of the academy is prioritized, with democratic civic engagement, where the focus is shifted to "inclusive, collaborative, and problem-oriented work in which academics share knowledge generating tasks with the public and involve community partners as participants in public problem-solving" (p. 9). The latter approach differs from normative engagement across dimensions of community relationships, knowledge production, epistemology, political purposes, and outcomes (see Table 16.1). These distinctions help to redefine and refocus the approach, purpose, and use of CES. It also raises important questions concerning the necessary response to the outcomes of CES work.

TABLE 16.1	Comparing Civic Engagement Frameworks	
	Civic Engagement (Focus on Activity and Place)	**Democratic Civic Engagement (Focus on Purpose and Process)**
Community Relationships	• Partnerships and mutuality • Deficit-based understanding of community • Academic work done for the public	• Reciprocity • Asset-based understanding of community • Academic work done with the public
Knowledge Production/ Research	• Applied • Unidirectional flow of knowledge	• Inclusive, collaborative, problem-oriented • Multidirectional flow of knowledge
Epistemology	• Positivist/scientific/ technocratic • Distinction between knowledge producers and knowledge consumers • Primacy of academic knowledge • University as center of public problem-solving	• Relational, localized, contextual • Cocreation of knowledge • Shared authority for knowledge creation • University as part of an ecosystem of knowledge production addressing public problem-solving
Political Dimension	• Apolitical engagement	• Facilitating an inclusive, collaborative, and deliberative democracy
Outcome	• Knowledge generation and dissemination through community involvement	• Community change that results from the cocreation of knowledge

Source: Saltmarsh, Hartley, & Clayton, 2009, p. 11. Reprinted with permission.

RESPONSES TO DIVERSITY ENCOUNTERED THROUGH COMMUNITY-ENGAGED SCHOLARSHIP

Required to respond to the diversity encountered through CES across demographic, cultural, geographic, and epistemological dimensions are awareness, critical analysis, and both cultural and intellectual humility.

Awareness

Within CES, we must "take active measures to surface issues of difference between and among participants [and] . . . plan for the heterogeneity of community as well as the difficulties involved with identifying and representing a community's interests" (Dempsey, 2010, p. 383). Dempsey (2010) identifies dialogue and deliberation as the key processes for brokering such awareness. Mitchell et al. (2012) suggest that awareness comes from checking one's assumptions (e.g., about the identity of one's students) and from taking a reflective stance about one's own approach, thus setting the stage for the larger collaboration to behave reflectively. Differences within identity and experiences, particularly within an engagement paradigm, need to be understood in intersectional ways (Mitchell, 2017). In addition to exposing differences, we must also become aware of our own and other collaborators' biases. Bias awareness, or "the extent to which people are aware of and concerned about their own and others' subtle bias" (Perry, Murphy, & Dovidio, 2015, p. 65), is a critical factor in reducing and self-regulating prejudice. When combined with tenets of conflict resolution (Prutzman & Johnson, 1997), such as developing perspective (or taking alternative points of view) and growing the capacity to disrupt and resolve incidents of expressed bias, the conditions for inclusive, shared knowledge creation are possible. This acknowledges that awareness is a deliberate process that involves competency and capacity-building of people, processes, and paradigms.

Critical Analysis

CES requires critical analysis of the focal public problem being addressed as well as the methods used to do so. Once again, an intersectional understanding is used to locate the concerns being addressed within the "multiple, interconnected, and compounding...social aspects" shaping them and their interventions to avoid framing them "from a single position of marginalization and with a single identity solution" (Mitchell, 2017, p. 37). Conducting critical analysis across multiple dimensions is a complex process that may challenge existing tools and methodologies. Nonetheless, collaborators need to conduct critical analysis to identify the interconnected structural and systemic injustices surrounding the problems being addressed and uncover the structures of power to which those affected by the problems are subject (Mitchell, 2017; Wijeyesinghe & Jones, 2014).

Cultural and Intellectual Humility

Humility is colloquially defined as the characteristic of remaining teachable or knowing that one doesn't know everything and being open to learning from others. It is about developing an accurate appraisal or estimation of oneself; not thinking lowly about oneself (Richards, 1992). The practices of cultural and intellectual humility employ three interconnected dimensions to the contours of our cultural norms, knowledge, and beliefs about how we create knowledge: (a) self-awareness of one's abilities and limitations; (b) openness to new ideas, ways of knowing, and learning from others; and (c) transcendence, or forging a connection to a larger perspective (Morris, Brotheridge, & Urbanski, 2005). This applies to cultural as well as academic or intellectual aspects of community-based work.

Each person involved in CES carries with him or her a specific history; cultural influences; disciplinary training; and intersectionality of identity, perspective, and epistemology. We each "refract a topic or issue through a distorted conceptual lens" informed by these influences and must recognize that the problems we are working to address "exceed the limits of our individual capabilities" (Van de Ven et al., 2018, p. 454). Cultural humility requires a critical consciousness (Kumagai & Lypson, 2009) by which we are not only aware of our own cultural biases but also employ a consideration of power as a means to craft mutually respectful collaborations (Cross, Pickering, & Hickey, 2015).

Intellectual humility involves recognizing the limit of our knowing and accepting that not everything we know and believe is perfectly true and complete. In doing so, we become willing to consider alternative perspectives, look for insights in alternative views, and continually become more interested in evidence that contradicts currently held beliefs or thoughts (Spiegel, 2012). Put another way, the problems of the world require a diversity of knowledge to understand and approaches to solve that often challenge our existing perspectives, assumptions, and biases. We each make specific contributions but need to be part of a much larger team of problem-solvers. Cultivating cultural and intellectual humility allows us to integrate our perspectives and approaches with those of others whose perspectives and experiences may differ from our own.

Awareness, critical analysis, and cultural and intellectual humility are not ideals to which we in CES aspire; instead, they are practical skills that are developed and that should be exercised regularly and refined over time. It is vital to develop a reflective practice that equips us with key questions for consideration as we move through any CES project:

- Reflect on one's proximity to the issue via one's social identity (Mitchell, 2017, p. 39): "Who am I? Why am I here? What can I do to effect change on this issue?"
- Conduct collaborative power-mapping: Identify how problems manifest in the community; identify what resources already exist within the community to respond to issues; and identify groups and individuals who are key decision-makers (Mitchell, 2017).
- Define problems through an intersectional and systemic model (Mitchell, 2017): Which structures of inequality (e.g., racism, clas-

sism, sexism, heterosexism) contribute to this problem? How are these structures interconnected?

- Examine cultural bias and the presence of power (Cross et al., 2015): How is my preferred approach to working on this problem influenced by my culture? Within this collaboration, what power do I hold? What power do my collaborators hold? How can we move closer to sharing power?

- Approach the problem and colleagues with humility (Spiegel, 2012): What perspectives and beliefs about this problem do my collaborators bring that may be alternative or contradictory to my own? How can those differences be leveraged for success? What are the limits of my knowledge and experience with this community? How may my worldview color the way I frame the problems we are addressing and starting points for addressing them?

CONCLUSION AND FUTURE DIRECTIONS

This chapter intentionally uses the language of "encounter" within its title to underscore the importance of anticipating, preparing for, and being responsive to a range of diversity within CES. Encounter means to unexpectedly meet. For those who attempt to undertake CES without a reflective posture that anticipates a range of diversity (intersectional identities among our collaborators, differences in agendas, and differences among the disciplinary lenses and epistemologies that are brought to bear on the problems being addressed), our efforts will likely be rendered ineffective and perhaps be harmful.

When we undertake inclusive and collaborative approaches to CES, it moves us from an application model of knowledge production to one that is cocreated. Effectively cocreating knowledge with community stakeholders requires us to acknowledge the diversity among collaborators and within our respective spheres of problem-solving, invoke critical analysis about the problem being addressed, and cultivate cultural and intellectual humility, not as ideals but as practicable skills.

REFERENCES

Arnstein, S. R. (1969). A ladder of citizen participation. *Journal of the American Institute of Planners, 35*(4), 216–224.

Banks, J. A. (1998). The lives and values of researchers: Implications for educating citizens in a multicultural society. *Educational Researcher, 27*(7), 4–17.

Biggs, S. D. (1989). Resource-poor farmer participation in research. A synthesis of experiences from nine agricultural research systems. *International Service for*

National Agricultural Research. Retrieved from http://ebrary.ifpri.org/cdm/ref/collection/p15738coll11/id/92

Butin, D. W. (2007). Focusing our aim: Strengthening faculty commitment to community engagement. *Change: The Magazine of Higher Learning, 39*(6), 34–39.

Campus Compact. (n.d.). *TRUCEN.* Retrieved from https://compact.org/initiatives/trucen

Clinical and Translational Science Awards Consortium Community Engagement Key Function Committee Task Force on the Principles of Community Engagement. (2011). *Principles of community engagement* (2nd ed.). Retrieved from https://www.atsdr.cdc.gov/communityengagement/pdf/pce_report_508_final.pdf

Collins, P. H. (2000). *Black feminist thought: Consciousness and the politics of empowerment* (Rev. 2nd ed.). New York, NY: Routledge.

Cornwall, A., & Jewkes, R. (1995). What is participatory research? *Social Science & Medicine, 41*(12), 1667–1676.

Cross, J. E., Pickering, K., & Hickey, M. (2015). Community-based participatory research, ethics, and institutional review boards: Untying a Gordian knot. *Critical Sociology, 41*(7–8), 1007–1026.

Dei, G. J. S., Hall, B. L., & Rosenberg, D. G. (2000). Introduction. In G. J. S. Dei, B. L. Hall, and D. G. Rosenberg (Eds.), *Indigenous knowledges in global contexts: Multiple readings of our world* (pp. 3–17). Toronto, Canada: University of Toronto Press.

Dempsey, S. E. (2010). Critiquing community engagement. *Management Communication Quarterly, 24*(3), 359–390.

Gordon da Cruz, C. (2018). Community-engaged scholarship: Toward a shared understanding of practice. *Review of Higher Education, 41*(2), 147–167.

Hollander, E., & Hartley, M. (2009). Introductory essay: Reimagining the civic imperative of higher education. In D. W. M. Barker & D. W. Brown (Eds.), *A different kind of politics* (pp. 1–14). Dayton, OH: Kettering Foundation Press.

International Association for Public Participation. (n.d.). *Public participation pillars.* Retrieved from https://cdn.ymaws.com/www.iap2.org/resource/resmgr/Communications/A3_P2_Pillars_brochure.pdf

Kumagai, A. K., & Lypson, M. L. (2009). Beyond cultural competence: Critical consciousness, social justice, and multicultural education. *Academic Medicine, 84*(6), 782–787.

Lorde, A. (1984). *Sister outsider: Essays and speeches.* Freedom, CA: Crossing Press.

Mathews, D. (1996). The public's disenchantment with professionalism: Reasons for rethinking academe's service to the country. *Journal of Public Service & Outreach, 1*(1), 21–28.

Merton, R. K. (1972). Insiders and outsiders: A chapter in the sociology of knowledge. *American Journal of Sociology, 78*(1), 9–47.

Miller, K. W., Wilder, L. B., Stillman, F. A., & Becker, D. M. (1997). The feasibility of a street-intercept survey method in an African-American community. *American Journal of Public Health, 87*(4), 655–658.

Mitchell, T. D. (2017). Teaching community on and off campus: An intersectional approach to community engagement. *New Directions for Student Services, 2017*(157), 35–44.

Mitchell, T. D., Donahue, D. M., & Young-Law, C. (2012). Service learning as a pedagogy of Whiteness. *Equity & Excellence in Education, 45*(4), 612–629.

Moraga, C., & Anzaldúa, G. (Eds.). (1983). *This bridge called my back: Writings by radical women of color.* New York, NY: Kitchen Table.

Morris, J. A., Brotheridge, C. M., & Urbanski, J. C. (2005). Bringing humility to leadership: Antecedents and consequences of leader humility. *Human Relations, 58*(10), 1323–1350.

National Task Force on Civic Learning and Democratic Engagement. (2012). *A national call to action: A crucible moment: College learning and democracy's future.* Retrieved from https://www.aacu.org/sites/default/files/files/crucible/Crucible_508F.pdf

Perry, S. P., Murphy, M. C., & Dovidio, J. F. (2015). Modern prejudice: Subtle, but unconscious? The role of bias awareness in Whites' perceptions of personal and others' biases. *Journal of Experimental Social Psychology, 61,* 64–78.

Prutzman, P., & Johnson, J. (1997). Bias awareness and multiple perspectives: Essential aspects of conflict resolution. *Theory Into Practice, 36*(1), 26–31.

Richards, N. (1992). *Humility.* Philadelphia, PA: Temple University Press.

Saltmarsh, J., Hartley, M., & Clayton, P. H. (2009). *Democratic engagement White Paper.* Boston, MA: New England Resource Center for Higher Education.

Scotland, J. (2012). Exploring the philosophical underpinnings of research: Relating ontology and epistemology to the methodology and methods of scientific, interpretive, and critical research paradigms. *English Language Teaching, 5*(9), 9–16.

Silver, H. (2003). Does a university have a culture? *Studies in Higher Education, 28*(2), 157–169.

Smith, L. T. (1999). *Decolonizing methodologies: Research and indigenous peoples.* New York, NY: Zed Books.

Spiegel, J. S. (2012). Open-mindedness and intellectual humility. *Theory and Research in Education, 10*(1), 27–38.

Sullivan, W. M. (2000). Institutional identity and social responsibility in higher education. In T. Ehrlich (Ed.), *Civic responsibility and higher education* (pp. 19–36). Phoenix, AZ: Oryx Press.

Sutton, S. E., & Kemp, S. P. (2006). Integrating social science and design inquiry through interdisciplinary design charrettes: An approach to participatory community problem solving. *American Journal of Community Psychology, 38*(1–2), 125–139.

Tajfel, H., & Turner, J. C. (1979). An integrative theory of intergroup conflict. In W. G. Austin & S. Worchel (Eds.), *The social psychology of intergroup relations* (pp. 33–47). Monterey, CA: Brooks/Cole.

Weaver, H. N. (2001). Indigenous identity: What is it, and who really has it? *American Indian Quarterly, 25*(2), 240–255.

Wijeyesinghe, C. L., & Jones, S. R. (2014). Intersectionality, identity, and systems of power and inequality. In D. Mitchell, C. Y. Simmons, & L. A. Greyerbiehl (Eds.), *Intersectionality and higher education: Theory, research, and praxis* (pp. 9–19). New York, NY: Peter Lang.

Van de Ven, A. H., Meyer, A. D., & Jing, R. (2018). Opportunities and challenges of engaged indigenous scholarship. *Management and Organization Review, 14*(3), 449–462.

CHAPTER 17

THE CRITICAL DEMOGRAPHY PARADIGM

Informing Instructional Strategies on Diversity and Inclusion in Higher Education

Geoffrey L. Wood
University of Pittsburgh, Greensburg

ABSTRACT

This chapter examines critical demography and extends the paradigm to inform research methods and instructional strategies on diversity and inclusion across disciplines in higher education. Data gathered from previous research serves as the background for the development of templates to inform and transform the ways in which the critical demography paradigm can elaborate research methods and instructional strategies on diversity and inclusion. Preliminary findings from a pilot study are presented in this chapter and implications for future work are discussed.

A central goal of this work is to elucidate critical demography and extend the paradigm to inform instructional strategies on diversity and inclusion

Diversity Across the Disciplines, pages 261–272

across disciplines in higher education. Critical demography begins with the basic premises of demography, which historically has been to count and record demographic characteristics of a population. Then, critical demography extends these premises by examining not just the numerical counts, but also the power and social structures in place, which may impact the abilities of people to be counted (Horton, 1999; Wood, 2017). By examining power and social structures, critical demography allows for explanatory and historical analysis, rather than simply descriptive analysis based on counts. Critical demography further argues that in order to measure concepts such as race, gender, and class, one must also examine racism, sexism, and classism in the context of the power in these categories and how these impact outcomes. So, in the case of examining diversity and inclusion in a classroom setting, critical demography allows for the exploration of historical power and social structure differences, which are not well captured by conventional demography. Tenets of critical demography can be used to improve efforts toward diversity and inclusion on college campuses by infusing instructional strategies with better ways of conceptualizing and operationalizing student perceptions and outcomes (Wood, 2017). Importantly, critical demography examines explicitly the ways in which social structure differentiates dominant and subordinate groups. Power is a crucial element missing in conventional demography, but essential in critical demography.

Further, the development of instructional strategies through the lens of critical demography will allow the extension of research on race, gender, class, religion, and immigration to enable conversations about diversity and inclusion in the classroom and future research. A pilot study, funded by the University of Pittsburgh, following a faculty retreat on diversity and inclusion, was an important first step in clarifying how to better design curricula and research methods in order to capture dimensions of power and social structures often missing from the typical discussions on diversity and inclusion in the classroom. The pilot study consisted of a faculty survey, an analysis of course syllabi, and focus groups with faculty to discuss ways in which to increase diversity and inclusion in the classroom. As the pilot study concluded, we are optimistic that our findings will show ways in which diversity and inclusion can be addressed and expanded in a multidisciplinary fashion across the curriculum for the benefit of our students. In later sections, a discussion of the highlights of the pilot study will be presented. These results are preliminary as we continue to conduct workshops with faculty and seek feedback on actual changes made in course curricula or syllabi, based on our initial discussions with faculty on the results of the pilot study.

BACKGROUND

In the Summer of 2017, the David Berg Center for Ethics and Leadership at the Joseph M. Katz Graduate School of Business and College of Business Administration at the University of Pittsburgh held a faculty retreat for those interested in exploring how to advance diversity research across the curriculum at the University of Pittsburgh. The 2-day retreat allowed faculty from various disciplines within the university to have candid and progressive conversations on how we can increase diversity and inclusion in both curricula and research. Following the retreat, faculty were invited to submit proposals on how we could increase interdisciplinary diversity and inclusion at our own campuses.

At the Greensburg campus, three faculty, Melissa J. Marks, Olivia S. Long, and Geoffrey L. Wood, combined experiences and resources from the faculty retreat to consider how we might impact diversity and inclusion in the curriculum. Given our small class sizes and strong connections to students, we thought we had a unique opportunity to examine how much diversity and inclusion was present in our classrooms, and then discover ways in which this could be improved. The Greensburg campus is not very diverse. Our student population is 78% White and 22% minority (University of Pittsburgh, Greensburg, 2018). However, this is a great deal of diversity when compared to Westmoreland County, Pennsylvania, which is about 96% White (United States Census Bureau, 2016). However, the amount of actual diversity on campus and in the classroom is far less important than the ways that diversity and inclusion are conceptualized into our curricula.

THE PROBLEM

Historically, counting the number of minority students in classes and in the population in general has been the work of conventional demographers (Horton, 1999; Wood, 2017, 2018). But when it came to examining diversity and inclusion actually present in the classroom, it was clear that simply counting students would not allow us to measure diversity in a meaningful way (Wood, 2017). In response to this, we revisited work previously published on critical demography in public education to see how these conceptualizations might allow us to better explore the presence of actual diversity and inclusion, as well as some ways we could go about measuring it (Wood, 2017).

In earlier work, the paradigm of critical demography was introduced as an alternative to conventional demography in addressing potential social disparities in education (Horton, 1999). Over time, demography has become the research method of choice for developments in urban sociology, residential neighborhood studies, and population outcomes in public education. In America, demography has been used historically to count and divide people into groups based on the socially constructed categories of race, gender, and class (Horton, 1999). However, this method of counting and dividing ignores historical dimensions of power and social structure in the process (Horton, 1999; Horton, Martin, & Fasching-Varner, 2017). So, rather than use conventional demography, we decided to use critical demography because of its ability to better conceptualize and operationalize historical changes over time with respect to power and social structure.

TAKING STOCK: RESEARCH QUESTIONS

Informed by the previous discussion on critical demography, we examined the degree of diversity and inclusion in Pitt-Greensburg courses taught by full-time faculty. We did this by developing and implementing a faculty survey on classroom diversity, analyzing course syllabi, and conducting focus groups. In addition to presenting the tools developed for the pilot study, a discussion of highlights of the findings as well as next steps and future work are included in this narrative.

In efforts to measure diversity and inclusion in curricula and classrooms, research methods that would allow us to describe our findings across multiple methodologies were considered. Using a faculty survey, analysis of course syllabi, and focus groups with faculty would allow for discovery of the nuances of translating diversity and inclusion practices into course design and curricula.

There were three steps used in the pilot study. Our first step toward discovering the degree of diversity and inclusion in the classroom was to implement a survey of faculty. In the survey, we asked faculty about the ways in which diversity and inclusion topics were included in their teaching materials, instruction, syllabus, and course requirements. We asked which division they were in, how many years they had taught at Pitt-Greensburg, and how they would define their race. We then asked questions on how they would define diversity and which academic division they believed would have the most and least levels of diversity included. Next, we asked questions on how they would implement diversity into their own classes. Finally, we asked if they would be willing to attend a follow-up focus group to provide more details on diversity and inclusion in the classroom. The faculty survey allowed for the initial measurement of faculty opinions on the importance of diversity and inclusion. A copy of the faculty survey is included in Appendix A to illustrate the wording and response categories for each question.

For the second step, we conducted focus groups with faculty, grouped by academic divisions. We conducted three focus groups, one with each division. Overall, 33 respondents completed the focus groups. Questions asked included the following:

- Do you include issues of diversity within any of your courses?
- How do you include issues of diversity in your course(s)?
- Do you feel that your pedagogy (instructional methods) or materials promote diverse viewpoints in your course(s)?
- Would you be interested in integrating more diversity into your course(s)? Why or why not?

The focus group with faculty allowed for the discussion of how diversity was conceptualized and operationalized in courses. Rather than answering closed-ended survey questions, the focus group gave faculty the opportunity to expand their responses on the topic. A copy of the faculty survey is included in Appendix B.

The third step in our approach was to analyze course syllabi to discover the presence and degree of diversity and inclusion as part of the course design. For the course syllabi analyses, we asked three undergraduate students of various racial, ethnic, and gender backgrounds to evaluate these. We felt students might show less bias and evaluate more objectively, as they were not involved in the development of the syllabi and did not have a stake in the process. We also believed that having diversity represented among the student analysis team would result in less biased and more accurate analysis. We analyzed a sample of course syllabi across the three academic divisions at Pitt-Greensburg. Students examined the course description, rationale, philosophy, and objectives for mentions of diversity and inclusion. Students also looked at course assignments and topics of discussion in classes for the presence of key diversity and inclusion language. This language included items such as gender and sexism; race and racism; ethnicity, language, and nationality; globalization and immigration; religion; sexual orientation and sexuality; disability; wealth and social class; culture; diversity in general; and social justice and oppression. These topics were selected to discover concepts representative of diversity and inclusion in courses taught by full-time faculty within our academic divisions. Keeping with the premises of critical demography, this approach allowed for the discovery of power and social structure differentiations more fully. In this third step, students examined course syllabi to assess the presence of diversity and inclusion in the classroom. A copy of the coding sheet used to analyze syllabi is in Appendix C.

PRELIMINARY FINDINGS FROM THE PILOT STUDY

Although analysis work on the survey, focus groups, and syllabi analysis are not complete, there are a number of highlights that can be discussed at this point. Each of the instruments used to measure diversity and inclusion in the classroom yielded important and surprising results. In terms of the faculty survey, we found there was a great range in how faculty defined diversity. Some faculty defined concepts such as "worldview," while others defined concepts with different language such as "variety of races," "ethnicities," or even "political discourses." Most participants expected that the Behavioral Sciences Division would have the most diversity integrated into its courses, followed by the Humanities Division, with the Natural Sciences Division having the least. Most respondents believed that teaching diversity was important for university courses. When asked which topic area of diversity was included in course materials, 7 of 33 respondents indicated that they included none, whereas 26 respondents provided specific examples of types. Similarly, when asked whether their instruction showed aspects of diversity, 6 respondents claimed their instruction did not include aspects of diversity, while the other 27 respondents provided a variety of types. A question on the importance of teaching diversity was split along similar lines. When asked if they would be interested in adding diversity issues to their classes, 19 respondents answered definitely or probably, with 14 answering either maybe or probably not.

For the faculty focus groups, each of the three groups answered that Pitt-Greensburg is not diverse. Lack of diversity on campus was mentioned repeatedly by faculty, and this lack of diversity was noted to exist among faculty, students, and staff. In the Natural Sciences Division, comments were made that the textbooks available did not allow for much diversity. Faculty also stated that science disciplines have only recently recognized contributions by women. Also, some faculty mentioned that Chinese students are sometimes segregated by language in science labs so that these students can learn through their preferred language. In the Behavioral Sciences and Humanities divisions, faculty stated that diversity was often integrated into course content. Suggestions for improvements on diversity issues included hiring more diverse faculty, providing more diversity readings or speakers, and increasing the numbers of international students and study abroad opportunities for students.

For the syllabi analysis, several highlights are important. First, even on syllabi that were relatively specific, syllabi showed little inclusion of diversity. Even for some classes where we would expect more diversity coverage, we were surprised at how little diversity was portrayed in the syllabi. There was also a lack of focus on religion, sexual orientation, wealth/class, and social justice/oppression in the syllabi. However, there were a couple of surprises. English literature courses concentrated almost entirely on White males as both the authors and the protagonists. Often, the diversity concepts in these courses were almost entirely gender, such as female writers or female protagonists. Also, syllabi analysis revealed that some courses were European art and literature, as opposed to arts and literature more generally. Other findings from the syllabi analysis were expected but confirmed. In their focus group, Behavioral Sciences participants concurred that, "English wouldn't be hard [to integrate diversity into], humanities wouldn't be hard, but math and science might be harder, and math is probably impossible." Natural Sciences (save for environmental science) contained almost no mention of diversity, save for infrequent references to "women in science" or "women in mathematics." Behavioral Sciences, especially sociology, psychology, and education, had a broader focus on diversity. For example, criminal justice courses focused on race-related actions and psychology courses focused on the variety of understandings within diverse cultures. The preliminary findings of the survey, focus groups, and syllabi analysis showed both expected findings and surprises when examining diversity and inclusion issues on campus.

After the survey, focus groups, and course syllabi evaluation, a faculty training workshop on diversity and inclusion was offered to review our efforts, gather faculty feedback, and focus on ways of increasing diversity and inclusion in the classroom. We had 28 faculty attend this diversity inclusion workshop. One of the items focused on in the workshop was the creation of a diversity and inclusion statement, which could be placed in a course syllabus to advise students of the importance of diversity and inclusion, as well as the open and accepting environment of a given class toward diversity and inclusion. Although we are still evaluating the ideas generated from the workshop, there was a positive view of creating a unifying statement on diversity and inclusion for placement in course syllabi.

FUTURE WORK

In the future, we plan to expand on our preliminary findings from this study and offer recommendations on ways in which diversity and inclusion can better be incorporated into course curricula, syllabi, and course diversity statements. We also plan to draw conclusions from our analyses and consider ways to develop templates for assisting faculty in developing stronger approaches toward increasing levels of diversity and inclusion. If so, this approach will allow for the measurement and evaluation of power and social structure differentiation when looking at curricula for teaching and studying diversity and inclusion in the classroom.

Once instructional strategies to promote diversity and inclusion based on critical demography have been developed based on our pilot study, these can then be used to design templates for integrating diversity and inclusion into instructional and research strategies. There is also much promise that strategies may lead to improvements in the methods used to evaluate diversity and inclusion in the classroom. Data gathered from the Pitt-Greensburg research study on diversity and inclusion will be examined in the development of approaches to teaching effectiveness based on evaluations of syllabi, curricula, and teaching methods. The findings from the pilot study can inform the ways in which the critical demography paradigm elaborates on research methods and instructional strategies on diversity and inclusion. This book chapter is consistent with the goals and objectives of the volume in that it will build on foundations of collaborative, interdisciplinary work across demography, education, history, political science, and sociology. Our diversity and inclusion pilot study was a direct effect of the 2-day retreat on diversity and inclusion we attended through the University of Pittsburgh. Future work on this topic includes the development of another manuscript that will include more detailed analysis of the findings from the pilot study, evaluations of faculty diversity statements to assess effectiveness, and the development of templates that can be used across university settings to address issues of diversity and inclusion in the classroom.

APPENDIX A
Pitt-Greensburg Faculty Survey of Diversity and Inclusion

Page 1: Demographics

1. To what division do you belong? (Check all that apply.)
   _____ Behavioral Sciences
   _____ Humanities
   _____ Natural Sciences

2. How many years have you taught at Pitt-Greensburg?
   _____ 0–5
   _____ 6–10
   _____ 11–20
   _____ More than 20

3. What is your gender?
   _____ Female
   _____ Male
   _____ Non-binary
   _____ Choose not to answer

4. How do you define your race?
   _____ Black/African American
   _____ Latino/Hispanic
   _____ Caucasian
   _____ Native American
   _____ Asian
   _____ Biracial/multiracial
   _____ Other

Page 2: Definition

    5. How would you define the term "diversity"?

Page 3: Questions About Implementation by Division

    6. Which division would you expect to teach the most about diversity?
        _____ Behavioral Sciences
        _____ Humanities
        _____ Natural Sciences

    7. Which division would you expect to teach the least about diversity?
        _____ Behavioral Sciences
        _____ Humanities
        _____ Natural Sciences

    8. Do you believe that your content area is an appropriate one in which to teach concepts from diversity? (1 represents definitely not, and 5 represents definitely yes.)

                    1   2   3   4   5

Page 4: Questions About Your Implementation

    9. Do you feel you implement concepts from diversity into any of your classes? (1 represents not so well, and 5 represents exceptionally well.)

                    1   2   3   4   5

   10. Do you feel you implement concepts from diversity into any of your classes? (1 represents not so well, and 5 represents exceptionally well.)

                    1   2   3   4   5

   11. Which of the following areas of diversity are included in any of your classes through the textbook(s) or content materials?
        _____ Gender
        _____ Race
        _____ Religion
        _____ Sexual orientation
        _____ Social class/wealth
        _____ Social justice/oppression

   12. Which of the following areas of diversity are included in any of your classes through your instruction?
        _____ Gender
        _____ Race
        _____ Religion
        _____ Sexual orientation
        _____ Social class/wealth
        _____ Social justice/oppression

13. How important is teaching diversity to you? (1 represents not so much, and 5 represents very much.)

1 2 3 4 5

14. Are you interested in adding more content or examples regarding diversity to your course(s)? (1 represents not so much, and 5 represents very much.)

1 2 3 4 5

Last Page

15. Would you be willing to be part of a focus group to discuss diversity in the classroom?

_____ Yes
_____ No

If yes, please leave your name. (This will not be connected in any way to the answers provided).

APPENDIX B
Pitt-Greensburg Outline of Questions for Focus Groups With Each Division

1. Do you include issues of diversity within any of your courses?
2. If yes, which course(s)?
3. How do you include issues of diversity in your course(s)?
4. Do you feel that your pedagogy (instructional methods) or materials promote diverse viewpoints in your course(s) (e.g., working with others, students sharing experiences, materials used)?
5. Would you be interested in integrating more diversity into your course(s)? Why or why not?

APPENDIX C
Pitt-Greensburg Coding Template
for Evaluating Course Syllabi

Faculty/Course Discipline		
• Discipline code		
• Division (1 = NS, 2 = Hum, 3 = Behavior)		
• Faculty of visible minority (1 = female, 2 = person of color, 3 = both, 0 = none)		
Class Description		
• Course topic/description creates expectation of integration about diversity (high expectation = 3, possibility = 2, low expectation = 1)		
Course Description/Rationale/Philosophy		
Objectives/Goals		
Assignments/Assessments (List of Assignments/Assessments)		
Topics/Discussions/In-Class, Based on Below		
• Gender/sexism		
• Race		
• Ethnicity/nationality/language		
• Globalism (non-U.S. focused)/immigration		
• Religion		
• Sexual orientation/sexuality		
• (Dis)ability		
• Wealth/class		
• Culture		
• Diversity in general		
• Social justice/oppression		
Ratings		
• Section not included = 0		
• Not mentioned = 1		
• Mentioned/if time allows = 2		
• 1-day focus = 3		
• Multiday focus/integrated = 4		

Behavior—Behavioral Sciences; Hum—Humanities; NS—Natural Sciences

REFERENCES

Horton, H. D. (1999). Critical demography: The paradigm of the future? *Sociological Forum, 14*(3), 363–367.

Horton, H. D., Martin, L. L., & Fasching-Varner, K. J. (Eds.). (2017). *Race, population studies, and America's public schools.* Lanham, MD: Lexington Books.

United States Census Bureau. (2016). *American community survey.* Retrieved from https://www.census.gov/acs/www/data/data-tables-and-tools/data-profiles/2016

University of Pittsburgh, Greensburg. (2018). *Pitt-Greensburg fact book.* Retrieved from https://prc.ir.pitt.edu/wp-content/uploads/2018/12/FactBook2018.pdf

Wood, G. L. (2017). Seventeen years later: Revisiting the critical demography paradigm to examine public education in American schools. In H. D. Horton, L. L. Martin, & K. J. Fasching-Varner (Eds.), *Race, population studies, and America's public schools* (pp. 7–16). Lanham, MD: Lexington Books.

Wood, G. L. (2018) Historical categorical inequality: The creation of two segregated cities within an urban centre. In K. J. Fasching-Varner, K. Tobin, & S. Lentz (Eds.), *#BRoken promises: Black deaths and blue ribbons: Understanding, complicating, and transcending police–community violence* (pp. 19–22). Leiden, The Netherlands: Brill.

CHAPTER 18

INTEGRATING DIVERSITY AND ETHICS INTO PALLIATIVE CARE FOR AFRICAN AMERICANS

John C. Welch
Pittsburgh Theological Seminary

ABSTRACT

Research has shown that African-Americans are least likely to receive adequate palliative interventions leading to concerns about the quality of health care in general and palliative care in particular for this population. Acknowledging patient preferences are essential in administering quality health care especially when a patient's condition is terminal. But when African-Americans are least likely to complete living wills or durable power of attorneys for health care and more likely to continue to request life sustaining treatments when near death, conflicts between patients and medical professionals can result. This chapter focuses on recognizing patient spirituality and addressing their spiritual needs as a more effective approach to diversity and inclusion within palliative care. An argument for a paradigm shift is presented such that models and approaches used to assess the spirituality of African-American

Diversity Across the Disciplines, pages 273–284
Copyright © 2020 by Information Age Publishing
All rights of reproduction in any form reserved.

patients must be culturally appropriate and performed by professionals with interpersonal communications skills and an awareness of how their implicit bias can impede the integrity of the clinician–patient interaction.

Although there is no absolute definition of palliative care, some equate it with hospice and end-of-life care, while others argue that it must include a holistic approach to the continuity of care for the chronically ill (Crawley, 2002). Recently, scholars have argued that the key to effective palliative care is to introduce diverse and interdisciplinary perspectives into the focus and function of the medical care team (Proulx & Jacelon, 2004). However, palliative care in its early iterations was almost exclusively focused on end-of-life care as the death and dying process (Finlay, 2001). Palliative care was viewed as a medical response to aggressive treatment for terminally ill patients (Proulx & Jacelon, 2004). This shift in perspective brings a natural tension between traditional end-of-life care models and emerging perspectives that challenge and introduce notions of quality of life, spirituality, culture, and advocacy to protect the rights of the patient and family (Crawley, 2002). These issues are at the interface of diversity and ethical perspectives within the emerging context of palliative care (van Ryn & Burke, 2000).

This chapter explores this shift in an attempt to better articulate a more inclusive approach to palliative care to meet the needs of diverse patients, families, and communities. This includes an explicit focus that expands beyond merely addressing short-term or long-term physical needs and moves toward including psychosocial and spiritual needs of diverse patient populations. This chapter specifically focuses on African Americans as one context in which notions of end of life, family, community, and spirituality have traditionally been ignored. In addition, the notion of changing models of palliative care for diverse populations is examined from an ethical lens as future directions for research and practice are explored.

CHALLENGING TRADITIONAL MODELS
OF PALLIATIVE CARE

Traditional palliative care models have their origins within a medical hospice care approach that has been recently subject to criticism in terms of serving the needs of diverse patient populations (Barrett & Heller, 2004). Some argue that for poor or minoritized communities, palliative care suffers from the same disparities—based on lack of access, financial resources, and inadequate cultural competence of providers—that have been noted within primary care service delivery (Betancourt, Green, Carrillo, & Ananeh-Firempong, 2003). In addition, traditional approaches to palliative care are limited by existing stereotypes, such as the use of medication for pain management, cultural definitions of quality of life, and lack of autonomy in medical decisions for those with limited financial resources. Disparities based on income, ethnicity, and/or culture are at the forefront of contemporary discussion of palliative care as providers attempt to take into account the needs of patients' families and the broader community, which have been excluded from consideration. Thus, there is growing consensus on the need to move beyond an exclusive focus on physical well-being and toward a more holistic approach that includes psychosocial, community, and spiritual dimensions of well-being (Puchalski et al., 2009).

Some argue that meeting the palliative care needs of diverse populations is fundamentally about changing notions of what "dignity" means across different patient populations. This means that the experience of dignity is differently defined and experienced across diverse patient groups, making effective communication among patients, family, and health care providers essential (Washington, 2003). For example, Dula (2004) contends that African Americans view dignity in a different manner than does the dominant racial/ethnic culture. Because of the history of what some see as neglect of African Americans by the medical and healthcare delivery systems, it is not uncommon for African Americans to view health care suspiciously. High mortality and morbidity rates, along with shorter lifespans, also increase suspicion and mistrust (Rhodes & Teno, 2009). Therefore, recommendations of care, various options presented to patients, and the actions of the care team are under scrutiny by diverse patient populations. This lack of trust and suspicion can also interfere with effective communication among patients, families, and the care team, which is critical to effective treatment.

For patients that are nearing the end of life and their families, communication is very important. Washington (2003) finds that doctors do not "hear" their patients. This is especially true among African American patients. Washington (2003) surveyed over 2,300 participants (1,429 patients and 963 physicians) from across the United States, with 85% of those targeted responding to the questionnaires examining patient–physician communication. Of the patient respondents, 34% claimed that their doctors do not listen to them, and 23% felt that their doctors do not spend enough time with them. In contrast, 90% of the doctors surveyed reported that they always listen and that they feel constrained by healthcare regulations, policies, and procedures (Washington, 2003). These challenges in communication among patients, physicians, and care teams have led to a strong outcry for greater cultural competency in communication to be a required element of healthcare education, training, and practice (Betancourt et al., 2003).

In addition to lack of trust and problems in communication, the history of negative experiences by both patients and physicians also leads to stereotyped views of diverse patients by medical professionals and physicians. For example, the literature indicates that physicians are still undertreating pain for some patients, which has been connected to the stereotype of African Americans having a high risk or propensity to become addicts. This leads to a greater risk of undertreatment for racial and ethnic minorities with chronic pain, which has been shown in research on African American patients (Anderson et al., 2002; Green, Baker, Smith, & Sato, 2003). Others find that physicians rated African American patients as less intelligent than White patients, even when patient sex, age, income, and education are controlled (van Ryn & Burke, 2000). This perception could lead to the assumption that African American patients are not able to understand treatment options, which could result in a lack of adequate information being shared concerning a range of treatment plans and options. For example, limited formularies and prescription drug coverage, expensive co-payments, complicated referral systems, and extensive paperwork have been found to contribute to the suboptimal options that physicians offer to their patients; these also have been shown to produce difficulties in communication (Barrett & Heller, 2004). Glasson et al. (1995) points out that patient knowledge of emerging trends, such as incentive-driven care, can dramatically impact the integrity of the patient–physician relationship for diverse populations (Turner, 2002).

The critical issues of historic mistrust, poor communication, persistent stereotypes, and financial barriers all impact the quality of the interaction and the palliative care that is provided to diverse patients. These issues tend to focus on how care is delivered. It is also true that the notions of dignity and quality of life within the context of end-of-life care for African Americans are viewed very differently by the medical profession and the patient (Proulx & Jacelon, 2004). This reveals a fundamental disconnect in how research and medical practice acknowledge diverse definitions of quality of life that include notions of connectedness and spirituality, which are not often taught in traditional medical training or included in medical practice. This exclusion is problematic, especially for African American patients because of the central role that spirituality often plays in family and community. Thus, it is critical that emerging models and approaches to palliative care take into account, integrate, and value the role that spirituality holds within the African American experience. Ignoring the importance of spirituality can jeopardize the quality of patient care but also ignore the needs of the family and the community, who are inextricably linked to the patient's well-being during periods of health and life transitions.

SPIRITUALITY AND PALLIATIVE CARE FOR AFRICAN AMERICANS

Spirituality is one of the trilateral components of palliative care alongside physical and psychosocial support, especially for diverse patient populations. Unlike any other field in health care, training in the relevance of spirituality and religion within the practice of palliative care is important but often ignored (Sulmasy, 1999; Walter, 2002). For example, among African Americans, when a family member dies there is often what is called a "home-going" service (Barrett & Heller, 2004). The phrase "going home" is a vernacular term commonly used by African Americans who are terminal and are ready to die. The difference in vocabulary here is critical because "going home" reflects a significant view among African Americans that contrasts with the notion or term "end of life."

Spirituality and religion are often conflated and used synonymously but over the years the two terms have become distinctly defined. Spirituality, religion in health care has been studied extensively over the years with the goal of trying to understand how this construct effects patient decision-making and postoperative recovery as well has how they are resourced for strength in coping through life's difficult situations. While, it should also be noted that although spirituality and religion are often referred to interchangeably, there is a difference. In agreeing with the distinction that spirituality is broader than religion, Sulmasy offers that not everyone is religious but all are spiritual, even in the sense that those who may reject the notion of a transcendent being whether or not they call the transcendent "God" are in relationship with the transcendent by their mere rejection (Sulmasy, 1999). Smith has examined numerous sources and has found a collection of definitions for religion which include: an obligation to a particular organization or tradition of faith, the codification of spiritual experiences into a system, an integrated set of beliefs and activities, and lastly, a search for significance (Smith, 2007). Within African American culture, this represents a considerable shift in focus from who an individual is in relation to God to a personal purpose and meaning even without godly relevance (Walter, 2002). This shift in definition and meaning coincides with the emergence of the philosophical movement in the area of pain and suffering (Green et al., 2003). However, this shift was devoid of extensive consideration of how diverse populations are viewed by traditional palliative care models, as well as how the medical profession disregards the role that spirituality plays, especially for African Americans. As a result, a type of schism was placed within theory and practice related to palliative care that often has a detrimental impact on diverse patient populations. Addressing this difference in perspectives clearly calls for a greater attention to diversity matters in the understanding and treatment of African Americans and other diverse patient groups. Including the central role that spirituality plays for African Americans within emerging models of palliative care is an essential starting point.

A number of studies have indicated that patients, particularly African Americans, with terminal and other advanced illnesses view spirituality and religion as very important to them in helping to cope with their condition

(Barrett & Heller, 2004; Puchalski, 2006b; Olson, Sandor, Sierpina, Vander-pool, & Dayao, 2006). Including spirituality in the delivery of care has been met with resistance or has received minimal attention among healthcare professionals, despite evidence supporting patient reliance (Walter, 2002). For spirituality to be effectively integrated within palliative care, it is important to understand the role and responsibility of medical professionals and all members of the care team in providing this holistic approach for diverse populations in general and African Americans in particular. This may at first appear to be a simple solution, but obstacles and oppositions remain.

Since its inception, the palliative care paradigm in healthcare delivery has utilized a care team approach; however, to some, the integration of spirituality has been controversial, and healthcare professionals still challenge its relevance (Curlin, Roach, Gorawara-Bhat, Lanton, & Chin, 2005; Glasson et al., 1995). Some medical professionals avoid inquiring about a patient's spirituality because they view such an inquiry to be an invasion of privacy. Others suggest that resistance to including notions of spirituality correlate with how medical professionals reflect (or fail to reflect) on their own spirituality; this may allow the caregiver to comfortably enter into a dialogue with the patient about the influence his or her own spirituality has had on medical decision-making (Brett & Jersild, 2003). According to Olson et al. (2006), some degree of openness to discussions of spirituality contributes to better health and better patient–physician relationships (Finlay, 2001).

Thus, spirituality in this context is not only important for the patient but may also be beneficial for members of the care team, as it can help them deal with resulting stress from this type of emotional work (Puchalski, 2006a). These various reasons why medical professionals will not actively engage in discussions of patient spirituality or push for its inclusion as a legitimate part of holistic care can negatively impact the quality of patient care. Some also argue that it can be seen as a violation of social responsibility and ethics surrounding patient care (Puchalski, 2006b). Regardless of the factors that may explain this resistance, addressing the issue of death and dying cannot be untangled from the centrality of spirituality within the African American experience (Barrett & Heller, 2004).

One way to bridge the difficulty that medical professionals may face while integrating spirituality into diverse patient care may begin with viewing care as not only a physical practice but also a spiritual practice as providers attempt to mitigate the injury to the "embodied spiritual" body that disease causes (Sulmasy, 1999, p. 1003). However, this perspective has been advocated by only a few medical professionals and has not been widely incorporated into the core of medical theory, training, and practice (Pellegrino, 1998; Pelligrino & Thomasma, 1981).

However, making this shift is not without debate. On one hand, Walter (2002) argues that moving away from traditional medical models and including spirituality within palliative care creates an unwelcome burden on medical personnel, especially since they are the least skilled at addressing the spiritual needs of patients. On the other hand, Puhalski (2006b) asserts that despite a lack of comfort or competence, it is the ethical responsibility of healthcare professionals to acknowledge this reality and assist patients as they explore their spiritual interests in the context of their care. Giblin (2002) comments that effective palliative care requires less technical expertise and more professional willingness to share in the experience of human suffering. Furthermore, to accentuate and expect professionals to only operate in their areas of expertise and not become caring companions "medicalizes the dying process," "disempowers everyone" on the care team, and "heightens the isolation" of patients and their families (Giblin, 2002, p. 237).

When medical professionals are unable to follow through with a holistic care plan for the patient that includes spiritual support—solely because of misalignment in personal values or lack of regard for spiritual and religious beliefs—patient care is impacted and an ethical dilemma can result. This also puts responsibility on the medical institution, not just on the individual physician, to foster an environment responsive to the spiritual needs of patients, their families, and their communities (Cotton et al., 2006). Placing the spiritual needs of patients on the same level as their physical needs is part of ongoing efforts to look at mind, body, and spirit as one whole that cannot and should not be disconnected in terms of patient care and especially palliative care (Olson et al., 2006).

If palliative care aims to alleviate the physical, psychosocial, and spiritual suffering of the chronically ill, and if a disproportionate amount of African Americans fall into this category, is there a moral obligation to shift attention and, subsequently, resources to address this disparity? If issues such as miscommunication, stereotypes, and lack of cultural competency lead to disparities in the quality of care for African Americans and other diverse populations, does this pose a challenge to the medical ethic of care? Is there a responsibility of the healthcare profession to provide adequate awareness and training in cultural competency to meet the needs of diverse patient groups and their families (Crawley, 2002)? Lastly, is there a case to be made that failure to address the issues that have historically been seen as diversity issues should now be viewed at the intersection of diversity and ethics in the area of palliative care for African Americans?

INTEGRATING DIVERSITY AND ETHICS INTO PALLIATIVE CARE

In addressing diverse needs within palliative care, it is important to include a review of the definition of palliative care through an ethical lens. Health care is a system, while palliative care is a delivery mechanism that should be both patient centered and culturally relevant. As patients face life-threatening illnesses, palliative care needs to exhibit nimbleness and flexibility to adapt to the unique needs of each patient, as opposed to the patient having to adapt to the care available (Barrett & Heller, 2004; Betancourt et al., 2003). Therefore, to think of palliative care as a philosophy of care is to run the risk of palliative care becoming an ideology (Ferrell et al., 2007). Furthermore, seeing palliative care as an ideology could silence the voices of diverse patients and their families, thereby severely affecting medical decision-making (Pellegrino, 1998; Pelligrino & Thomasma, 1981).

Brett and Jersild (2003) discuss medical ethics in general as the product of how the conjoining of theological and philosophical worldviews has become its own enterprise. They further argue for the need to consider the ethics of palliative care differentiated from traditional medical ethics. From this perspective, one of the things not often mentioned when addressing the ethics of palliative care is the ethics of virtue or personal character. This means including what have been described as natural and supernatural virtues, which lay the groundwork for virtue ethics. Natural virtues are those characteristics guided by reason and unaided by biblical scripture that compel an individual to seek the good, while supernatural virtues are aided by biblical scripture (Pellegrino, Thomasma, & Miller, 1996). However, it was during what has been referred to as the Period of Enlightenment when medical ethics shifted its focus from the kind of person one ought to be to the kind of decisions one ought to make. This necessarily included a shift from the virtues one should cultivate to the principles, duties, and rules one ought to respect (Pellegrino et al., 1996). Because spirituality is one of the critical areas of focus within palliative care, it would seem only natural to adjoin the relevance of virtue and character to this context. Giblin (2002) explicitly calls for us to expand our principles-based ethical frameworks to include virtue when evaluating end-of-life care. From this perspective, relationships are defined as an important driver in palliative care and are even more important in hospice care. Thus, the virtues and personal character of medical practitioners will determine if and how those relationships develop (Giblin, 2014). Virtue ethics is less about the act or the decisions of right and wrong and more about the traits of the person that lead to the decisions made or the acts committed. This suggests that the principled nature of medical ethics, as it is now practiced, focuses more on the process of decision-making and therefore offers little insight into the right and/or proper conduct of physicians, especially with diverse patient populations. Although the subjects of principle and duty pervade traditional discussions on health care, there is a need to inject notions of virtue within dialogues on palliative care and end-of-life care. This area of ethics is critical in the analysis of and treatment for diverse populations in general and African Americans specifically.

Consider the disparity in the number of hospitals that offer palliative care programs. This brings forth the important ethical issue of access. The fact that there are some patients who are denied this type of care in certain parts of the country creates a clear ethical dilemma, especially from a virtue ethics perspective. This is highlighted by the fact that African Americans are more likely to lack access or receive substandard end-of-life care for a variety of reasons including but not limited to racism and lack of cultural competence among providers (Turner, 2002). According to a state-by-state report card published by the Center to Advance Palliative Care and the National Palliative Care Research Center, along with 2013 population estimates from U.S. census data, of 17 states in the South with an average African American population above 22%, only Maryland and North Carolina were given a B or better among hospitals with palliative care programs (Voelker, 2011). This means that lack of access to quality and culturally competent palliative care cannot be simply viewed as an economic issue. It must instead be framed as an issue of ethics and social responsibility; the medical profession and healthcare providers must address the historic and contemporary disparities in lack of access to this care, viewing it as a human right not an economic privilege (Payne, Payne, & Heller, 2002). Thus, the notion of ethics must be integrated with aspects of diversity if we are to adequately conceptualize and address the needs of African American patients and families now and into the future.

FUTURE CONSIDERATIONS FOR PALLIATIVE CARE PRACTICE

There have been some efforts to operationally deliver palliative care services to African Americans and other populations with traditionally minimal access to quality health care. Three of those examples are the Harlem Palliative Care Network; the Balm of Gilead Center at Cooper Green Hospital in Birmingham, Alabama; and Hospice of the Valley in Santa Clara County (Payne et al., 2002). The Harlem Palliative Care Network was a collaborative project among North General Hospital in Harlem, Memorial Sloan Kettering Cancer Center, and the Visiting Nurse Service of New York. While most of the patients seen in this program were patients with cancer, its target population consisted of patients with HIV/AIDs, end-stage renal disease, and chronic obstructive pulmonary disease. Some of this organization's success can be attributed to identifying and including community stakeholders on an active advisory board, offering palliative care training to North General Hospital medical professionals, and establishing relationships with community clergy. The Balm of Gilead Center also experienced success before closing in 2013 and used similar equity in access and diversity orientation strategies. Through its care-sharing initiative, volunteers were mobilized through two programs, the CareTeam Program and the Adopt-a-Room Program. In the palliative care unit of Cooper Green Hospital, patients were cared for in rooms furnished by local churches and community groups. At Hospice of the Valley, improving the cultural competency of the hospice staff was important and so a handbook was created for the use of all hospice workers. Although these three examples were limited in reach in terms of number of patients impacted, they are nonetheless specific examples of how communities and medical practices can work collaboratively to address the diversity and ethical challenges that limit access to and availability of palliative care for African Americans.

Thus, much needed changes in the definitions, perspectives, and delivery of palliative care are gaining some momentum in the United States and other parts of the world. Addressing deficits in patient care for African Americans requires considering their use of spirituality to cope with illness, as well as validating their distrust of the healthcare system; both are needs and barriers that must be recognized in the provision of quality palliative care. The positive healthcare outcomes, from the use of spirituality, continues to be an area that requires more attention by research and practice, particularly with the African American and other diverse patient populations.

However, diversity is not simply about changing the numbers in terms of access to this type of care. The right of people to have access to quality palliative care, especially African Americans, must also be examined as future efforts attempt to correct the inconsistent delivery of palliative care for diverse patients. The fact that there seems to be a pattern that the fewest number of hospitals with palliative care programs coincide with states with the highest population of African Americans leaves open a number of ethical concerns. It can also be viewed as an ethical dilemma when the failure of health care to fully identify, address, and alleviate the suffering of diverse patients within holistic care is seen as an issue of social inequality and not merely as gaps in service delivery.

Perhaps it is time to designate the lack of understanding and awareness of the experiences of diverse patients, including their mistrust of the healthcare system and their religious and cultural beliefs, as a breach of both virtue ethics and social responsibility. Future developments in palliative care ethics must consider how to separate from a medical ethics paradigm and into an ethical identity of its own and, in doing so, determine how diversity and ethics can be integrated to provide an effective holistic approach to care. This clearly means challenging stereotypes of specific patient populations, reducing disparities in access to quality care, increasing the cultural competence of those within the care team, and removing the stigma of discussing issues of spirituality in the treatment experience. This will not only improve outcomes for African Americans and their families but also lead to innovations related to how palliative care is defined, delivered, and distributed across an increasingly diverse patient population.

REFERENCES

Anderson, K. O., Richman, S. P., Hurley, J., Palos, G., Valero, V., Mendoza, T. R., . . . Cleeland, C. S. (2002). Cancer pain management among underserved minority outpatients: Perceived needs and barriers to optimal control. *Cancer, 94*(8), 2295–2304.

Barrett, R. K., & Heller, K. S. (2004). Death and dying in the Black experience. *Journal of Palliative Medicine, 5*(5), 793–799.

Betancourt, J. R., Green, A. R., Carrillo, J. E., & Ananeh-Firempong, O., II. (2003). Defining cultural competence: A practical framework for addressing racial/ethnic disparities in health and health care. *Public Health Reports, 118*(4), 293–302.

Brett, A. S., & Jersild, P. (2003). "Inappropriate" treatment near the end of life: Conflict between religious convictions and clinical judgment. *Archives of Internal Medicine, 163*(14), 1645–1649.

Cotton, S., Puchalski, C. M, Sherman, S. N., Mrus, J. M., Peterman, A. H., Feinberg, J., . . . Tsevat, J. (2006). Spirituality and religion in patients with HIV/AIDS. *Journal of General Internal Medicine, 21*(Suppl. 5), S5–S13.

Crawley, L. M. (2002). Palliative care in African American communities. *Journal of Palliative Medicine, 5*(5), 775–779.

Curlin, F. A., Roach, C. J., Gorawara-Bhat, R., Lanton, J. D., & Chin, M. H. (2005). How are religion and spirituality related to health? A study of physicians' perspectives. *Southern Medical Journal, 98*(8), 761–766.

Dula, A. (2004). Bioethics: African-American perspectives. In S. G. Post (Ed.), *Encyclopedia of bioethics* (pp. 287–292). New York, NY: Macmillan Reference USA.

Ferrell, B., Connor, S. R., Cordes, A., Dahlin, C. M., Fine, P. G., Hutton, N., . . . Zuroski, K., (2007). The national agenda for quality palliative care: The National Consensus Project and the National Quality Forum. *Journal of Pain and Symptom Management, 33*(6), 737–744.

Finlay, I. (2001). UK strategies for palliative care. *Journal of the Royal Society of Medicine, 94*, 437–441.

Giblin, M. J. (2002). Beyond principles: Virtue ethics in hospice and palliative care. *American Journal of Hospice and Palliative Medicine, 19*(4), 235–239.

Glasson, J., Plows, C. W., Clarke, O. W., Ruff, V., Fuller, D., Kliger, C. H., . . . Leslie, J. (1995). Ethical issues in managed care: Council on Ethical and Judicial Affairs, American Medical Association. *JAMA, 273*(4), 330–335.

Green, C. R., Baker, T. A., Smith, E. M., & Sato, Y. (2003). The effect of race in older adults presenting for chronic pain management: A comparative study of Black and White Americans. *Journal of Pain, 4*(2), 82–90.

Olson, M. M., Sandor, M. K., Sierpina, V. S., Vanderpool, H. Y., & Dayao, P. (2006). Mind, body, and spirit: Family physicians' beliefs, attitudes, and practices regarding the integration of patient spirituality into medical care. *Journal of Religion and Health, 45*(2), 234–247.

Payne, R., Payne, T. R., & Heller, K. S. (2002). The Harlem Palliative Care Network. *Journal of Palliative Medicine, 5*(5), 781–792.

Pellegrino, E. D., Thomasma, D. C., & Miller, D. G. (1996). *The Christian virtues in medical practice.* Washington, DC: Georgetown University Press.

Pellegrino, E. D. (1998). Emerging ethical issues in palliative care. *JAMA, 279*(19), 1521–1522.

Pellegrino, E. D., & Thomasma, D. C. (1981). *A philosophical basis for medical practice: Toward a philosophy and ethics of the healing profession.* New York, NY: Oxford University Press.

Proulx, K., & Jacelon, C. (2004). Dying with dignity: The good patient versus the good death. *American Journal of Hospice and Palliative Care, 21*(2), 116–120.

Puchalski, C. M. (2006a). The role of spirituality in the care of seriously ill, chronically ill, and dying patients. In *A time for listening and caring: Spirituality and the care of the chronically ill and dying* (pp. 5–26). New York, NY: Oxford University Press.

Puchalski, C. M. (2006b). Spirituality in palliative care: An ethical imperative. In *A time for listening and caring* (pp. 27–38). New York, NY: Oxford University Press.

Puchalski, C., Ferrell, B., Virani, R., Otis-Green, S., Baird, P., Bull, J., . . . Sulmasy, D. (2009). Improving the quality of spiritual care as a dimension of palliative care: The report of the consensus conference. *Journal of Palliative Medicine, 12*(10), 885–904.

Rhodes, R., & Teno, J. M. (2009). What's race got to do with it? *Journal of Clinical Oncology, 27*(33), 5496–5498.

Smith, L. C. (2007). Conceptualizing spirituality and religion in counseling: Where we've come from, where we are, and where we are going. *Journal of Pastoral Counseling, 42,* 4–21.

Sulmasy, D. P. (1999). Is medicine a spiritual practice? *Academic Medicine, 74*(9), 1002–1005.

Turner, L. (2002). Bioethics and end-of-life care in multi-ethnic settings: Cultural diversity in Canada and the USA. *Mortality, 7*(3), 285–301.

van Ryn, M., & Burke, J. (2000). The effects of patient race and socio-economic status on physicians' perceptions of patients. *Social Science & Medicine, 59*(6), 813–828.

Voelker, R. (2011). Hospital palliative care programs raise grade to B in new report card on access. *JAMA, 306*(21), 2313–2314.

Walter, T. (2002). Spirituality in palliative care: Opportunity or burden? *Palliative Medicine, 16*(2), 133–139.

Washington, M. S. (2003). *Doctor, can you hear me? Patient, are you listening?* Pittsburgh, PA: Washington Associates.

CHAPTER 19

ENHANCING DIVERSITY WITHIN ACADEMIC HEALTH CENTERS

Moving From Obstacles to Opportunities

Jeannette E. South-Paul
University of Pittsburgh

Kendall M. Campbell
East Carolina University

Audrey J. Murrell
University of Pittsburgh

ABSTRACT

This chapter examines the underrepresentation of minorities in medicine in Academic Health Centers. Historical and systemic obstacles towards greater representation of underrepresented minorities in medicine (URMMs) are introduced and analyzed. The authors then present current transformations in the recruitment and advancement process of URMMs. The authors conclude

Diversity Across the Disciplines, pages 285–294
Copyright © 2020 by Information Age Publishing
All rights of reproduction in any form reserved.

by providing specific examples and models of practice to improve the representation of URMMs in Academic Health Centers to transform the paradigm of clinical care delivery to be more inclusive of the needs of diverse patient populations.

Academic health centers (AHCs) provide patients and the community with healthcare services and support often not available elsewhere, as well as education and training for the next generation of healthcare providers. The dynamic changes occurring in the healthcare industry are having a dramatic impact on AHCs, especially concerning their workforce development efforts. These changes include the evolving structure of healthcare delivery, the entrance of advanced practice providers into the market, and expanding models of insurance coverage. Furthermore, the increasingly diverse patient population is more technologically savvy and interconnected than ever before. To effectively manage these changes, AHCs must strategically plan how to provide clinical care while fulfilling their responsibility for training the next generation of diverse healthcare providers. It is important for this next generation of healthcare providers to more closely reflect the demographics of their communities, hence the need to increase representation of underrepresented minorities in medicine (URMMs). URMMs include African Americans or Blacks, Latinos, and Native Americans. This challenge may appear straightforward; however, given the current status of diversity within the field, it poses significant barriers as well as obstacles.

The overall percentage of URMMs within health care remains low, at only 8.9% of physicians in practice in 2013 (Nivet, 2015). In addition, from 1993 to 2013, there was only a 1% increase in URMM faculty in academic medicine, which is far behind parity for this group in the U.S. general population (Guevara, Adanga, Avakame, & Carthon, 2013). Fewer URMMs and particularly African American males are matriculating in medical schools today than in 1978, resulting in limited representation for this entire group and leaving glaring omissions in perspectives in clinical care, medical education, and research (Association of American Medical Colleges, 2015; Lautenberger, Moses, & Castillo-Page, 2016). Some argue that academic medicine is at a crossroads, with attempts to meet the needs of AHCs and to address changes in the field as a result of healthcare reform, economic priorities, and changing patient needs (Block, Sonnino, & Bellini, 2015).

At the apex of this crossroads is the challenge of increasing the diversity of AHC faculty, which is critical to managing and enhancing the knowledge base and comfort of health professional teams, as well as to building trust between patients and healthcare professionals. Thus, this chapter examines the trends, barriers, and underlying factors related to the lack of diversity and poor representation of URMMs within AHCs and offers key considerations for increasing numbers of URMs within academic medicine faculty.

A HISTORY OF OBSTACLES TO DIVERSITY

There are many reasons for poor representation of URMMs within AHCs. One reason is the difficulty in quantifying workforce needs by race/ethnicity. Recent analyses indicate challenges in predicting how many providers of which disciplines will be needed not only now but also in the future (Grover, Orlowski, & Erikson, 2016). This challenge is compounded by the difficulty in projecting workforce needs in general, let alone with respect to race/ethnicity or other diversity characteristics. Important questions include considering how workforce needs are defined for URMMs, as well as whether they can or should be, and how parity can be reached with the U.S. population. Should parity be the goal? Research is needed to more clearly define the disparity, determine goals, and develop solutions. Despite these unanswered questions, it is still the case that the diversity of AHCs does not reflect the diversity of the patient population that requires high-quality and culturally competent care.

This leads to another key reason for poor representation of URMM faculty in AHCs: the challenge of overcoming historical derailments to workforce diversity. Structural barriers imbedded in the U.S. social and political systems have significantly delayed progress toward diversifying the healthcare workforce. Historical injustices, such as the removal of American Indians from their homelands and slavery, framed core elements of American society—agriculture, construction, service, and education, to name a few. Majority members of the population received the benefits of land, voting rights, educational opportunity, access to certain industries, and paid employment that resulted in structural privilege that contributes to the current uneven playing field (Adelman, 2007).

Many public institutions and state universities did not matriculate African American or Latino students until the late 1960s or early 1970s, hindering access and the growth of minority populations into higher education, especially in pathways within the healthcare profession. The influential 1910 Flexner Report (also called the Carnegie Foundation Report) called on U.S. medical schools to put into place high admission and graduation standards to promote the strict standing of science in both research and teaching. The result was a centralization of medical institutions when many fell short of these enhanced standards, leading to large-scale mergers and closures of AHCs and medical schools. A devastating consequence was also the closure of all but two medical schools embracing African American students, thus limiting the potential production of diverse physicians focused on serving a diverse patient population (Steinecke & Terrell, 2010). The repercussions of the Flexner Report have produced far-reaching consequences for the pipeline of diverse faculty representation, but would eventually spark the creation of organizations dedicated to reversing these negative trends.

Ironically, the impact of these historical educational inequities remain invisible to many nonminority faculty, leaders, and AHC administrators. As Peggy McIntosh (1998) so clearly describes, people who benefit most from systems of privilege are mostly unaware of and blind to the existence of privilege systems, thus preserving the myths of moral and managerial meritocracy. Imposing standards that ignore the unique needs of diverse populations can serve to homogenize the profession in ways that may be unintended but are nonetheless devastating. Perhaps viewing the medical profession as a privileged class serves as a hidden barrier that perpetuates the historical inequities and lack of diversity representation with AHCs. For example, it is well documented that the Flexner Report viewed Blacks as inferior and thus strongly advocated the closing of historically Black medical schools. It also led to barriers for women's admittance into U.S. medical schools. Although quality was the explicit goal, the consequences of this effort toward medical reform would be to set back the profession for several decades in terms of creating a highly skilled and well-trained pipeline of medical professionals, physicians, and healthcare leaders.

As the demand for greater numbers within the healthcare profession increases, the profession appears ill-equipped to meet these demands in a way that removes the historical barriers faced by URMMs and their access to healthcare careers and influential leadership roles within AHCs. In response to this demand, institutions and public entities embraced affirmative action in the early 1970s to address historical underrepresentation of minorities in higher education, public contracts, and hiring. Organizations such as the Association of American Medical Colleges adopted strategies to increase diversity, creating a Division of Minority Health, Education and Prevention in 1988 and developing the Project 3000 by 2000 initiative in 1990 to increase the number of minority students matriculating in medical schools (Association of American Medical Colleges, 1992). Unfortunately, the efforts of higher educational institutions and other public organizations were severely hampered by a series of ballot initiatives, lawsuits, and legislation. Efforts to derail affirmative action began in 1996 with the passage of Proposition 209 in California, which outlawed consideration of race and ethnicity in admissions to the state's institutions of higher education (Steinecke & Terrell, 2010). These historical, structural, and political obstacles are some key explanations for why the profession has been slow to diversify its ranks, particularly among faculty and leadership within AHCs.

A CALL FOR ACTION AND TRANSFORMATION

URM faculty openly acknowledge a devaluing of their professional contributions and a discounting of those whose scholarly work focuses on reducing health disparities in minority communities. URM faculty also confront ongoing discrimination, racism, disrespect and bias, and demands for excessive committee service (Pololi, Cooper, & Carr, 2010; Price et al., 2005). Furthermore, minority faculty note characteristics of their identities as minorities that impact their interactions in the professional world. For example, they feel that they represent an entire race or ethnic group and thus experience a higher level of scrutiny by peers and supervisors. They feel particularly responsible for supporting a spouse or partner's career, not just their own. If one member of the couple is unhappy or feels professionally unsupported or even harassed, he or she must consider the implications of leaving the institution on the ability of the spouse or partner to keep his or her position or to advance professionally. Minority faculty describe a distrust of the motives and actions of those of discordant cultural backgrounds who are their peers or superiors. This results in an elevated sense of anxiety related to how their missteps will be viewed with less tolerance than if they were majority professionals, resulting in even more pressure to excel.

These perceptions are consistent with the work of Nunez-Smith et al. (2007) whose qualitative study of physicians of African descent in the northeast United States revealed an awareness of race that permeated their professional lives and influenced the institutional climate. Responses to perceived racism at work varied from minimization to confrontation and included a feeling of racial fatigue that resulted from collective race-related experiences (Nunez-Smith et al., 2007). Despite facing these persistent personal barriers, Cora-Bramble, Zhang, and Castillo-Page (2010) note that minority faculty members who are academically productive are more likely to have personal resilience when they possess specific personal and/or cultural characteristics that are enablers. Indeed, certain nontraditional, resilience-centered intervention strategies may positively affect the advancement of minority faculty in academic medicine in a way that can help with the need for transformation across the profession and within AHCs. Block et al. (2015) argue that academic medicine has entered into a critical period of evolution and transformation. Attention to the mission of academic medicine reveals the need for focused efforts on meeting the needs of a more diverse patient population by diversifying the workforce and increasing cultural competence. The challenge of meeting the core mission of academic medicine has intensified due to factors such as healthcare reform, revenue prioritization, technology changes, and consumer access to healthcare information. Clearly the landscape is changing. In addition, within the United States, there is a projected shortfall of nurses and physicians, especially among diverse populations (Kirch, Henderson, & Dill, 2012). How quality health care is delivered, by whom, and with what methods are causes of uncertainty for AHCs, but also a call for action and transformation. As AHCs evaluate their mission, capabilities, and opportunities, we look to individual, instructional, and organizational initiatives that can help to shape positive transformation as we move forward.

MOVING FROM OBSTACLES TO OPPORTUNITIES

Attention to reducing recruitment and advancement barriers for URM health professionals and faculty is likely to increase numbers, as was seen with women faculty. For example, commitment to improving the historic underrepresentation of women in medicine, science, and leadership has resulted in evaluation of the causes of this underrepresentation and implementation of interventions to achieve change. Much of the literature focused on the need for new types of mentorship, work–family balance, salary equity, academic productivity, and other factors that influence or contribute to women's success (Adelman, 2007). The extensive body of literature and analyses focusing on women's issues emphasizes the importance of improving the culture for equitable advancement of women: equal access to resources and opportunities, minimization of unconscious gender bias, enhancement of work–life balance, and leadership engagement (McIntosh, 1998). A similarly intense approach would likely improve minority faculty representation as well. This means looking at focused initiatives that seek to transform the profession as well as reshape AHCs to meet the current and future demands of this professional environment.

Even before the entrance of other professionals into the clinical workforce, URMM numbers (especially African Americans and Latinos) were not increasing as rapidly as might be predicted, given advances in minority medical student enrollment. Institutions have a role to play in finding a way forward. Multiple studies have identified a lack of mentoring, role models, and social capital for URM trainees and faculty alongside the burden of increased social and civic responsibilities (Beech et al., 2013). This challenge gives institutions the ability to increase URMM faculty representation through inclusiveness, support, and the creation of guidelines that promote change.

National and regional conferences that offer a public health focus directly addressing health disparities and promoting networking and collaboration are a critical avenue for developing URMM faculty. In spite of heavy clinical responsibilities, attendance at similar gatherings will promote the exchange of creative ideas and professional cross-institutional programs and centers that benefit faculty who focus on health disparities and their institutions. Academic institutions that promote faculty career development—such as what McGee and his colleagues (Thakore et al., 2014) have developed at Northwestern University for biomedical scientist faculty—demonstrate the success derived from an intense multifocal institutional approach. The Northwestern program (Thakore et al., 2014) is based on a novel application of deploying highly skilled coaches to complement, rather than be a substitute for, traditional mentoring in biomedical research training.

Individual professional societies have also identified the lack of diversity in their disciplines and have incorporated offerings in their annual meeting programs to offer support and guidance for members from underrepresented groups; these include the Society of Teachers of Family Medicine (STFM), the Society of General Internal Medicine, and the American Psychiatric Association (APA). Others have formed committees (e.g., the STEM's Minority and Multicultural Health Collaborative) to assess the needs of members and guide the programs of the larger organization. Others have created fellowship programs for students and residents to explore issues related to diversity (e.g., APA's Diversity Leadership Fellowship).

Most notably, the Association of American Medical Colleges was founded as a not-for-profit association dedicated to improving health care by transforming medical education, improving patient care, and facilitating impactful medical research. Membership consists of 152 accredited U.S. and 17 accredited Canadian medical schools, as well as major teaching hospitals, health systems, and other academic societies. One of their major areas of focus is also to increase the pipeline of diversity within the medical profession, and within AHCs more specifically. An example of these efforts is their annual Minority Faculty Leadership Development Seminar that brings together junior faculty from across the United States and provides them with real-world guidance and tools for pursuing career advancement in academic medicine. In addition, several ongoing efforts by the Association of American Medical Colleges support developing critical professional competencies, such as research, grant writing, communications, mentoring, and navigation of the complexity of academic and clinical responsibilities within AHCs.

At the macro level, Centers of Excellence programs, funded by the Health Resources and Services Administration (HRSA) have incorporated robust faculty development initiatives into their funding priorities. Health Resources and Services Administration's Title VII programs have supported infrastructure development and undergraduate and graduate medical training for more than 30 years (HRSA, n.d.). This effort was enhanced as a result of the passage of the Patient Protection and Affordable Care Act in 2010. Several initiatives were launched by HRSA, including enhancement of the Centers of Excellence programs. This initiative specifically supports efforts to address the lack of diversity within the profession as well as ongoing disparities in health outcomes based on race, socioeconomic status, ethnicity, and gender. Most recently, this effort has drawn an important and critical link between diversity within the healthcare workforce and achievement of the goal of high-quality, safe, and accessible care for a diverse patient population. In addition, diversity of healthcare professionals has been broadened to include the need for greater cultural competence across all sections of healthcare delivery, academic medicine, and research. Having a substantial increase in a diverse and culturally competent health professions workforce as a contributing factor to effectively addressing the healthcare needs of URM populations has the potential to significantly transform the way that healthcare institutions overall, and in AHCs in particular, conduct their work and evaluate their outcomes.

These examples serve as models for the necessary changes, structures, and resources that are needed to transform AHCs to be more inclusive in their workforce and leadership. There is no one-shot solution to this challenge. Thus, initiatives at the organizational, institutional, and societal levels are necessary for long-term and significant change to occur. While this may appear to reflect a daunting endeavor, there are opportunities for innovation as part of ongoing efforts to diversify academic medicine.

CONCLUSIONS

The central focus of this chapter is to better understand the dynamic changes occurring in the healthcare industry have with regard to their workforce development efforts. Block et al. (2015) offer the insight that the evolving professional landscape is not merely an obstacle but a driver and an opportunity for innovation. For example, rethinking the definition, role, and reward structure for faculty within AHCs will be necessary as we increase diversity in the health professions. Pathways for promotion, the role of the clinician–educator, and the need for greater community engagement are all reshaping the role of those involved within AHCs, especially faculty of color. Faculty whose backgrounds and experiences reflect the communities served by the AHC will add understanding and expertise to AHCs committed to addressing unique community needs. The Affordable Care Act requirement for hospitals to conduct community health needs assessments every 3 years was a significant step in acknowledging the need for identifying, understanding, and addressing unique community needs. How we define the role of physician faculty, the value of research, and the need for more collaboration between institutions and the communities in which they reside are all transformative forces that are reshaping the defined mission of AHCs. This suggests that the diversification of AHCs must quickly transform from being merely a question of diversity workforce or leadership and to one of diversity in thought, approach, pedagogy, and practice. In the future, we are likely looking at a redefinition of the role and structure of medical education and scholarly activities within academic medicine.

If we do not shift our focus and increase our efforts to diversify faculty within academic medicine, the nation's rapidly changing demographics will result in missed opportunities to develop clinicians from an increasingly larger segment of the population. We risk training more clinicians who do not possess the cultural competence to care for our current population. These skills are important if we are to maintain our national competitive edge for advancement in what has become one of the nation's leading industries: health care.

REFERENCES

Adelman, L. (2007). Unnatural causes: Is inequality making us sick? *Preventing Chronic Disease: Public Health Research, Practice and Policy, 4*(4), 1–2. Retrieved from https://www.ncbi.nlm.nih.gov/pmc/articles/PMC2134831/pdf/PCD44A116 .pdf

Association of American Medical Colleges. (1992). *Project 3000 by 2000 technical assistance manual: Guidelines for action.* Washington, DC: Author.

Association of American Medical Colleges. (2015). *Altering the course: Black males in medicine.* Retrieved from https://store.aamc.org/altering-the-course-black -males-in-medicine.html

Beech, B. M., Calles-Escandon, J., Hairston, K. G., Langdon, S. E., Latham-Sadler, B. A., & Bell, R. A. (2013). Mentoring programs for underrepresented minority faculty in academic medical centers: A systematic review of the literature. *Academic Medicine, 88*(4), 541–549. https://doi.org/10.1097/acm.0b013 e31828589e3

Block, S. M., Sonnino, R. E., & Bellini, L. (2015) Defining "faculty" in academic medicine: Responding to the challenges of a changing environment. *Academic Medicine, 90*(3), 279–282.

Cora-Bramble, D., Zhang, K., & Castillo-Page, L. (2010). Minority faculty members' resilience and academic productivity: Are they related? *Academic Medicine, 85*(9), 1492–1498. https://doi.org/10.1097/acm.0b013e3181df12a9

Grover, A., Orlowski, J. M., & Erikson, C. E. (2016). The nation's physician workforce and future challenges. *American Journal of the Medical Sciences, 351*(1), 11–19. https://doi.org/10.1016/j.amjms.2015.10.009

Guevara, J. P., Adanga, E., Avakame, E., & Carthon, M. B. (2013). Minority faculty development programs and underrepresented minority faculty representation at US medical schools. *JAMA, 310*(21), 2297–2304. https://doi.org/10.1001/ jama.2013.282116

Health Resources and Services Administration. (n.d.). *Centers of excellence.* Retrieved from https://bhw.hrsa.gov/fundingopportunities/?id=fabd901d-f6b1 -45eb-913b-d491c1e6a747

Kirch, D. G., Henderson, M. K., & Dill, M. J. (2012). Physician workforce projections in an era of health care reform. *Annual Review of Medicine, 63*, 435–445.

Lautenberger, D., Moses, A., & Castillo-Page, L. C. (2016). An overview of women full-time medical school faculty of color. *Analysis in Brief, 16*(4), 1–2.

McIntosh, P. (1998). White privilege, color and crime: A personal account. In C. R. Mann & M. S. Zatz (Eds.), *Images of color, images of crime: Readings* (pp. 207–216). Los Angeles, CA: Roxbury.

Nivet, M. A. (2015). A diversity 3.0 update: Are we moving the needle enough? *Academic Medicine, 90*(12), 1591–1593. https://doi.org/10.1097/acm.0000000000000950

Nunez-Smith, M., Curry, L. A., Bigby, J., Berg, D., Krumholz, H. M., & Bradley, E. H. (2007). Impact of race on the professional lives of physicians of African descent. *Annals of Internal Medicine, 146*, 45–51. https://doi.org/10.7326/0003-4819-146-1-200701020-00008

Pololi, L., Cooper, L. A., & Carr, P. (2010). Race, disadvantage and faculty experiences in academic medicine. *Journal of General Internal Medicine, 25*(12), 1363–1369. https://doi.org/10.1007/s11606-010-1478-7

Price, E. G., Gozu, A., Kern, D. E., Powe, N. R., Wand, G. S., Golden, S., & Cooper, L. A. (2005). The role of cultural diversity climate in recruitment, promotion, and retention of faculty in academic medicine. *Journal of General Internal Medicine, 20*(7), 565–571. https://doi.org/10.1111/j.1525-1497.2005.0127.x

Steinecke, A., & Terrell, C. (2010). Progress for whose future? The impact of the Flexner Report on medical education for racial and ethnic minority physicians in the United States. *Academic Medicine, 85*(2), 236–245. https://doi.org/10.1097/acm.0b013e3181c885be

Thakore, B. K., Naffziger-Hirsch, M. E., Richardson, J. L., Williams, S. N., & McGee, R., Jr. (2014). The Academy for Future Science Faculty: Randomized controlled trial of theory-driven coaching to shape development and diversity of early-career scientists. *BMC Medical Education, 14*, 160. https://doi.org/10.1186/1472-6920-14-160

CHAPTER 20

DELIBERATIVE COMMUNITY FORUMS AS INCLUSIVE PUBLIC WORK

Collaborations That Engage Difference as a Resource

Tim Dawson
The Art of Democracy, Pittsburgh, PA

ABSTRACT

The principles and practices of deliberative democracy present a uniquely valuable framework for supporting interdisciplinary, public work projects that can benefit diverse communities and the scholars and students with whom they work. This chapter describes Deliberative Community Forums as an inclusive public work project bringing together students on campus at Carnegie Mellon University and diverse groups of citizens from Pittsburgh neighborhoods engaging with policy makers on matters such as affordable housing, climate change, community-police relations, community redevelopment, healthcare ethics, municipal budgets, and natural gas drilling. Individual public work projects brought together scholars from across disciplines

Diversity Across the Disciplines, pages 295–311
Copyright © 2020 by Information Age Publishing
295

and from across universities, including bioethicists, climate scientists, civil and environmental engineers, designers, philosophers, rhetoricians, social scientists, and theater artists. Drawing insights from more than a decade of community-engaged research, the authors present a framework for creating inclusive public work using Deliberative Community Forums which engage difference and support agency.

For more than a decade, I, along with my colleagues at Carnegie Mellon University's Program for Deliberative Democracy and, for the last several years, at the Art of Democracy, have worked in collaboration with community leaders, elected officials, nonprofit organizations, and residents of diverse communities to make Pittsburgh, Pennsylvania, a center for deliberative democracy. This work has involved organizing opportunities for everyday people and policymakers to engage in informed and inclusive public deliberations. Specific projects we have organized differed in terms of their outcomes and the issues on which they were focused. Despite this variability, those with whom we collaborate invariably identify similar objectives for our work together: to create a public engagement experience that is meaningfully different, in several specific ways, from past experiences. First, our collaborators wish to bring together a diversity of people and perspectives. Second, this desire for diversity is often expressed as a goal that our engagement will involve more than the usual suspects (e.g., activists, lobbyists, community development professionals). What our partners seek is an engagement that elicits the voices of everyday people from diverse backgrounds. In particular, they want to hear from people whose perspectives are often absent from or silenced by traditional forms of public engagement. Third, project organizers look for a public engagement experience that will nurture connections and establish relationships among the people involved. Furthermore, these organizers hope that collaborations will foster connections, commitment, and a communal identity that provides a shared sense of community among those who participate.

One result of our collaborations is a protocol called Deliberative Community Forums. Our experience teaches us that individuals, policymakers, and policy-making processes benefit from public engagement that employ this protocol. These benefits serve to strengthen democracy and a commitment to democratic processes in the places and among the people with whom we have worked. Moreover, the protocol provides a framework for structuring interdisciplinary community-engaged public work (Ackerman & Coogan, 2010; Boyte, 2011) that enables those involved to experience a type of citizenship that entails people sharing in communal labor that is focused on promoting inclusion by engaging diversity as a resource (Young, 2000) and supporting the agency of diverse individuals involved in the process (Flower, 2008).

DELIBERATIVE COMMUNITY FORUMS

As a field of inquiry, deliberative democracy has been under concerted development, within the United States and internationally, since at least the early 1990s (Bachtiger, Dryzak, Mansbridge, & Warren, 2018). Through theory and practice, deliberative theorists and practitioners pursue the realization of three principles: inclusion, reciprocity, and legitimacy (Gutmann & Thompson, 2004). Our Deliberative Community Forum protocol includes the general features of engagement that reflect these principles (i.e., deliberative engagement), as outlined by Leighninger (2012) in the edited collection Democracy in Motion. Commenting on the wide range of practices chronicled in this collection, Leighninger (2012) identifies the features that indicate how the principles of inclusion, reciprocity, and legitimacy are pursued through deliberative engagement.

- Inclusion is supported by active efforts to recruit a group of people reflective of the diversity of the communities impacted by the outcomes of the deliberation (Karpowitz & Raphael, 2016).
- Reciprocity is supported by engagement that provides opportunities for a diverse group to consider a range of policy options, to engage relevant arguments and information, to compare values and experiences, and to share their reasons, reasoning, and justifications for their preferences (Gutmann & Thompson, 1997).
- Inclusion and reciprocity are supported by structured discussions.
- Legitimacy is supported by efforts to ensure that open and inclusive engagement is connected to and directed at tangible actions and outcomes related to specific decision- or policy-making processes.

Provided as a list of features that characterize deliberative engagement, this list works well as a series of questions that should be addressed during the process of organizing opportunities for deliberative engagement. That is, as organizers begin their work, they should add "How will we . . ." to the beginning of each item on this list.

Reflecting these general features, Deliberative Community Forums seek to engage a diverse group of people in structured conversations that are geared toward providing individuals with an opportunity to understand and consider multiple, diverse perspectives in their process of developing an informed opinion. Significantly, participants in these forums do not pursue consensus, nor is their engagement intended to result in a specific decision. Rather, as an opportunity for public engagement that can be incorporated into decision-making processes that include other types of engagement (e.g., individuals and groups making presentations to a city council), Deliberative Community Forums provide people with the opportunity to understand and learn from one another as they engage collaboratively in reflection on and consideration of their needs, the needs of others, and the needs of their community. The results of Deliberative Community Forums create a resource for policymakers, organizations, and individuals who are seeking to devise strategies to address particular challenges facing their community.

Figure 20.1 details the key elements of a Deliberative Community Forum, which include a diverse group of participants, briefing materials containing information relevant to the issue being discussed, small-group discussions facilitated by trained moderators, a question and answer session with a resource panel of people with diverse types of expertise relevant to the issue(s), and a post-deliberation survey. Together, these elements provide resources for individuals to develop and record an opinion informed by relevant facts, expert information, and an understanding of the effects that issues and policy options can have on diverse members of a community.

This protocol has been used to structure forums on the campus of Carnegie Mellon University and in neighborhoods throughout Pittsburgh and southwestern Pennsylvania. On campus, through an initiative called Campus Conversations, participants have deliberated a range of issues, including climate change, free speech on college campuses, and marriage equality. Off campus, forums have focused on regional issues, such as the financial constraints on local governments and the challenges associated with natural gas drilling; they have also focused on more localized issues, such as neighborhood redevelopment, priorities for the City of Pittsburgh's Capital Budget, and the selection of a new chief of police for the City of Pittsburgh. In several publications, scholars have detailed the process and results of particular projects, including Campus Conversations on climate change (Canfield, Klima, & Dawson, 2015) and marriage equality (Bridges & Dickert, 2011), deliberations on neighborhood revitalization in Pittsburgh (Crowley, 2011), and deliberations on ethical frameworks for how to allocate scarce medical resources during a flu pandemic (Daugherty Biddison et al., 2014).

In addition to documenting participants' views on particular issues, these publications include assessments of the forums that are exemplary of more

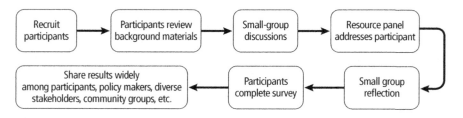

Figure 20.1   Elements of a Deliberate Community Forum.

general findings. When asked in surveys to assess their experience, most participants find these forums engaging, informative, and worthwhile. Participants report that these forums enable their voice to be heard while also providing them an opportunity to learn information and understand perspectives with which they had previously not been familiar. An overwhelming majority of participants indicate that, based on their experience with one forum, they are likely to attend a similarly structured forum in the future.

Comments gathered in surveys or in conversation with community partners offer similar assessments. Participants in these forums express a desire for more forums. During one forum on how to promote equity in our region, one human rights activist identified our ongoing collaboration supporting the City of Pittsburgh's use of Deliberative Community Forums as a key governance innovation that has made our region better. For their part, public officials we have worked with say they value these forums as a process ensuring that "all voices, not just the loudest, have a chance to be heard" (Program for Deliberative Democracy & Art of Democracy, n.d., p. 41).

These positive assessments, however, must be considered alongside concerns participants have also expressed. While recognizing the value of the engagement enabled by the forums—in fact, it would seem, precisely because they recognize its value—participants have identified important voices missing from specific deliberations. These include youth, young adults, and people who find it difficult to make time to attend public meetings, such as parents with young children. In addition, for particular forums, people have identified missing stakeholders, such as oil and gas industry representatives at a forum on natural gas drilling, abortion opponents at a forum on abortion clinic regulations, conservatives at a forum on free speech, and absentee landlords at a forum on affordable housing. These latter examples suggest that those who have participated believe deliberative forums provide a useful means to engage productively with people whose perspectives and privilege are reinforced by the status quo.

While the desire for more diverse voices suggests that participants believe the forums are a valuable means for engaging with divergent views, some participants have suggested that the protocol functions to silence already marginalized perspectives. In a recent meeting of the City of Pittsburgh's Public Engagement Working Group, for example, one of the working group members said that deliberative forums "do not let groups find themselves." In fact, the protocol does emphasize engagement among individuals rather than groups. For example, those who arrive at a forum together are asked (but not forced) to join different small groups for discussion. This is done with the assumption that those who come together have a similar perspective to share and it is better if that perspective is shared more broadly among the small groups. As was suggested to one group of participants that was reluctant to disband, more of the final surveys might reflect their group's perspective if it was given voice at multiple tables. Nevertheless, as I discuss more fully later, the group's reluctance to disband and thereby isolate its members and possibly have its voice diluted indicates that the forum protocol presents a challenge to certain ideas about agency and how to gain agency within a diverse public.

The concerns reviewed raise important questions about how to promote inclusive deliberative engagement. On the one hand, there is the question of how to recruit more diverse voices. On the other hand, there is the question of how to create opportunities for deliberative engagement that people from diverse backgrounds will perceive as a legitimate means to assert their agency. Reflecting on comments like those discussed, one of our closest long-term partners, the former director of the City of Pittsburgh's Office of Community Affairs, offered the following sobering reflection: "It's not the protocol by itself that guarantees diversity or inclusion." As she went on to point out, while the protocol can capitalize on whatever diversity is available in the room, it is only when strategies of inclusion are employed in the process of organizing a forum that the conditions are created for the forum itself to realize the benefits of deliberative engagement.

As a response to the concerns raised by some participants and the questions they raise about how to promote inclusion, we have found it useful to pursue our collaborations as public work and to maintain, throughout the process of organizing a forum, a focus on two actions: (a) engaging difference as a resource in order to (b) support the agency of those involved. More than the forum protocol, it is pursuit of these actions in the process of organizing a forum that enables those who become involved to experience the particular type of citizenship enabled by Deliberative Community Forums.

INCLUSIVE PUBLIC WORK: ENGAGING DIFFERENCE AS A RESOURCE AND SUPPORTING AGENCY

Deliberative Community Forums provide people with an opportunity to have an influence on their community's decision-making processes. To help ensure that the opportunity is meaningful and that participants will recognize the forum as a meaningful and legitimate opportunity to make their voice heard, organizers, especially when they are academics collaborating with community partners, must take pains to avoid the pitfall of participants being engaged as subjects in a research project. We take steps away from this this pitfall by pursuing Deliberative Community Forums as public work. As defined by Boyte (2011), public work is a "normative, democratizing ideal of citizenship generalized from communal labors of making and tending the commons" (p. 5). Ackerman and Coogan (2010) caution that university partners involved in public work (e.g., faculty, students) should expect to engage community partners not as experts or service providers; instead, they should engage in collaborative projects as "citizen-scholars" (p. 8). Accordingly, university partners should expect to join in communal labor to "solve public problems and create things of lasting civic value both material and symbolic" (Boyte, 2011, p. 5). Like the others involved, university partners should expect to contribute their expertise and resources toward advancing collective objectives and goals as these are determined through deliberation and negotiation with community partners. To best understand how a concept of public work can inform practice, it is useful to understand more about the actions we pursue as we engage in communal labor with our community partners.

Engaging Difference as a Resource

A diverse group of people engaging in deliberation will need to adopt a productive way of thinking about difference. This can be difficult, Young (2000) argues, because historically, theories and practices of democratic deliberation have been undermined by two persistent assumptions regarding difference. The first is that people's differences are a problem and necessarily a source of conflict; the second is that difference equals abnormal or deficient. These assumptions are reflected in the idea that the knowledge and expertise people develop as a result of their particular experience, what Young (following Haraway, 1988) calls "situated knowledge" (p. 76), is not as valuable as the knowledge of experts or as knowledge that is purportedly universally true for all humans. Young argues that any theory proposed as a model for inclusive democratic deliberation must dispel both of these assumptions. She proposes that, to address these assumptions, people must be enabled to engage difference as a resource when they gather to deliberate about what ought to be done to address problems in their own community.

Young's (1990) proposal for engaging difference as a resource is premised on what she calls a "relational understanding of difference" (p. 171). This is in contrast to essentializing notions that encourage people toward the belief that an individual's race, ethnicity, gender, sexuality, or social position relative to others provides some indication of how a person will behave or what a person will believe. As a contrast, Young proposes a view that regards difference as both a resource and a subject for public inquiry and reflection. As a resource, individuals bring to engagement a wealth of practical wisdom derived from their experience interacting within and among a community's various associational networks. Because people's experience and interactions will differ, people will have differing practical, or situated, knowledge that informs what they think about problems and how they can best be addressed. Moreover, while individuals' practical knowledge reflects their experience of membership in particular social groups, Young maintains that a group's needs cannot be assumed prior to engagement. Rather, people can discover what differences are important to consider in relation to specific issues or problems during their public engagement. During an engagement focused on inquiry and understanding, people come to comprehend which differences are salient and significant in their community. I, for example, am a heterosexual middle-aged White man who is a parent, theater artist, and teacher. In any given situation, one, several, or none of these things may prove to be the basis of my experience of affinity with or estrangement from others. As Young (1990) describes it, in specific contexts people will experience affinity through "a flowing process in which individuals identify themselves and others" (p. 172), and it is this experience of individuals recognizing affinity with some and estrangement from others that serves to differentiate one group from another in the time and for the purposes relevant to the specific context of their engagement.

Following from this relational understanding of difference, Young (2000) argues that, to engage difference as a resource, public resources should be dedicated to creating institutional mechanisms that enable individuals to articulate their practical wisdom so that diverse groups can collaboratively develop a "collective social wisdom" (p. 76). The type of collective wisdom Young imagines is not available prior to deliberative engagement, nor does it belong to or reflect the experience of any one individual or group. Rather, through processes that involve individuals sharing their particular wisdom as a diverse group engages in collaborative dialogue, collective social wisdom emerges as a resource. This resource is one that all participants can use as they consider how to address problems in their community.

Deliberative Community Forums are designed to engage difference as a resource in the ways imagined by Young (2000). The organizational process preceding these forums involves coordinating resources (e.g., people, information, money) to support the forums. Moreover, ongoing collaboration with our partners help to ensure that these forums become something like the institutionalized mechanisms Young imagines. For example, Pittsburgh now holds Deliberative Community Forums about the capital budget annually, the City of Pittsburgh's Office of Community Affairs worked with us to develop a how-to manual for organizing the forums, and the protocol and the how-to manual will be identified as a key tool in the City of Pittsburgh's forthcoming public engagement strategy document.

Supporting Agency

To engage in public work, people need to be able to regard one another as competent and capable individuals whose concerns are valid and whose knowledge and experience are valuable. As a result, public work projects require means that enable people from diverse backgrounds to engage and support one another as agents.

This challenge can manifest in a number of ways. People can find attributing agency to others difficult, especially when they are attempting to work with one another across the boundaries of difference (Flower, 2008). Young (2000) points out, for example, that traditional processes of public engagement often marginalize individuals and groups because the norms of deliberation are biased against some forms of expression. The silencing effect of dominating discourses can block or interfere with efforts to support the agency of individuals. Dominating discourses, however, are just one of what can be a diverse range of scripts of agency that can be influencing people's interaction during public engagement (Flower, 2008).

Through their lived experience in various contexts, people develop a range of ideas about what actions will enable their voice to be heard and valued. Those who have enjoyed success with the rules of engagement privileged by schools and other elite institutions may attribute agency only to civil discourse, understood as dispassionate critical-rational argumentation (Higgins, Long, & Flower, 2006). Those who have achieved success through activism, protest, and agitation may prefer these strategies, and they may be suspicious of any suggestion that they adopt different strategies (Young, 2003). People experiencing marginalization may bring to an engagement a more circumspect script of agency. Cushman's (1998) ethnographic study of poor women in under-resourced urban communities, for example, found that these women asserted their agency by avoiding the institutions or agents of government or by maintaining a tight control over how much information they shared when they had to interact with these agents and institutions. Even if people with this experience were somehow convinced to attend a public forum, they could not be expected to readily share their practical wisdom with unfamiliar others. Public engagement projects that welcome diversity in the service of promoting inclusion may find that competing ideas of what counts as agency can function to undermine efforts to engage across the boundaries of difference.

After forums on natural gas drilling, for example, a debrief of small-group facilitators revealed that anti-drilling activists had sought to take over small-group discussions with coordinated messaging; these same activists took a confrontational stance during the question and answer session with the forum's panelists, refusing to accept panelists' answers and not giving up the microphone to allow questions from others. Facilitators also reported, however, that while they had struggled to manage the coordinated efforts of these activists, some other participants spoke out against these tactics; that is, some participants pointed out to the activists that these tactics made it difficult for them to share their perspectives. Interestingly, several of the activists involved later trained and participated as volunteers for subsequent forums on different topics, and, years later, it was one of these activists who identified Deliberative Community Forums as a regional asset.

We have seen others follow a trajectory similar to that of these activists several times. Individuals who come to one forum prepared to assert their agency through strategies they have used successfully in other contexts seem to experience as valuable the forum's focus on inquiry and developing understanding of multiple perspectives (rather than their being focused on debate, persuasion, or a drive to consensus). This attribution of value seems evident in the choice some individuals make to participate in subsequent forums but in a different role. Many of the people who train as facilitators do so after they have attended a forum as a participant. However, in choosing to train as a facilitator, they are choosing a role that functions to support the agency of others. Thus, they seem to attribute value to the forums as a useful means that supports the articulation of multiple perspectives in inclusive ways.

An important way inclusion is fostered during the forums involves facilitation that supports what Young (2000) would call "an expanded repertoire" of democratic communication, or the acceptance of diverse modes of speaking in addition to the inclusion of diverse speakers (p. 80). For example, Young (2000) suggests that embracing narrative as a means of engagement promotes inclusion in ways that support the agency of individuals who may be marginalized by norms of communication more comfortable and familiar to elites (p. 76). Researchers who have drawn on Young's theories (1997) when devising community-engaged research projects involving deliberative engagement find that narrative can be useful. Having, in various community-engaged projects, employed numerous ways of documenting and sharing narratives, from facilitation that elicits narratives during a deliberative conversation, to stories shared in briefing documents, to the development and performance of short skits, Higgins et al. (2006) find that narrative is, in fact, "a powerful tool" for engaging difference as a resource and for turning "individual knowledge into a communal resource" (p. 21).

Based on varied experiences, Flower (2008) cautions that "acknowledging agency in the actions of someone else is not the automatic outcome of political correctness, liberal beliefs, or goodwill" (p. 198). Flower notes, for example, that the narratives of children, urban youth, or "project mothers" may be received as charming or heartwarming; however, others may not regard the people who develop and share these narratives as agents because the style, diction, or grammar they employ may encourage others to perceive them as marginally literate (p. 192). People of goodwill may regard what has been created as good for those involved (e.g., good for building their self-esteem), but they may not engage it as a spur to deliberation. That is, people may appreciate what has been created as the revelation of a different identity, experience, or perspective, but they may not make the deliberative leap to move beyond acknowledgement of differences and engage these differences as a resource for reflection on and reconsideration of the ideas and practices they value and to which they are committed. Responding in this way, people fail to attribute agency to others. Because people may find it difficult to engage individual narratives as a resource for deliberative reflection in contexts where engagement is influenced by differing scripts of agency, Flower contends that those with privilege must employ strategies that help people to affirm, document, and support the agency of the individuals involved.

THREE PHASES FOR ENGAGING DIFFERENCE AND SUPPORTING AGENCY

Capitalizing on the insights described above—that engaging difference as a resource requires affirming, documenting, and supporting the agency of diverse participants—we have found it useful to distinguish three phases in the process of organizing a Deliberative Community Forum: (a) establishing an agenda for deliberation, (b) capturing the current conversation, and (c) holding the Deliberative Community Forum.

Establishing an Agenda for Deliberation

Whereas many people may be able to identify issues or problems in a community, their perspectives on the problems and what might be done to address them will differ. These perspectives will be informed by the practical wisdom people derive from their personal experience as well as their involvement (or lack of involvement) in a community's past efforts to address problems. As a result, while many people may agree that deliberative public engagement about a problem is necessary, people are unlikely to agree on an agenda for that deliberation. To establish an agenda, we find it important to engage with diverse stakeholders at the outset of every project to clarify objectives, priorities, and desired outcomes. The brief examples that follow provide a glimpse into this aspect of the process:

- Collaborating with the League of Women Voters of Greater Pittsburgh to organize a forum on gun safety, we began the process of setting an agenda by reaching out to people or organizations that had publicly spoken out from diverse perspectives on issues related to gun safety. We interviewed law enforcement officers, government officials, gun club members, violence prevention groups, groups advocating for gun control legislation, and groups advocating for the rights of gun owners. When reaching out to these people and organizations, we invited them to answer the following question: What conversation can we have at this time that will help us reduce gun violence in our communities? The resulting agenda for deliberation outlined four approaches: a public health approach, an approach addressing the root causes of poverty and inequality, a law enforcement approach, and an approach focusing on promoting safe and responsible gun ownership.

- Collaborating with the public television station in Pittsburgh to organize deliberative engagement about how to address poverty in our region, we hosted two deliberative sessions involving, among others, service providers, city and county officials, directors of community-based organizations, documentary filmmakers, and individuals who experienced poverty. The resulting agenda focused on the following two questions: How can we move past stigma and help people to understand the truth about the experience of poverty? How can we build coalitions that enable us to combat poverty as a systemic problem?

- Collaborating with a local philanthropic foundation to organize deliberative forums about how to address the challenges facing service members, veterans, and military families, we engaged a range of stakeholders whose everyday work involved addressing these challenges, many of whom were veterans themselves. The resulting agenda involved the following three questions: How can the region best nurture the strengths service members or veterans contribute to the region? What challenges make it difficult for service members, veterans, and their families to thrive in our region? How might service providers better connect with and help service members, veterans, and their families?

In each case, when discussing an agenda, we focused not on what could be discussed but instead on what local people with a range of expertise, grounded in their particular wisdom, believe needed to be discussed at this time in our community. In addition, having been involved in helping to set the agenda, these stakeholders join in the communal labor as partners, providing information for the forum's briefing materials, helping to recruit participants from among their particular associational networks, and even serving as resource panelists to address the questions participants had after their small-group deliberations.

Capturing the Current Conversation

Once an agenda has been established, we work with our community partners to develop resources that will enable those participating in the forum to join the conversation. At minimum, our work involves developing four resources that work together to affirm, document, and support the agency of those who participate: a very brief written document (somewhere between one to five pages), a presentation that provides an overview of the forum's agenda and the briefing document's contents, an annotated agenda that identifies which sections of the briefing document are relevant to which of the agenda's questions, and a survey for participants to complete after deliberating.

Capturing in these materials the current conversations circulating in our community about a problem is an important way to document, affirm, and support the agency of our community partners and those who will participate in a forum. Capturing these conversations involves providing information about differing perspectives in ways that will be acceptable to those who voice these perspectives. To develop the resources, we rely on our community partners to help us identify people to interview and information to gather. Reports developed by public and private agencies and organizations are always useful, but there are also community meetings to attend, documentaries to watch, and neighborhood walking tours to participate in, with our community partners as guides. Developing these materials is also an iterative process. Collaborating partners are invited to participate in creating the materials (e.g., drafting text; providing graphs, charts, or images; nominating questions for the surveys), and, throughout the process, partners are provided with drafts to review and revise.

When developing materials for a forum on poverty, for example, after each of the two deliberative sessions among stakeholders that occurred in the agenda-setting phase, participants were invited to review, revise, or amend meeting notes. Once these stakeholders agreed on an agenda, they participated in individual interviews with our public media partners and facilitated interviews with people representing perspectives that the stakeholders thought were missing from the meetings we had held (e.g., those experiencing poverty in suburban or rural communities). Having arrived at an agenda focused on addressing stigma and combating poverty as a systemic problem, the stakeholders, now serving more as collaborating partners, determined that the briefing materials should identify persistent stereotypes and myths about poverty, provide data that would help to dispel these myths, and provide an explanation for what it would mean to understand and address poverty as a systemic problem rather than as an individual's personal problem. In addition, the partners identified and helped recruit panelists for the forum. Among others, these panelists were provided an opportunity to review and suggest revisions to the briefing materials and surveys as they were developed. Ultimately, the collaborating partners decided that the best venue for the forum would be an annual Thanksgiving food distribution event organized by one of the partners that provided food and access to service providers to people from throughout southwestern Pennsylvania who were experiencing poverty.

Through the second phase of this project, the collaborating partners helped create briefing materials that identified problems with the current conversation and provided information and a new perspective that people could use to move beyond these problems toward a more productive discussion about how to address poverty. Through this process, the partners also came to be more invested to the point, in this case, that one was willing to add the forum as a new element to their organization's major annual event.

Holding the Deliberative Community Forum

Throughout the first two phases, partners work together to engage their differences as a resource and to support one another's agency. Through an iterative process, they elicit and document the diversity of each partner's particular wisdom, affirming the value of that wisdom by working with each partner to ensure that the collective wisdom, which emerges as the agenda and the briefing materials, reflects and is responsive to what we have learned from one another. The resources developed through this process, in turn, represent, among other things, the collaborating partners' efforts to support the agency of those who gather to deliberate. Informed by the expertise of diverse stakeholders, the briefing materials provide resources that enable people to enter the conversation in ways that will address the community's specific needs and concerns. During the forum, participants receive further support from facilitators and from resource panelists who, serving as teachers not pundits, answer the particular questions raised by the participants after they have deliberated in small groups. The agency of the forum participants is supported as well by the process that preceded the forum in another way. Because decision-makers and key stakeholders are engaged from the outset, they are invested in learning from the outcomes.

CONCLUDING THOUGHTS

Positioning the protocol of a Deliberative Community Forum within this three-phase process promotes inclusion and provides a framework for interdisciplinary teams to pursue community-engaged public work that integrates education and research. Our collaborations have involved faculty and students, both undergraduate and graduate, from multiple disciplines and institutions. Our public work has benefited from the expertise of artists, bioethicists, climate scientists, designers, economists, historians, philosophers, social scientists, theater artists, urban planners, and many others. To this public work, individuals have made contributions appropriate to their backgrounds, disciplines, and expertise. Like our community partners off campus, they have assisted in the work of establishing an agenda for deliberation, developing briefing materials, crafting surveys, devising strategies for recruiting participants, training facilitators, and serving as panelists during the forums. Through this public work, the collaborating partners have had the opportunity to experience a relationship as citizens that involves inquiry, invention, and deliberation directed at fostering inclusion by engaging difference as a resource and supporting the agency of those who participate.

Results from our public work are consistent with more general findings about the benefits of deliberative engagement. Two review articles, published more than a decade apart, derive similar conclusions from a review of deliberative practices in multiple countries (Carpini, Cook, & Jacobs, 2004, Kuyper, 2018). The most recent considers the effects of public deliberation on individuals, on groups or collectives, and on a polity. This review finds that research reveals a "strong link" between deliberation and the following outcomes (Kuyper, 2018, p. 15):

- for individuals: knowledge gain, changes in opinion or preference;
- for groups and collectives: reduced polarization, social learning, and a deeper understanding of the views of others; and meta-consensus, or a shared understanding of the nature of an issue and an agreement on a limited range of preferred outcomes (Niemeyer & Dryzek, 2007); and
- for polities: increased perception of legitimacy of decisions.

For our ongoing work of refinement and revision, in the future, we want to learn more about the engagement enabled by the protocol. For each of the outcomes he reviews, for example, Kuyper (2018) emphasizes that future research should focus on disaggregating deliberative protocols and illuminating what the effects are of specific elements. For our work, this will mean understanding more about how individual elements of our protocol (i.e., recruiting participants; developing briefing materials; and facilitating small-group discussions, resource panel question and answer sessions, and surveys) can or can do more to promote inclusion, engage difference as a resource, and support the agency of those who participate.

To improve the process of inclusive public work within which we have embedded our protocol, we believe we need to know more about the existing "participation infrastructure" (Nabatchi & Leighninger, 2015, p. 287) in the communities where we work. We expect that efforts to engage diverse stakeholders in agenda-setting and to capture the diversity of the current conversation can be improved by efforts to map the existing participation infrastructure in terms of the places where people engage, the associational networks of those who engage in specific places, the types of engagement occurring in different places, and how (or if) information travels from one arena of engagement to others, with a particular focus on detailing how (or if) the results of engagement can or does influence policymakers, policymaking, and policies. By mapping the existing infrastructure, we hope to discover opportunities for collaborating and for renovating or creating pathways that connect public engagement to the decision-making processes occurring within our community.

REFERENCES

Ackerman, J. M., & Coogan, D. J. (Eds.). (2010). *The public work of rhetoric: Citizen-scholars and civil engagement*. Columbia: University of South Carolina Press.

Bachtiger, A., Dryzak, J. S., Mansbridge, J., & Warren, M. E. (Eds.). (2018). *The Oxford handbook of deliberative democracy*. New York, NY: Oxford University Press.

Boyte, H. C. (2011). *We the people politics: The populist promise of deliberative public work.* Dayton, OH: Kettering Foundation.

Bridges, M., & Dickert, J. (2011). Deliberative polling in Pennsylvania: From student senate to state senate. In R. Cavalier (Ed.), *Approaching deliberative democracy: Theory and practice* (pp. 199–222). Pittsburgh, PA: Carnegie Mellon University Press.

Canfield, C., Klima, K., & & Dawson, T. (2015). Using deliberative democracy to identify energy policy priorities in the United States. *Energy Research & Social Science, 8*, 184–189.

Carpini, M. D. X., Cook, F. L., & Jacobs, L. R. (2004). Public deliberation, discursive participation, and citizen engagement: A review of the empirical literature. *Annual Review of Political Science, 7*, 315–344.

Crowley, G. (2011). Building trust through inclusion: Reflections on the practice of deliberative democracy. In R. Cavalier (Ed.), *Approaching deliberative democracy: Theory and practice* (pp. 179–198). Pittsburgh, PA: Carnegie Mellon University Press.

Cushman, E. (1998). *The struggle and the tools: Oral and literate strategies in an inner city community*. Albany: State University of New York Press.

Daugherty Biddison, E. L., Gwon, H., Schoch-Spana, M., Cavalier, R., White, D. B., Dawson, T., . . . Toner, E. S. (2014). The community speaks: Understanding ethical values in allocation of scarce lifesaving resources during disasters. *Annals of the American Thoracic Society, 11*(5), 777–783.

Flower, L. (2008). *Community literacy and the rhetoric of public engagement*. Carbondale: Southern Illinois University Press.

Gutmann, A., & Thompson, D. (1997). Deliberating about bioethics. *Hastings Center Report, 27*(3), 38–41.

Gutmann, A., & Thompson, D. (2004). *Why deliberative democracy?* Princeton, NJ: Princeton University Press.

Haraway, D. (1988). Situated knowledges: The science question in feminism and the privilege of partial perspective. *Feminist Studies, 14*(3), 575–599.

Higgins, L., Long, E., & Flower, L. (2006). Community literacy: A rhetorical model for personal and public inquiry. *Community Literacy, 1*(1), 9–43.

Karpowitz, C. F., & Raphael, C. (2016). Ideals of inclusion in deliberation. *Journal of Public Deliberation, 12*(2), 1–21.

Kuyper, J. W. (2018). The instrumental value of deliberative democracy—Or, do we have good reasons to be deliberative democrats? *Journal of Public Deliberation, 14*(1), 1–33.

Leighninger, M. (2012). Mapping deliberative engagement: Pictures from a revolution. In T. Nabatchi, J. Gastil, M. Leighninger, & G. M. Weiksner (Eds.), *Democracy in motion: evaluating the practice and impact of deliberative civic engagement* (pp. 19–39). New York, NY: Oxford University Press.

Niemeyer, S., & Dryzek, J. S. (2007). The ends of deliberation: Meta-consensus and intersubjective rationality as ideal outcomes. *Swiss Political Science Review, 13*(4), 497–526.

Nabatchi, T., & Leighninger, M. (2015). *Public participation for 21st century democracy.* San Francisco, CA: Jossey-Bass.

Program for Deliberative Democracy & Art of Democracy. (n.d.). *A handbook for deliberative community forums.* Retrieved from http://hss.cmu.edu/pdd/cities/handbook.pdf

Young, I. M. (1990). *Justice and the politics of difference.* Princeton, NJ: Princeton University Press.

Young, I. M. (1997). Difference as a resource for democratic communication. In J. Bohman & W. Rehg (Eds.), *Deliberative democracy: Essays on reason and politics* (pp. 383–406). Cambridge, MA: MIT Press.

Young, I. M. (2000). *Inclusion and democracy.* New York, NY: Oxford University Press.

Young, I. M. (2003). Activist challenges to deliberative democracy. In J. J. Fishkin & P. Laslett (Eds.), *Debating deliberative democracy* (pp. 102–120). Malden, MA: Blackwell.

EPILOGUE

THE EVOLVING PARADIGM OF DIVERSITY AND INCLUSION

Where Are We Headed?

Ableism. Latinx. Non-binary. Alternative spirituality. Transracial. Mansplain. The landscape of diversity and inclusion is no longer Black and White, or Female and Male; it requires the ability to navigate culture in a manner that is vastly different today than ever before. But just wait until tomorrow!

Countless studies have shown that diverse employee representation at all levels of an organization has a quantifiable impact on financial performance. In fact, it is now commonly acknowledged that diversity and inclusion serve as the engine for many corporations to ensure the knowledge, critical thinking, and innovation required to successfully achieve business and mission-critical objectives. But haven't we been talking about "the business case" for diversity and inclusion for some time? How much progress have we, as diversity practitioners, really made in our corporations and more broadly throughout society? And does the next generation of diversity leaders have a different agenda from that which we are immersed in today?

Diversity and inclusion started receiving widespread use throughout corporate America in the early 1990s. At that time, efforts to advance this work

Diversity Across the Disciplines, pages 313–315
Copyright © 2020 by Information Age Publishing
All rights of reproduction in any form reserved.

were largely compliance-related and focused on equal employment opportunity laws, which initially concentrated on limited protected classes. Fast forward nearly 30 years later and we have made great strides. Or have we?

- Only 2 of the 300 case studies read by first-year Harvard Business School students include illustrations of Black executives.
- In 28 states, there are no explicit statewide laws protecting people from discrimination on the basis of sexual orientation or gender identity in employment, housing, and public accommodations.
- Despite growth in recent years, only 6.6% of Fortune 500 CEOs are women.
- Thirty percent of workers fits the federal definition of having a disability yet less than half disclose that information to their employer which exemplifies the absence of a culture of inclusion and safety in the workplace.

Earlier this year, I tuned-in to watch the reboot of comedy pioneer, Norman Lear's "All in the Family" and its spinoff series "The Jeffersons." The live event recreated the original episode from both of the Emmy-winning comedies which debuted nearly 50 years ago. The brash comedy illustrated in both sitcoms played on the politically charged, and oftentimes bigoted and sexist, environment of the time. Strikingly, amidst the contemporary backdrop of today's #MeToo, #LoveWon, and #BlackLivesMatter movements, Archie Bunker is still relevant. The more things change, the more they stay the same.

Over the past 30 years, we have looked at diversity as an approach to foster representation and ensure access into the workplace. Moving forward, diversity emphasis will continue to shift towards strategies that drive equity, inclusion, and social justice. When you focus on inclusion, diversity often comes naturally. Representation will also look different for tomorrow's workforce. We are already learning expectations from the newest generation to enter the workforce. Generation Zers self-identify as competitive, spontaneous, adventuresome, and curious, not to mention multicultural with membership and belonging to various diverse communities. Investments from younger generations, and the positions they occupy, will affect how companies make business decisions.

Transformation is an urgent business requirement, and cultural competency will be fundamental to that transformation. Developing integrated business strategies to level the playing field across cultures with metrics such as employee engagement, customer satisfaction, impact on bottom-line, as well as retention and termination rates, will be instrumental in accelerating the development of culturally proficient and nimble organizations. Companies that actively accelerate transformation are dedicated to fostering a work environment where people from diverse backgrounds work comfortably in teams to achieve shared goals. These organizations recognize that talent and ability are not limited, but enhanced by the diversity and cultural expertise that individuals bring to the workplace.

While we have made tremendous progress, we realize that diversity and inclusion is a journey, not a destination, where no one, myself-included, knows everything there is to know about every single culture. Instead, we have to collectively develop the cultural humility to learn that which we do not know with the end goal of enhancing the level of respect, civility, and dignity that we demonstrate to one another—at work and in our communities.

—**James E. Taylor, PhD**
Chief Diversity, Inclusion,
and Talent Management Officer
UPMC

ABOUT THE EDITORS

Audrey J. Murrell, conducts research, teaching, and consulting that helps organizations better utilize and engage their most important assets—their human and social capital. She is currently acting dean of the University Honors College and professor of business administration, psychology, public and international affairs at the University of Pittsburgh, Katz/CBA School of Business. She is also the senior research fellow of the David Berg Center for Ethics and Leadership at the University of Pittsburgh. Her research focuses on mentoring, careers in organizations, workplace–supplier diversity, and social issues in management. This work has been published widely in management and psychology journals as well as book chapters and special issues. Popular media has also highlighted this work including the *Wall Street Journal, Pittsburgh Post-Gazette, Atlanta Journal and Constitution, Pittsburgh Business Times, Cleveland Plain Dealer, Black Enterprise, Jet Magazine,* and *Vida Executive* (in Brazil). Dr. Murrell is the author (along with Crosby and Ely) of the book entitled, *Mentoring Dilemmas: Developmental Relationships Within Multicultural Organizations* (1999, Erlbaum); "*Intelligent Mentoring: How IBM Creates Value Through People, Knowledge, and Relationships*"with Forte-Trummel and Bing (2008, Prentice-Hall); and the most recent book with Blake-Beard, *Mentoring Diverse Leaders: Creating Change for People, Processes, and Paradigms* (2017, Routledge).

Jennifer L. Petrie-Wyman is the assistant director at the University of Pittsburgh's David Berg Center for Ethics and Leadership. She researches global competency, service learning, leadership, and international education policy with attention to Africa. In Ghana, her current project focuses on im-

Diversity Across the Disciplines, pages 317–318
Copyright © 2020 by Information Age Publishing
All rights of reproduction in any form reserved.

proving policy, educational outcomes, and resources for music and dance education. She has coauthored a policy brief for the National Education Policy Center and edited work for the Ohio Department of Education, the World Association of Arts Education, and Azaguno.

Abdesalam Soudi earned his PhD in sociolinguistics from the University of Pittsburgh. His research focuses on the human-computer interface in doctors' consultations, provider-patient conversation, and cultural and linguistic diversity. Dr. Soudi holds a full-time faculty appointment with the Department of Linguistics at the University of Pittsburgh. He is also a faculty affiliate with Medical Humanities at Pitt's center for bioethics, and Family Medicine at the University of Pittsburgh School of Medicine. He co-directs a master's-level cultural and linguistic competency course, and also serves as the advisor for the Linguistic Internship and Consulting; a program he created in 2012 to connect linguistics to the community and industry. In 2016, Dr. Soudi directed a unique, collaborative work with the school of medicine to design and host a first-ever Humanities in Health Conference at Pitt as part of the Provost's Year of the Humanities Initiative. In 2017, he chaired another interdisciplinary conference on "Cultural and Linguistic Diversity: Living and Working Together." As part of the conference, he produced and directed a short documentary on the meaning and value of diversity. A special collection on humanities in health he led appeared in 2017 in the *European Journal of Person Centered Healthcare*. Dr. Soudi has published his research in several other journals.

ABOUT THE CONTRIBUTORS

CHAPTER 1

Z. Yasemin Kalender obtained a BS degree from Boğaziçi University in Istanbul with a focus on experimental particle physics during which she worked as a collaborator in several projects at CERN. Later, she moved to the United States to continue her education as a PhD student at the University of Pittsburgh with a research focus on physics education. Her current research interest is investigating motivational characteristics of students, diversity issues in the physics discipline, and incorporating big data analysis techniques into the area of physics education research. After earning her PhD in 2019, she will continue her academic training as a postdoctoral research associate at Cornell University.

Emily Marshman is an assistant professor in the physics department at Community College of Allegheny County. She obtained a BS in physics education from California University of Pennsylvania and a PhD in physics with a focus on physics education research from the University of Pittsburgh. After obtaining her PhD, she worked as a postdoctoral teacher scholar, assessment consultant, and associate director at the Discipline Based Science Education Research Center at the University of Pittsburgh. She then became a faculty member at the Community College of Allegheny County. Her research focuses on improving teaching and learning in upper division

Diversity Across the Disciplines, pages 319–340
Copyright © 2020 by Information Age Publishing

physics courses, enhancing teaching assistants' teaching approaches, and addressing issues related to student motivation in physics courses.

Timothy J. Nokes-Malach is an associate professor of psychology and a research scientist at the Learning Research and Development Center at the University of Pittsburgh. He received his bachelor's degree from the University of Wisconsin-Whitewater, PhD from the University of Illinois at Chicago, and postdoctoral training at the Beckman Institute for Advanced Science and Technology at the University of Illinois at Urbana-Champaign. His research focuses on human learning, problem solving, and knowledge transfer, and most recently on the interactive effects of motivation and social interaction on those processes. His work has been supported with grants from the Pittsburgh Science of Learning Center, the National Science Foundation, and the Department of Education's Institute for Education Sciences (http://www.lrdc.pitt.edu/nokes/CSL-lab-home.html).

Christian Schunn obtained his PhD from Carnegie Mellon in 1995. He currently is a senior scientist at the Learning Research and Development Center and a Professor of Psychology, Learning Sciences and Policy, and Intelligent Systems at the University of Pittsburgh. Most recently he became co-director of the Institute for Learning. He has led many research and design projects in science, mathematics, engineering, technology, and writing education. His current research interests include STEM reasoning (particularly studying practicing scientists and engineers) and learning (developing and studying integrations of science and engineering or science and math), neuroscience of complex learning (in science and math), peer interaction and instruction (especially for writing instruction), and engagement and learning (especially in science). He is a fellow of several scientific societies (AAAS, APA, APS) as well as a fellow and executive member of the International Society for Design & Development in Education. He has served on three National Academy of Engineering committees. Finally, he has launched a startup called Peerceptiv that is based upon his research on technology-based peer assessment in high school and college settings.

Chandralekha Singh is a professor in the Department of Physics and Astronomy and the director of the Discipline-Based Science Education Research Center at the University of Pittsburgh. She obtained her PhD in theoretical condensed matter physics from the University of California Santa Barbara and was a postdoctoral fellow at the University of Illinois Urbana Champaign, before joining the University of Pittsburgh. She has been conducting research in physics education for 2 decades. She was elected to the Presidential-Line of the American Association of Physics Teachers and is currently serving as the president-elect. She was one of the two team leaders of the U.S. team to the 6th International Conference on Women in

Physics (ICWIP) in Birmingham United Kingdom in 2017 and is an editor of the 6th ICWIP proceedings. She held the Chair-line of the American Physical Society Forum on Education from 2009–2013 and was the chair of the editorial board of Physical Review Special Topics Physics Education Research from 2010–2013. She has co-organized two physics education research conferences in 2006 and 2007 and was the co-chair of the 2010 Gordon Conference on Physics Research and Education. She co-chaired the first conference which brought together physicists, chemists, and engineers from various engineering departments to discuss the future of materials science and engineering education in 2008. She was the co-organizer of the first and third conferences on graduate education in physics in 2008 and 2017 and chaired the second conference on graduate education in physics in 2013. She is a Fellow of the American Physical Society, American Association of Physics Teachers and the American Association for the Advancement of Science. More information about her can be found here https://sites.google.com/site/professorsinghswebpage/

CHAPTER 2

Katherine Bogen is a clinical research program coordinator in the Department of Psychiatry at Rhode Island Hospital, where she works with Dr. Lindsay Orchowski to implement and evaluate dating violence and sexual assault prevention programming. Her work focuses on the long-term impacts of sexual trauma on women's health, as well as disparities between in-person and online trauma disclosure patterns. Ms. Bogen is particularly interested in the utilization of social media analysis to inform research, practice, and interventions supporting survivors of violence who lack access to in-person resources. In her free time, Ms. Bogen is a vocal social justice activist, focusing on advocating for survivors of sexual violence, celebrating the LGBTQ+ community, engaging in anti-racist efforts, and combating antisemitism.

Lisa D. Brush holds appointments as professor of sociology and of gender, sexuality, and women's studies at the University of Pittsburgh in Pittsburgh, PA. Her first book, *Gender and Governance*, documents and explains the ways contemporary capitalist welfare/workfare states and social policies produce and position women and men as different and unequal, and the ways gender difference and inequality organize states and social policies. Her second book, *Poverty, Battered Women, and Work in U.S. Public Policy*, investigates what happens when "work–family conflict" becomes literal; how men's control, coercion, and sabotage trap women in poverty and abuse; and how "domestic" violence moves out of the home and follows women to work. Current collaborations investigate primary prevention of violence and abuse by engaging high school and middle school boys and their athletic program coaches in transforming gender.

Samantha Ciaravino is a senior research analyst within the reproductive health and family formation program area at Child Trends. In this capacity, Ms. Ciaravino contributes to a variety of projects focused on promoting healthy marriage and co-parenting relationships and teen pregnancy prevention. She earned a Master of Public Health degree with a focus on behavioral and community health sciences from the University of Pittsburgh. Prior to joining Child Trends, Ms. Ciaravino worked as a clinical research coordinator at the University of Pittsburgh, where she oversaw the evaluation of several school and community-based violence prevention programs. Ms. Ciaravino's graduate studies and prior work experience have provided her training in both quantitative and qualitative research methods as well as project management. She is particularly interested in male engagement in initiatives and programming aimed at violence prevention and promoting healthy relationships.

Maria Catrina D. Jaime's research and work experience spans over the past 15 years. She began her research career working on multidisciplinary research at the University of California Davis Medical Center and received her Master of Public Health. Later, Dr. Jaime worked for the University of Pittsburgh and the Division of Adolescent Medicine, Children's Hospital of Pittsburgh. She oversaw community-based and federally funded research grants, focusing on prevention and interventions with community-partnered approaches to reach vulnerable populations. Dr. Jaime also served on the Community PARTners Core through the Clinical Translational Science Institute, University of Pittsburgh. She developed guidelines and trainings to assist investigators and community members on community-based projects.

Dr. Jaime completed her doctoral studies at the University of Pittsburgh, Graduate School of Public Health, in the Department of Behavioral and Community Health Sciences. She examined masculinity norms and gender inequitable attitudes associated with sexual risk behaviors among young men involved in the juvenile justice system. Dr. Jaime is a T32 postdoctoral scholar for the Quality, Safety, and Comparative Effectiveness Research Training at University of California, Davis through the Center for Healthcare Policy and Research. Her primary research focus is improving the health of marginalized adolescents and young adults, specifically related to sexual and reproductive health.

Heather L. McCauley is a social epidemiologist and assistant professor in the College of Social Science at Michigan State University. Her research focuses on social and structural determinants of sexual violence and sexual violence prevention, with emphasis on communities that experience marginalization (e.g., sexual and gender minorities). As principal investigator, Dr. McCauley's work has been funded by the National Institutes of Health, the Michigan Department of Health and Human Services, Center for Victim Research, and the National Resource Center on Domestic Violence. Nationally, Dr. McCauley serves on grant review panels for the National Institute of Justice and the National Institutes of Health. She is an associate editor of the multidisciplinary research journal *Psychology of Violence.* She earned her MS in global health and ScD in social epidemiology from Harvard University and completed postdoctoral training in adolescent and young adult health at the University of Pittsburgh School of Medicine. From 2014–2016, she was an assistant professor of pediatrics and psychiatry at the University of Pittsburgh before moving to Michigan State in 2016.

Elizabeth Miller is professor of pediatrics, public health, and clinical and translational science at the University of Pittsburgh School of Medicine, director of adolescent and young adult medicine, and director of community and population health at UPMC Children's Hospital Pittsburgh and holds the Edmund R. McCluskey Endowed Chair in pediatric medical education. Trained in internal medicine and pediatrics and medical anthropology, she has over 15 years of practice and research experience in addressing interpersonal violence prevention and adolescent health promotion in clinical and community settings, with funding from the National Institutes of Health, National Institute of Justice, Office on Women's Health, and foundations. Her research focuses on the impact of gender-based violence on adolescent and young adult health, with an emphasis on reproductive and sexual health. She is also involved in developing and testing primary sexual violence prevention programs, including one titled "Coaching Boys Into Men" which involves training coaches to talk to their male athletes about stopping violence against women, funded by the Centers for Disease Control and Prevention.

CHAPTER 3

Cynthia Croot is a director, deviser, and social practice artist. As co-founder of the artist-activist collective *Ifyoureallyloveme* and resident director of the experimental theater company *Conni's Avant Garde Restaurant* (winner of two New York Innovative Theater Awards) her critically-acclaimed site-specific and immersive performances have been seen throughout the United States and abroad. Productions in NYC include work at PS122, HERE, Town Hall, Symphony Space, and the Guggenheim Museum. Regional and international credits include the Windybrow Theatre and Eastern Cape Opera Company in South Africa, Colorado Shakespeare Festival, Stonington Opera House, Cleveland Public Theatre, Actor's Theater of Louisville, and ART's Club Oberon. Since first visiting Syria in 2004 she returned to the region for research in Syria, Jordan, Israel, Palestine, and Iran and subsequently orchestrated *Taking Refuge*, a multidisciplinary performance series in the United States and the United Kingdom focused on humanizing the Syrian refugee crisis. In 2018 she staged *"Mirror Butterfly: Migrant Liberation Movement Suite,"* a new jazz hip-hop opera composed by Ben Barson with libretto by Ruth Margraff, at the Kennedy Center Millennium Stage. Ongoing research includes her latest devised work: *Recoil* (exploring the U.S. love-affair with guns), featured at the Smithsonian American History Museum this spring as part of the ACCelerate Conference. www.cynthiacroot.com

CHAPTER 4

Clark Chilson is an associate professor in the Department of Religious Studies at the University of Pittsburgh, where he teaches on religion in Asia and the relationship between Buddhism and psychology. He is the author of *Secrecy's Power: Covert Shin Buddhists in Japan and Contradictions of Concealment* (2014) and the co-editor of two books: *The Nanzan Guide to Japanese Religions* (with Paul Swanson), and *Shamans in Asia* (with Peter Knecht). He has published articles on Shin Buddhism, Kuya, Ikeda Daisaku, and nonreligious spiritual care in Japan.

Among his recent publications is an article titled "Naikan: A Meditation Method and Psychotherapy" in *Oxford Research Encyclopedia of Religion* (Oxford University Press, 2018). He is a founding member of the North American Naikan Council and has given presentations on Naikan in Japan, Canada, Denmark, and the United States. He has done intensive Naikan five times at two different Naikan centers in Japan.

CHAPTER 5

Katrina Bartow Jacobs is an assistant professor of practice in language, literacy, and culture within the Department of Instruction and Learning at the University of Pittsburgh's School of Education. Dr. Jacobs earned her PhD in reading/writing/literacy at the Graduate School of Education at the University of Pennsylvania. She was formerly a first grade and fourth grade teacher in California.

Her research centers on the integration of sociocultural and critical perspectives of literacy and practitioner research within teacher education programs and in early childhood educational contexts, with a particular emphasis on how these frameworks impact the ways that literacy educators define their profession and their classroom practice within urban contexts. She focuses both on the nature of children's learning with and from texts, and on how to integrate these perspectives within teacher preparation. Within this area of research her current work focuses on the intersections of practice, theory, and policy; the ways that children take up issues of gender and identity during the reading of texts; and the ways that early career teachers develop, make sense of, and enact critical literacy pedagogies.

Thomas M. Hill Jr. is a doctoral student in language, literacy, and culture within the Department of Instruction and Learning at the University of Pittsburgh's School of Education. Thomas is a former early childhood educator in Pennsylvania and New Mexico where he earned an MA in language, literacy, and sociocultural studies from the University of New Mexico.

His research interests include representations within children's literature and curricular materials centered on critical indigenous theory. Previous research has included the role of play-based learning in vocabulary instruction as well as student and teacher talk about gender during English/language arts activities.

CHAPTER 6

Lori Delale-O'Connor is an assistant professor of urban education at the University of Pittsburgh. She received a PhD in sociology from Northwestern University where she was a certificate fellow in the multidisciplinary program in education sciences—a pre-doctoral training program funded by the Institute of Education Sciences. Dr. Delale-O'Connor also holds an MEd in secondary education from Boston College where she was a Donovan Urban Scholar. Dr. Delale-O'Connor's work has received support from the National Science Foundation, the Spencer Foundation, and the Institute of Education Sciences (IES). Her research has appeared in publications including *Urban Education, Teachers College Record, Equity and Excellence in Education, Education and Urban Society,* and *Theory Into Practice.* Her current teaching, research, and policy interests focus on the social contexts of education with a focus on caregiver and community engagement. Dr. Delale-O'Connor previously worked as an evaluator to both in and out-of-school time programs.

Ira E. Murray holds a bachelor's degree in business administration from Florida A&M University, a master of education degree from Vanderbilt University's Peabody College, and a Doctor of Philosophy in education from the University of Pittsburgh. Dr. Murray is an education scholar, with expertise in issues of race, equity, and achievement in urban schools, districts, and communities. Dr. Murray is currently a member of the Mississippi Commission on the Status of Women, the 100 Black Men of Jackson, and the board of directors of Excel by 5. Dr. Murray is also a member of the American Educational Research Association and the American Educational Studies Association. Dr. Murray is the recipient of numerous recognitions, including being named a 2014 *Mississippi Business Journal* Top 40 Under 40 business leader.

CHAPTER 7

Abdesalam Soudi earned his PhD in sociolinguistics from the University of Pittsburgh. His research focuses on the human-computer interface in doctors' consultations, provider-patient conversation, and cultural and linguistic diversity. Dr. Soudi holds a full-time faculty appointment with the Department of Linguistics at the University of Pittsburgh. He is also a faculty affiliate with Medical Humanities at Pitt's center for bioethics, and Family Medicine at the University of Pittsburgh School of Medicine. He co-directs a master's-level cultural and linguistic competency course, and also serves as the advisor for the Linguistic Internship and Consulting; a program he created in 2012 to connect linguistics to the community and industry. In 2016, Dr. Soudi directed a unique, collaborative work with the school of medicine to design and host a first-ever Humanities in Health Conference at Pitt as part of the Provost's Year of the Humanities Initiative. In 2017, he chaired another interdisciplinary conference on "Cultural and Linguistic Diversity: Living and Working Together." As part of the conference, he produced and directed a short documentary on the meaning and value of diversity. A special collection on humanities in health he led appeared in 2017 in the *European Journal of Person Centered Healthcare*. Dr. Soudi has published his research in several other journals.

Leyan deBorja is a project coordinator with the Department of Family Medicine at the University of Pittsburgh. She graduated from the University of Maryland with a bachelor's degree in general biology and received a Master of Public Health degree from the University of Pittsburgh Graduate School of Public Health with a focus in behavioral and community health sciences. Her work in the Department of Family Medicine has involved conducting a teen mentoring program, as well as a study investigating the acceptability of long-acting reversible contraception. She has a strong interest in the areas of women's health, primary care, and cultural competence in medicine.

Jeannette South-Paul is responsible for the educational, research, and clinical activities of the undergraduate and graduate medical education, faculty practice, and community arms of 3 family medicine residencies and seven ambulatory clinical sites in Allegheny County (Pittsburgh), Pennsylvania, as well as provides the academic leadership for 5 additional UPMC family medicine residencies in Mercer, Blair, Lycoming, and Lancaster counties. She is a practicing family physician who includes maternity care, as well as an academician with specific research interests in the areas of cultural competence, maternity care, and health disparities in the community.

Dr. South-Paul has served in leadership positions in the Society of Teachers of Family Medicine (STFM), the American Academy of Family Physicians (AAFP), the Association of American Medical Colleges (AAMC), and the Association of Departments of Family Medicine (ADFM) to include president of the Uniformed Services of American Family Physicians (USAFP) and president of the STFM.

Dr. South-Paul earned her BS degree from the University of Pennsylvania, her MD at the University of Pittsburgh School of Medicine and was elected to the Institute of Medicine (now National Academy of Medicine) in 2011. In 2012, Dr. South-Paul received the Dr. Wangari Maathai Humanitarian Award from Workforce Development Global Alliance (WDGA), a Pittsburgh-based organization that helps disadvantaged youth in the United States and Africa.

In 2013, Dr. South-Paul received the University of Pittsburgh 225th Anniversary Chancellor's Medallion. In 2015, Dr. South-Paul was elected to the Gold Humanism Honor Society through the Arnold P. Gold Foundation. Also, in 2015 Dr. South-Paul received the Chapel of Four Chaplains' Legion of Honor Award. In February 2018, Dr. South-Paul received the Allegheny County Medical Society Richard Dietrick Humanitarian Award.

CHAPTER 8

Mario C. Browne is the director of Health Sciences Diversity at the University of Pittsburgh Schools of the Health Sciences. In this role he manages and monitors several diversity and inclusion, and cultural competency initiatives within the schools of the health Sciences. Mr. Browne is an affiliate faculty member of the Center for Health Equity in the Graduate School of Public Health, and a faculty fellow in the Center for Urban Education in the School of Education. Mr. Browne's expertise is in community engagement with a primary interest in translating research and theory of the social determinants of health into practice, and building community capacity to eliminate disparities and achieve equity. Mario is a Certified Diversity Practitioner and holds a BS in biology and a BS in medical technology from Salem International

University and a MPH from the University of Pittsburgh's Graduate School of Public Health. He is a member of the Delta Omega Honors Society for Public Health Excellence, an alumnus of the Emerging Leaders in Public Health Scholars program at UNC Chapel Hill, and the Minority Training Program in Cancer Control Research at UCLA. He served as public health administrator for the Allegheny County Health Department's Department of Epidemiology and Biostatistics, responsible for promoting county-wide public health promotion/disease prevention programs.

Prior to that, Mario served as project director and community health coordinator for the University of Pittsburgh Center for Minority Health, now known as the Center for Health Equity (CHE). He was responsible for engaging community-based organizations as partners to eliminate health disparities and conducted community outreach, education, and health promotion related to the national health disparity priority areas. Mario currently serves as the co-chair for the CHE's Community Research Advisory Board (CRAB), the advisory board for the Pennsylvania Department of Health Equity, and previously on the Pennsylvania Department of Environmental Justice and the Consumer Health Coalition board of directors. Mario is a member of the American Public Health Association where he serves on the Black Caucus of Health Workers board of directors, and the Society of Public Health Education where he serves as the co-chair of the Health Equity Community of Practice.

Erika Gold Kestenberg, is a part-time faculty member in the Center for Urban Education at the University of Pittsburgh School of Education and a diversity, inclusion, equity, and justice consultant through her Courageous Hearts Company. Erika Gold Kestenberg's degrees include a PhD in education with a multidisciplinary focus on social justice, a master's degree and teaching certificate in secondary education social studies and a dual bachelor's degree in political science and history with a minor in psychology. She also has a certificate in diversity and inclusion as well as extensive training in transformative intergroup dialogues and conflict mediation.

Dr. Kestenberg was the associate director of Educator Development and Practice for the Center for Urban Education and a visiting assistant professor of urban education at the University of Pittsburgh for 7 years. During that time she designed a certificate in urban education program as well as developed and managed the urban scholars program. She also taught undergraduate and graduate students interested in becoming teachers in urban schools and in higher education. Her courses included Identity, Power, and Privilege; Culturally Relevant and Responsive Teaching; Relationship Building With Students, Families, and Communities; Social Foundations of Education; Urban Scholars Seminars; and Becoming a Change Agent, all with a focus on urban contexts grounded in equity and justice. She also trained and coached in-service educators and leaders around a variety of equity-based issues through multiple methods and approaches. Her earlier work at the university also included research in Pitt's Learning Research and Development Center as well as the Center on Race and Social Problems.

In addition to working in higher education, Dr. Kestenberg is and has been a teacher, trainer, advocate, coach, creator, and administrator in traditional and nontraditional mostly urban educational and nonprofit spaces in the United States and Israel. In those spaces, she teaches/taught about issues related to diversity, inclusion, equity and justice, social studies, English language arts, English as a second language, service learning, and cross-cultural communication. Dr. Kestenberg has received an Outstanding Service Award, a Program Innovation Award and has been recognized twice by the city of Pittsburgh's city council for her service learning work with youth across the city. She also co-authored a book with Milner, Cunningham, Delale-O'Connor, and Kestenberg entitled *"These Kids Are Out of Control:" Why We Must Reimagine Classroom Management for Equity* (2018, Corwin Press). At the core, Dr. Kestenberg is a critically conscious, compassionate, and passionate social justice educator advocate who honors our collective humanity and strives to embrace courageous imperfection, all anchored in love.

CHAPTER 9

Shelome Gooden is an associate professor of linguistics at the University of Pittsburgh. Her research centers in part on issues of (socio)cultural and linguistic diversity and on how these intersect with linguistic structures. These themes are similarly embedded in her teaching and service activities. She currently serves on the executive board of the Society for Pidgin and Creole Languages and the advisory board for Creative Multilingualism (https://www.creativeml.ox.ac.uk).

Shelome has published research articles on intonation and prosody, segmental variation and language and identity focusing on languages such as Jamaican Creole, Trinidadian Creole, African American Language, and Yami. She received her MA and PhD from The Ohio State University.

Abdesalam Soudi earned his PhD in sociolinguistics from the University of Pittsburgh. His research focuses on the human-computer interface in doctors' consultations, provider-patient conversation, and cultural and linguistic diversity. Dr. Soudi holds a full-time faculty appointment with the Department of Linguistics at the University of Pittsburgh. He is also a faculty affiliate with Medical Humanities at Pitt's center for bioethics, and Family Medicine at the University of Pittsburgh School of Medicine. He co-directs a master's-level cultural and linguistic competency course, and also serves as the advisor for the Linguistic Internship and Consulting; a program he created in 2012 to connect linguistics to the community and industry. In 2016, Dr. Soudi directed a unique, collaborative work with the school of medicine to design and host a first-ever Humanities in Health Conference at Pitt as part of the Provost's Year of the Humanities Initiative. In 2017, he chaired another interdisciplinary conference on "Cultural and Linguistic Diversity: Living and Working Together." As part of the conference, he produced and directed a short documentary on the meaning and value of diversity. A special collection on humanities in health he led appeared in 2017 in the *European Journal of Person Centered Healthcare*. Dr. Soudi has published his research in several other journals.

Karen Elizabeth Park is an assistant professor of linguistics at the University of Pittsburgh and linguist for the Ethno-Ornithology World Archive (EWA). Her research interests include language change, documentation, and maintenance; generative syntax; historical linguistics; ethno-ornithology; and biocultural diversity.

With Dr. Andrew Gosler, Oxford University Research Lecturer in Ornithology and Conservation and director of EWA, she is a co-investigator on the Oxford-led research program, Creative Multilingualism (http://www.creativeml.ox.ac.uk/research/naming).

Prior to taking up her current post at the University of Pittsburgh, she held an American Council of Learned Societies fellowship with the Council of American Overseas Research Centers at the Smithsonian Museum of Natural History, where she also served as a research collaborator with Smithsonian anthropologist Dr. Bill Merrill, and a post-doctoral research fellowship directed by Dr. Gosler on the development of EWA, funded by the Arts and Humanities Research Council. She received her MPhil and DPhil from the University of Oxford and BA from Grinnell College.

Valerie Kinloch is the Renee and Richard Goldman Dean of the School of Education and professor at the University of Pittsburgh. She is the recipient of the 2018 Advancement of People of Color Leadership Award from the National Council of Teachers of English. Her scholarship examines literacy, language, and community engagement of youth and adults inside and outside school systems. She has published books and research articles on race, place, literacy, and equity. Her book, *Harlem On Our Minds* (2012, Teachers College Press), received the Outstanding Book of the Year Award from the American Educational Research Association (AERA); and her book *Crossing Boundaries: Teaching and Learning with Urban Youth* (2012, Teachers College Press), was named a 2013 "Staff Pick for Professional Development" by the *Teaching Tolerance Education Magazine.*

In 2015, Valerie received the Rewey Belle Inglis Award for Outstanding Women in English Education from the National Council of Teachers of

English (NCTE), and in 2016, was awarded the Distinguished Faculty Advising Award from the Council of Graduate Students at Ohio State. She has received grants from the Spencer Foundation, National Council of Teachers of English, Corporation for National and Community Service, and the Battelle Endowment for Technology. She received her MA and PhD from Wayne State University.

CHAPTER 10

Nisha Nair is a clinical assistant professor of business administration at the Katz Graduate School of Business at the University of Pittsburgh. She has previously taught as a visiting faculty at the Cotsakos College of Business at William Paterson University and served as a tenured faculty member at the Indian Institute of Management (IIM) Indore. Her research interests are primarily in the dark side of employee behavior; namely, work alienation and deviance. She is also interested in diversity and inclusion, and organizational development in the nonprofit sector.

Deborah Cain Good is a faculty member at the Joseph M. Katz Graduate School of Business, University of Pittsburgh teaching staffing, training, compensation, employee and labor relations, interpersonal skills, ethics, sports management, business communication, and organizational behavior courses in the undergraduate, MBA, and Executive MBA programs. She has worked with Westinghouse, ALCOA, Arconic, Aon, and RTI Metals among other clients in a training and consulting capacity. She was a former research associate at the National Education Center for Women in Business. Her current research interests include generational differences in the workplace, integrating analytics into the curriculum, microaggressions and their impacts and experiential learning activities and assessments. Good has a PhD in human resource management and industrial relations from the University of Pittsburgh. She was an eight year member of the Franklin Regional School Board where she served as president, vice president, and negotiation committee member. She has had numerous publications in various academic journals and has presented papers at multiple national, regional, and local conferences.

CHAPTER 11

Scott Morgenstern is professor of political science at the University of Pittsburgh, and past director of Pitt's Center for Latin American Studies. His research focuses on political parties, electoral systems, and legislatures, with a regional specialization in Latin America. His teaching focuses on these themes, plus U.S.–Latin American relations and democratic governance. Among his publications are: *Are Politics Local? The Two Dimensions of Party Nationalization Around the World* (Cambridge University Press, 2017), *Patterns of Legislative Politics: Roll Call Voting in the United States and Latin America's Southern Cone* (Cambridge University Press, 2004), *Legislative Politics in Latin America,* (coeditor and contributor; Cambridge University Press, 2002), *Pathways to Power* (coeditor and contributor, Pennsylvania State University Press, 2008), and *Cuba Reforming Communism Cuba in Comparative Perspective* (Pittsburgh University Press, 2018). His articles have appeared in the *Journal of Politics, Comparative Political Studies, Comparative Politics, Party Politics, Electoral Studies, Review of International Political Economy,* and other journals. He was also the primary investigator on a grant from the USAID to produce documents related to their political party development programs.

Kelly Morrison is a doctoral student in political science with specializations in international relations and comparative politics and a regional focus on Latin America. She is primarily interested in understanding the causes and consequences of political violence, and her dissertation work examines the determinants of electoral punishment for repressive leaders in democratic countries. In other collaborative research, she considers the relationship between elections and civil conflict onset and the determinants of compliance with decisions of the Inter-American Court of Human Rights. Before joining Pitt's graduate program, Kelly graduated from Lee University with degrees in political science and Spanish.

CHAPTER 12

Ralph Bangs has been employed at the University of Pittsburgh for more than 32 years. He is currently Study Abroad Faculty Leader (2015–present) at the University Center for International Studies and was associate director, Center on Race and Social Problems (2002–2014) and research associate, University Center for Social and Urban Research (1997–2002). His most recent book is *Race and Social Problems: Restructuring Inequality* (Springer Press, 2014) with Larry Davis. His awards include Ronald H. Brown Leadership Award by the Urban League of Pittsburgh (2016), "Best Researcher" by *In Pittsburgh* newspaper (2000), and Racial Justice Award by YWCA of Pittsburgh (1997). His doctorate is in public policy research and analysis from the University of Pittsburgh (1985).

Audrey J. Murrell conducts research, teaching, and consulting that helps organizations better utilize and engage their most important assets—their human and social capital. She is currently associate dean and professor of business administration, psychology, public and international affairs at the University of Pittsburgh, Katz/CBA School of Business. She is also the director of the David Berg Center for Ethics and Leadership at the University of Pittsburgh. Her research focuses on mentoring, careers in organizations, workplace–supplier diversity, and social issues in management. This work has been published widely in management and psychology journals as well as book chapters and special issues. Popular media has also highlighted this work including the *Wall Street Journal, Pittsburgh Post-Gazette, Atlanta Journal and Constitution, Pittsburgh Business Times, Cleveland Plain Dealer, Black Enterprise, Jet Magazine,* and *Vida Executive* (in Brazil). Dr. Murrell is the author (along with Crosby and Ely) of the book entitled, *Mentoring Dilemmas: Developmental Relationships Within Multicultural Organizations* (1999, Erlbaum); "*Intelligent Mentoring: How IBM Creates Value Through People, Knowledge, and Relationships*" with Forte-Trummel and Bing (2008, Prentice-Hall); and the most recent book with Blake-Beard, *Mentoring Diverse Leaders: Creating Change for People, Processes, and Paradigms* (2017, Routledge).

CHAPTER 13

Jennifer Petrie-Wyman is assistant director of the David Berg Center for Ethics and Leadership at the University of Pittsburgh. She also serves as adjunct faculty for the Katz Graduate School of Business teaching a Capstone Seminar on Leadership and Ethics. She received her Doctorate of Education (2015) and master's in African studies (2011) from Ohio University. At the University of Pittsburgh, she researches global competency, leadership, ethics education, and African development policy. In Ghana, Jennifer's current project focuses on understanding women's ethical leadership development. Her work has been presented at national and international conferences and published in *COMPARE: A Journal of Comparative and International Education,* the *Journal of Service Learning in Higher Education,* and at the National Education Policy Center. She is a 2019 CORO Women's Leadership Fellow and she serves on the Squirrel Hill Urban Coalition's Education Committee. Jennifer has also been performing dance as a member of *Azaguno,* a multicultural African performing arts ensemble, for the past 10 years.

CHAPTER 14

Rose E. Constantino is an associate professor at the University of Pittsburgh School of Nursing, Department of Health and Community Systems. She teaches forensic nursing to graduate students based on the content of her book (co-editor) entitled, *Forensic Nursing: Evidence-Based Principles and Practice* (2013, F. A. Davis). Her research focuses on examining the depth and breadth of the consequences of intimate partner violence (IPV) on the health, safety, and well-being of women, men, and children worldwide, is founded on her pro bono family law practice with women and girls in IPV. Her current research is in evaluating the effectiveness of online and mobile delivery of health interventions to survivors of IPV as a frugal innovation HELP zone in building healthy relationships and preventing relationship violence. She mentors numerous students, faculty, and friends locally, regionally, nationally, and globally.

In 1962, Rose graduated with her BSN degree from Philippine Union College in Manila now the Adventist University of the Philippines in Silang, Cavite, Philippines. In 1971 she completed her master's in nursing (MSN) degree from the University of Pittsburgh School of Nursing, her PhD from the University of Pittsburgh in 1979, and her Juris Doctor (JD) degree from Duquesne University in 1984. She is a fellow of the American Academy of Nursing and the American College of Forensic Examiners and a Board Certified Homeland Security Specialist. She has numerous publications, presentations, honors, and awards. In 2016, she was a Fulbright Scholar to the University of Jordan, Amman, Jordan and in 2017, she was *Balik* (Return) Scientist Fellow of the Philippines through the Philippine Council for Health Research Development, hosted by the Centro Escola University, Manila, Philippines.

Margarete L. Zalon is professor of nursing and director of the online Master of Science in health informatics program at the University of Scranton. Dr. Zalon worked in several major medical centers in New York City before moving to Pennsylvania. She teaches adult health nursing, professional issues and policy, research and evidence-based practice in nursing, and population health for health informatics. Dr. Zalon's research has focused on pain management, and vulnerable elders. She has received funding from the American Nurses Foundation, and the National Institutes of Health. More recently, her research focuses on the prevention of cognitive decline in the hospitalized elderly and delirium descriptors in the electronic health record.

Dr. Zalon is committed to advancing the nursing profession and helping nurses to be better advocates for their patients at the bedside and the boardroom. Dr. Zalon is co-editor of *Nurses Making Policy From Bedside to Boardroom* (2018, Springer), now in its second edition. She has served on the board of the American Nurses Association (ANA), as vice-president of the American Nurses Credentialing Center, and as the chairperson of the board of trustees of the American Nurses Foundation (ANA's charitable arm). Dr. Zalon is a past president of the Pennsylvania State Nurses Association. Currently, she serves on the American Academy of Nursing's Acute and Critical Care Expert Panel and is the president of the Nursing Foundation of Pennsylvania.

Dr. Zalon graduated with a BSN from Duke University, and her MA and PhD in nursing from New York University. She is certified as an adult health clinical specialist by the American Nurses Credentialing Center. She is a fellow of the American Academy of Nursing.

CHAPTER 15

Ray Jones teaches introductory undergraduate courses in business ethics and organizational behavior as well as advanced undergraduate courses in gender and diversity in management and governance and management. In the MBA program, he teaches the required organizational behavior core course. For the past several years, he has served as coordinator of the Certificate Program in Leadership and Ethics (CPLE), in which more than 60 undergraduate students work toward the completion of the certificate as an enhancement of their undergraduate major. In addition to teaching, he plays a variety of advisory roles in a number of different student activities and pursuits in the College of Business Administration. He current serves in the role of director for the David Berg Center for Ethics and Leadership at the University of Pittsburgh. He received his PhD from the University of Pittsburgh in the areas of ethics and organizational behavior.

Jones serves as the faculty advisor for the CBA chapter of Delta Sigma Pi, a role that puts him in contact with the 55–60 CBA students who belong to the fraternity. He has served in this role for the past several years and has watched the brothers reactivate the chapter on campus, and then subsequently establish the Lambda chapter as one of the strongest chapters in the entire country.

He is also the faculty advisor for the Department of Athletics' Academy of Sports Marketing, an internship program in which the Department of Athletics offers sports marketing internships exclusively to CBA students. In this program, CBA students are given responsibility for researching, designing, and implementing a marketing plan for one of the department's Olympic (i.e., nonrevenue) sports (women's soccer, men's soccer, swimming/diving, gymnastics, wrestling, baseball, and softball). The program has been in existence for several years, and academy students have been generating amazing results in terms of both increasing attendance at meets and matches, and in terms of establishing and enhancing team awareness and brand awareness for Pitt athletics.

Audrey J. Murrell conducts research, teaching, and consulting that helps organizations better utilize and engage their most important assets—their human and social capital. She is currently associate dean and professor of business administration, psychology, public and international affairs at the University of Pittsburgh, Katz/CBA School of Business. She is also the director of the David Berg Center for Ethics and Leadership at the University of Pittsburgh. Her research focuses on mentoring, careers in organizations, workplace–supplier diversity, and social issues in management. This work has been published widely in management and psychology journals as well as book chapters and special issues. Popular media has also highlighted this work including the *Wall Street Journal, Pittsburgh Post-Gazette, Atlanta Journal and Constitution, Pittsburgh Business Times, Cleveland Plain Dealer, Black Enterprise, Jet Magazine,* and *Vida Executive* (in Brazil). Dr. Murrell is the author (along with Crosby and Ely) of the book entitled, *Mentoring Dilemmas: Developmental Relationships Within Multicultural Organizations* (1999, Erlbaum); "*Intelligent Mentoring: How IBM Creates Value Through People, Knowledge, and Relationships*" with Forte-Trummel and Bing (2008, Prentice-Hall); and the most recent book with Blake-Beard, *Mentoring Diverse Leaders: Creating Change for People, Processes, and Paradigms* (2017, Routledge).

Jennifer Petrie-Wyman is assistant director of the David Berg Center for Ethics and Leadership at the University of Pittsburgh. She also serves as adjunct faculty for the Katz Graduate School of Business teaching a Capstone Seminar on Leadership and Ethics. She received her Doctorate of Education (2015) and master's in African studies (2011) from Ohio University. At the University of Pittsburgh, she researches global competency, leadership, ethics education, and African development policy. In Ghana, Jennifer's current project focuses on understanding women's ethical leadership development. Her work has been presented at national and international conferences and published in *COMPARE: A Journal of Comparative and International Education,* the *Journal of Service Learning in Higher Education,* and at the National Education Policy Center. She is a 2019 CORO Women's Leadership Fellow and she serves on the Squirrel Hill Urban Coalition's Education Committee. Jennifer has also been performing dance as a member of *Azaguno,* a multicultural African performing arts ensemble, for the past 10 years.

CHAPTER 16

Tim Dawson is co-founder and co-principal of the Art of Democracy, LLC, a consultancy designing civic engagement collaborations that practically realize principles of deliberative democracy and human centered design. Tim is an affiliate and former program manager at Carnegie Mellon University's Program for Deliberative Democracy (PDD), where he helped facilitate deliberative forums at the national, state, and local levels, including forums at fifteen university campuses across the United States, statewide forums in Pennsylvania and Maryland, and neighborhood-level forums throughout Southwestern Pennsylvania. Through the Art of Democracy, Tim regularly collaborates with artists, academics, public officials, and residents of diverse communities to design creative strategies for informed and inclusive public engagement. Since 2014, Tim has worked with the City of Pittsburgh to institutionalize Deliberative Community Forums as a best practice for soliciting residents' input.

Tim regularly speaks and conducts workshops at national and international conferences focused on the future of democracy, including presentations at the American Democracy Project/The Democracy Commitment, Frontiers of Democracy, Imagining America, the International Conference on Arts in Society, and the National Conference on Citizenship. Tim earned his PhD in Rhetoric at Carnegie Mellon University, where he has taught in the English Department, the humanities scholars program, and the School of Drama.

CHAPTER 17

Geoffrey L. Wood is assistant professor of sociology and director of the Center for Applied Research (CFAR) at Pitt-Greensburg. He earned a PhD in sociology from the University at Albany, State University of New York. He teaches courses in sociology and public policy, and directs research projects with CFAR, most recently a Community Health Needs Assessment (CHNA). Dr. Wood publishes articles and book chapters in the areas of historical social inequality, the impact of natural disasters on changes in social inequality, racialized segregation in public education, and applied research reports as part of his work with CFAR.

CHAPTER 18

John C. Welch is a native of Pittsburgh and product of its public and private education systems. A graduate of Central Catholic High School, he matriculated to Carnegie Mellon University where he received a BS in chemical engineering and economics. Rev. Welch received a Master of Divinity from Pittsburgh Theological Seminary and a PhD in healthcare ethics from Duquesne University.

CHAPTER 19

Lina Dee Dostilio is the associate vice chancellor for community engagement at the University of Pittsburgh. She is responsible for supporting community-facing work that includes community relations, cultivating strategic opportunities to advance Pitt's community engagement agenda, and implementing the university's place-based community engagement initiative through the development of neighborhood-based community engagement centers. Her previous administrative appointment was as director of Duquesne University's Center for Community-Engaged Teaching and Research.

Dostilio was named the Coalition of Urban and Metropolitan Universities Research Fellow in 2019. In this role, she investigates the impact of place-based community engagement on community capacities. She was previously the scholar in residence directing the Campus Compact's Project on the Community Engagement Professional, a national research project staffed by 19 research fellows across the country that has produced, *The Community Engagement Professional in Higher Education: A Competency Model for an Emerging Field* (2017, Stylus) and *The Community Engagement Professional Guidebook* (2019, Stylus). Dostilio has also served as a past-chair of the board of directors of the International Association for Research on Service-Learning and Community Engagement and is on the editorial board of the *Metropolitan Universities*. Her research as a scholar-administrator has focused on multi-sector partnership development, place-based community engagement, and the evolution of the community engagement profession within higher education.

CHAPTER 20

Jeannette South-Paul is responsible for the educational, research, and clinical activities of the undergraduate and graduate medical education, faculty practice, and community arms of 3 family medicine residencies and seven ambulatory clinical sites in Allegheny County (Pittsburgh), Pennsylvania, as well as provides the academic leadership for 5 additional UPMC family medicine residencies in Mercer, Blair, Lycoming, and Lancaster counties. She is a practicing family physician who includes maternity care, as well as an academician with specific research interests in the areas of cultural competence, maternity care, and health disparities in the community.

Dr. South-Paul has served in leadership positions in the Society of Teachers of Family Medicine (STFM), the American Academy of Family Physicians (AAFP), the Association of American Medical Colleges (AAMC), and the Association of Departments of Family Medicine (ADFM) to include president of the Uniformed Services of American Family Physicians (US-AFP) and president of the STFM.

Dr. South-Paul earned her BS degree from the University of Pennsylvania, her MD at the University of Pittsburgh School of Medicine and was elected to the Institute of Medicine (now National Academy of Medicine) in 2011. In 2012, Dr. South-Paul received the Dr. Wangari Maathai Humanitarian Award from Workforce Development Global Alliance (WDGA), a Pittsburgh-based organization that helps disadvantaged youth in the United States and Africa.

In 2013, Dr. South-Paul received the University of Pittsburgh 225th Anniversary Chancellor's Medallion. In 2015, Dr. South-Paul was elected to the Gold Humanism Honor Society through the Arnold P. Gold Foundation. Also, in 2015 Dr. South-Paul received the Chapel of Four Chaplains' Legion of Honor Award. In February 2018, Dr. South-Paul received the Allegheny County Medical Society Richard Dietrick Humanitarian Award.

Kendall M. Campbell earned his MD from the University of Florida College of Medicine and came to East Carolina University from Florida State University College of Medicine, where he served as co-founder and co-director for the Center for Underrepresented Minorities in Academic Medicine. He has interests in recruitment and retention of underrepresented minority students and faculty and has dedicated his research to this area and to the area of underrepresented patients in the clinical setting. He has over 50 publications and has spoken nationally on this topic. His professional career includes previous academic appointments at the University of Florida (UF) College of Medicine in the Department of Community Health and Family Medicine and as assistant dean for Minority Affairs. During this time, he also served as medical director and chief at Shands UF Eastside Community Practice, an interprofessional practice for the underserved. His clinical interests have traditionally been for underserved patients for which he has developed medication access initiatives, integrated pharmacy services and social services with primary care, and led community health education initiatives to benefit the community.

Dr. Campbell has received honors and awards for his service to the field of medicine including the Martin Luther King Jr. Distinguished Service Award, the Exemplary Teacher Award, and the Advancing the Mission of the College of Medicine Faculty Council Award. Dr. Campbell was also a 2014–2016 Fellow of the National Academy of Medicine (NAM), sponsored by the American Board of Family Medicine. He is a member of the NAM Roundtable on Health Equity, and has completed the Association of American Medical Colleges (AAMC) Leadership Education and Development (LEAD) certificate program.

Audrey J. Murrell conducts research, teaching, and consultii. organizations better utilize and engage their most important a.   -their human and social capital. She is currently associate dean and professor of business administration, psychology, public and international affairs at the University of Pittsburgh, Katz/CBA School of Business. She is also the director of the David Berg Center for Ethics and Leadership at the University of Pittsburgh. Her research focuses on mentoring, careers in organizations, workplace–supplier diversity, and social issues in management. This work has been published widely in management and psychology journals as well as book chapters and special issues. Popular media has also highlighted this work including the *Wall Street Journal, Pittsburgh Post-Gazette, Atlanta Journal and Constitution, Pittsburgh Business Times, Cleveland Plain Dealer, Black Enterprise, Jet Magazine,* and *Vida Executive* (in Brazil). Dr. Murrell is the author (along with Crosby and Ely) of the book entitled, *Mentoring Dilemmas: Developmental Relationships Within Multicultural Organizations* (1999, Erlbaum); "*Intelligent Mentoring: How IBM Creates Value Through People, Knowledge, and Relationships*" with Forte-Trummel and Bing (2008, Prentice-Hall); and the most recent book with Blake-Beard, *Mentoring Diverse Leaders: Creating Change for People, Processes, and Paradigms* (2017, Routledge).

Made in the USA
Monee, IL
21 November 2020